YOU'RE ALL I NEED

ただ、あなたのそばに – Just Being by Your Side

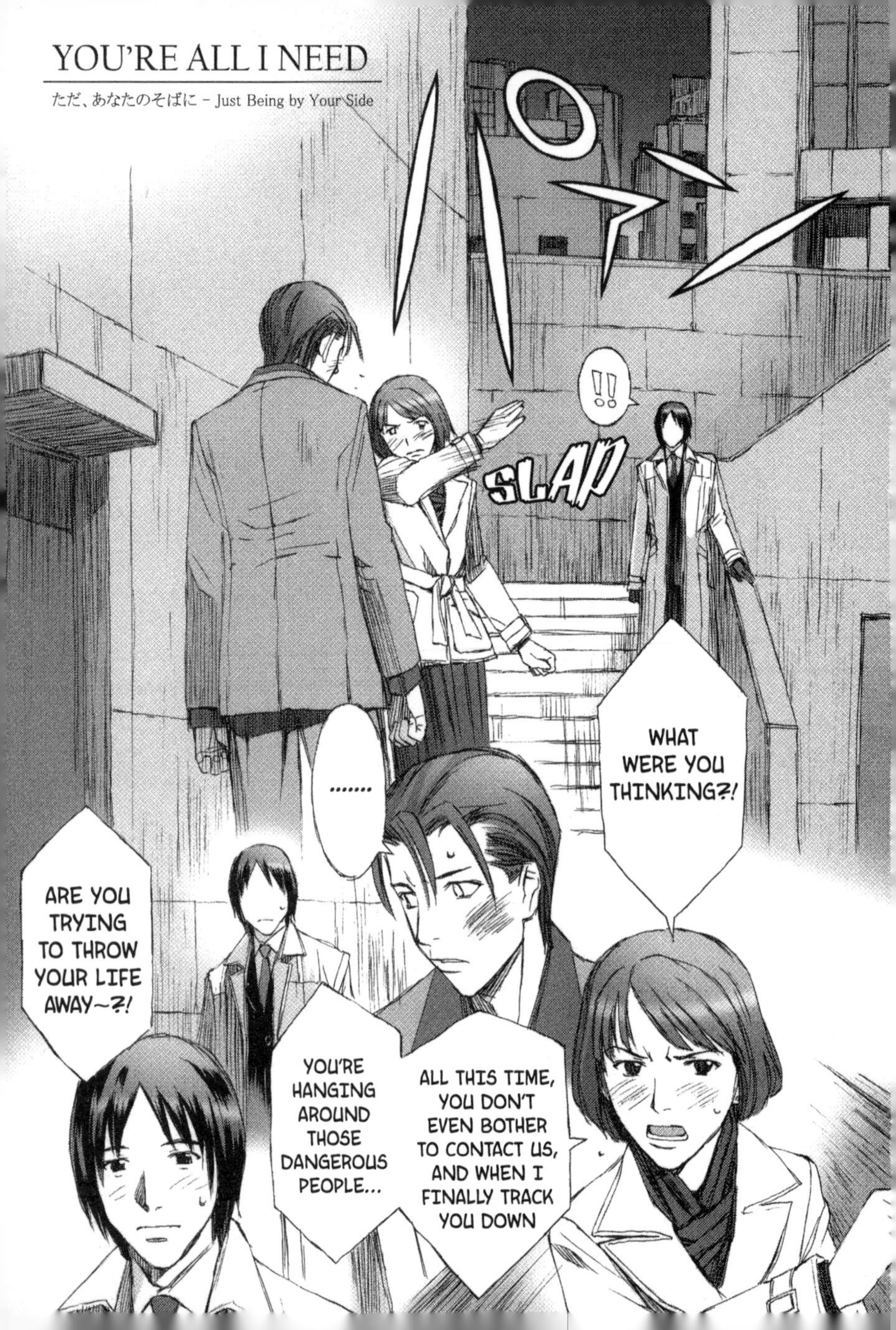
!!
SLAP
WHAT WERE YOU THINKING?!
....
ARE YOU TRYING TO THROW YOUR LIFE AWAY~?!
ALL THIS TIME, YOU DON'T EVEN BOTHER TO CONTACT US, AND WHEN I FINALLY TRACK YOU DOWN
YOU'RE HANGING AROUND THOSE DANGEROUS PEOPLE...

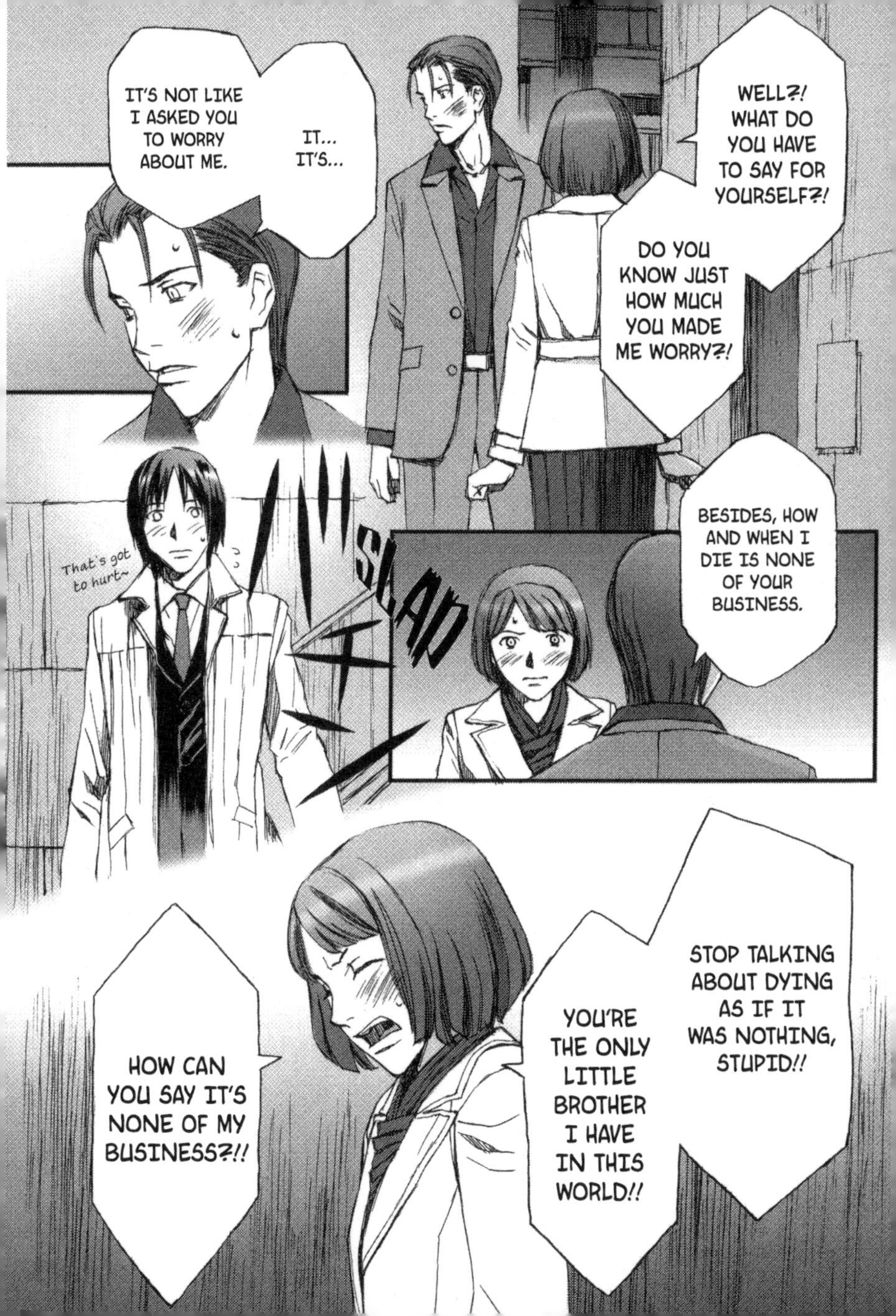
WELL?! WHAT DO YOU HAVE TO SAY FOR YOURSELF?!
DO YOU KNOW JUST HOW MUCH YOU MADE ME WORRY?!
IT... IT'S...
IT'S NOT LIKE I ASKED YOU TO WORRY ABOUT ME.
BESIDES, HOW AND WHEN I DIE IS NONE OF YOUR BUSINESS.
SLAP
That's got to hurt~
STOP TALKING ABOUT DYING AS IF IT WAS NOTHING, STUPID!!
YOU'RE THE ONLY LITTLE BROTHER I HAVE IN THIS WORLD!!
HOW CAN YOU SAY IT'S NONE OF MY BUSINESS?!!

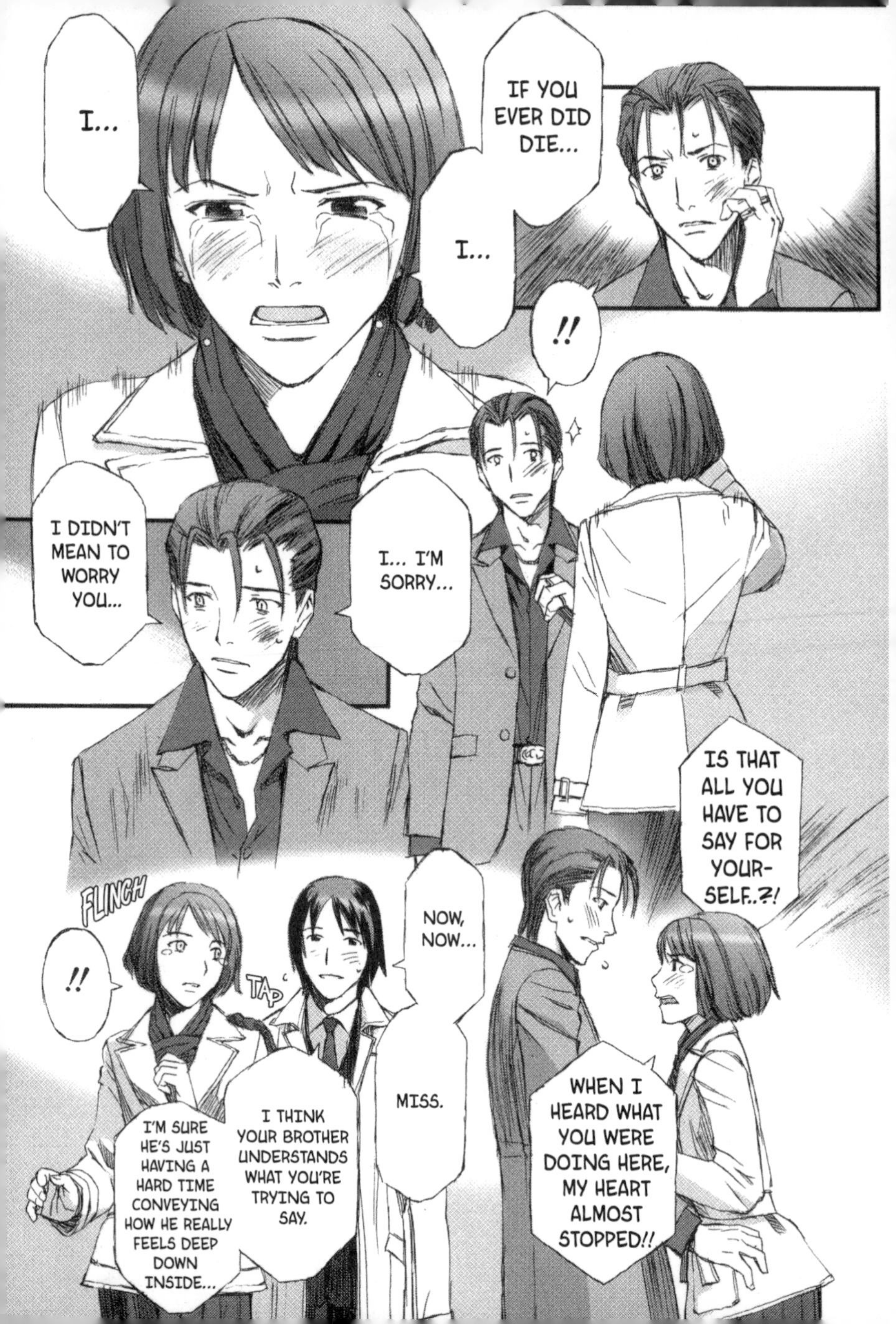
IF YOU EVER DID DIE...
I...
I...
!!
I... I'M SORRY...
I DIDN'T MEAN TO WORRY YOU...
IS THAT ALL YOU HAVE TO SAY FOR YOUR-SELF..?!
WHEN I HEARD WHAT YOU WERE DOING HERE, MY HEART ALMOST STOPPED!!
FLINCH
!!
NOW, NOW...
TAP
MISS.
I THINK YOUR BROTHER UNDERSTANDS WHAT YOU'RE TRYING TO SAY.
I'M SURE HE'S JUST HAVING A HARD TIME CONVEYING HOW HE REALLY FEELS DEEP DOWN INSIDE...

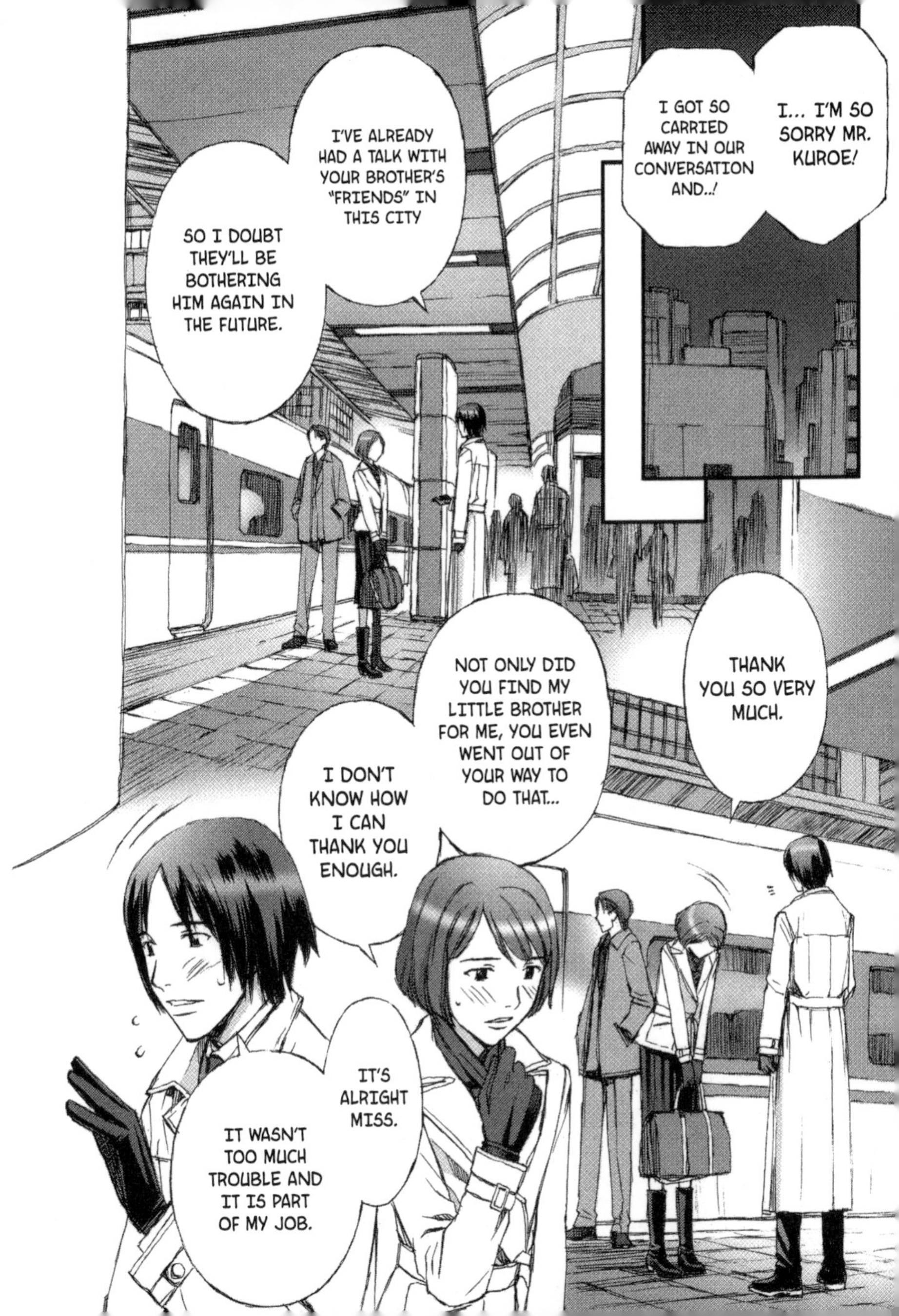
I... I'M SO SORRY MR. KUROE!
I GOT SO CARRIED AWAY IN OUR CONVERSATION AND..!
I'VE ALREADY HAD A TALK WITH YOUR BROTHER'S "FRIENDS" IN THIS CITY
SO I DOUBT THEY'LL BE BOTHERING HIM AGAIN IN THE FUTURE.
THANK YOU SO VERY MUCH.
NOT ONLY DID YOU FIND MY LITTLE BROTHER FOR ME, YOU EVEN WENT OUT OF YOUR WAY TO DO THAT...
I DON'T KNOW HOW I CAN THANK YOU ENOUGH.
IT'S ALRIGHT MISS.
IT WASN'T TOO MUCH TROUBLE AND IT IS PART OF MY JOB.

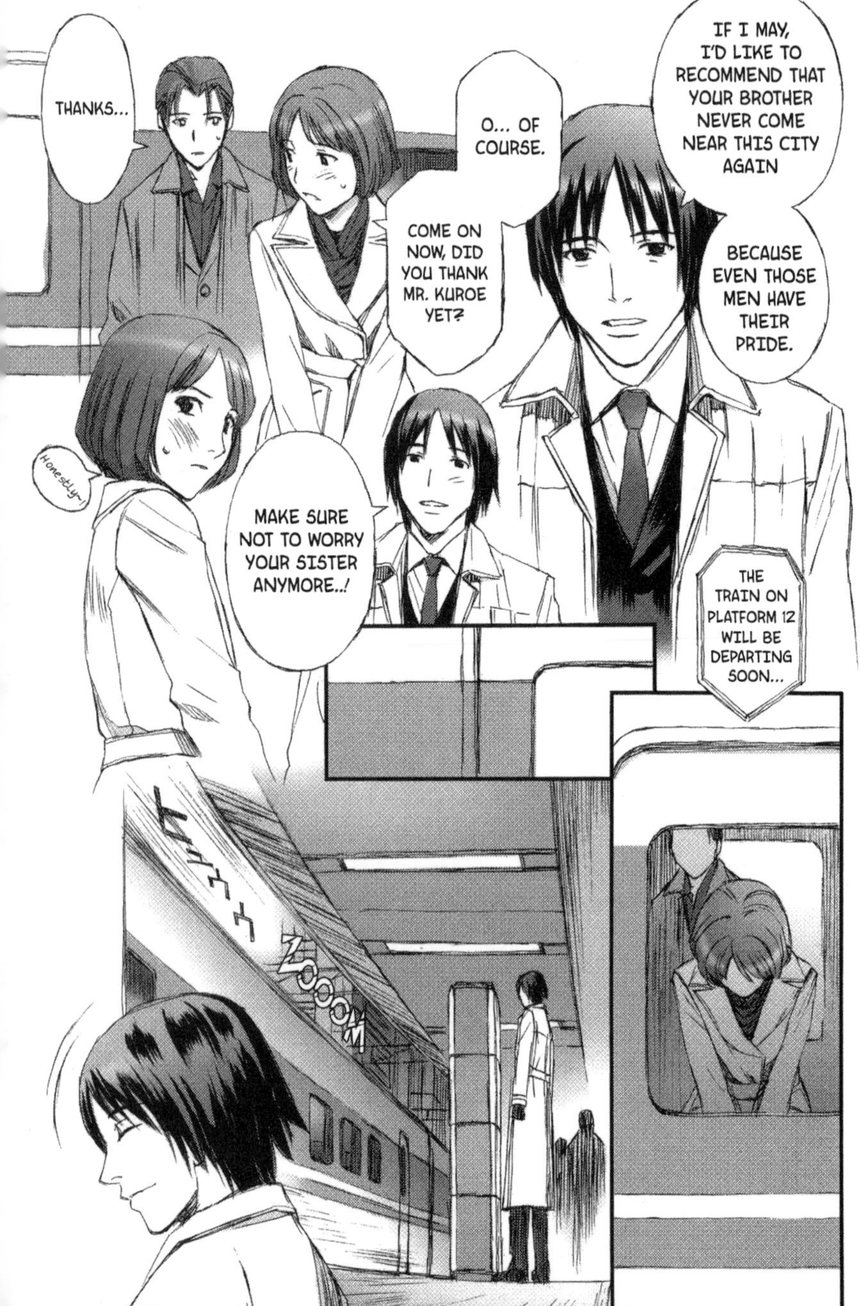
IF I MAY, I'D LIKE TO RECOMMEND THAT YOUR BROTHER NEVER COME NEAR THIS CITY AGAIN
BECAUSE EVEN THOSE MEN HAVE THEIR PRIDE.
O... OF COURSE.
COME ON NOW, DID YOU THANK MR. KUROE YET?
THANKS...
MAKE SURE NOT TO WORRY YOUR SISTER ANYMORE..!
Honestly~!
THE TRAIN ON PLATFORM 12 WILL BE DEPARTING SOON...
ZOOOM

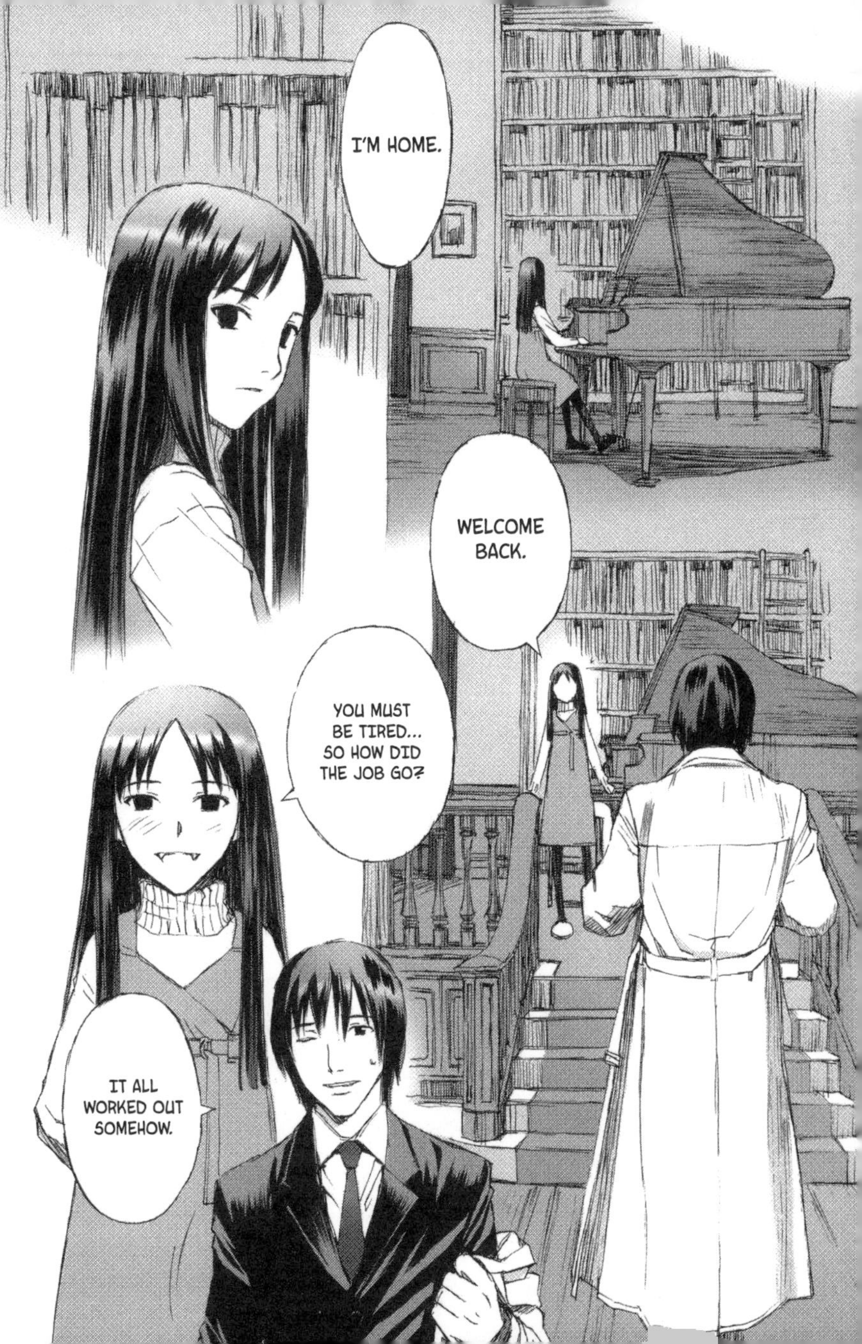
I'M HOME.
WELCOME BACK.
YOU MUST BE TIRED... SO HOW DID THE JOB GO?
IT ALL WORKED OUT SOMEHOW.

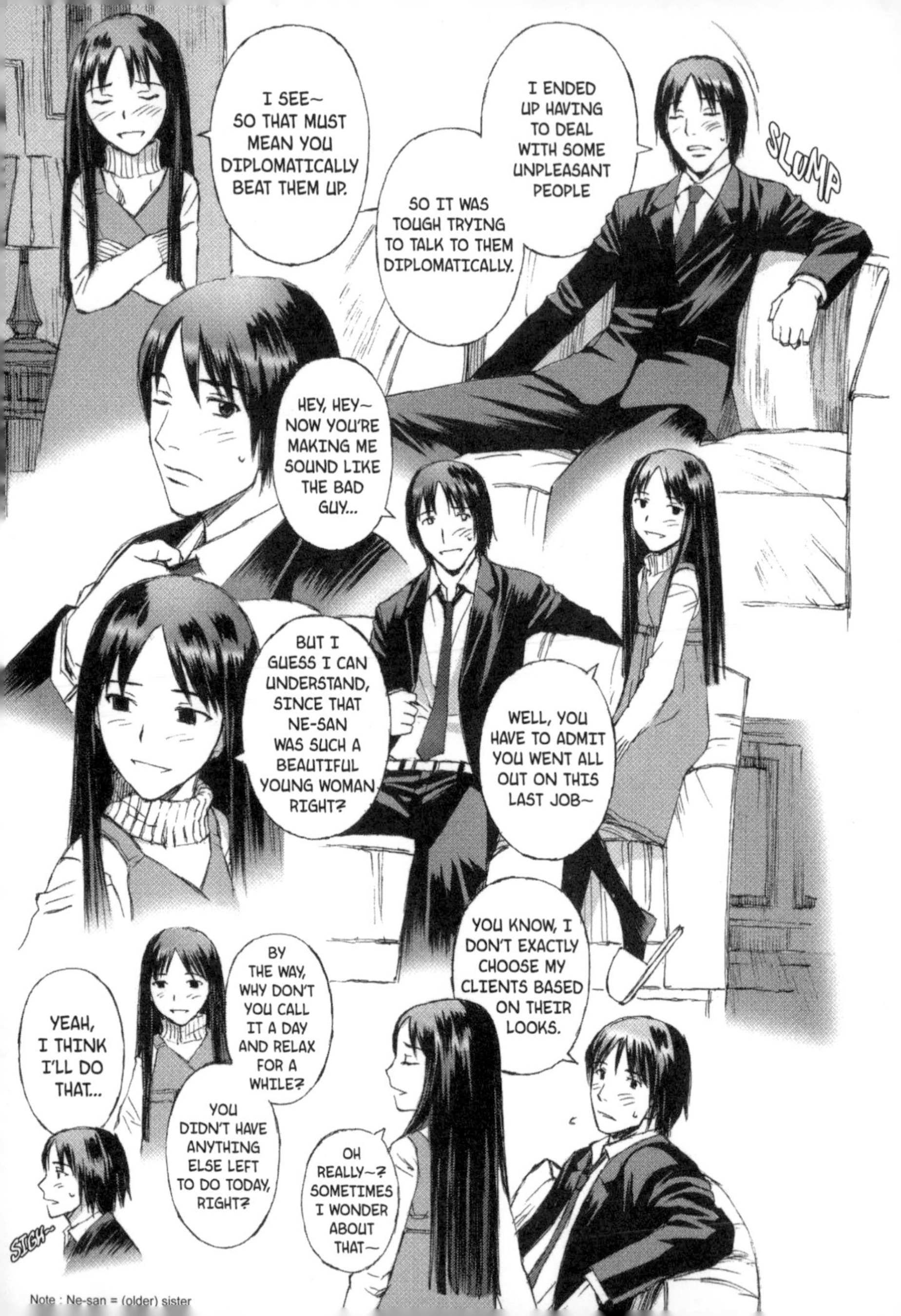
I ENDED UP HAVING TO DEAL WITH SOME UNPLEASANT PEOPLE
SO IT WAS TOUGH TRYING TO TALK TO THEM DIPLOMATICALLY.
SLUMP
I SEE~ SO THAT MUST MEAN YOU DIPLOMATICALLY BEAT THEM UP.
WELL, YOU HAVE TO ADMIT YOU WENT ALL OUT ON THIS LAST JOB~
YOU KNOW, I DON'T EXACTLY CHOOSE MY CLIENTS BASED ON THEIR LOOKS.
OH REALLY~? SOMETIMES I WONDER ABOUT THAT~
HEY, HEY~ NOW YOU'RE MAKING ME SOUND LIKE THE BAD GUY...
BUT I GUESS I CAN UNDERSTAND, SINCE THAT NE-SAN WAS SUCH A BEAUTIFUL YOUNG WOMAN, RIGHT?
BY THE WAY, WHY DON'T YOU CALL IT A DAY AND RELAX FOR A WHILE?
YOU DIDN'T HAVE ANYTHING ELSE LEFT TO DO TODAY, RIGHT?
YEAH, I THINK I'LL DO THAT...
SIGH~

Note : Ne-san = (older) sister

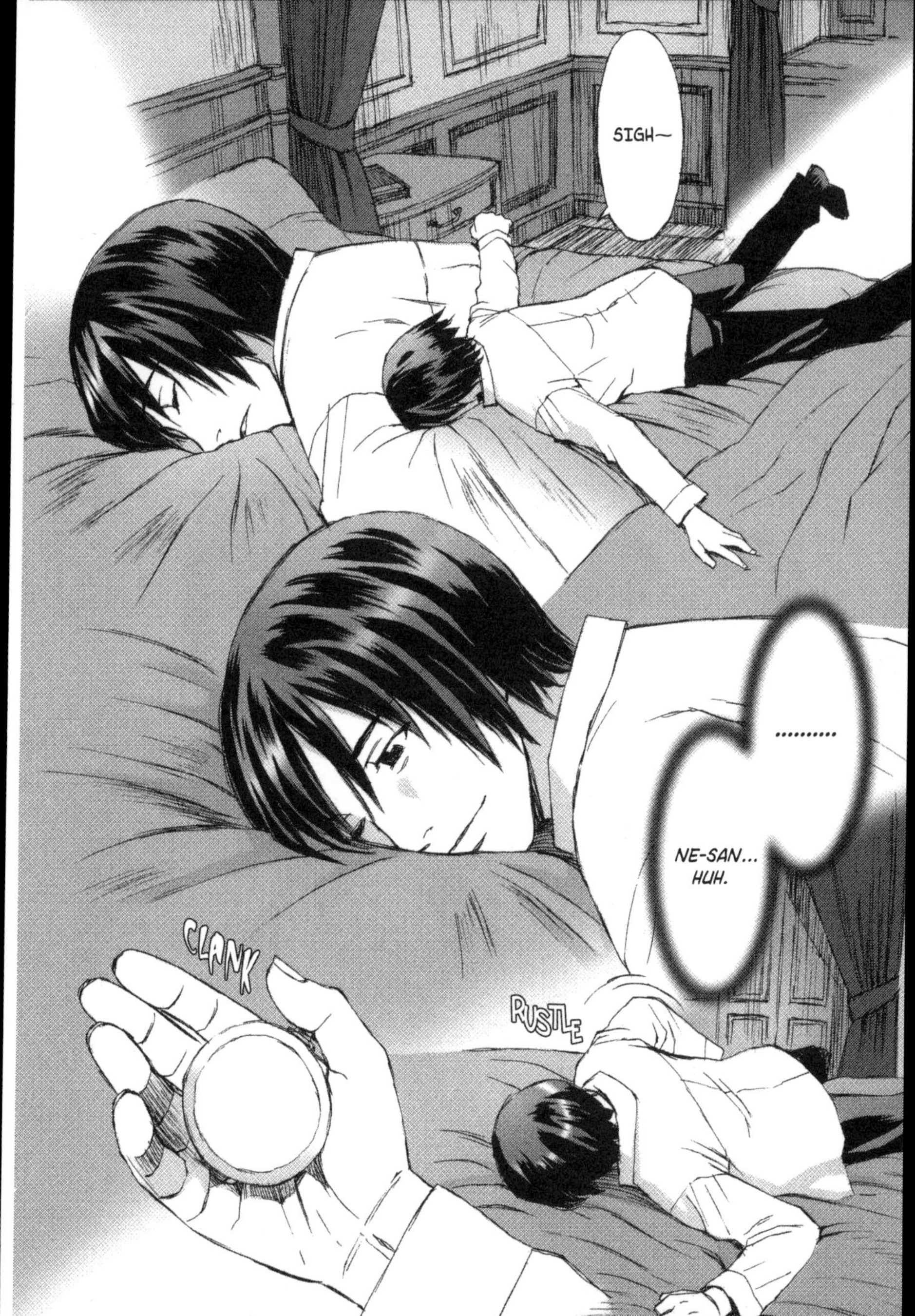
SIGH~
....
NE-SAN... HUH.
CLANK
RUSTLE

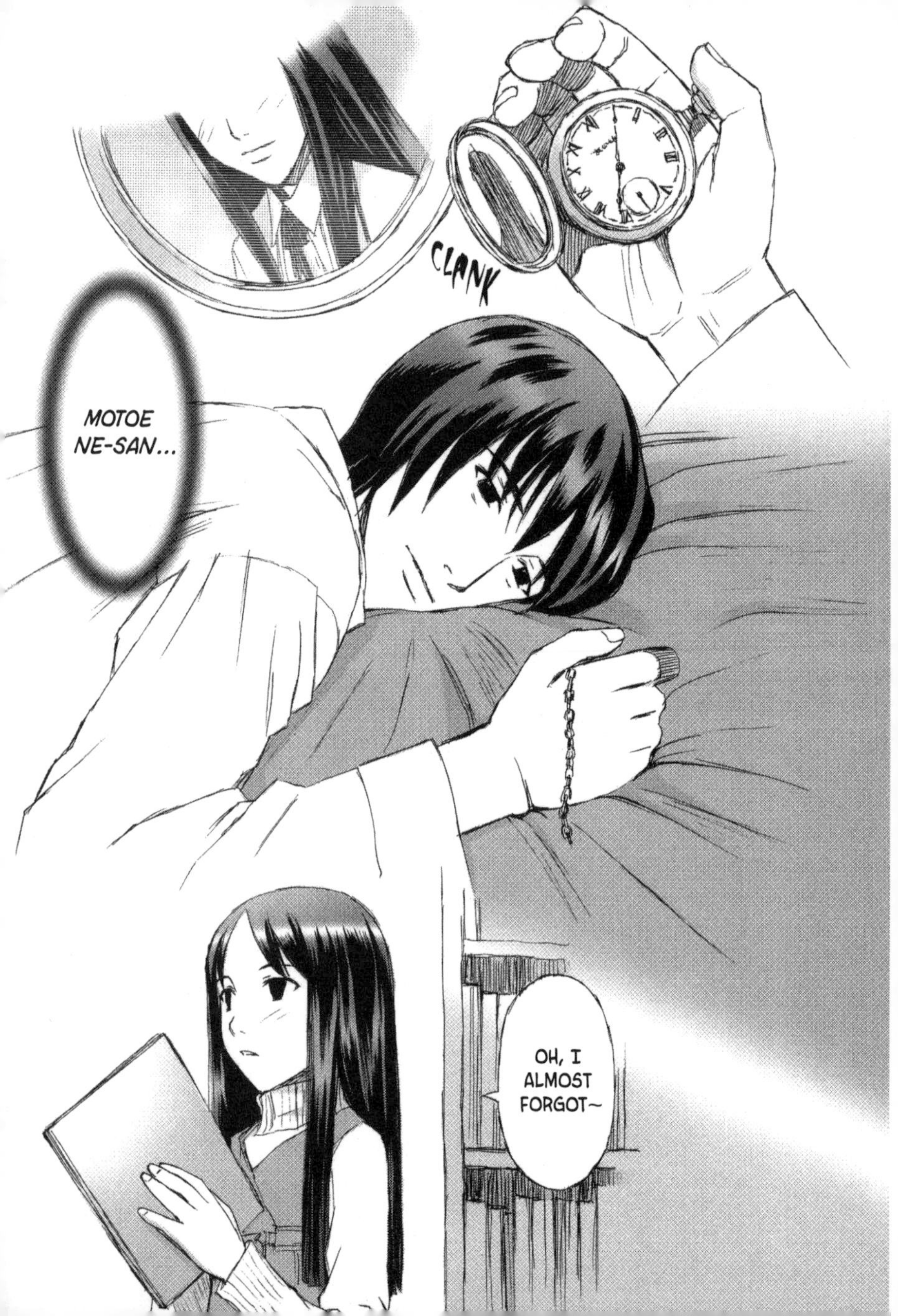
CLANK
MOTOE NE-SAN...
OH, I ALMOST FORGOT~

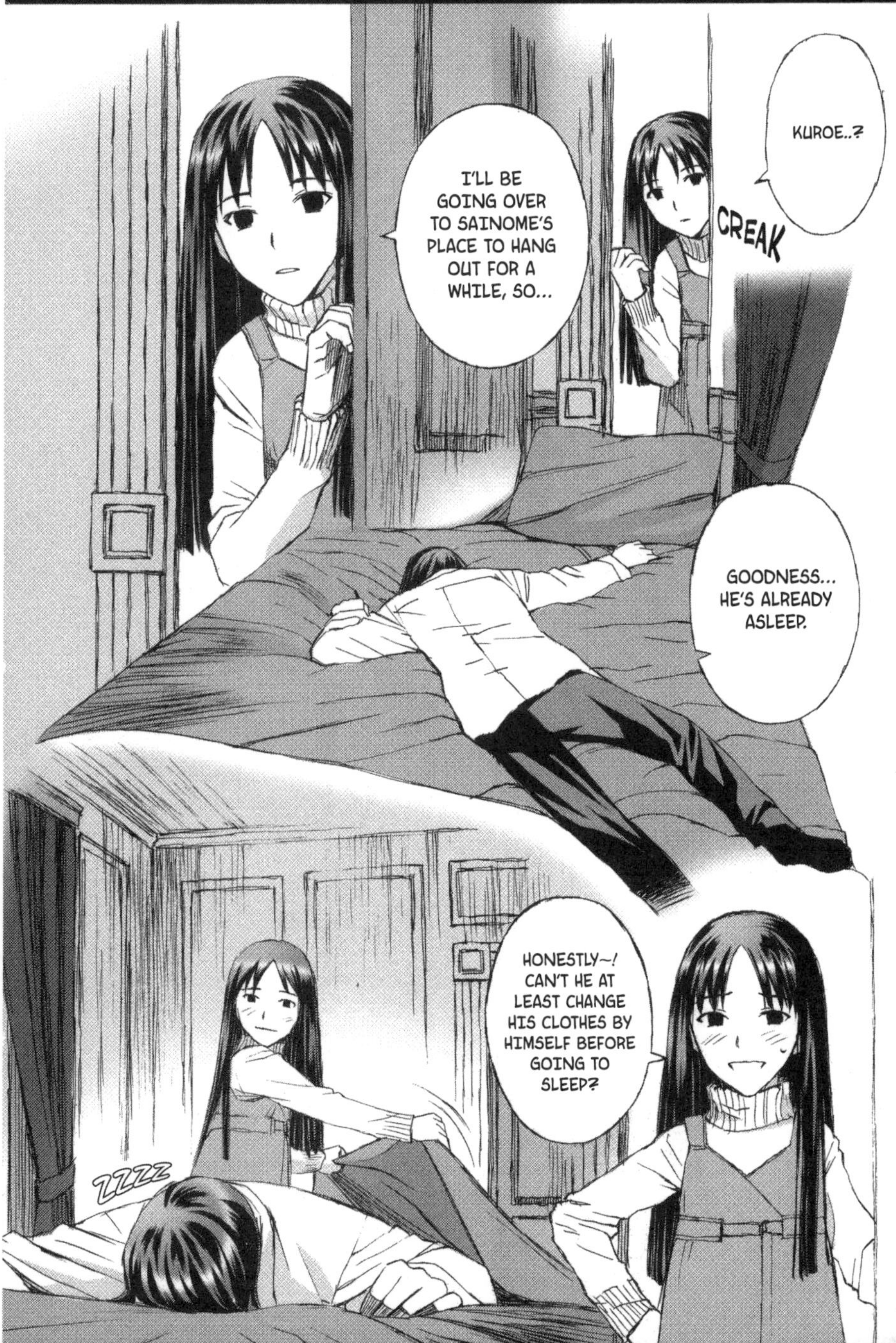
KUROE..?
CREAK
I'LL BE GOING OVER TO SAINOME'S PLACE TO HANG OUT FOR A WHILE, SO...
GOODNESS... HE'S ALREADY ASLEEP.
HONESTLY~! CAN'T HE AT LEAST CHANGE HIS CLOTHES BY HIMSELF BEFORE GOING TO SLEEP?
ZZZZ

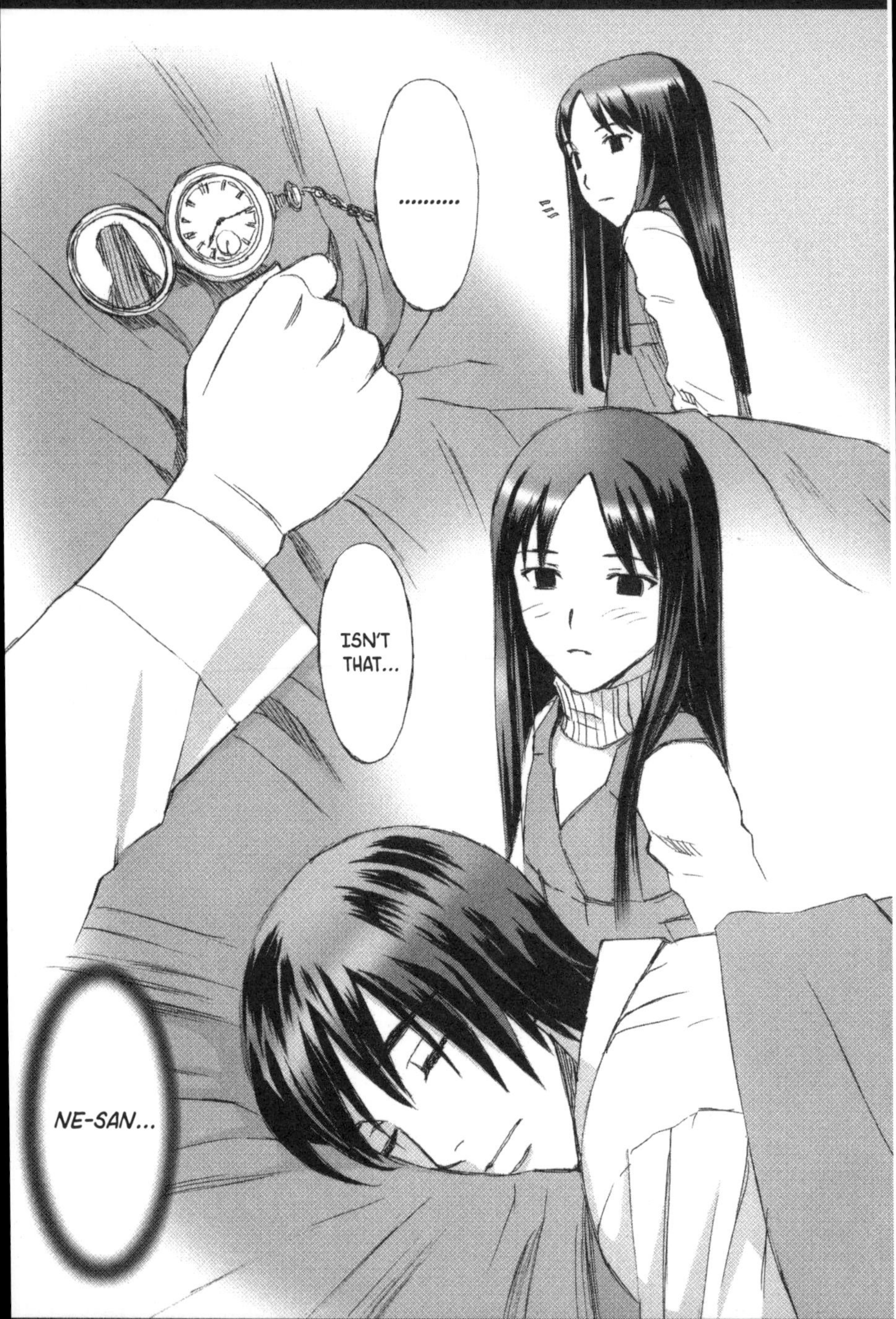
....
ISN'T THAT...
NE-SAN...

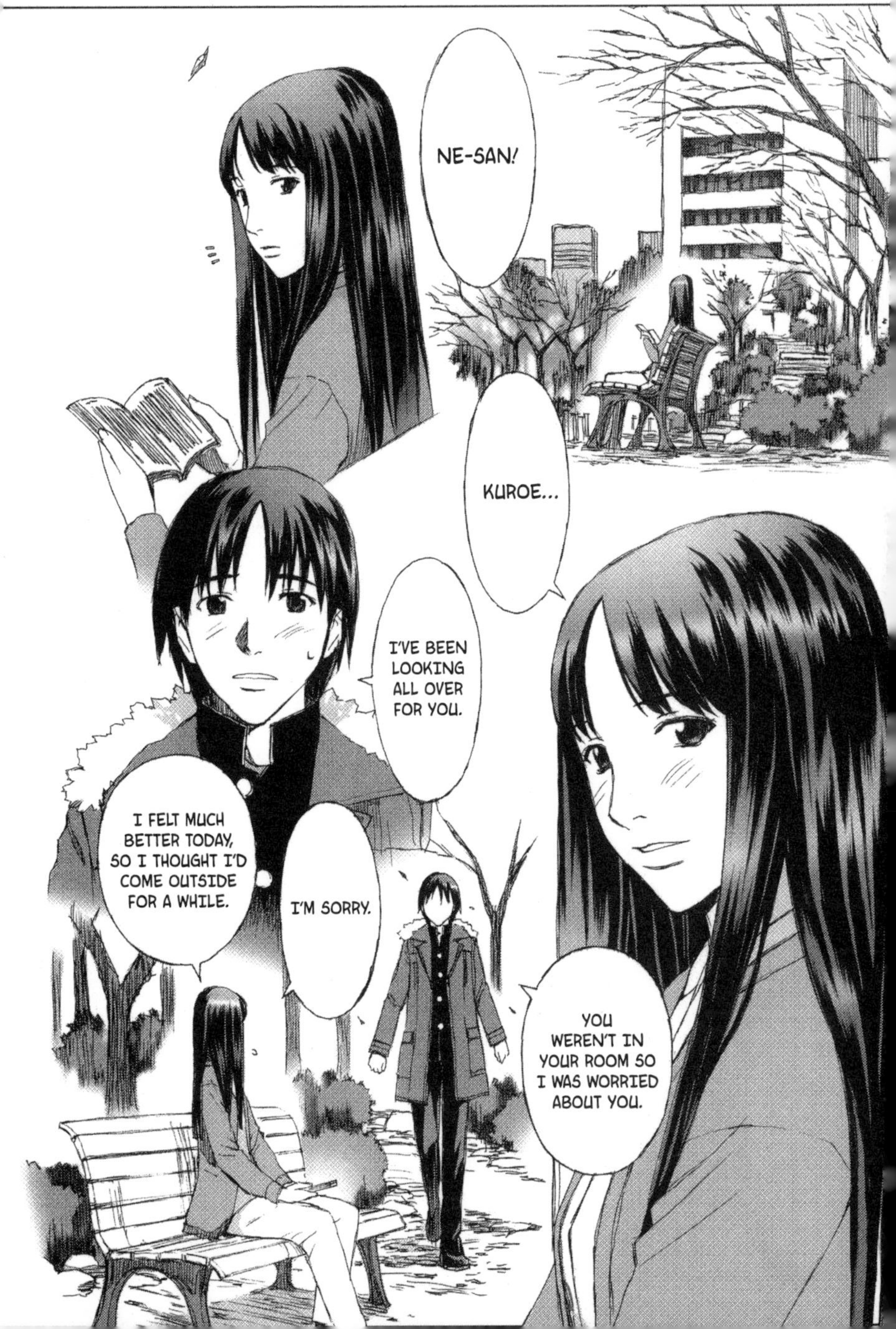

NE-SAN!
KUROE...
I'VE BEEN LOOKING ALL OVER FOR YOU.
YOU WEREN'T IN YOUR ROOM SO I WAS WORRIED ABOUT YOU.
I'M SORRY.
I FELT MUCH BETTER TODAY, SO I THOUGHT I'D COME OUTSIDE FOR A WHILE.

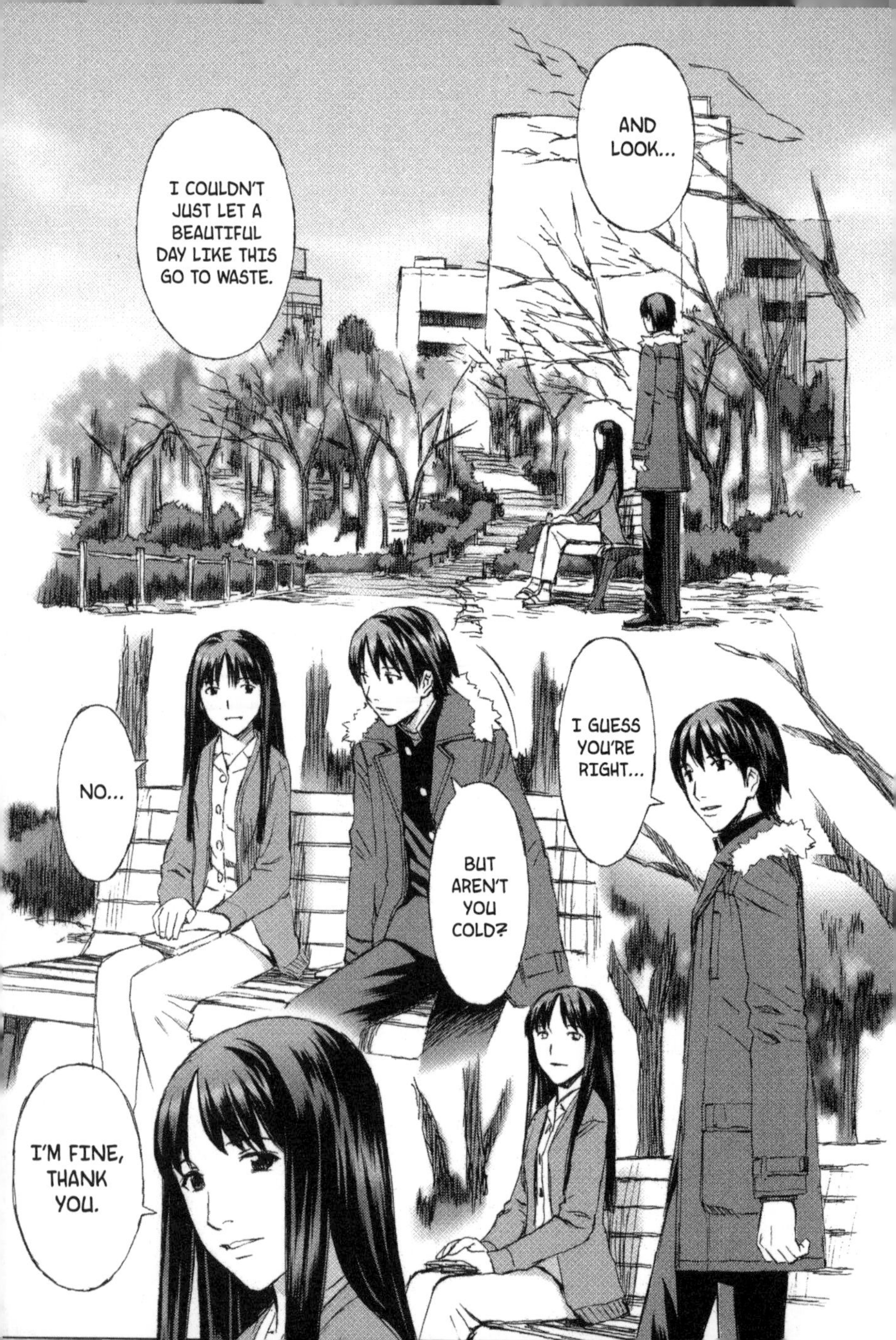
AND LOOK...
I COULDN'T JUST LET A BEAUTIFUL DAY LIKE THIS GO TO WASTE.
I GUESS YOU'RE RIGHT...
BUT AREN'T YOU COLD?
NO...
I'M FINE, THANK YOU.

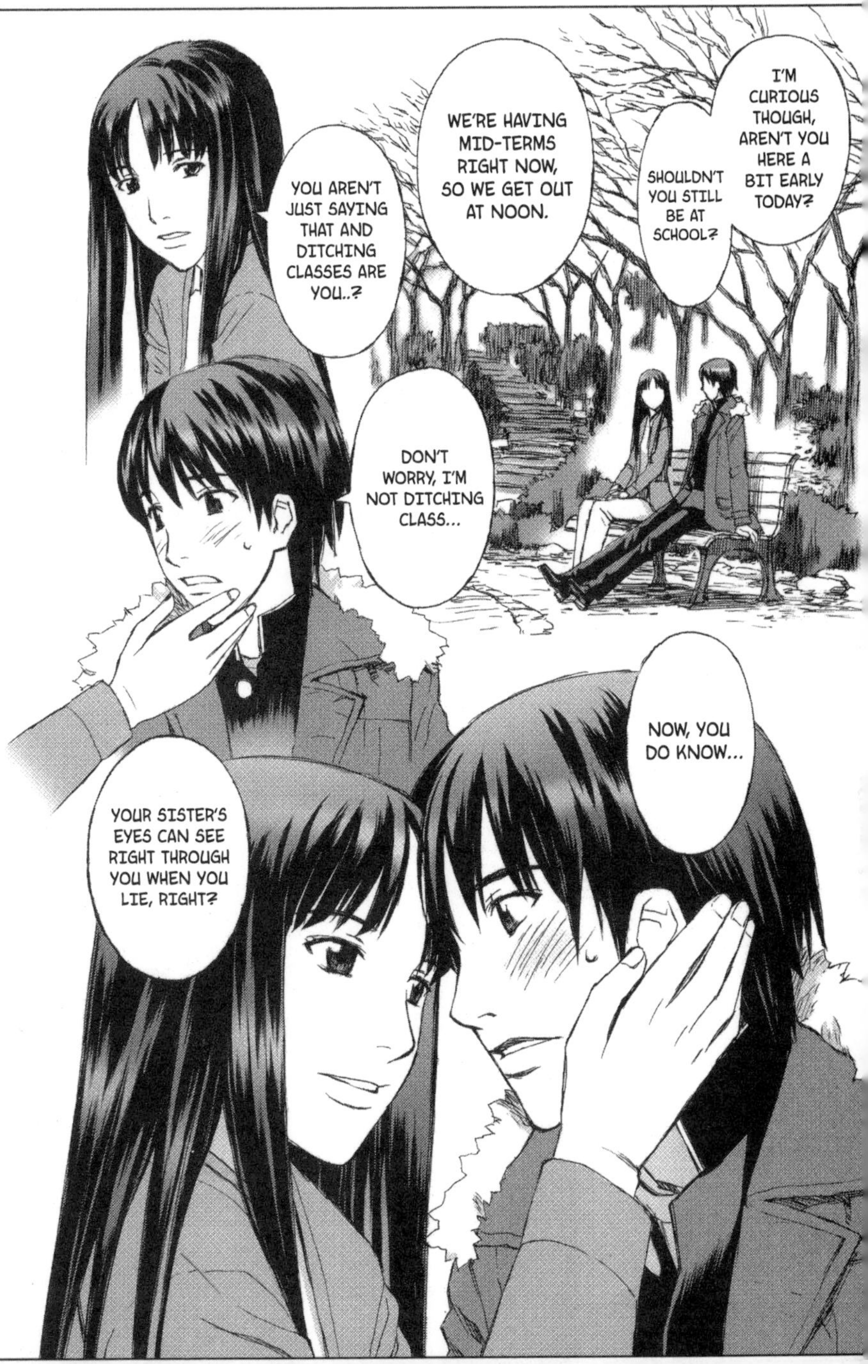
I'M CURIOUS THOUGH, AREN'T YOU HERE A BIT EARLY TODAY?
SHOULDN'T YOU STILL BE AT SCHOOL?
WE'RE HAVING MID-TERMS RIGHT NOW, SO WE GET OUT AT NOON.
YOU AREN'T JUST SAYING THAT AND DITCHING CLASSES ARE YOU..?
DON'T WORRY, I'M NOT DITCHING CLASS...
NOW, YOU DO KNOW...
YOUR SISTER'S EYES CAN SEE RIGHT THROUGH YOU WHEN YOU LIE, RIGHT?

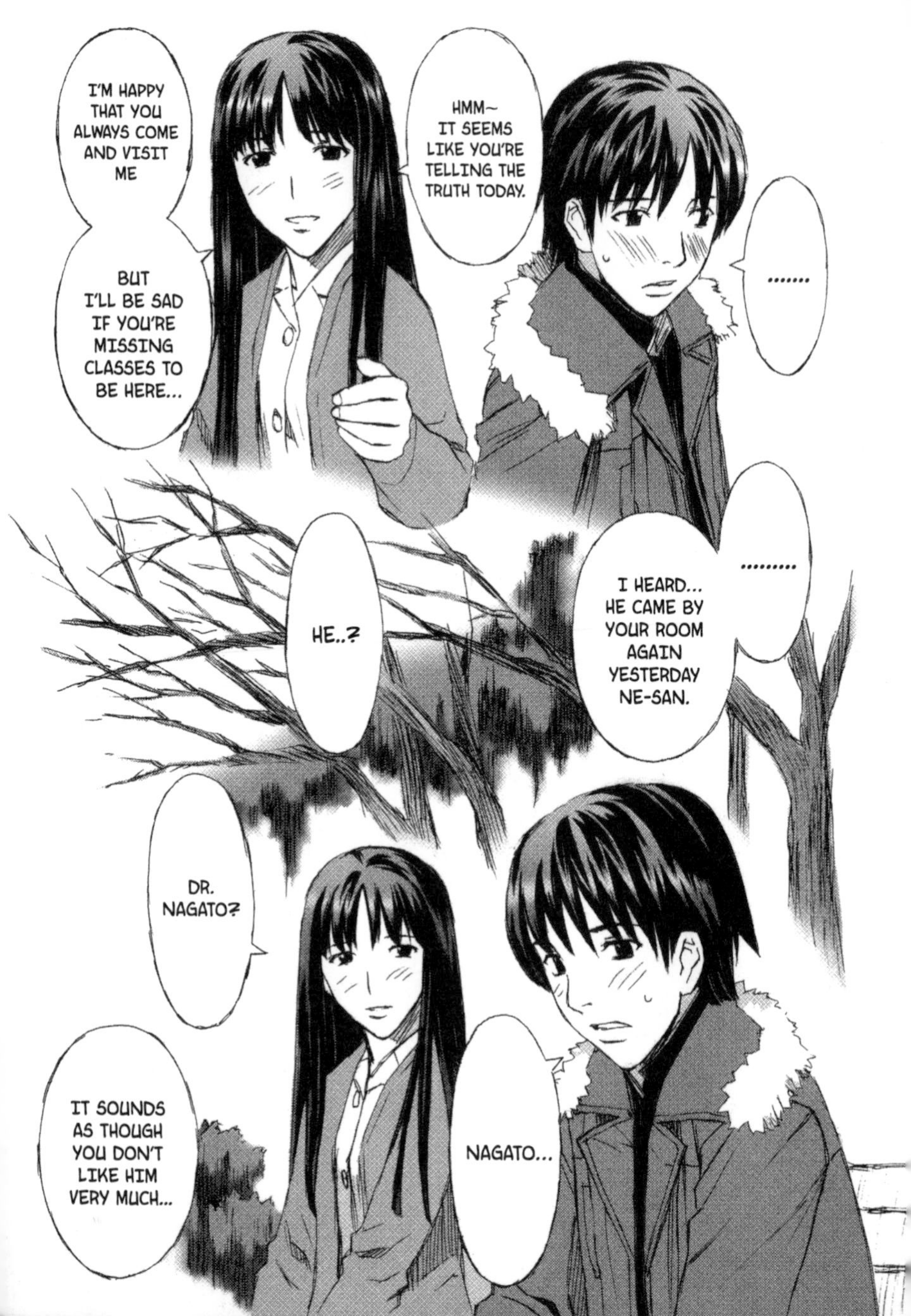
HMM~ IT SEEMS LIKE YOU'RE TELLING THE TRUTH TODAY.
I'M HAPPY THAT YOU ALWAYS COME AND VISIT ME
BUT I'LL BE SAD IF YOU'RE MISSING CLASSES TO BE HERE...
....
....
I HEARD... HE CAME BY YOUR ROOM AGAIN YESTERDAY NE-SAN.
HE..?
DR. NAGATO?
NAGATO...
IT SOUNDS AS THOUGH YOU DON'T LIKE HIM VERY MUCH...

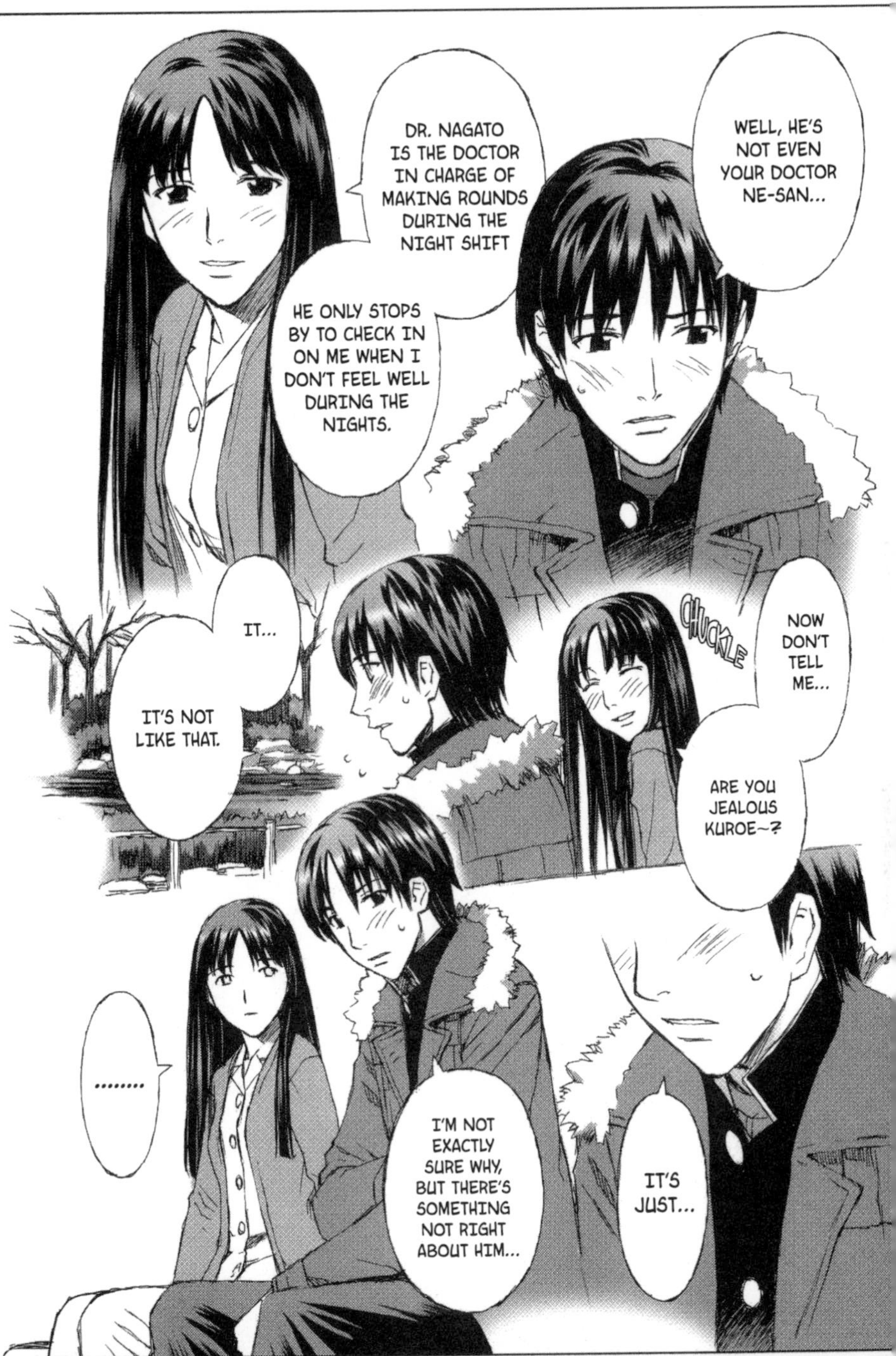
WELL, HE'S NOT EVEN YOUR DOCTOR NE-SAN...
DR. NAGATO IS THE DOCTOR IN CHARGE OF MAKING ROUNDS DURING THE NIGHT SHIFT
HE ONLY STOPS BY TO CHECK IN ON ME WHEN I DON'T FEEL WELL DURING THE NIGHTS.
CHUCKLE
NOW DON'T TELL ME...
ARE YOU JEALOUS KUROE~?
IT...
IT'S NOT LIKE THAT.
IT'S JUST...
I'M NOT EXACTLY SURE WHY, BUT THERE'S SOMETHING NOT RIGHT ABOUT HIM...
....

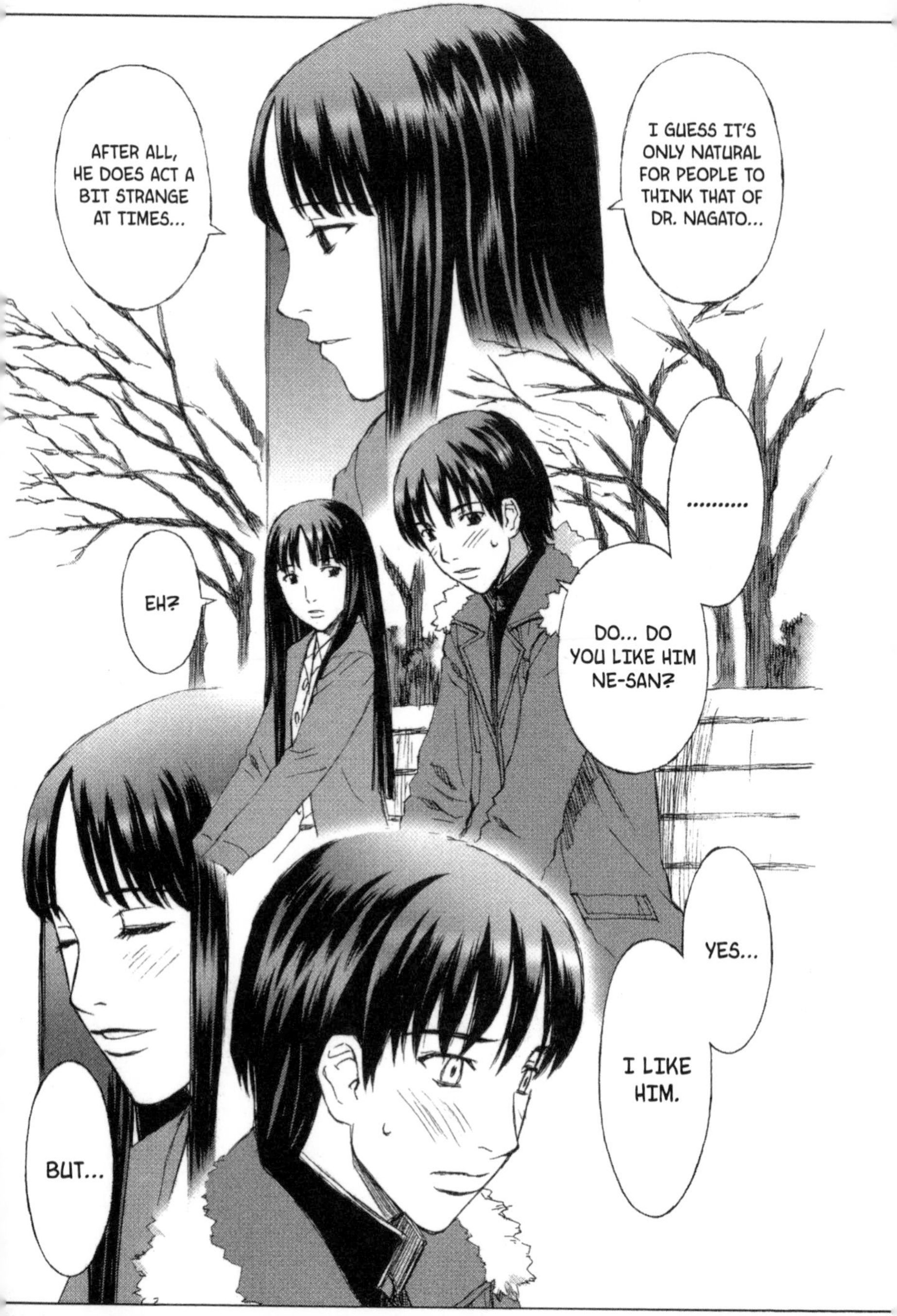
I GUESS IT'S ONLY NATURAL FOR PEOPLE TO THINK THAT OF DR. NAGATO...
AFTER ALL, HE DOES ACT A BIT STRANGE AT TIMES...
....
DO... DO YOU LIKE HIM NE-SAN?
EH?
YES...
I LIKE HIM.
BUT...

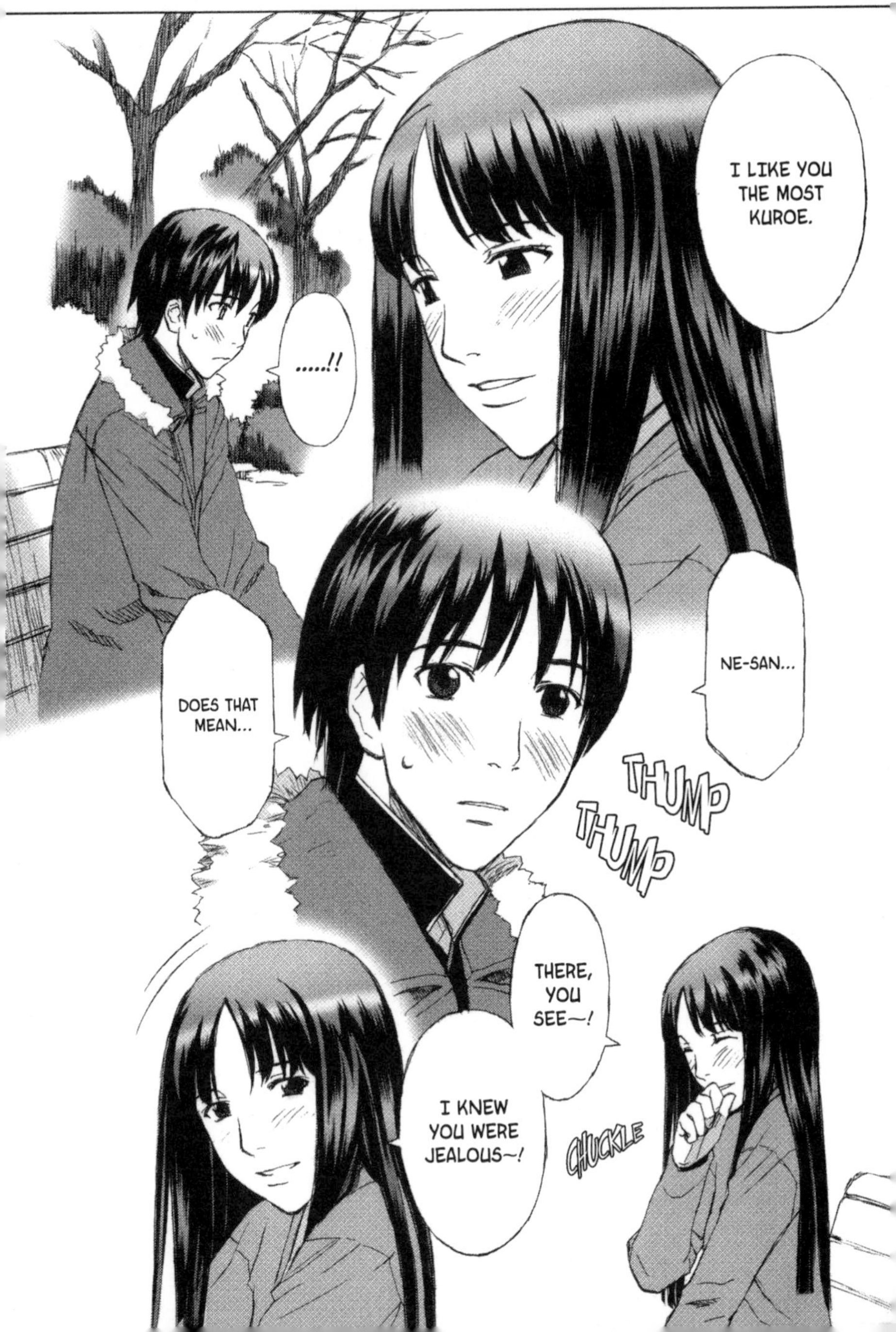
I LIKE YOU THE MOST KUROE.
......!!
NE-SAN...
DOES THAT MEAN...
THUMP
THUMP
CHUCKLE
THERE, YOU SEE~!
I KNEW YOU WERE JEALOUS~!

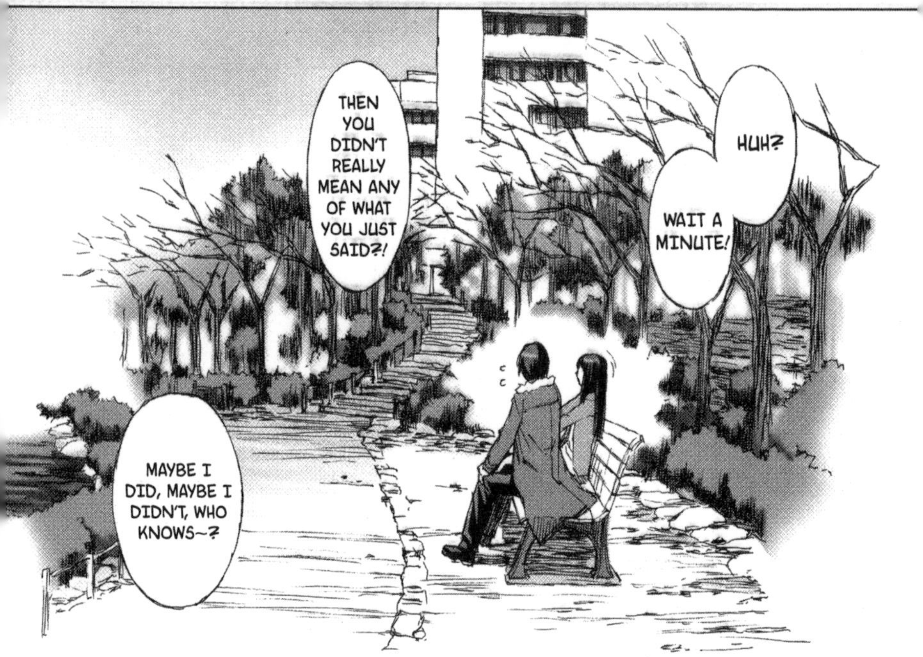
HUH?
WAIT A MINUTE!
THEN YOU DIDN'T REALLY MEAN ANY OF WHAT YOU JUST SAID?!
MAYBE I DID, MAYBE I DIDN'T, WHO KNOWS~?

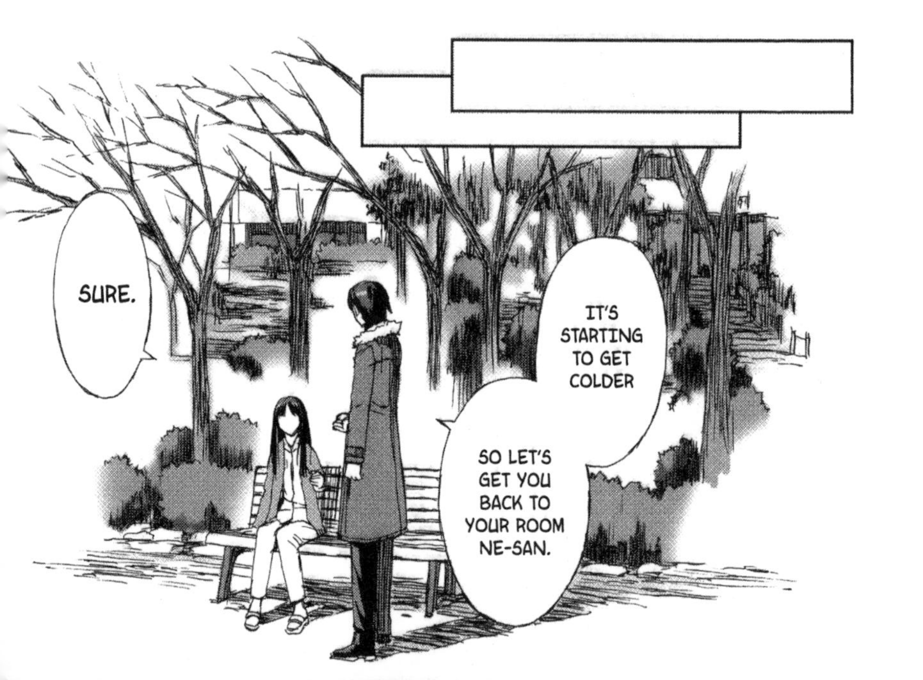
IT'S STARTING TO GET COLDER
SO LET'S GET YOU BACK TO YOUR ROOM NE-SAN.
SURE.

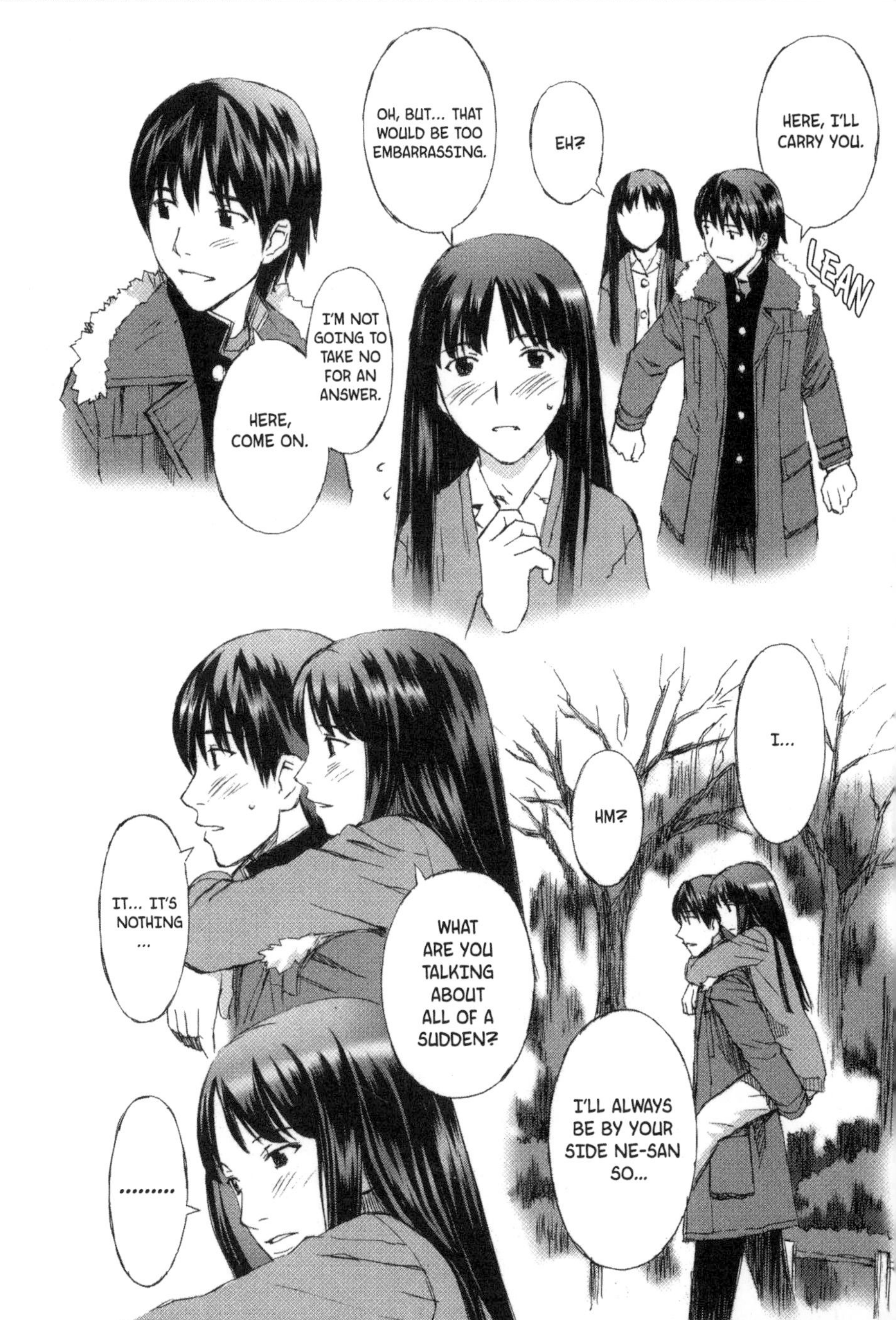
HERE, I'LL CARRY YOU.
LEAN
EH?
OH, BUT... THAT WOULD BE TOO EMBARRASSING.
I'M NOT GOING TO TAKE NO FOR AN ANSWER.
HERE, COME ON.
I...
HM?
I'LL ALWAYS BE BY YOUR SIDE NE-SAN SO...
WHAT ARE YOU TALKING ABOUT ALL OF A SUDDEN?
IT... IT'S NOTHING ...
....

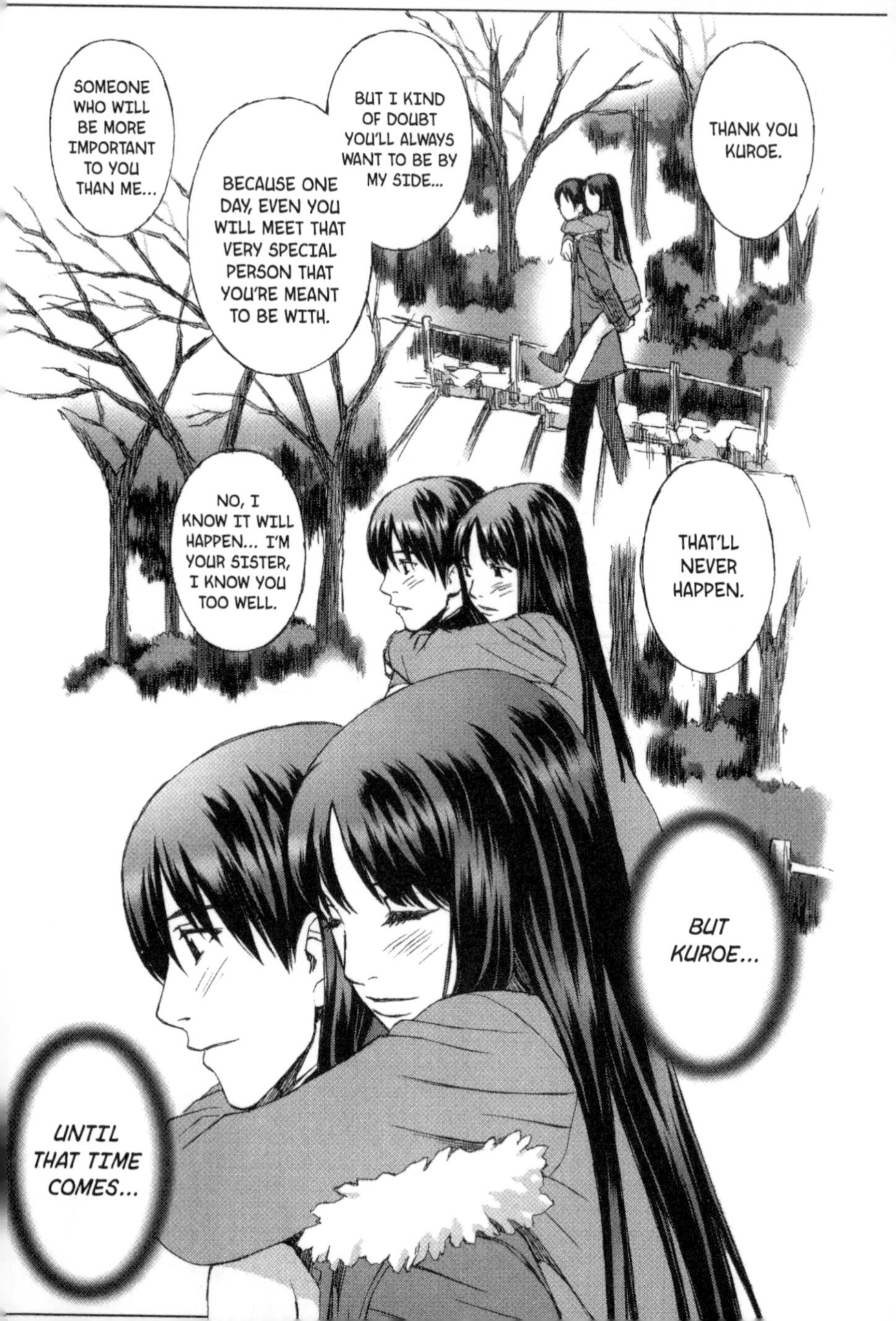
THANK YOU KUROE.
BUT I KIND OF DOUBT YOU'LL ALWAYS WANT TO BE BY MY SIDE...
BECAUSE ONE DAY, EVEN YOU WILL MEET THAT VERY SPECIAL PERSON THAT YOU'RE MEANT TO BE WITH.
SOMEONE WHO WILL BE MORE IMPORTANT TO YOU THAN ME...
THAT'LL NEVER HAPPEN.
NO, I KNOW IT WILL HAPPEN... I'M YOUR SISTER, I KNOW YOU TOO WELL.
BUT KUROE...
UNTIL THAT TIME COMES...

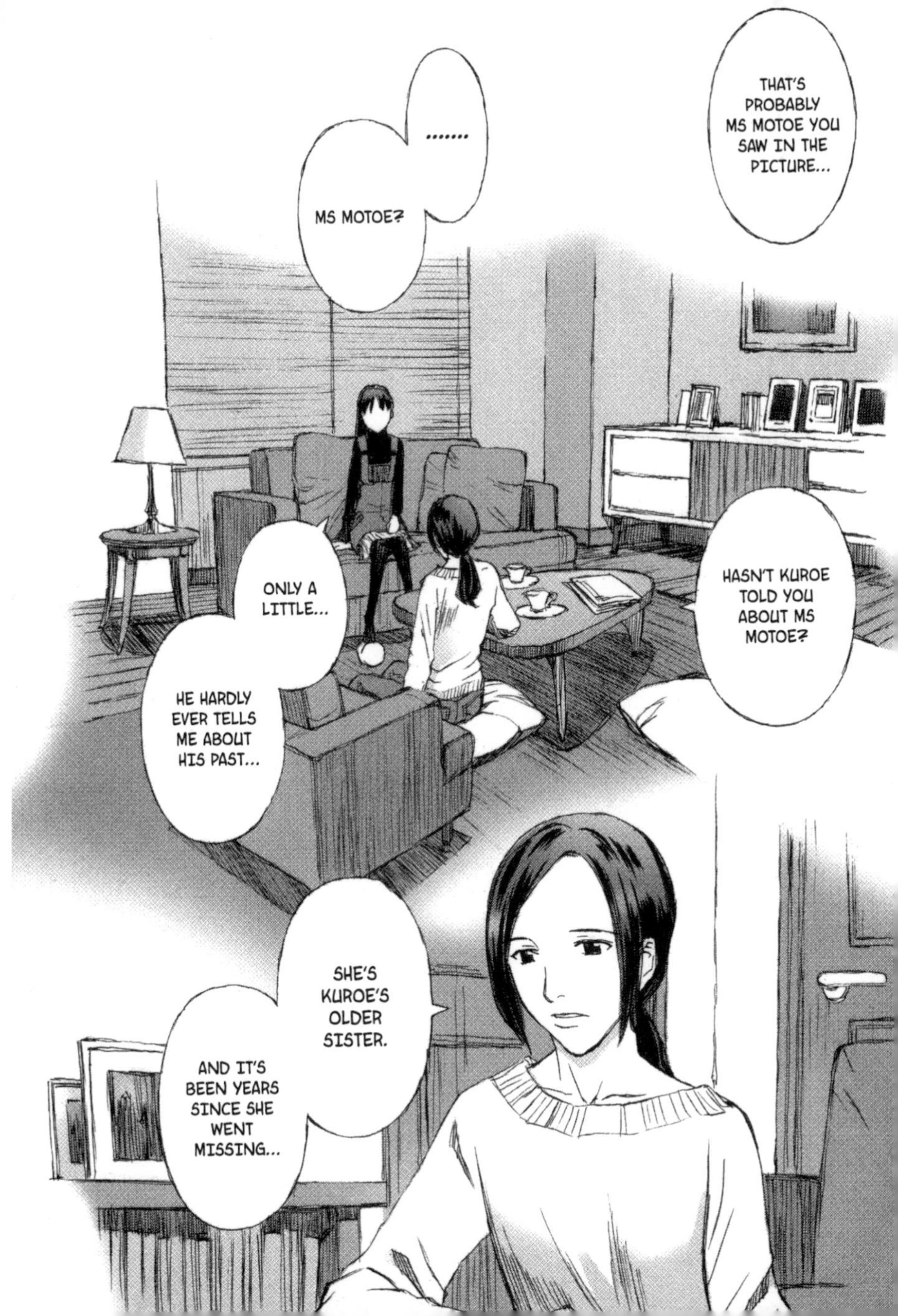
THAT'S PROBABLY MS MOTOE YOU SAW IN THE PICTURE...
....
MS MOTOE?
HASN'T KUROE TOLD YOU ABOUT MS MOTOE?
ONLY A LITTLE...
HE HARDLY EVER TELLS ME ABOUT HIS PAST...
SHE'S KUROE'S OLDER SISTER.
AND IT'S BEEN YEARS SINCE SHE WENT MISSING...

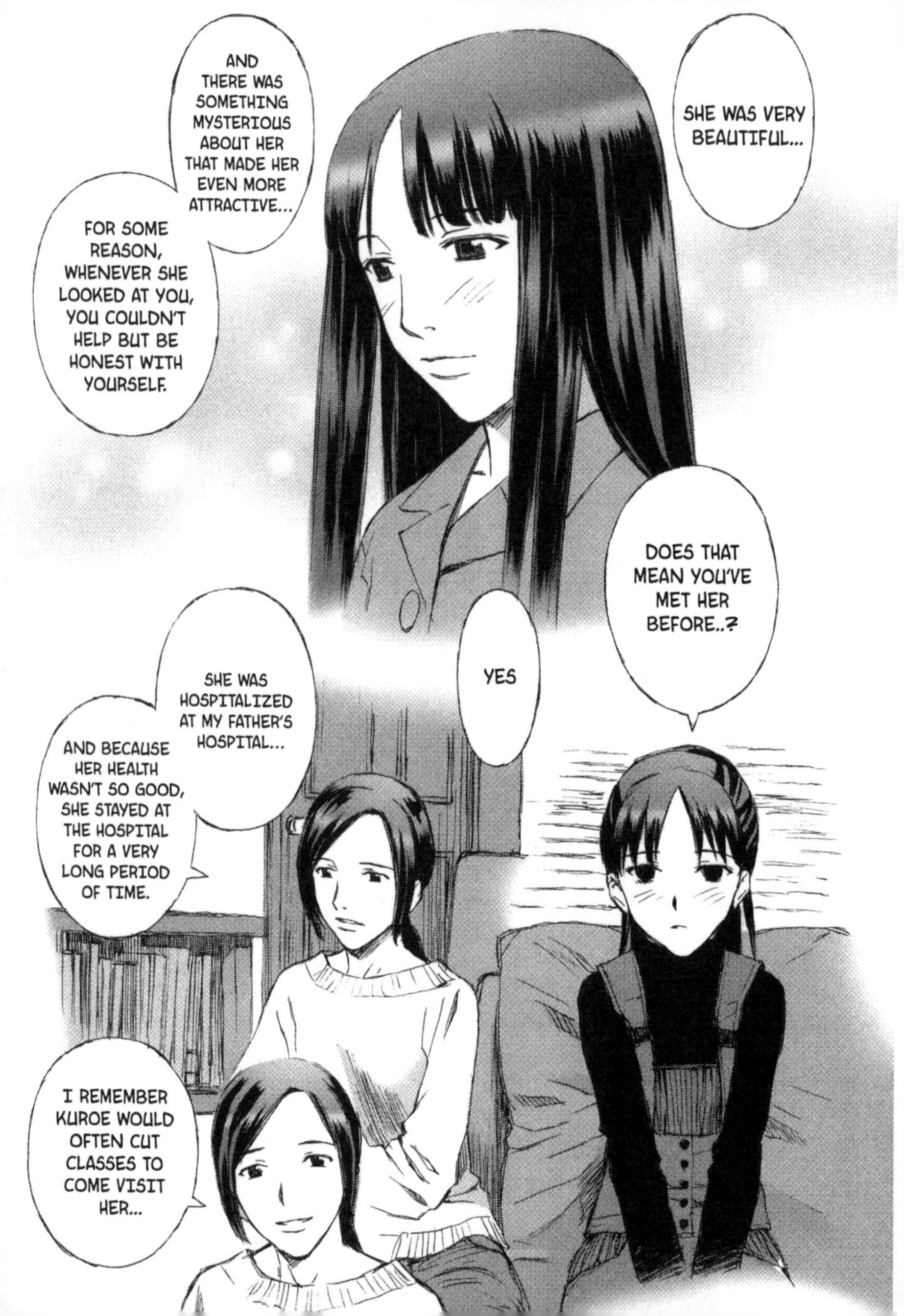
SHE WAS VERY BEAUTIFUL...
AND THERE WAS SOMETHING MYSTERIOUS ABOUT HER THAT MADE HER EVEN MORE ATTRACTIVE...
FOR SOME REASON, WHENEVER SHE LOOKED AT YOU, YOU COULDN'T HELP BUT BE HONEST WITH YOURSELF.
DOES THAT MEAN YOU'VE MET HER BEFORE..?
YES
SHE WAS HOSPITALIZED AT MY FATHER'S HOSPITAL...
AND BECAUSE HER HEALTH WASN'T SO GOOD, SHE STAYED AT THE HOSPITAL FOR A VERY LONG PERIOD OF TIME.
I REMEMBER KUROE WOULD OFTEN CUT CLASSES TO COME VISIT HER...

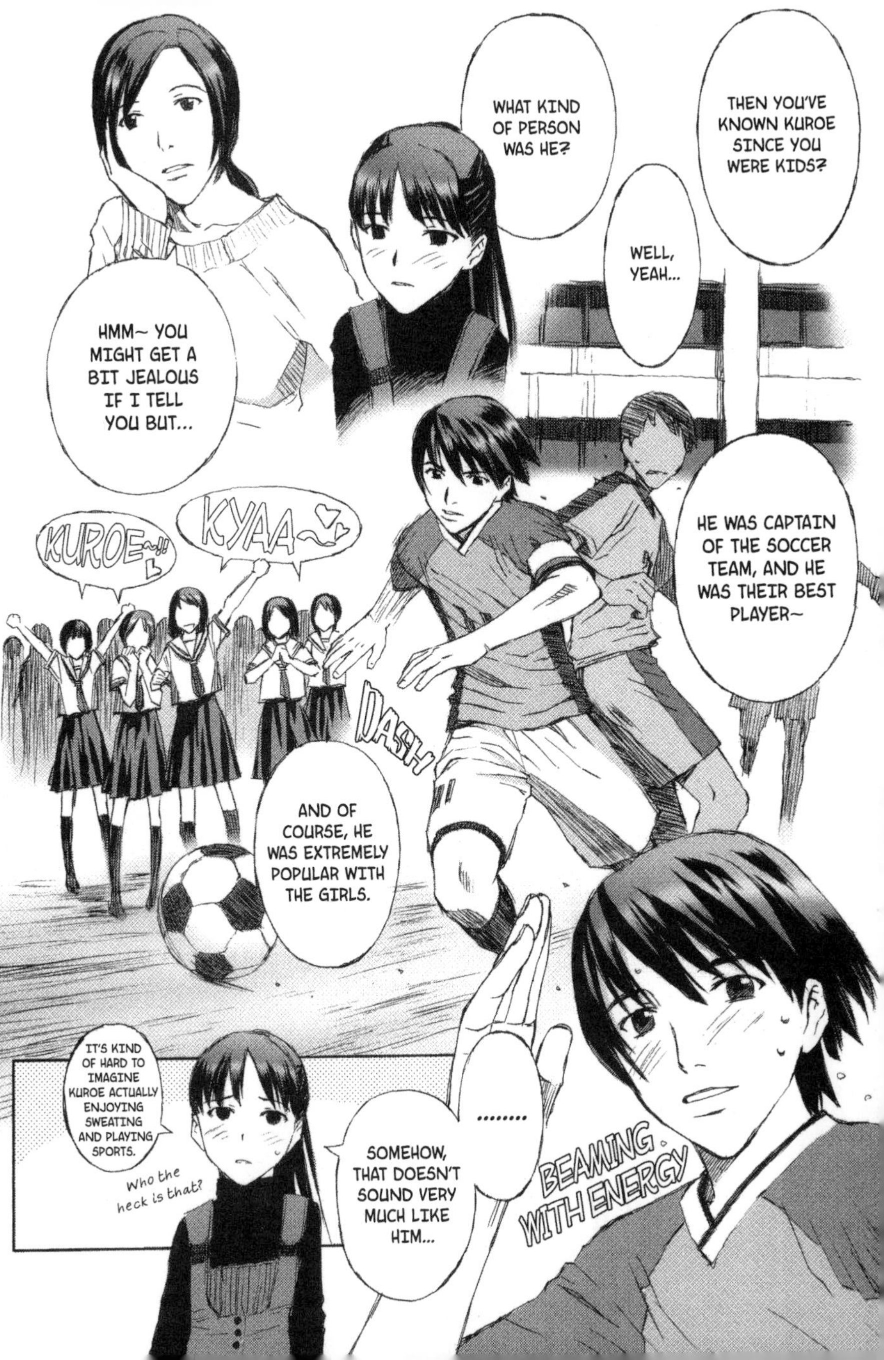
THEN YOU'VE KNOWN KUROE SINCE YOU WERE KIDS?
WELL, YEAH...
WHAT KIND OF PERSON WAS HE?
HMM~ YOU MIGHT GET A BIT JEALOUS IF I TELL YOU BUT...
HE WAS CAPTAIN OF THE SOCCER TEAM, AND HE WAS THEIR BEST PLAYER~
KYAA~
KUROE~!!
DASH
AND OF COURSE, HE WAS EXTREMELY POPULAR WITH THE GIRLS.
BEAMING WITH ENERGY
....
SOMEHOW, THAT DOESN'T SOUND VERY MUCH LIKE HIM...
IT'S KIND OF HARD TO IMAGINE KUROE ACTUALLY ENJOYING SWEATING AND PLAYING SPORTS.
Who the heck is that?

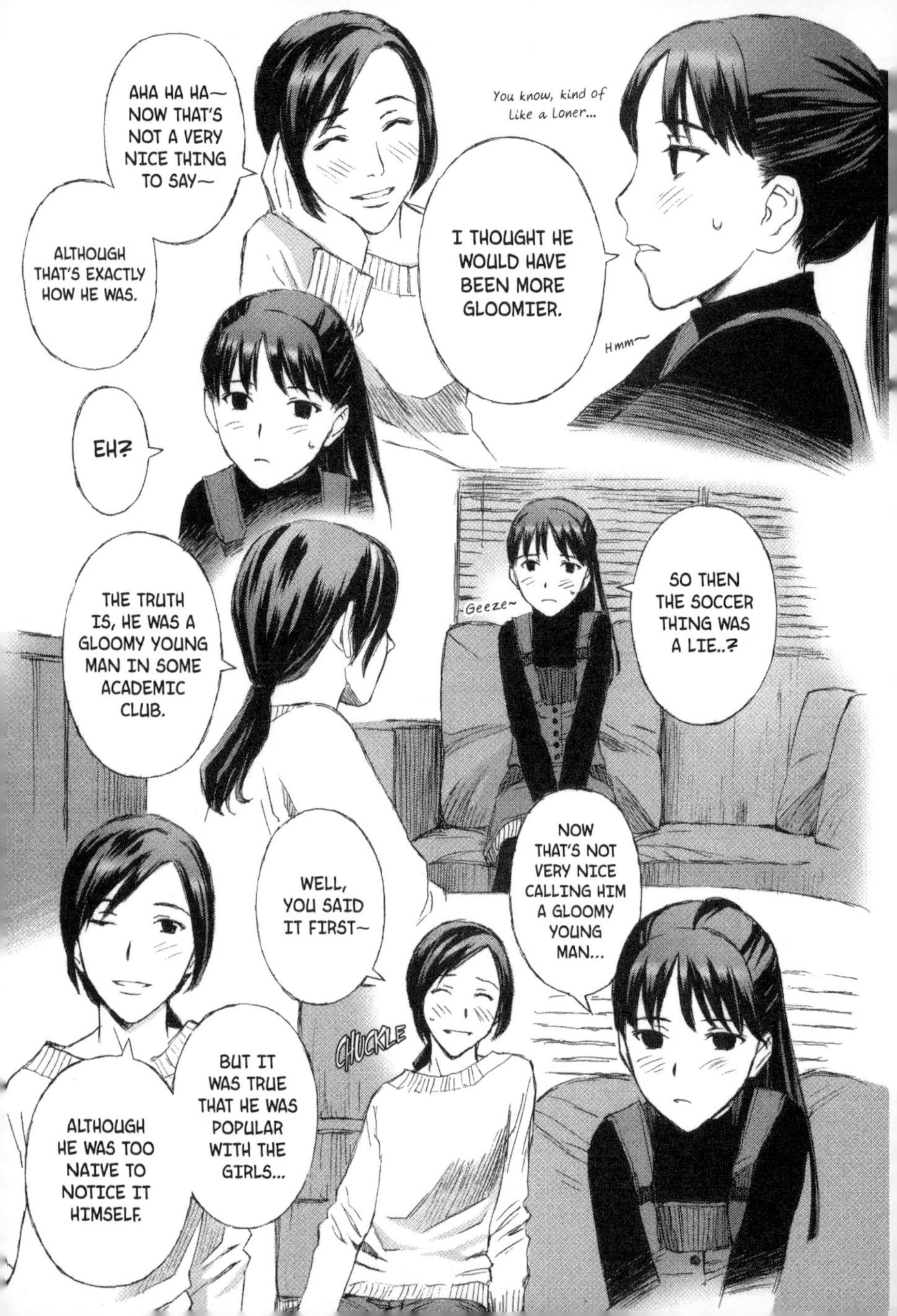
You know, kind of Like a Loner...
I THOUGHT HE WOULD HAVE BEEN MORE GLOOMIER.
Hmm~
AHA HA HA~ NOW THAT'S NOT A VERY NICE THING TO SAY~
ALTHOUGH THAT'S EXACTLY HOW HE WAS.
EH?
Geeze~
SO THEN THE SOCCER THING WAS A LIE..?
THE TRUTH IS, HE WAS A GLOOMY YOUNG MAN IN SOME ACADEMIC CLUB.
NOW THAT'S NOT VERY NICE CALLING HIM A GLOOMY YOUNG MAN...
CHUCKLE
WELL, YOU SAID IT FIRST~
BUT IT WAS TRUE THAT HE WAS POPULAR WITH THE GIRLS...
ALTHOUGH HE WAS TOO NAIVE TO NOTICE IT HIMSELF.

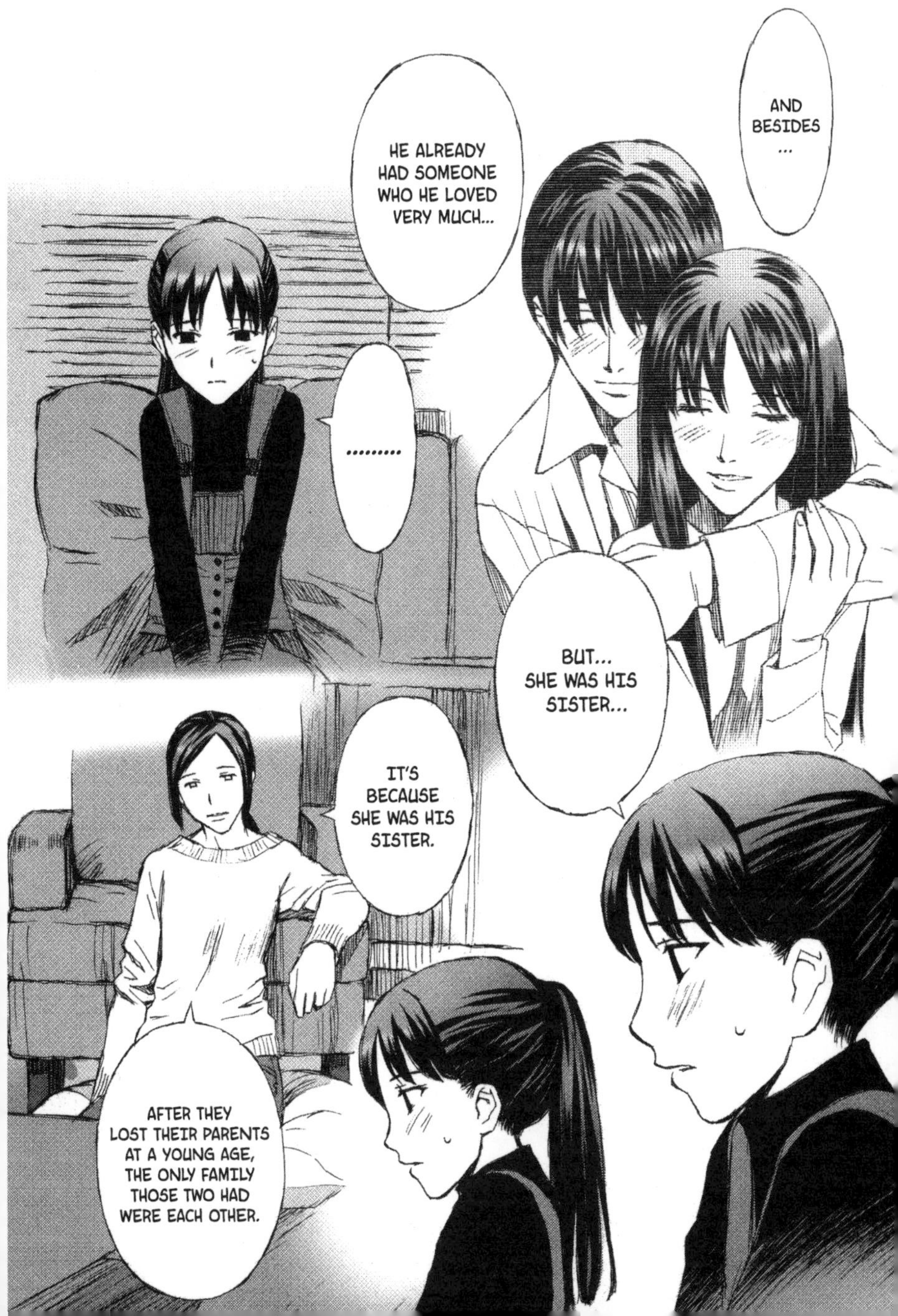
AND BESIDES ...
HE ALREADY HAD SOMEONE WHO HE LOVED VERY MUCH...
BUT... SHE WAS HIS SISTER...
....
IT'S BECAUSE SHE WAS HIS SISTER.
AFTER THEY LOST THEIR PARENTS AT A YOUNG AGE, THE ONLY FAMILY THOSE TWO HAD WERE EACH OTHER.

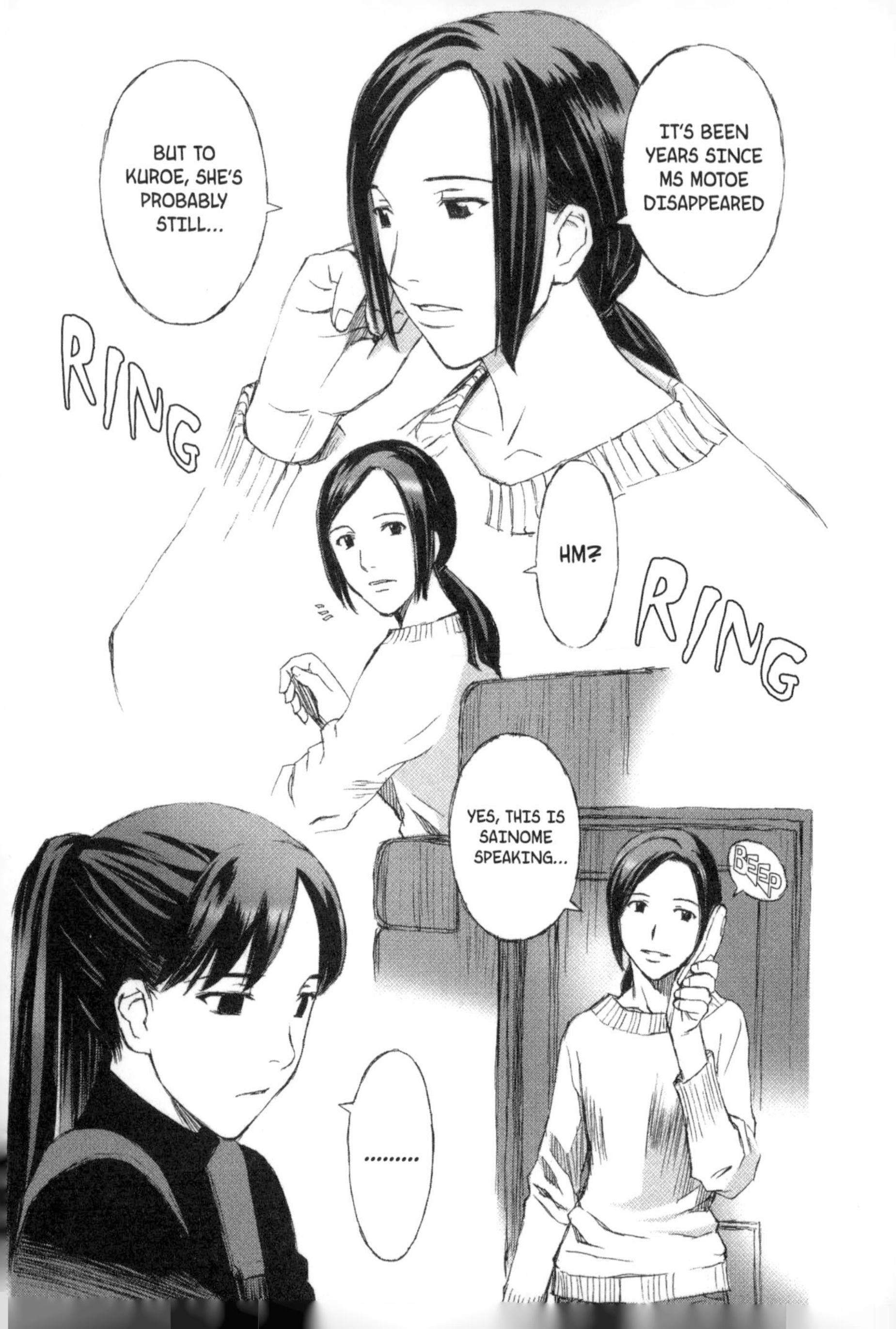
IT'S BEEN YEARS SINCE MS MOTOE DISAPPEARED
BUT TO KUROE, SHE'S PROBABLY STILL...
RING
RING
HM?
YES, THIS IS SAINOME SPEAKING...
BEEP
....

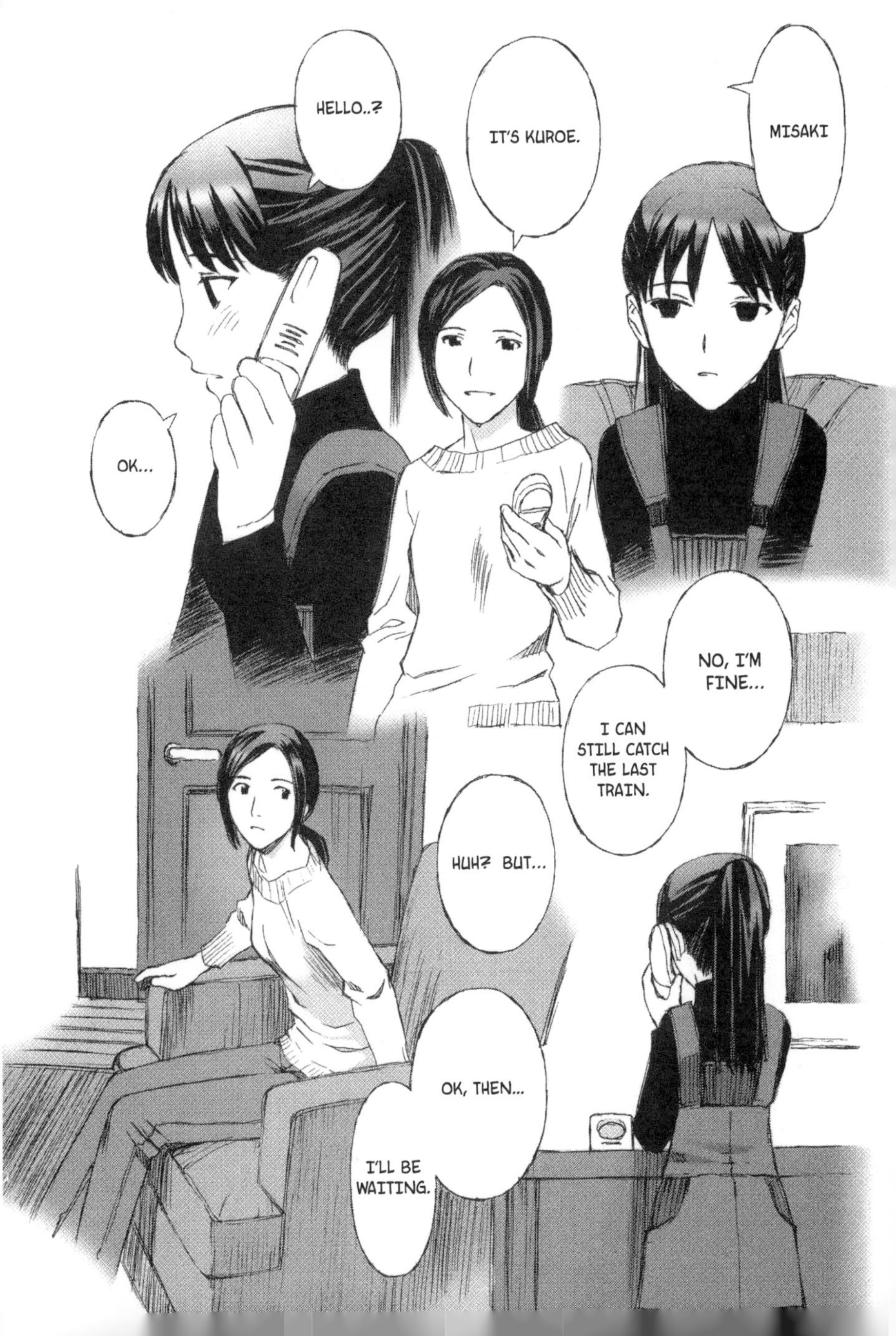
MISAKI
IT'S KUROE.
HELLO..?
OK...
NO, I'M FINE...
I CAN STILL CATCH THE LAST TRAIN.
HUH? BUT...
OK, THEN...
I'LL BE WAITING.

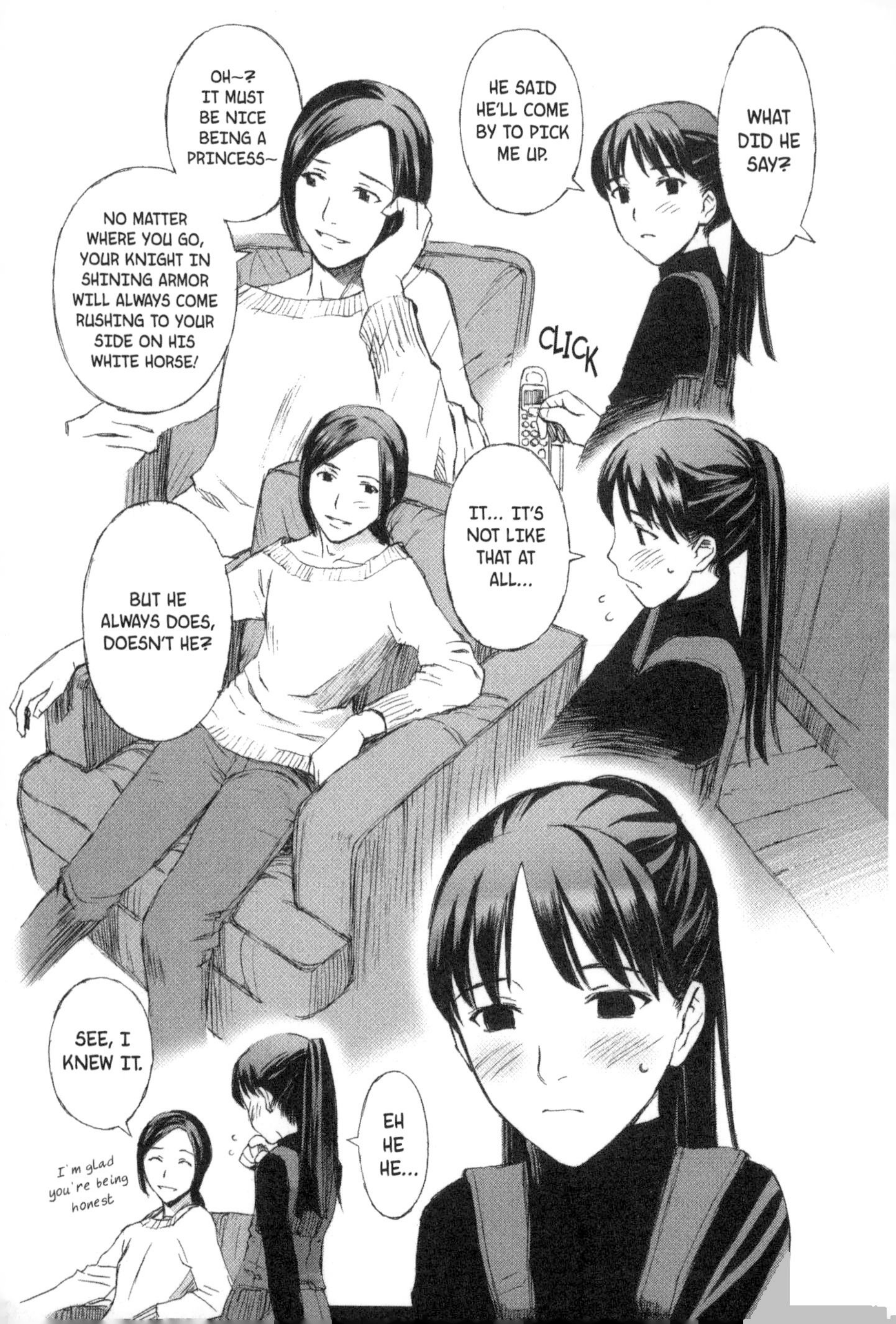
WHAT DID HE SAY?
HE SAID HE'LL COME BY TO PICK ME UP.
OH~? IT MUST BE NICE BEING A PRINCESS~
NO MATTER WHERE YOU GO, YOUR KNIGHT IN SHINING ARMOR WILL ALWAYS COME RUSHING TO YOUR SIDE ON HIS WHITE HORSE!
CLICK
IT... IT'S NOT LIKE THAT AT ALL...
BUT HE ALWAYS DOES, DOESN'T HE?
SEE, I KNEW IT.
EH HE HE...
I'm glad you're being honest

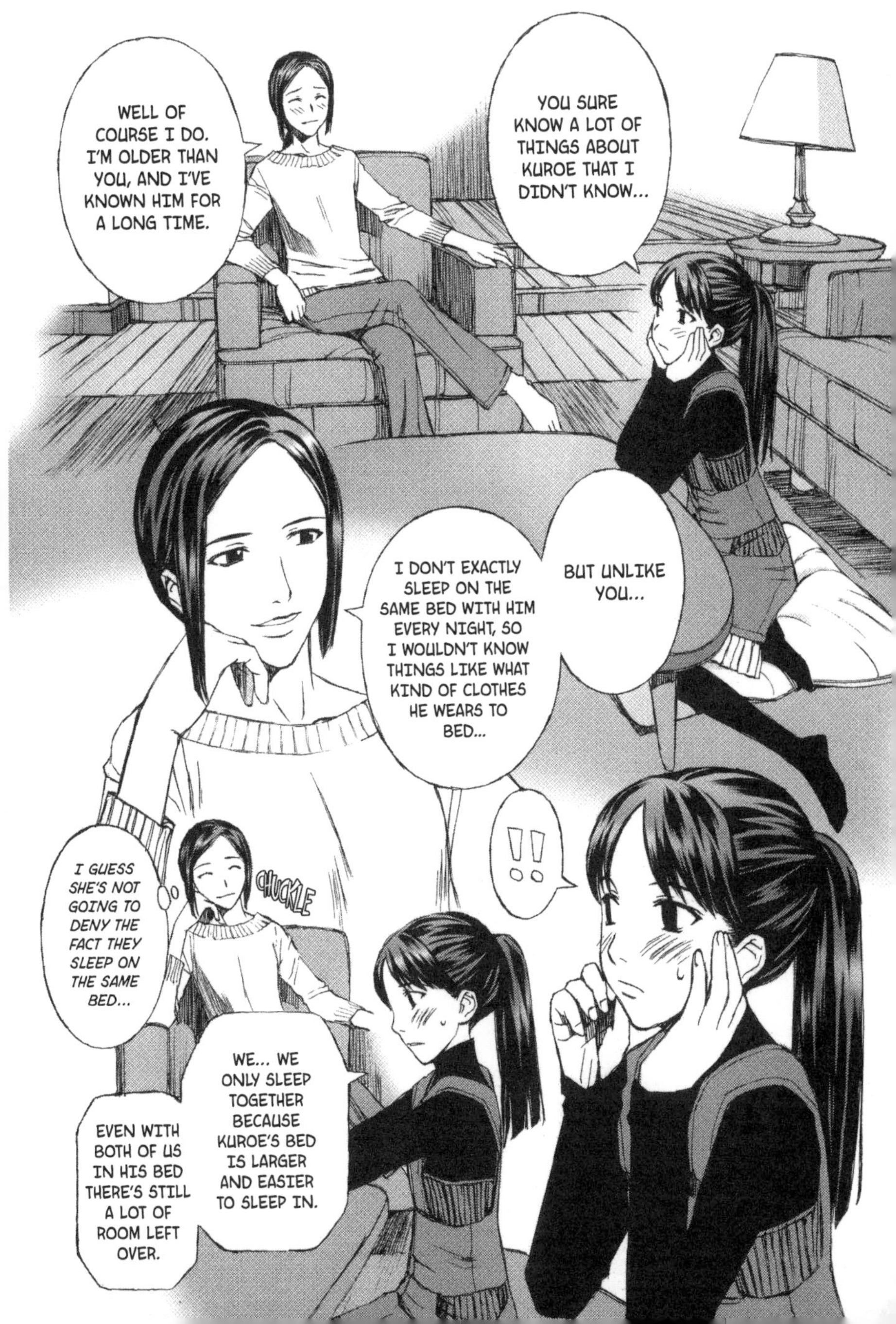
YOU SURE KNOW A LOT OF THINGS ABOUT KUROE THAT I DIDN'T KNOW...
WELL OF COURSE I DO. I'M OLDER THAN YOU, AND I'VE KNOWN HIM FOR A LONG TIME.
BUT UNLIKE YOU...
I DON'T EXACTLY SLEEP ON THE SAME BED WITH HIM EVERY NIGHT, SO I WOULDN'T KNOW THINGS LIKE WHAT KIND OF CLOTHES HE WEARS TO BED...
!!
CHUCKLE
I GUESS SHE'S NOT GOING TO DENY THE FACT THEY SLEEP ON THE SAME BED...
WE... WE ONLY SLEEP TOGETHER BECAUSE KUROE'S BED IS LARGER AND EASIER TO SLEEP IN.
EVEN WITH BOTH OF US IN HIS BED THERE'S STILL A LOT OF ROOM LEFT OVER.

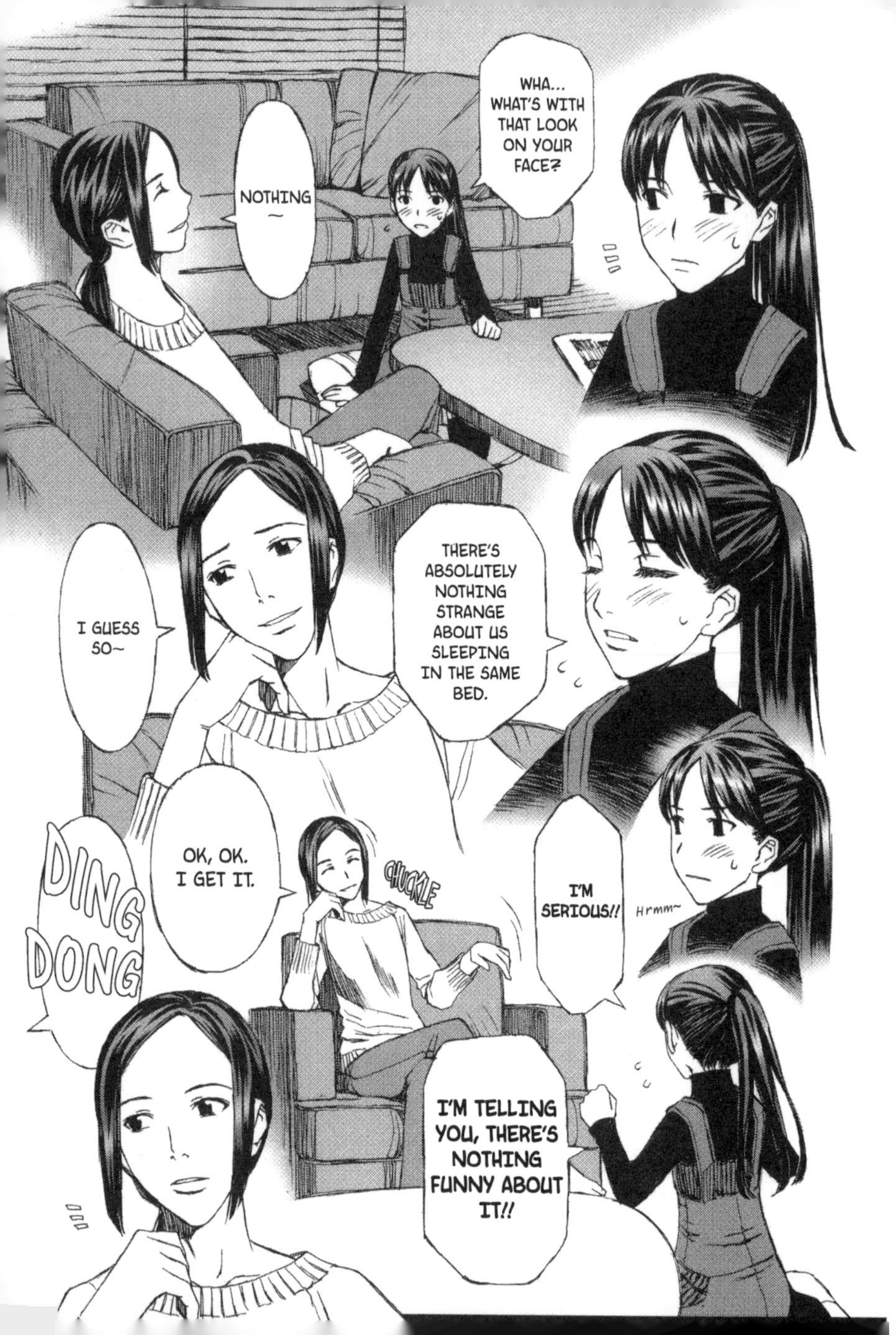
WHA... WHAT'S WITH THAT LOOK ON YOUR FACE?
NOTHING ~
THERE'S ABSOLUTELY NOTHING STRANGE ABOUT US SLEEPING IN THE SAME BED.
I GUESS SO~
I'M SERIOUS!!
Hrmm~
OK, OK. I GET IT.
CHUCKLE
I'M TELLING YOU, THERE'S NOTHING FUNNY ABOUT IT!!
DING DONG

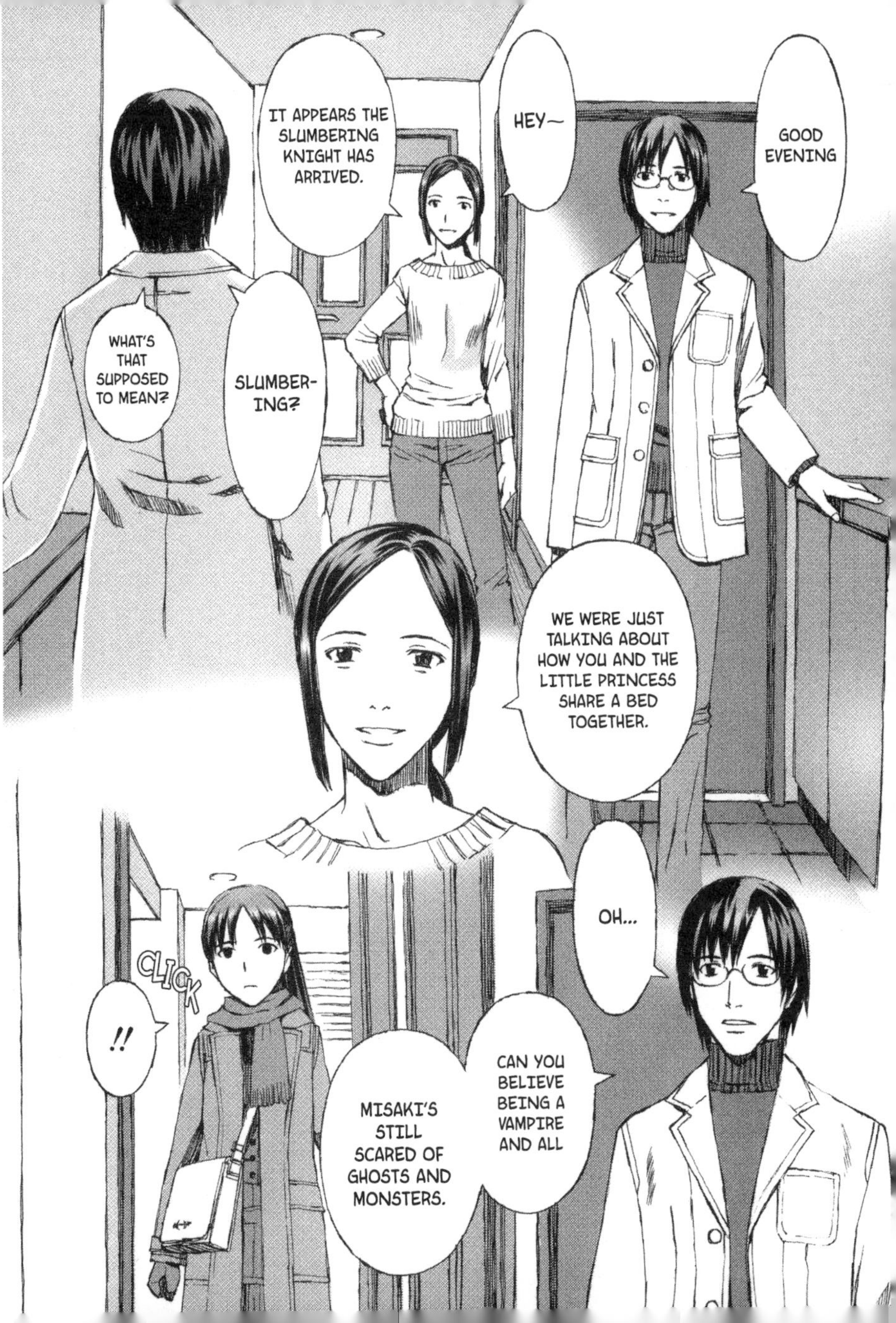
GOOD EVENING
HEY~
IT APPEARS THE SLUMBERING KNIGHT HAS ARRIVED.
SLUMBER-ING?
WHAT'S THAT SUPPOSED TO MEAN?
WE WERE JUST TALKING ABOUT HOW YOU AND THE LITTLE PRINCESS SHARE A BED TOGETHER.
OH...
CAN YOU BELIEVE BEING A VAMPIRE AND ALL
MISAKI'S STILL SCARED OF GHOSTS AND MONSTERS.
CLICK
!!

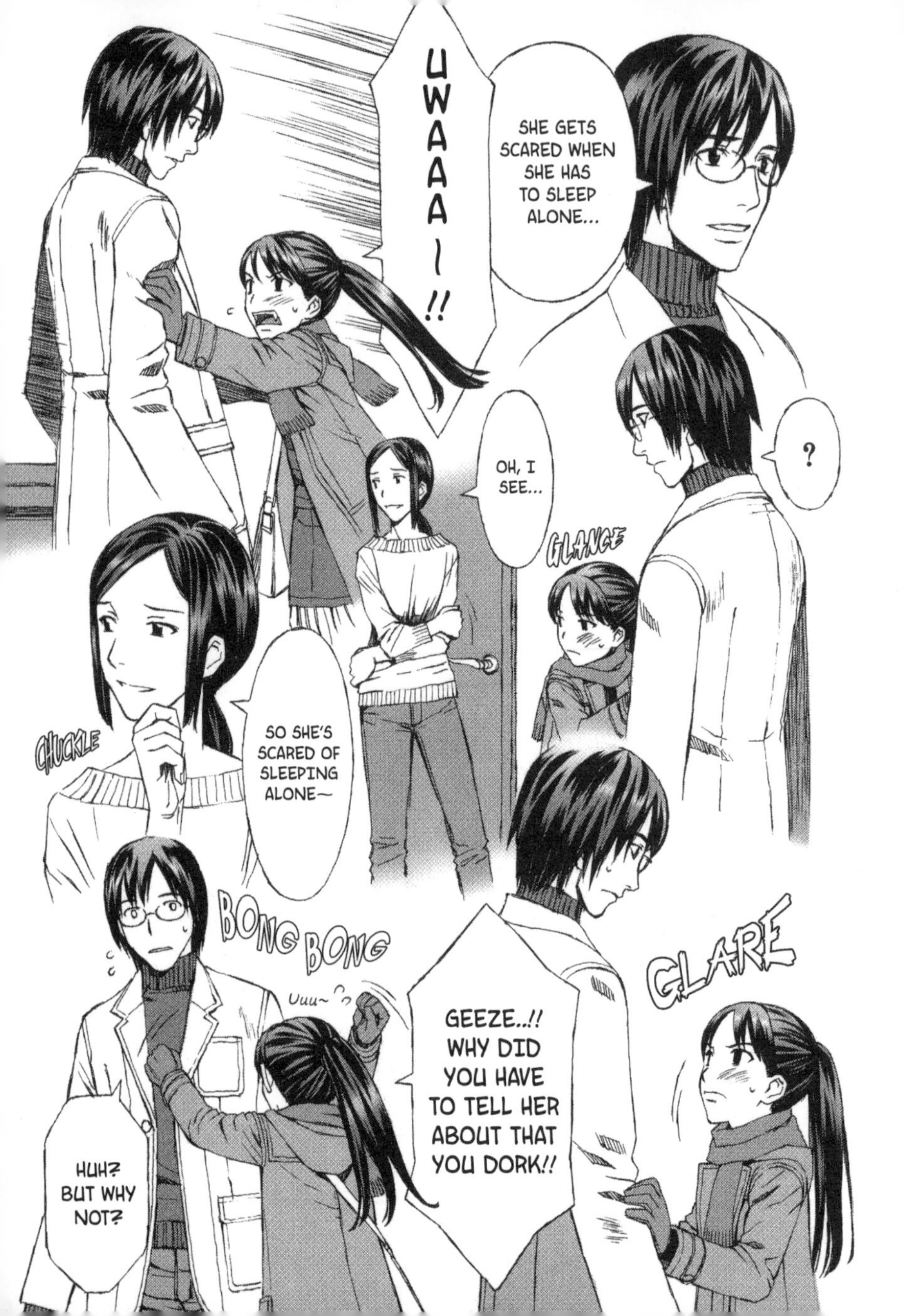
SHE GETS SCARED WHEN SHE HAS TO SLEEP ALONE...
UWAAA~!!
?
GLANCE
OH, I SEE...
SO SHE'S SCARED OF SLEEPING ALONE~
CHUCKLE
GLARE
GEEZE..!! WHY DID YOU HAVE TO TELL HER ABOUT THAT YOU DORK!!
Uuu~
BONG BONG
HUH? BUT WHY NOT?

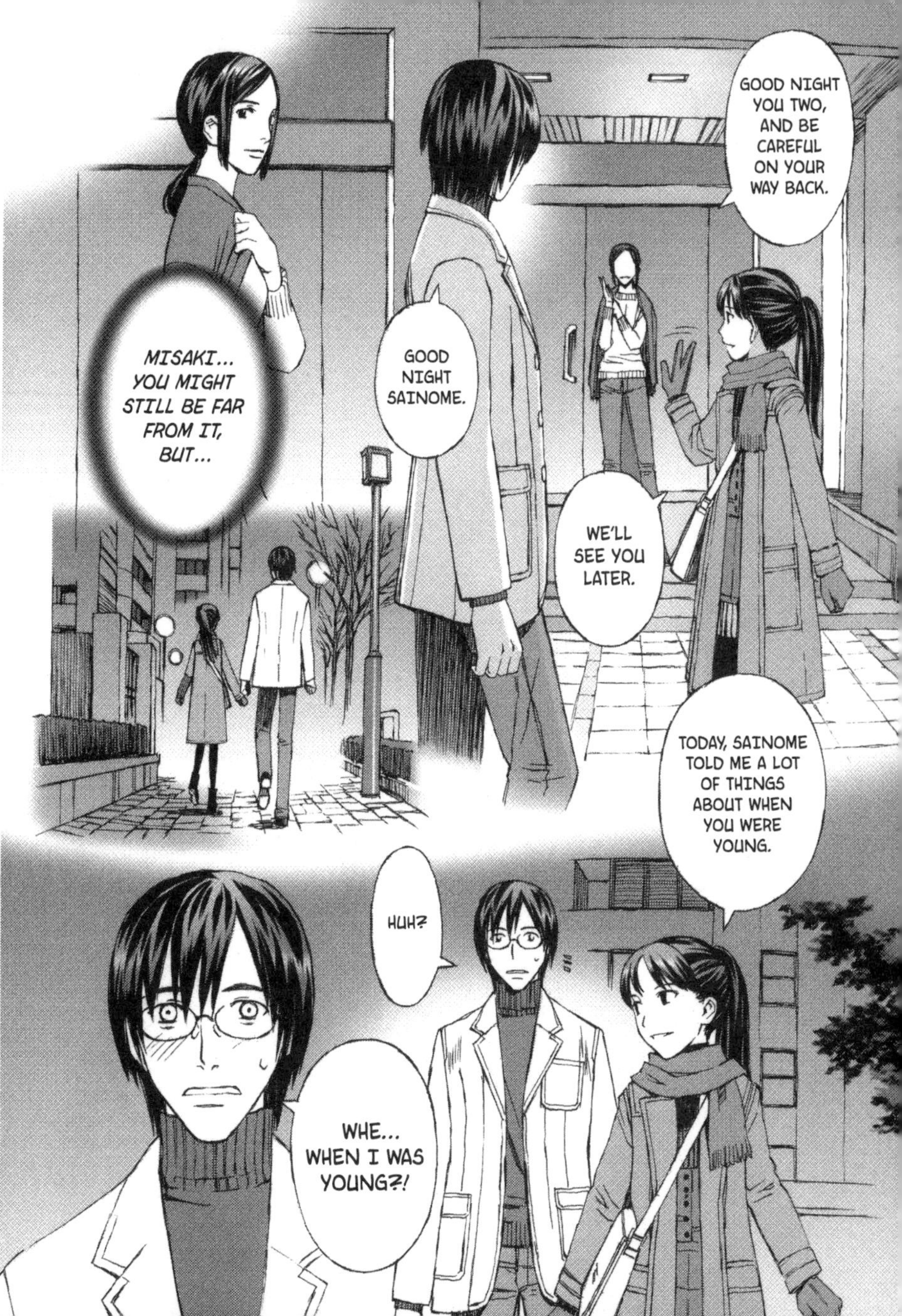
GOOD NIGHT YOU TWO, AND BE CAREFUL ON YOUR WAY BACK.
GOOD NIGHT SAINOME.
WE'LL SEE YOU LATER.
MISAKI... YOU MIGHT STILL BE FAR FROM IT, BUT...
TODAY, SAINOME TOLD ME A LOT OF THINGS ABOUT WHEN YOU WERE YOUNG.
HUH?
WHE... WHEN I WAS YOUNG?!

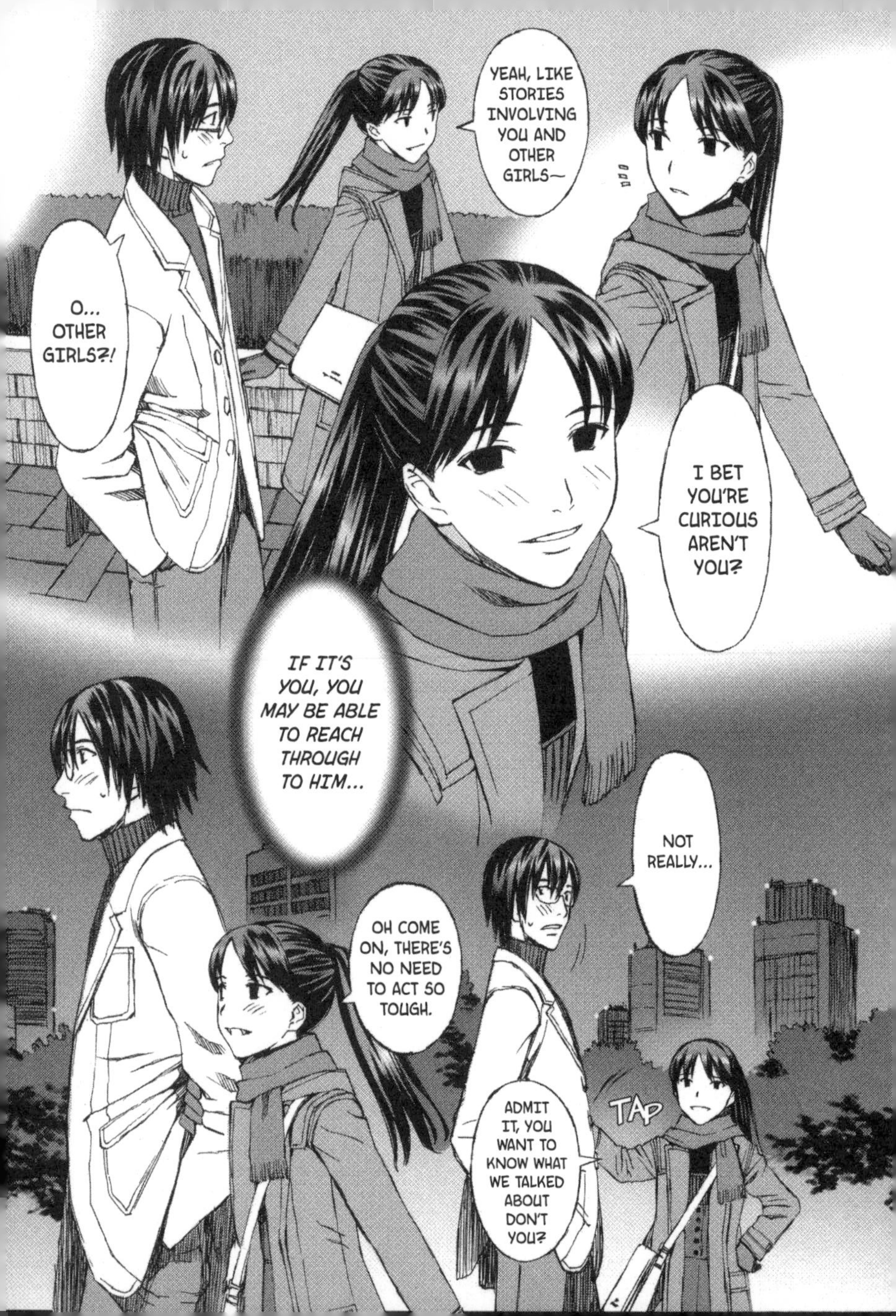
YEAH, LIKE STORIES INVOLVING YOU AND OTHER GIRLS~
O... OTHER GIRLS?!
I BET YOU'RE CURIOUS AREN'T YOU?
IF IT'S YOU, YOU MAY BE ABLE TO REACH THROUGH TO HIM...
NOT REALLY...
TAP
ADMIT IT, YOU WANT TO KNOW WHAT WE TALKED ABOUT DON'T YOU?
OH COME ON, THERE'S NO NEED TO ACT SO TOUGH.

Episode 8

YOUR SMILE

私の知らない笑顔 – A Smile I Never Knew About

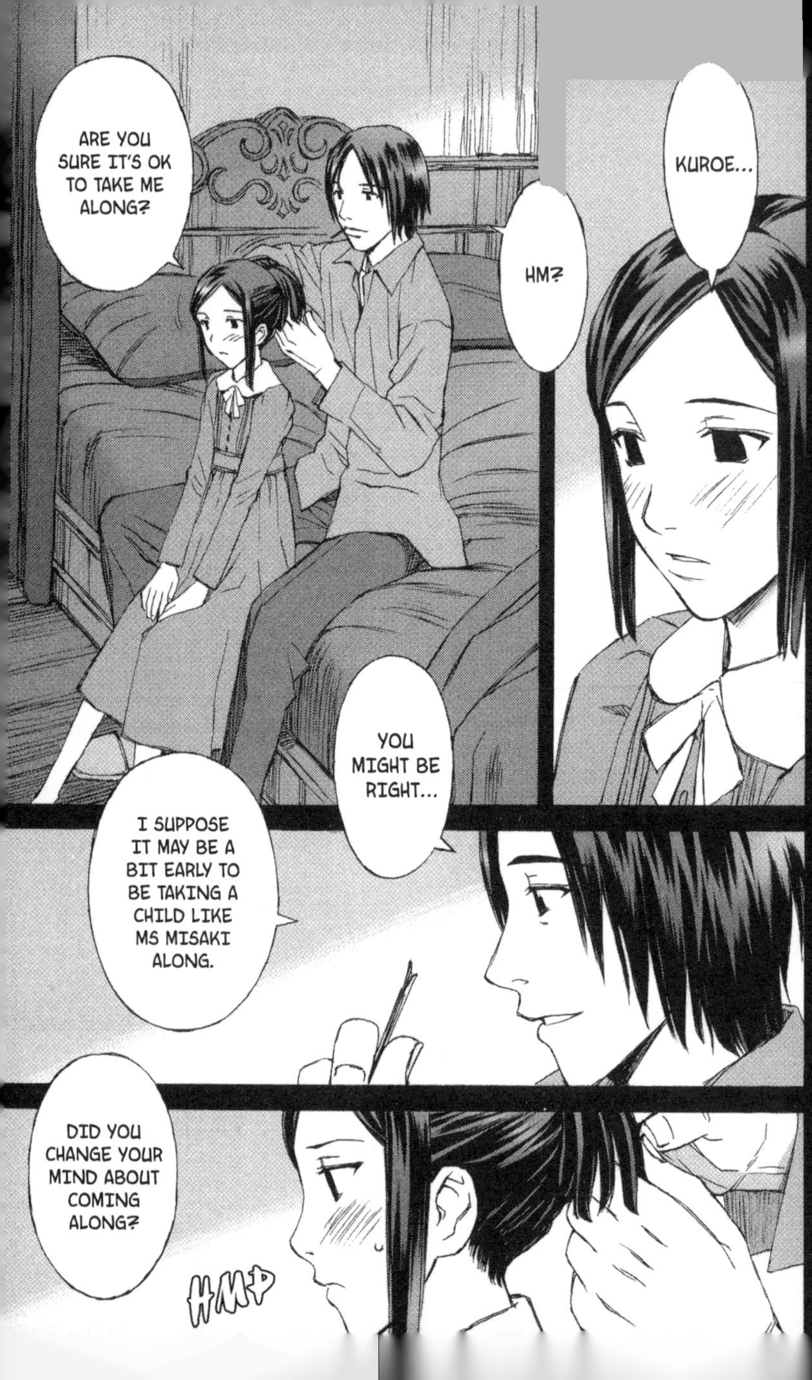
KUROE...
HM?
ARE YOU SURE IT'S OK TO TAKE ME ALONG?
YOU MIGHT BE RIGHT...
I SUPPOSE IT MAY BE A BIT EARLY TO BE TAKING A CHILD LIKE MS MISAKI ALONG.
DID YOU CHANGE YOUR MIND ABOUT COMING ALONG?
HMP

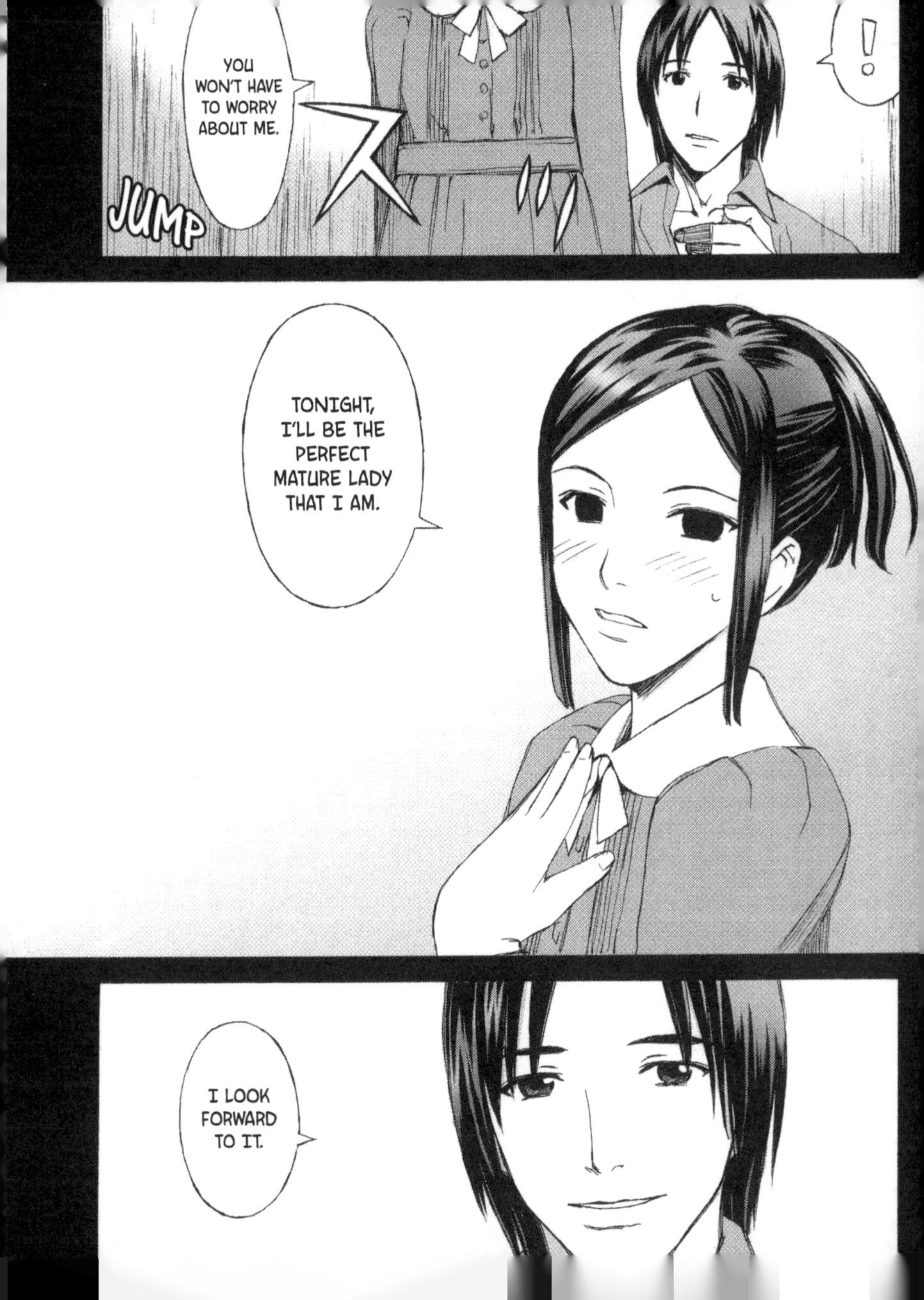
!
YOU WON'T HAVE TO WORRY ABOUT ME.
JUMP
TONIGHT, I'LL BE THE PERFECT MATURE LADY THAT I AM.
I LOOK FORWARD TO IT.

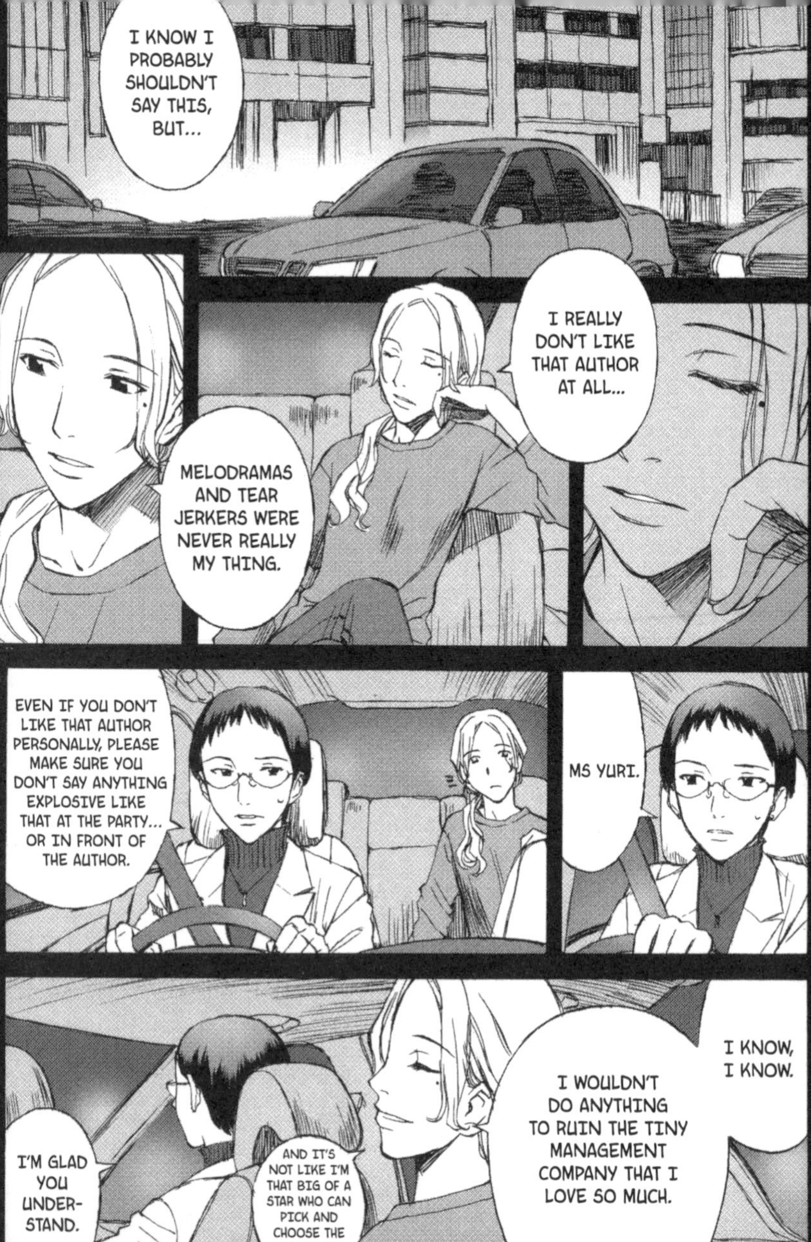
I KNOW I PROBABLY SHOULDN'T SAY THIS, BUT...
I REALLY DON'T LIKE THAT AUTHOR AT ALL...
MELODRAMAS AND TEAR JERKERS WERE NEVER REALLY MY THING.
MS YURI.
EVEN IF YOU DON'T LIKE THAT AUTHOR PERSONALLY, PLEASE MAKE SURE YOU DON'T SAY ANYTHING EXPLOSIVE LIKE THAT AT THE PARTY... OR IN FRONT OF THE AUTHOR.
I KNOW, I KNOW.
I WOULDN'T DO ANYTHING TO RUIN THE TINY MANAGEMENT COMPANY THAT I LOVE SO MUCH.
AND IT'S NOT LIKE I'M THAT BIG OF A STAR WHO CAN PICK AND CHOOSE THE PARTS I PLAY.
I'M GLAD YOU UNDER-STAND.

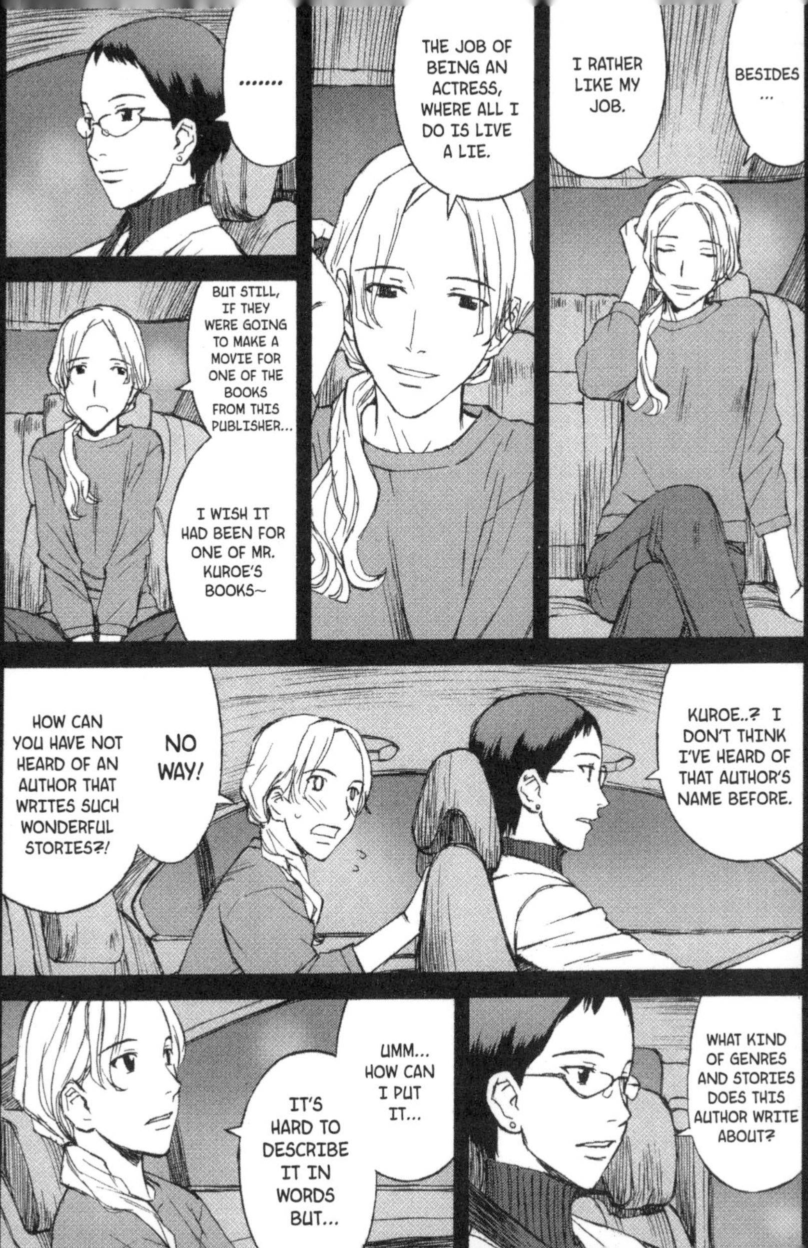
BESIDES...
I RATHER LIKE MY JOB.
THE JOB OF BEING AN ACTRESS, WHERE ALL I DO IS LIVE A LIE.
....
BUT STILL, IF THEY WERE GOING TO MAKE A MOVIE FOR ONE OF THE BOOKS FROM THIS PUBLISHER...
I WISH IT HAD BEEN FOR ONE OF MR. KUROE'S BOOKS~
KUROE..? I DON'T THINK I'VE HEARD OF THAT AUTHOR'S NAME BEFORE.
NO WAY!
HOW CAN YOU HAVE NOT HEARD OF AN AUTHOR THAT WRITES SUCH WONDERFUL STORIES?!
WHAT KIND OF GENRES AND STORIES DOES THIS AUTHOR WRITE ABOUT?
UMM... HOW CAN I PUT IT...
IT'S HARD TO DESCRIBE IT IN WORDS BUT...

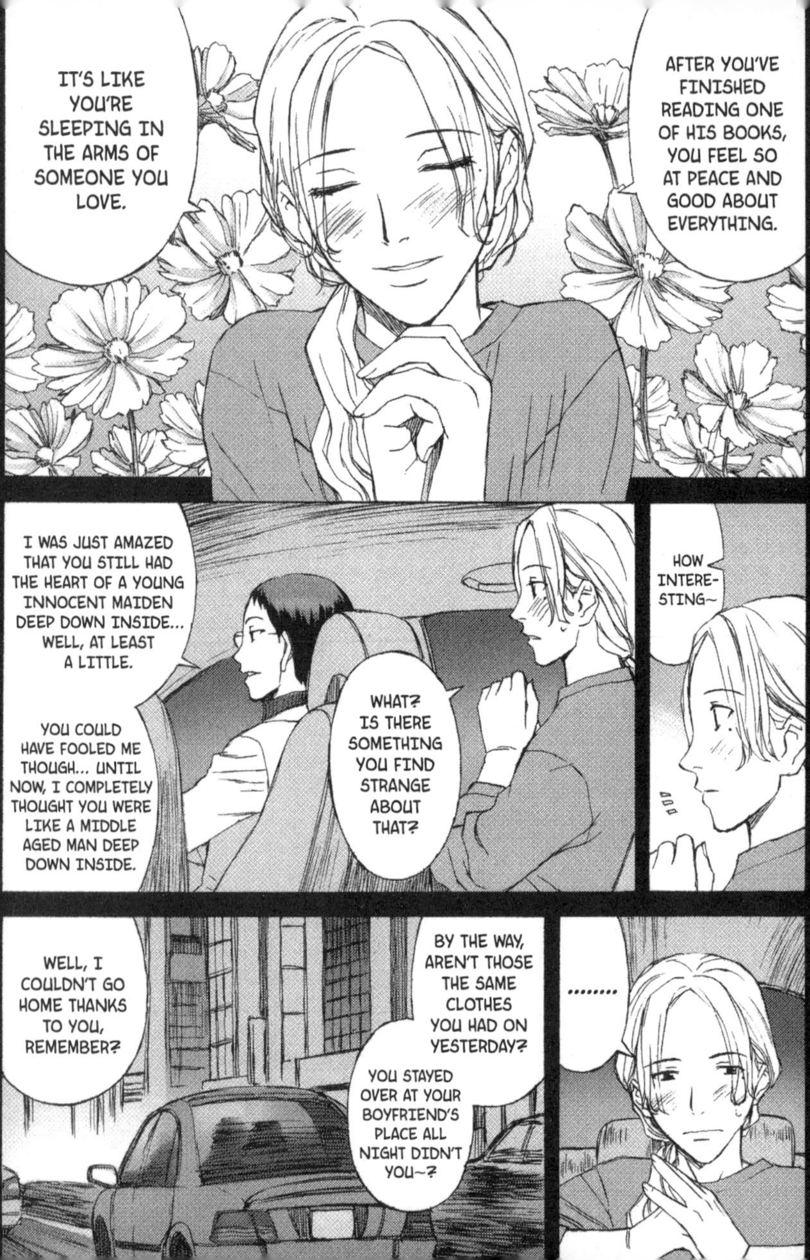
AFTER YOU'VE FINISHED READING ONE OF HIS BOOKS, YOU FEEL SO AT PEACE AND GOOD ABOUT EVERYTHING.
IT'S LIKE YOU'RE SLEEPING IN THE ARMS OF SOMEONE YOU LOVE.
HOW INTERE-STING~
I WAS JUST AMAZED THAT YOU STILL HAD THE HEART OF A YOUNG INNOCENT MAIDEN DEEP DOWN INSIDE... WELL, AT LEAST A LITTLE.
WHAT? IS THERE SOMETHING YOU FIND STRANGE ABOUT THAT?
YOU COULD HAVE FOOLED ME THOUGH... UNTIL NOW, I COMPLETELY THOUGHT YOU WERE LIKE A MIDDLE AGED MAN DEEP DOWN INSIDE.
....
BY THE WAY, AREN'T THOSE THE SAME CLOTHES YOU HAD ON YESTERDAY?
YOU STAYED OVER AT YOUR BOYFRIEND'S PLACE ALL NIGHT DIDN'T YOU~?
WELL, I COULDN'T GO HOME THANKS TO YOU, REMEMBER?

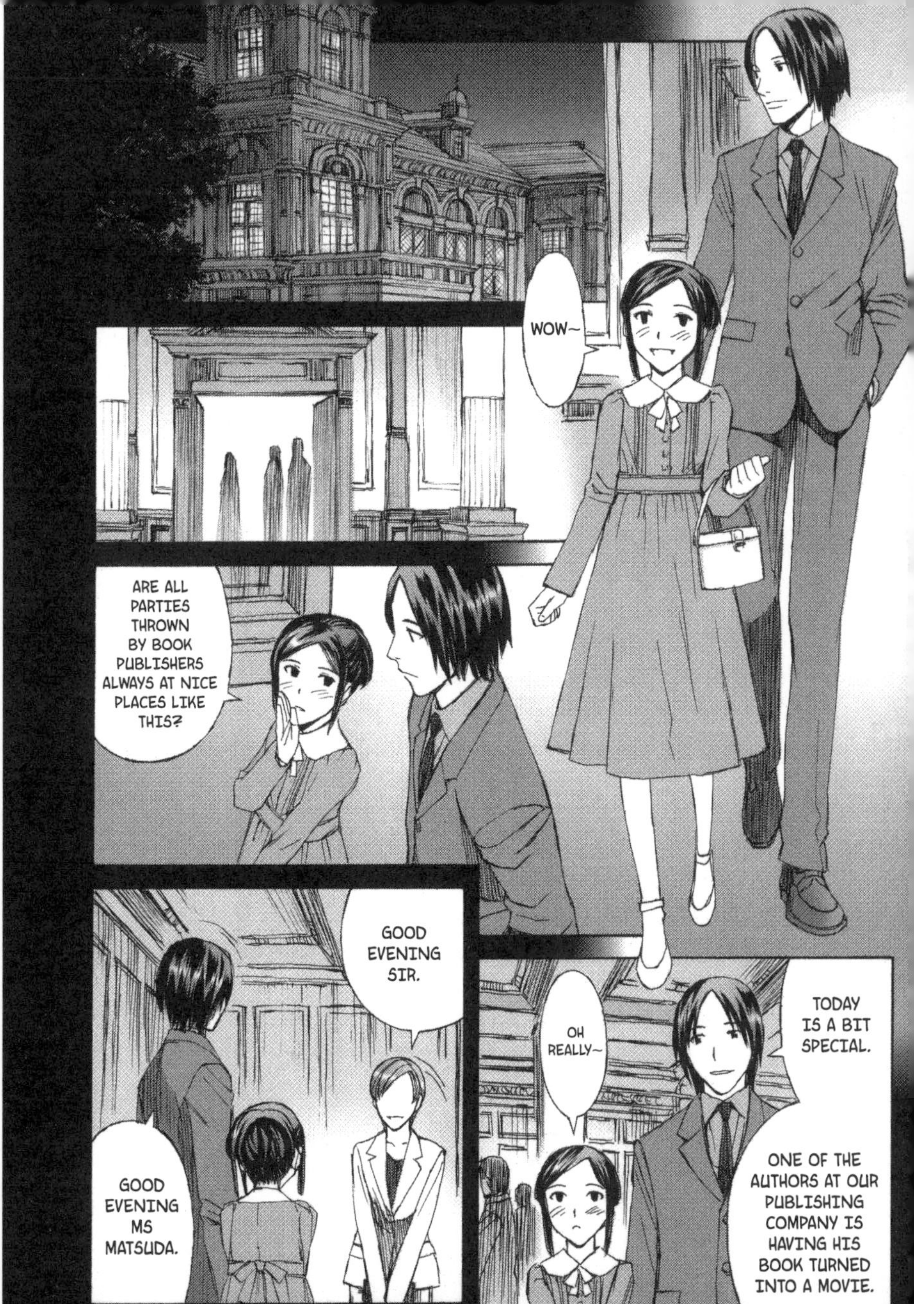
WOW~
ARE ALL PARTIES THROWN BY BOOK PUBLISHERS ALWAYS AT NICE PLACES LIKE THIS?
TODAY IS A BIT SPECIAL.
OH REALLY~
ONE OF THE AUTHORS AT OUR PUBLISHING COMPANY IS HAVING HIS BOOK TURNED INTO A MOVIE.
GOOD EVENING SIR.
GOOD EVENING MS MATSUDA.

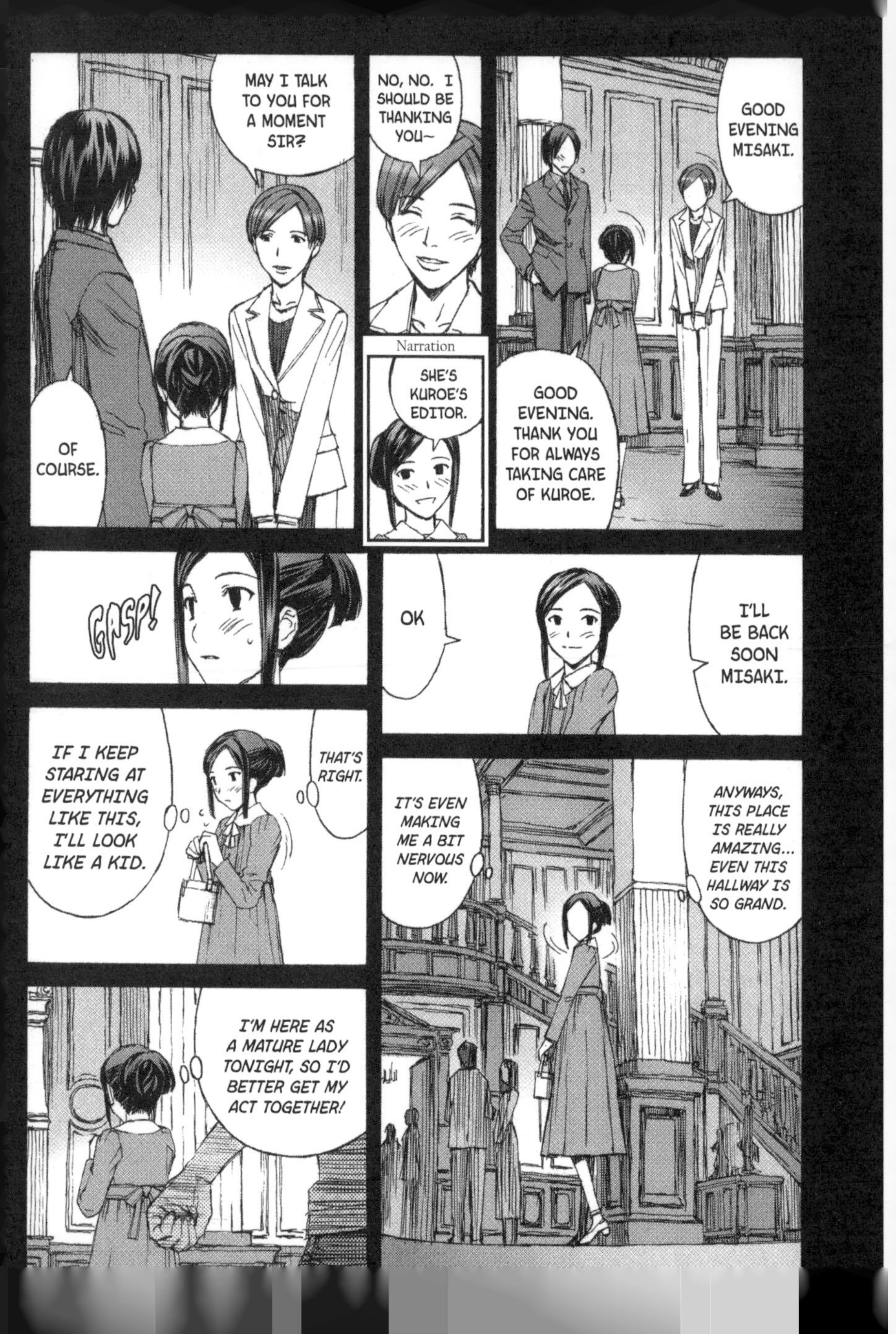
GOOD EVENING MISAKI.
GOOD EVENING. THANK YOU FOR ALWAYS TAKING CARE OF KUROE.
NO, NO. I SHOULD BE THANKING YOU~
Narration
SHE'S KUROE'S EDITOR.
MAY I TALK TO YOU FOR A MOMENT SIR?
OF COURSE.
I'LL BE BACK SOON MISAKI.
OK
GASP!
ANYWAYS, THIS PLACE IS REALLY AMAZING... EVEN THIS HALLWAY IS SO GRAND.
IT'S EVEN MAKING ME A BIT NERVOUS NOW.
THAT'S RIGHT.
IF I KEEP STARING AT EVERYTHING LIKE THIS, I'LL LOOK LIKE A KID.
I'M HERE AS A MATURE LADY TONIGHT, SO I'D BETTER GET MY ACT TOGETHER!

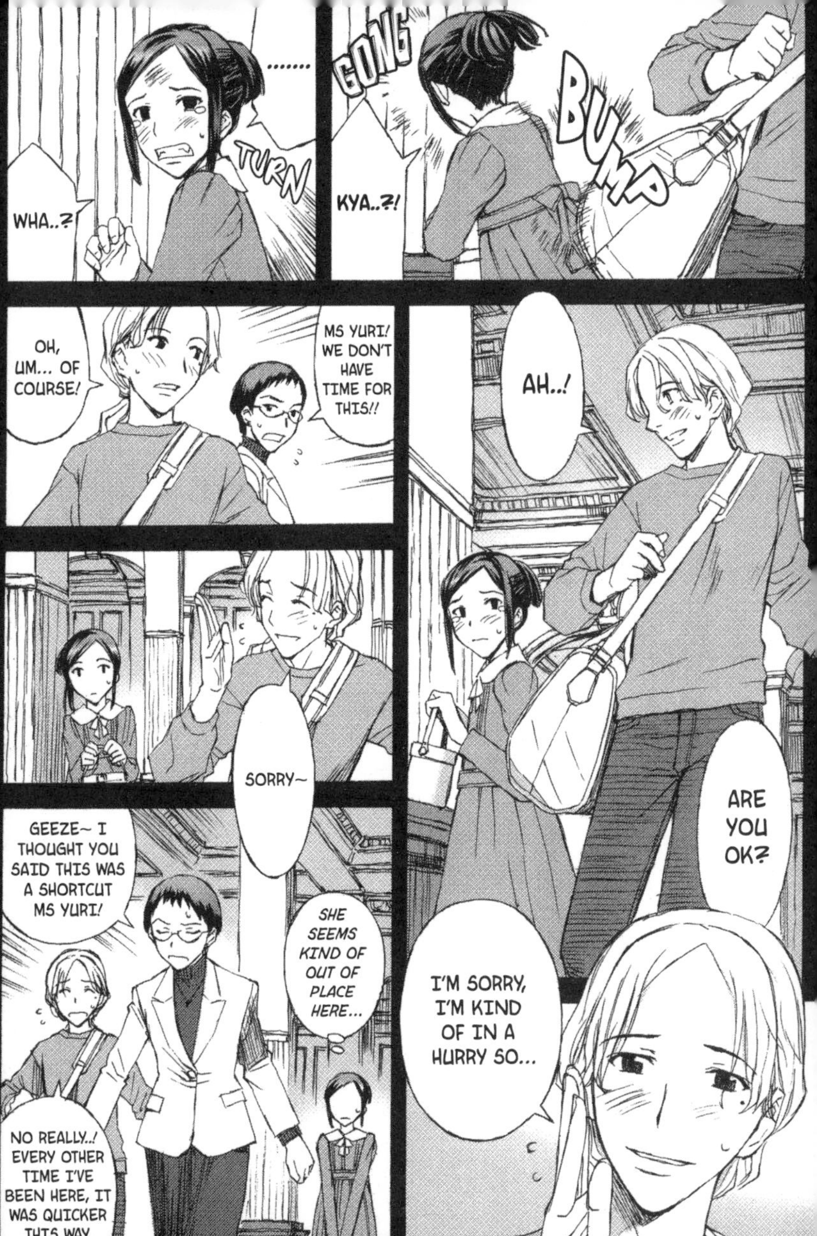
GONG
KYA..?!
BUMP
....
TURN
WHA..?!
AH..!
ARE YOU OK?
I'M SORRY, I'M KIND OF IN A HURRY SO...
MS YURI! WE DON'T HAVE TIME FOR THIS!!
OH, UM... OF COURSE!
SORRY~
GEEZE~ I THOUGHT YOU SAID THIS WAS A SHORTCUT MS YURI!
SHE SEEMS KIND OF OUT OF PLACE HERE...
NO REALLY..! EVERY OTHER TIME I'VE BEEN HERE, IT WAS QUICKER THIS WAY.

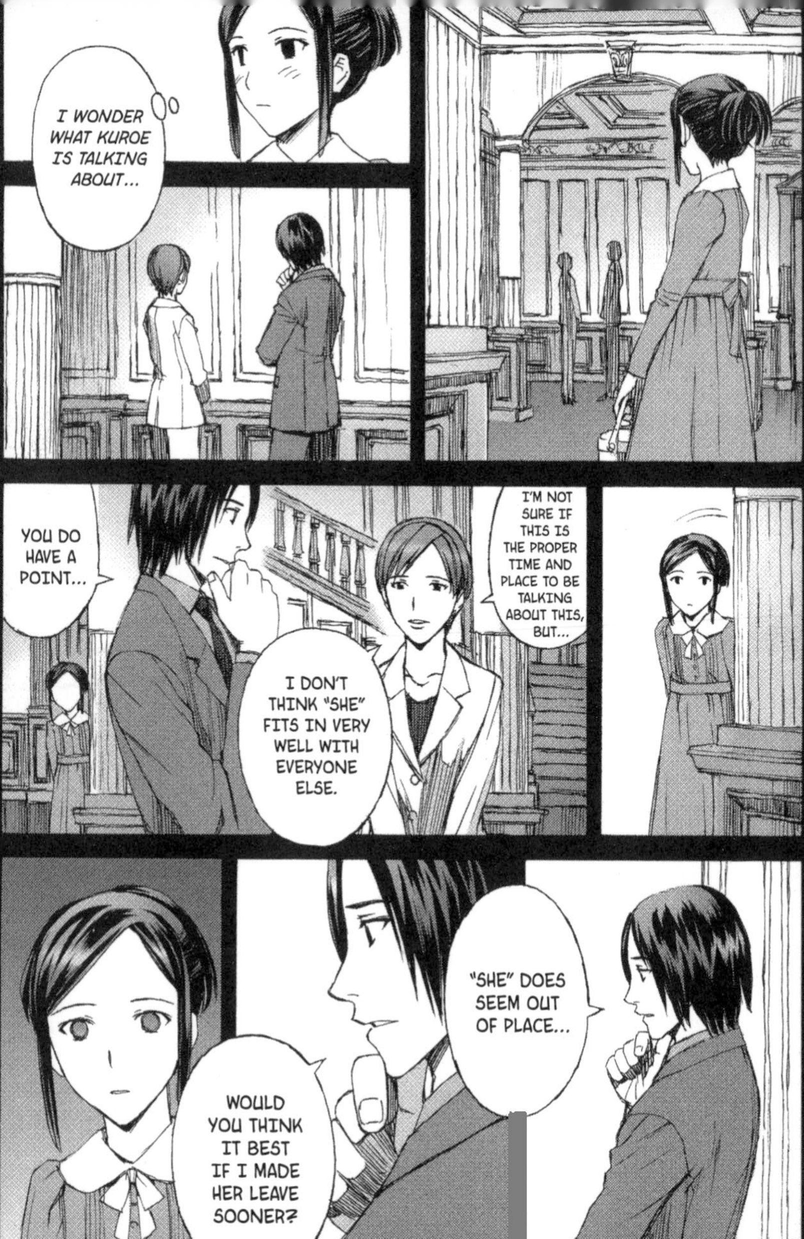
I WONDER WHAT KUROE IS TALKING ABOUT...
I'M NOT SURE IF THIS IS THE PROPER TIME AND PLACE TO BE TALKING ABOUT THIS, BUT...
I DON'T THINK "SHE" FITS IN VERY WELL WITH EVERYONE ELSE.
YOU DO HAVE A POINT...
"SHE" DOES SEEM OUT OF PLACE...
WOULD YOU THINK IT BEST IF I MADE HER LEAVE SOONER?

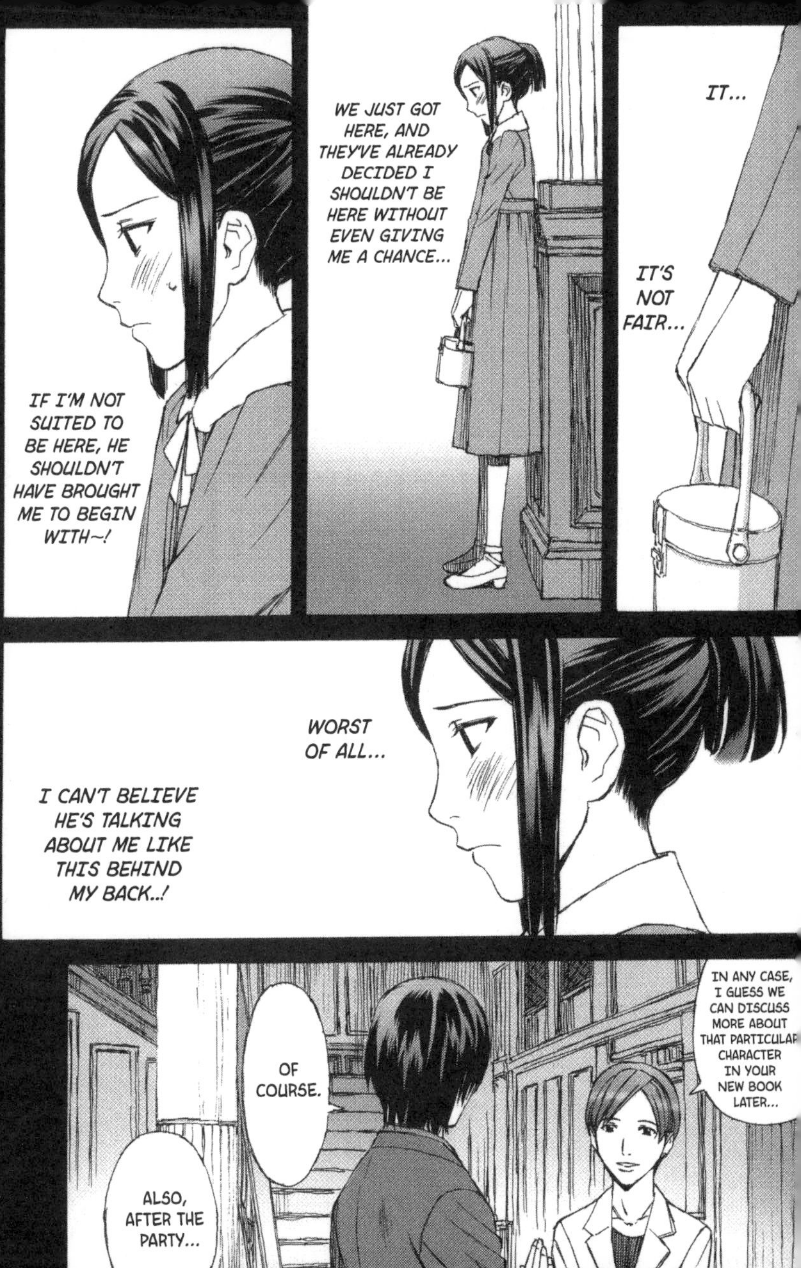
IT...
IT'S NOT FAIR...
WE JUST GOT HERE, AND THEY'VE ALREADY DECIDED I SHOULDN'T BE HERE WITHOUT EVEN GIVING ME A CHANCE...
IF I'M NOT SUITED TO BE HERE, HE SHOULDN'T HAVE BROUGHT ME TO BEGIN WITH~!
WORST OF ALL...
I CAN'T BELIEVE HE'S TALKING ABOUT ME LIKE THIS BEHIND MY BACK..!
IN ANY CASE, I GUESS WE CAN DISCUSS MORE ABOUT THAT PARTICULAR CHARACTER IN YOUR NEW BOOK LATER...
OF COURSE.
ALSO, AFTER THE PARTY...

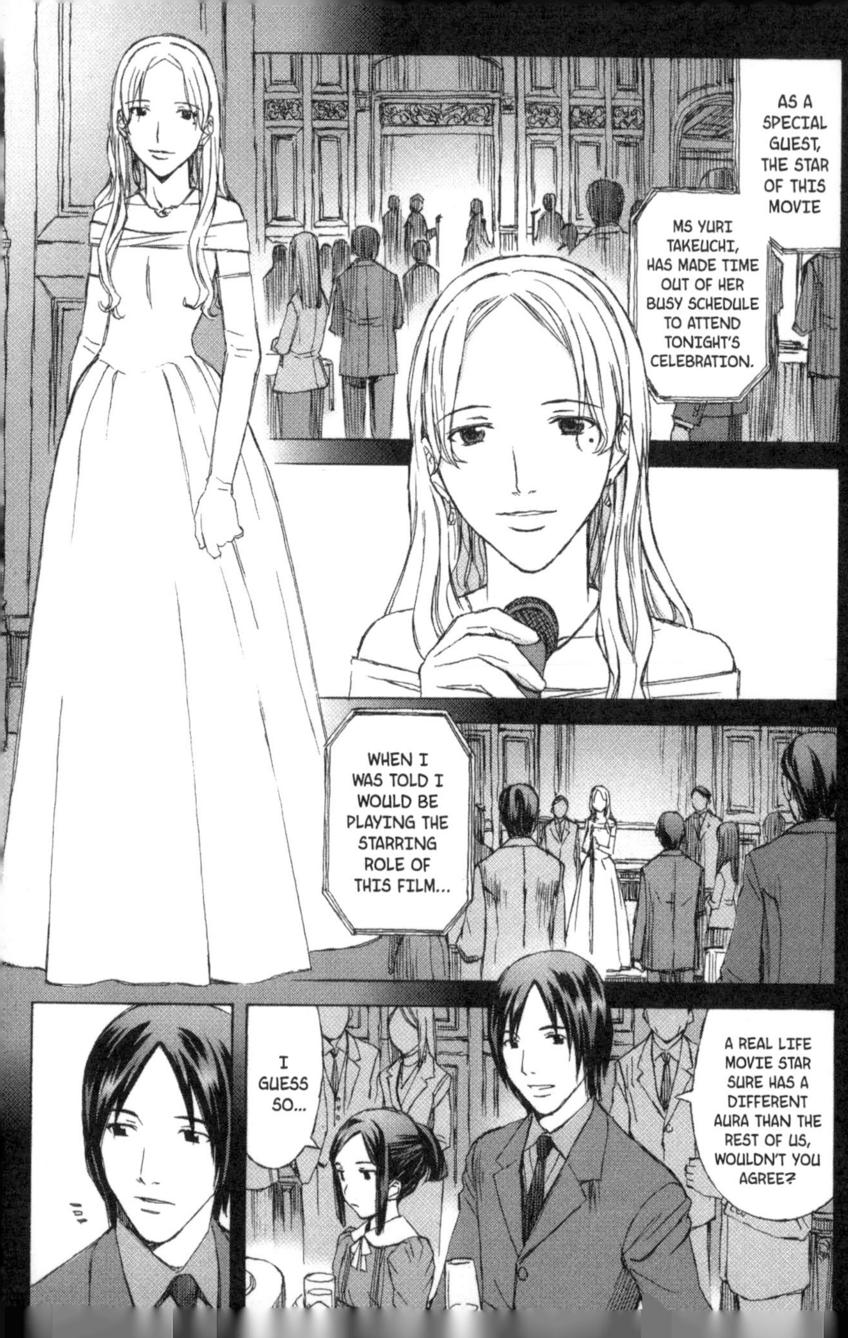
AS A SPECIAL GUEST, THE STAR OF THIS MOVIE
MS YURI TAKEUCHI, HAS MADE TIME OUT OF HER BUSY SCHEDULE TO ATTEND TONIGHT'S CELEBRATION.
WHEN I WAS TOLD I WOULD BE PLAYING THE STARRING ROLE OF THIS FILM...
A REAL LIFE MOVIE STAR SURE HAS A DIFFERENT AURA THAN THE REST OF US, WOULDN'T YOU AGREE?
I GUESS SO...

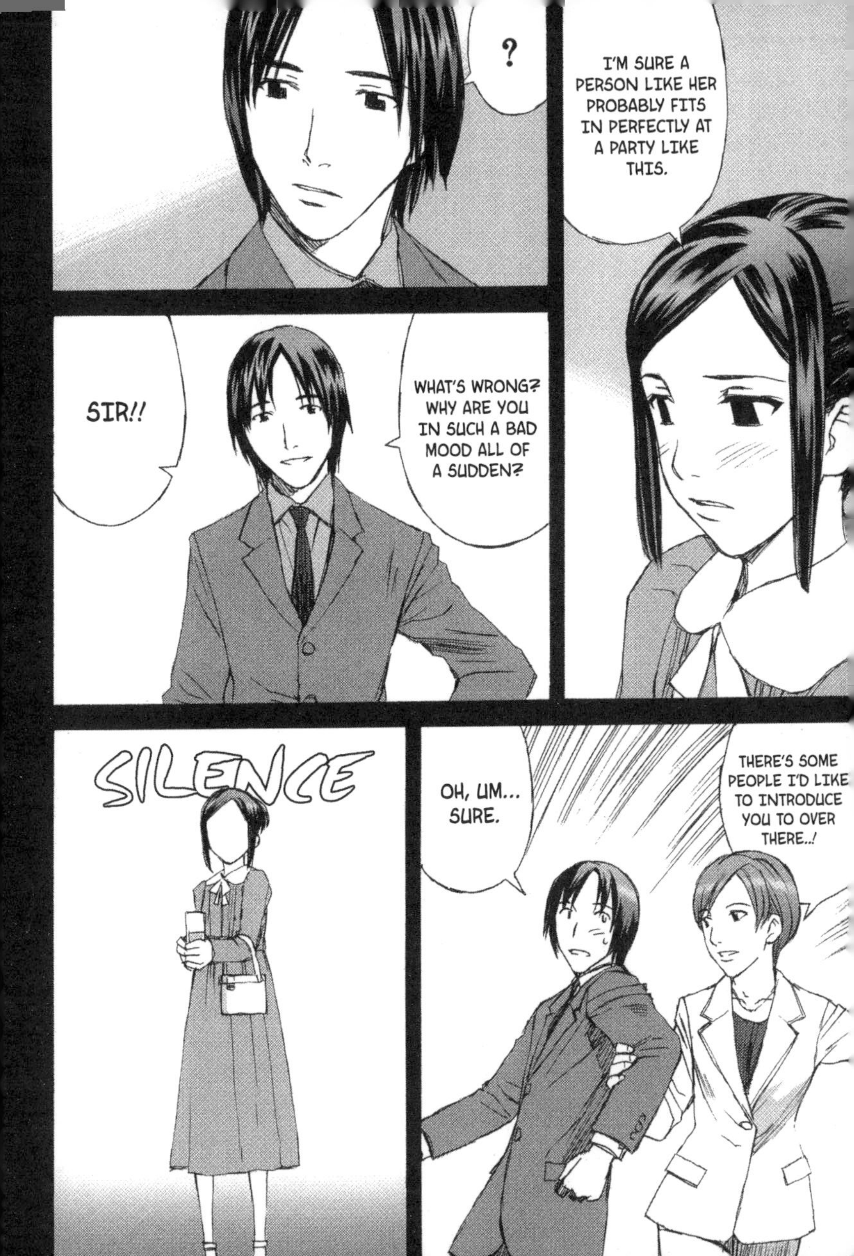
I'M SURE A PERSON LIKE HER PROBABLY FITS IN PERFECTLY AT A PARTY LIKE THIS.
?
WHAT'S WRONG? WHY ARE YOU IN SUCH A BAD MOOD ALL OF A SUDDEN?
SIR!!
THERE'S SOME PEOPLE I'D LIKE TO INTRODUCE YOU TO OVER THERE..!
OH, UM... SURE.
SILENCE

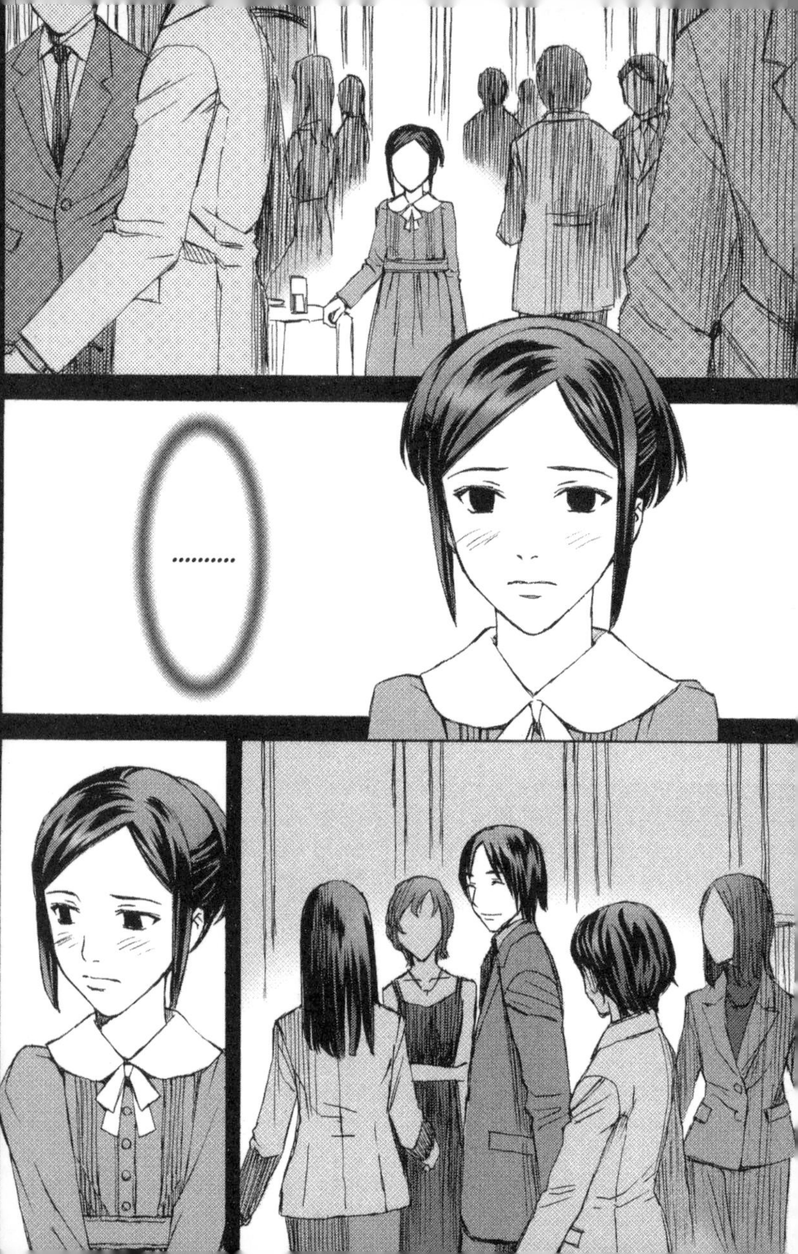
……….

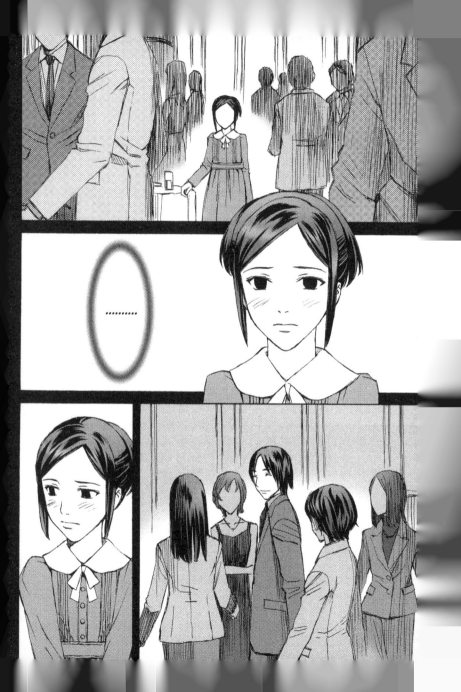

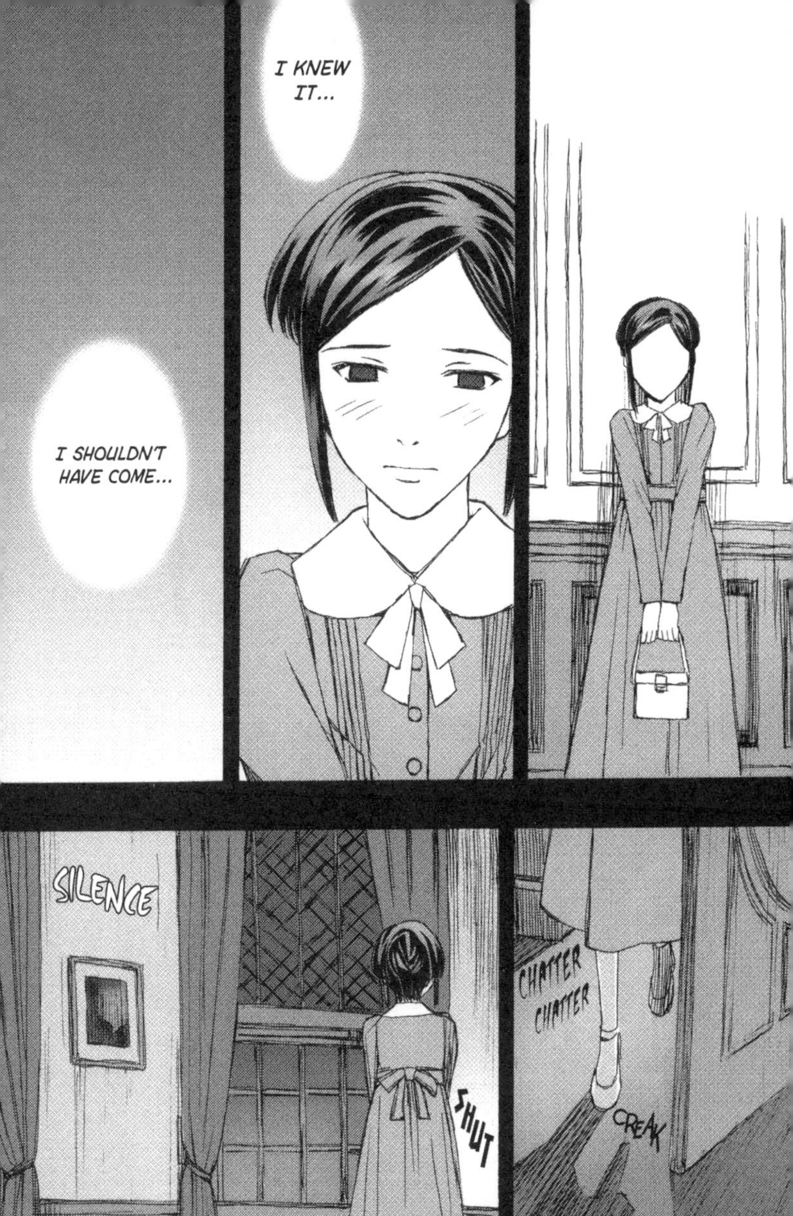
I KNEW IT...
I SHOULDN'T HAVE COME...
CHATTER CHATTER
CREAK
SILENCE
SHUT

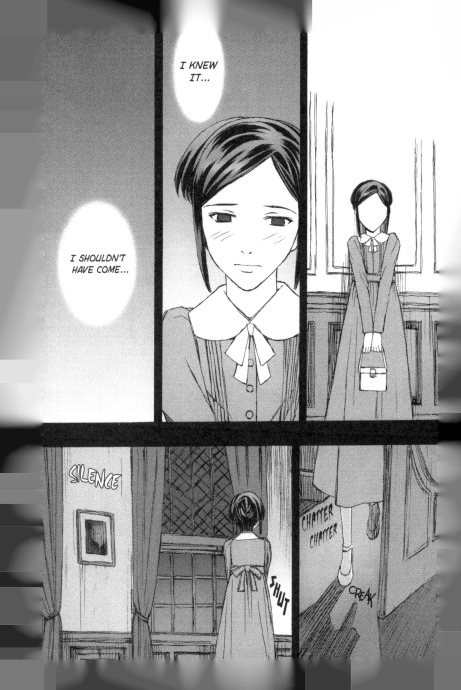

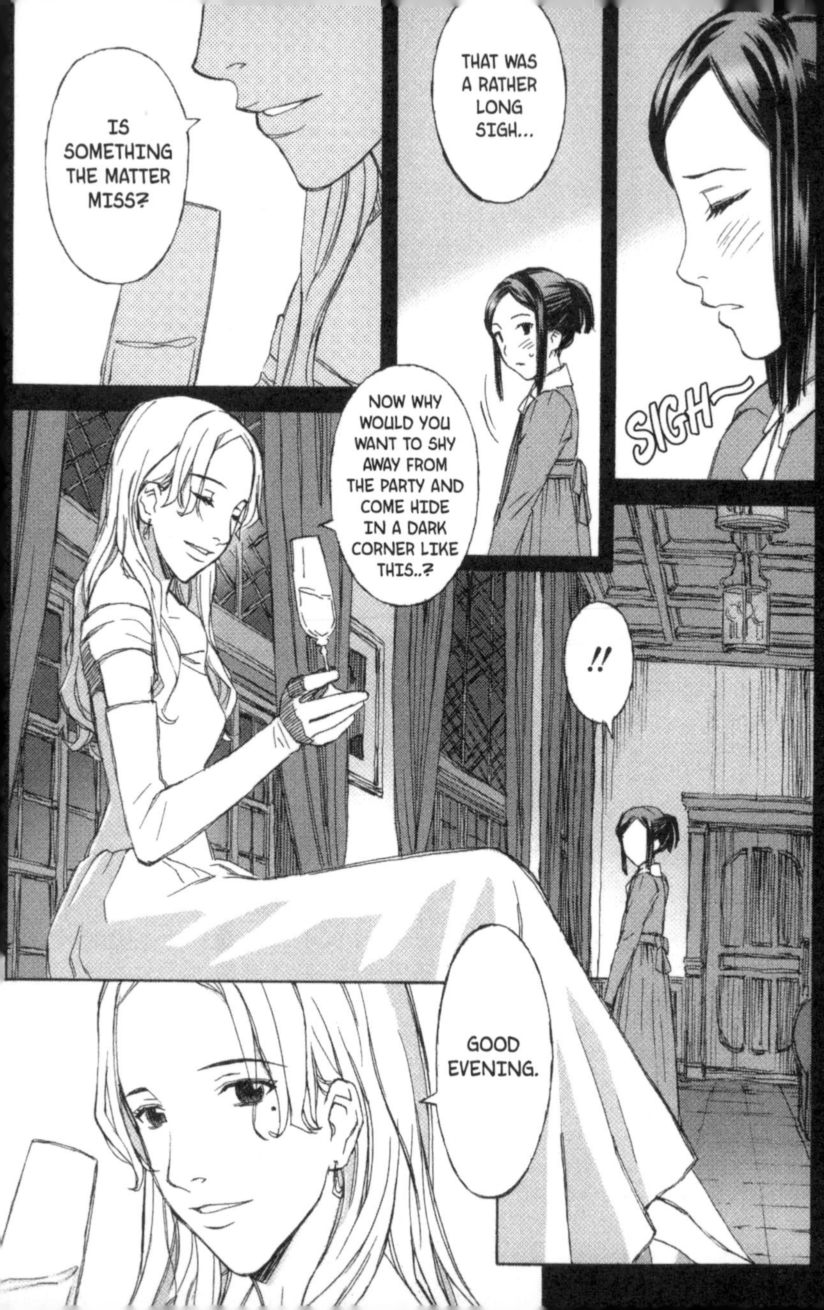
SIGH~
THAT WAS A RATHER LONG SIGH...
IS SOMETHING THE MATTER MISS?
!!
NOW WHY WOULD YOU WANT TO SHY AWAY FROM THE PARTY AND COME HIDE IN A DARK CORNER LIKE THIS..?
GOOD EVENING.

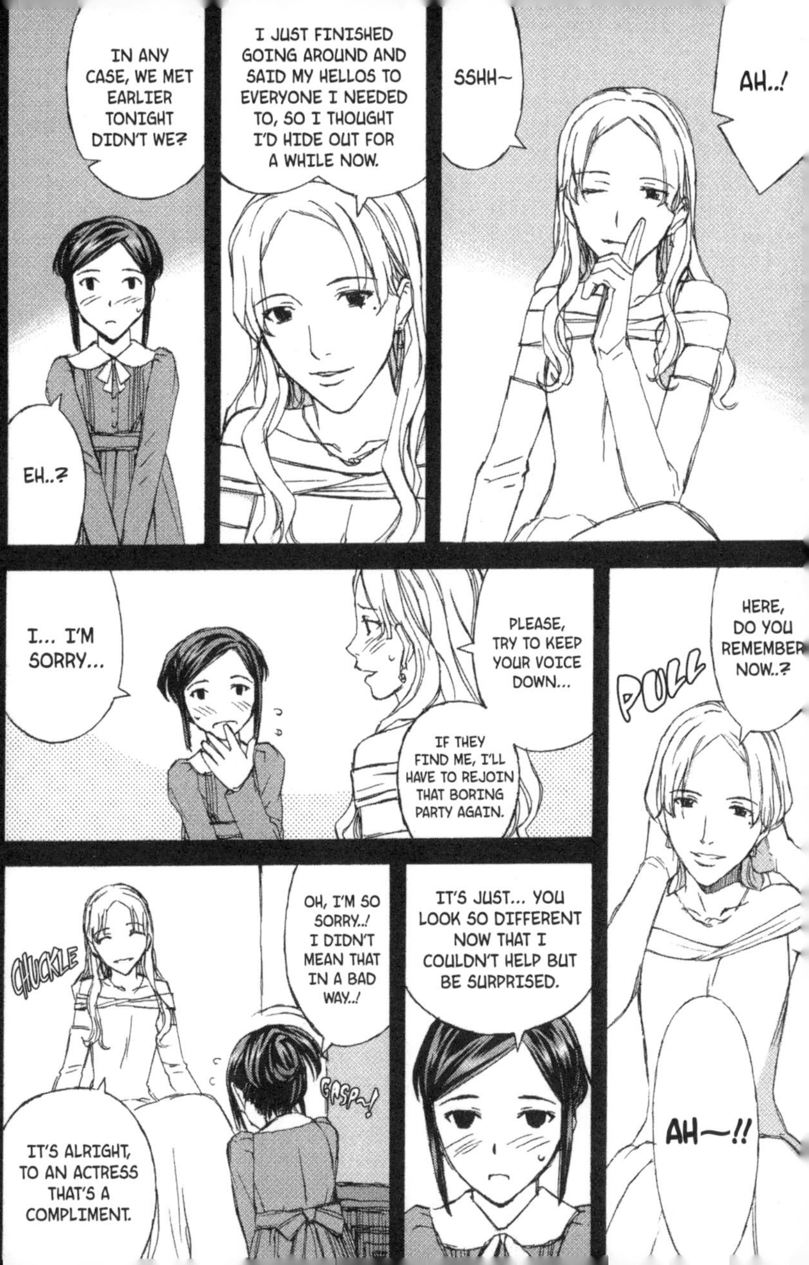
AH..!
SSHH~
I JUST FINISHED GOING AROUND AND SAID MY HELLOS TO EVERYONE I NEEDED TO, SO I THOUGHT I'D HIDE OUT FOR A WHILE NOW.
IN ANY CASE, WE MET EARLIER TONIGHT DIDN'T WE?
EH..?
HERE, DO YOU REMEMBER NOW..?
PULL
AH~!!
PLEASE, TRY TO KEEP YOUR VOICE DOWN...
IF THEY FIND ME, I'LL HAVE TO REJOIN THAT BORING PARTY AGAIN.
I... I'M SORRY...
IT'S JUST... YOU LOOK SO DIFFERENT NOW THAT I COULDN'T HELP BUT BE SURPRISED.
OH, I'M SO SORRY..! I DIDN'T MEAN THAT IN A BAD WAY..!
GASP~!
CHUCKLE
IT'S ALRIGHT, TO AN ACTRESS THAT'S A COMPLIMENT.

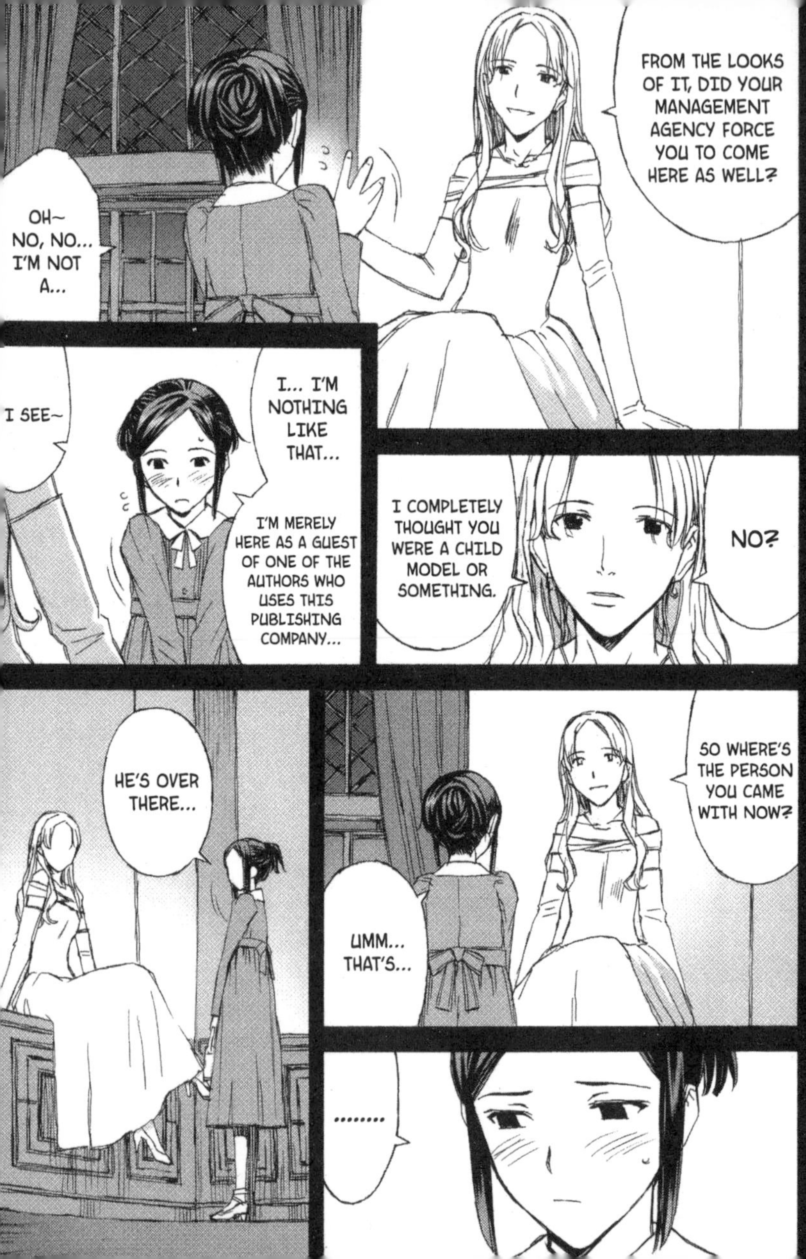
FROM THE LOOKS OF IT, DID YOUR MANAGEMENT AGENCY FORCE YOU TO COME HERE AS WELL?
OH~ NO, NO... I'M NOT A...
NO?
I COMPLETELY THOUGHT YOU WERE A CHILD MODEL OR SOMETHING.
I... I'M NOTHING LIKE THAT...
I'M MERELY HERE AS A GUEST OF ONE OF THE AUTHORS WHO USES THIS PUBLISHING COMPANY...
I SEE~
SO WHERE'S THE PERSON YOU CAME WITH NOW?
UMM... THAT'S...
....
HE'S OVER THERE...

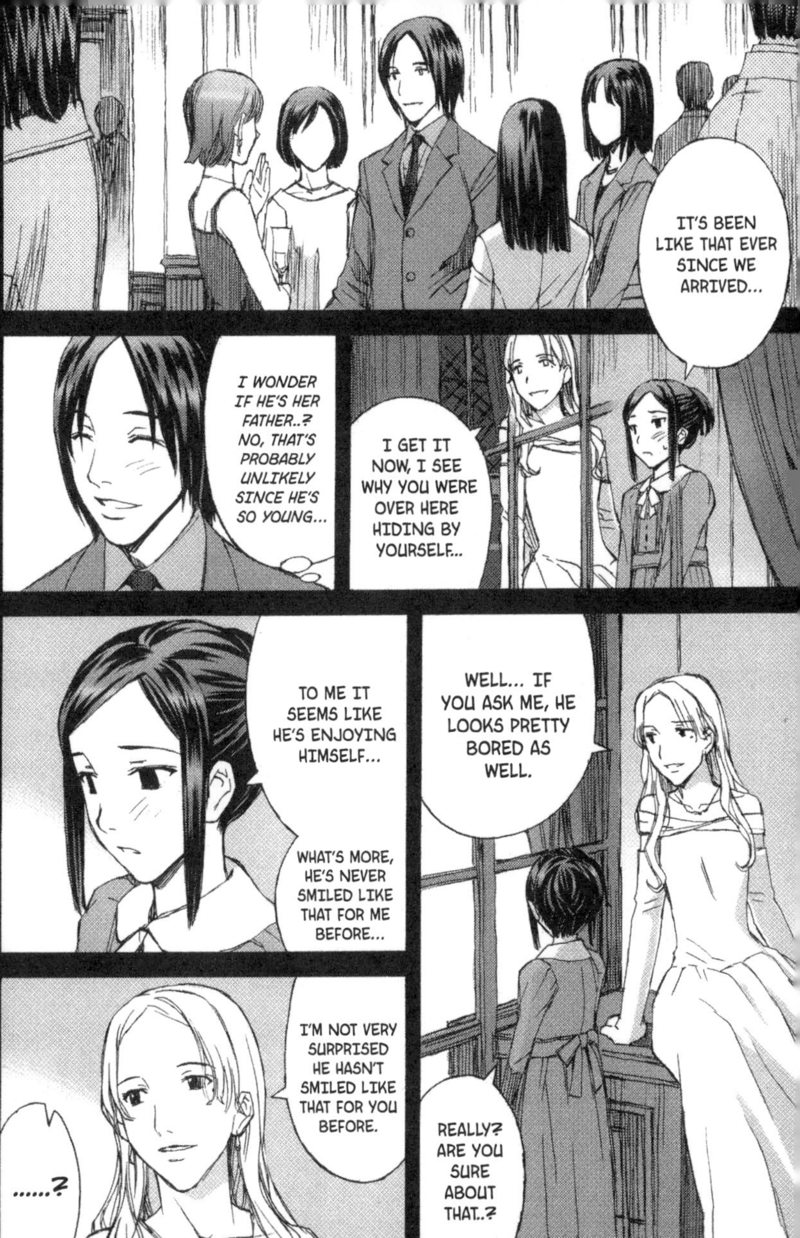
IT'S BEEN LIKE THAT EVER SINCE WE ARRIVED...
I GET IT NOW, I SEE WHY YOU WERE OVER HERE HIDING BY YOURSELF...
I WONDER IF HE'S HER FATHER..? NO, THAT'S PROBABLY UNLIKELY SINCE HE'S SO YOUNG...
WELL... IF YOU ASK ME, HE LOOKS PRETTY BORED AS WELL.
REALLY? ARE YOU SURE ABOUT THAT..?
TO ME IT SEEMS LIKE HE'S ENJOYING HIMSELF...
WHAT'S MORE, HE'S NEVER SMILED LIKE THAT FOR ME BEFORE...
I'M NOT VERY SURPRISED HE HASN'T SMILED LIKE THAT FOR YOU BEFORE.
......?

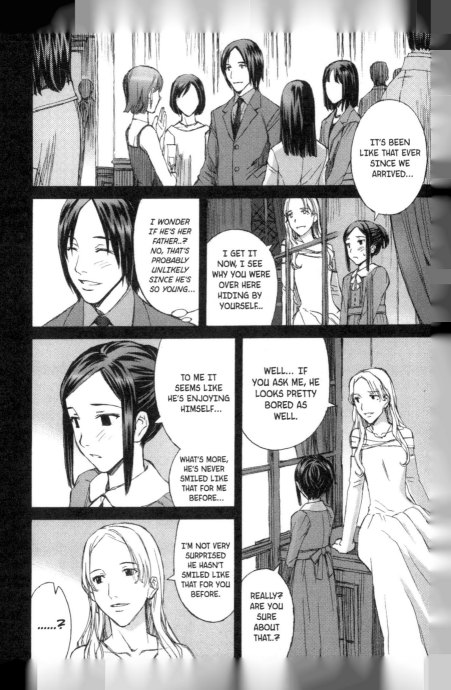

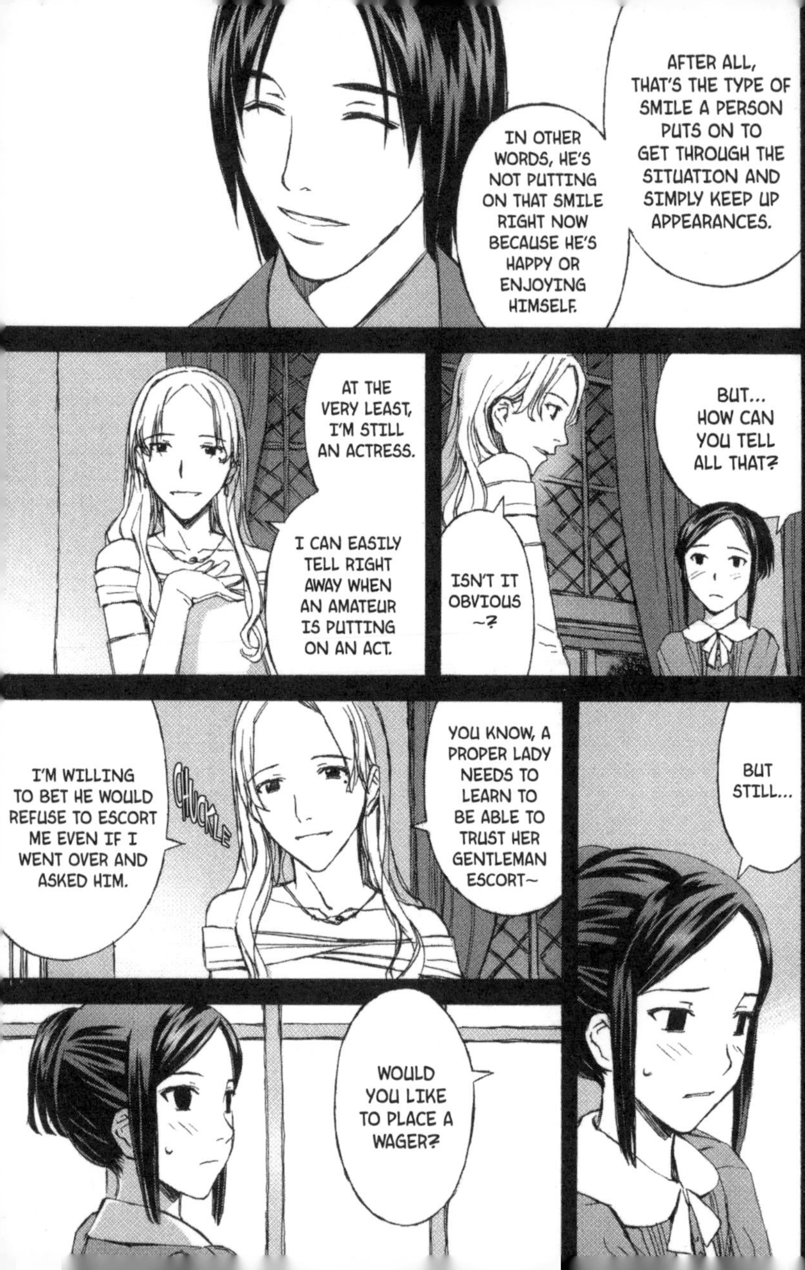
AFTER ALL, THAT'S THE TYPE OF SMILE A PERSON PUTS ON TO GET THROUGH THE SITUATION AND SIMPLY KEEP UP APPEARANCES.
IN OTHER WORDS, HE'S NOT PUTTING ON THAT SMILE RIGHT NOW BECAUSE HE'S HAPPY OR ENJOYING HIMSELF.
BUT... HOW CAN YOU TELL ALL THAT?
ISN'T IT OBVIOUS ~?
AT THE VERY LEAST, I'M STILL AN ACTRESS.
I CAN EASILY TELL RIGHT AWAY WHEN AN AMATEUR IS PUTTING ON AN ACT.
BUT STILL...
YOU KNOW, A PROPER LADY NEEDS TO LEARN TO BE ABLE TO TRUST HER GENTLEMAN ESCORT~
CHUCKLE
I'M WILLING TO BET HE WOULD REFUSE TO ESCORT ME EVEN IF I WENT OVER AND ASKED HIM.
WOULD YOU LIKE TO PLACE A WAGER?

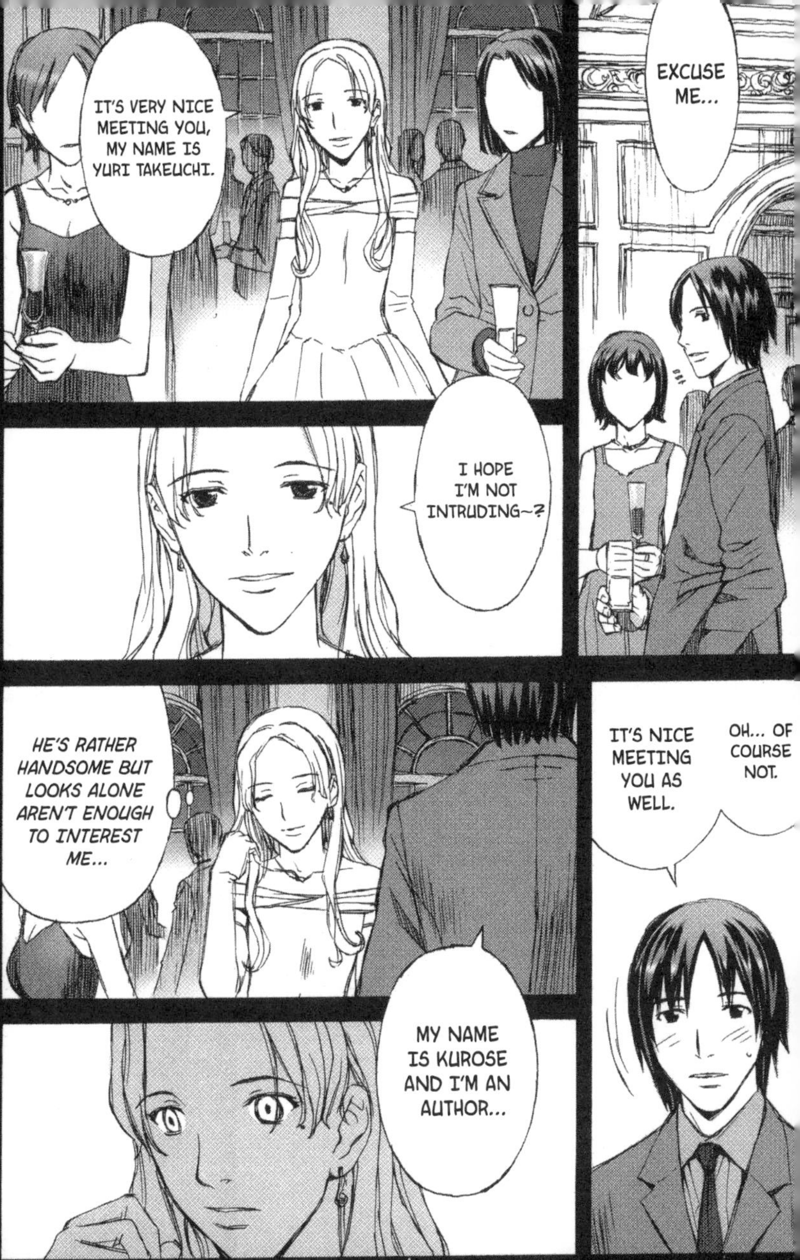
EXCUSE ME...
IT'S VERY NICE MEETING YOU, MY NAME IS YURI TAKEUCHI.
I HOPE I'M NOT INTRUDING~?
OH... OF COURSE NOT.
IT'S NICE MEETING YOU AS WELL.
HE'S RATHER HANDSOME BUT LOOKS ALONE AREN'T ENOUGH TO INTEREST ME...
MY NAME IS KUROSE AND I'M AN AUTHOR...

Note : The author has yet to specify whether "Kurose" is Kuroe's pen name, last name, or nickname.

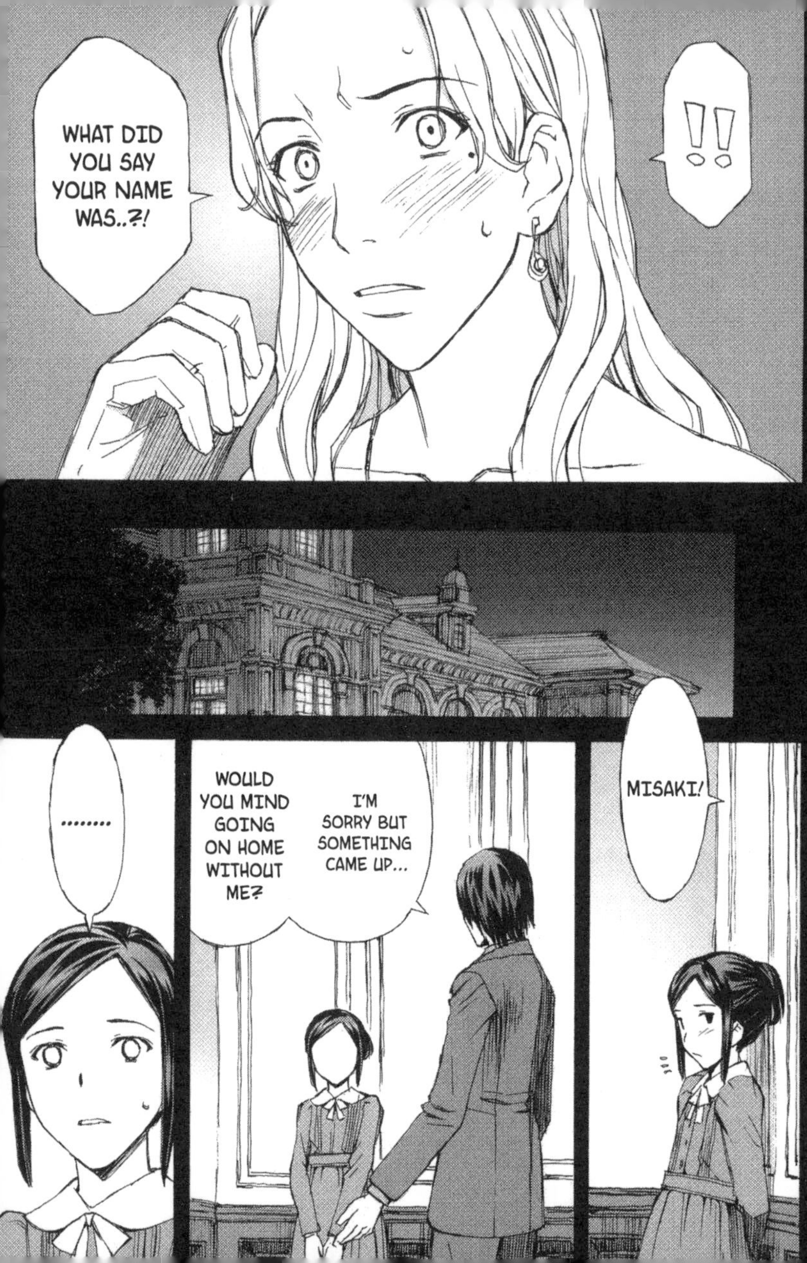
!!
WHAT DID YOU SAY YOUR NAME WAS..?!
MISAKI!
I'M SORRY BUT SOMETHING CAME UP...
WOULD YOU MIND GOING ON HOME WITHOUT ME?
....

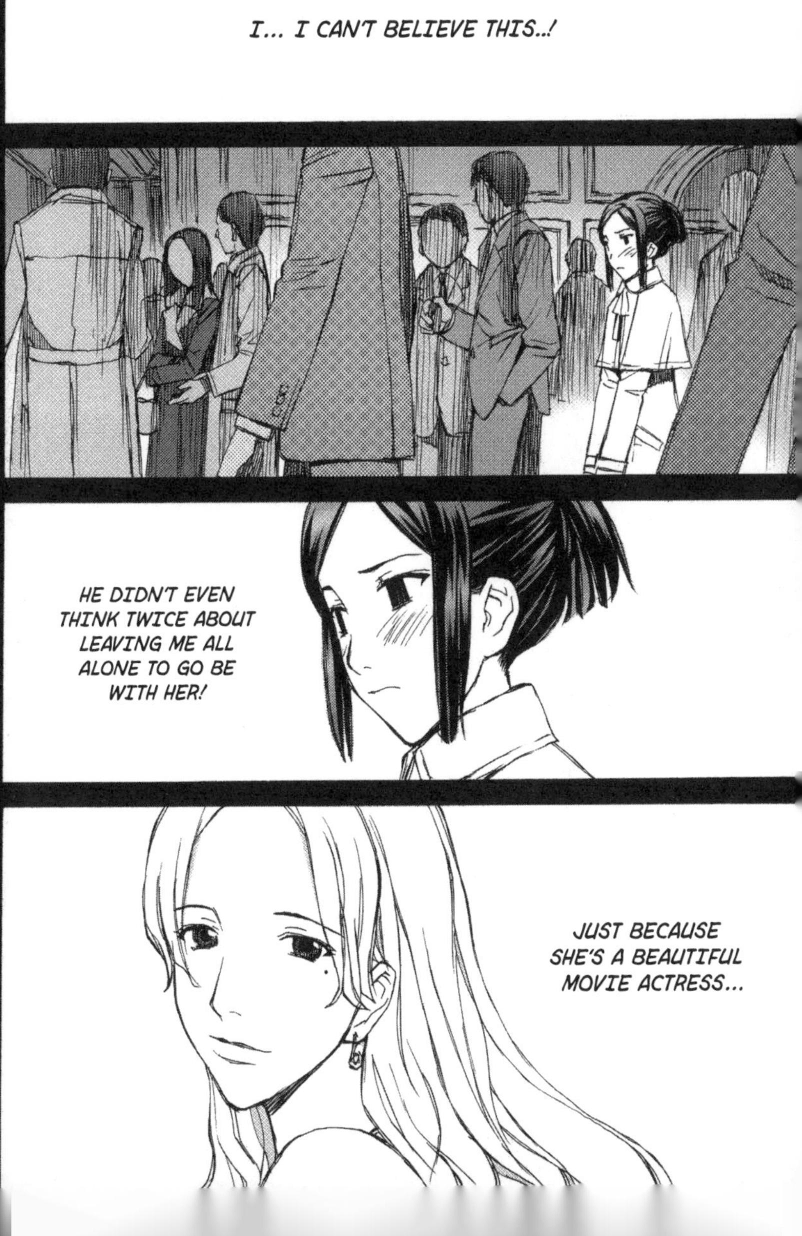
I... I CAN'T BELIEVE THIS..!
HE DIDN'T EVEN THINK TWICE ABOUT LEAVING ME ALL ALONE TO GO BE WITH HER!
JUST BECAUSE SHE'S A BEAUTIFUL MOVIE ACTRESS...

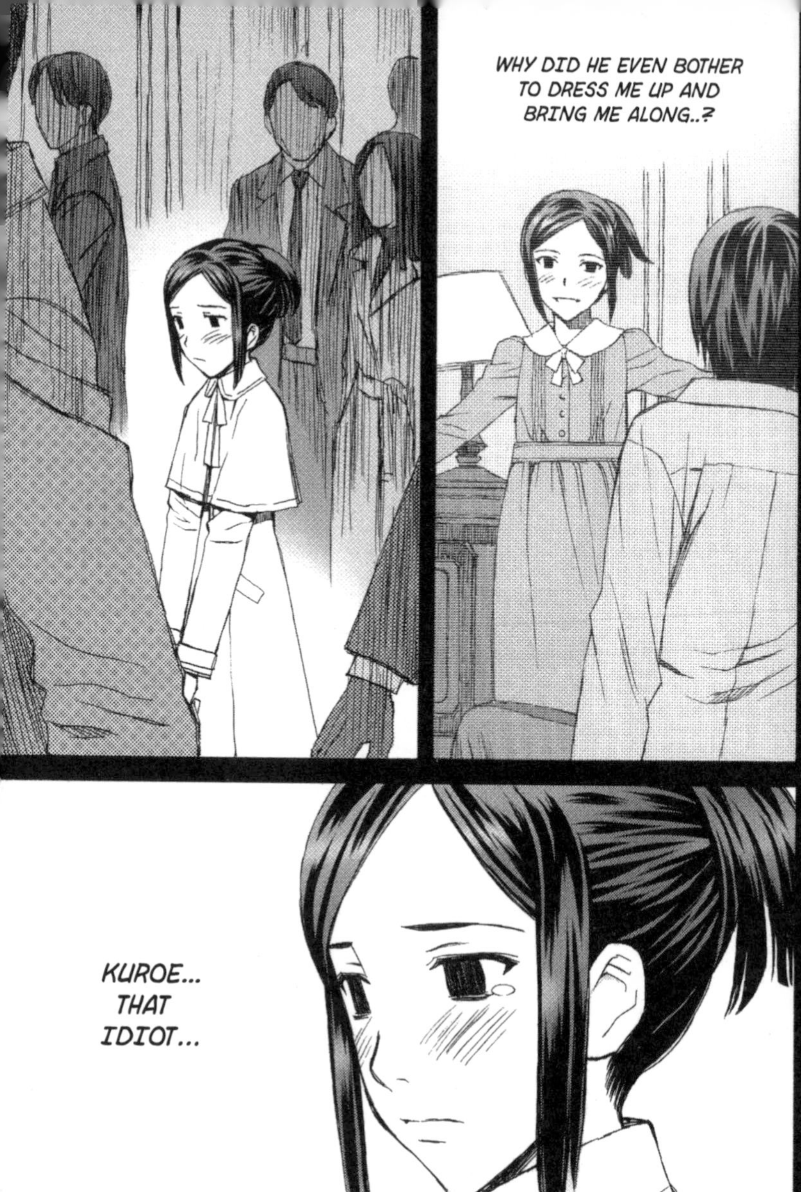
WHY DID HE EVEN BOTHER TO DRESS ME UP AND BRING ME ALONG..?
KUROE... THAT IDIOT...

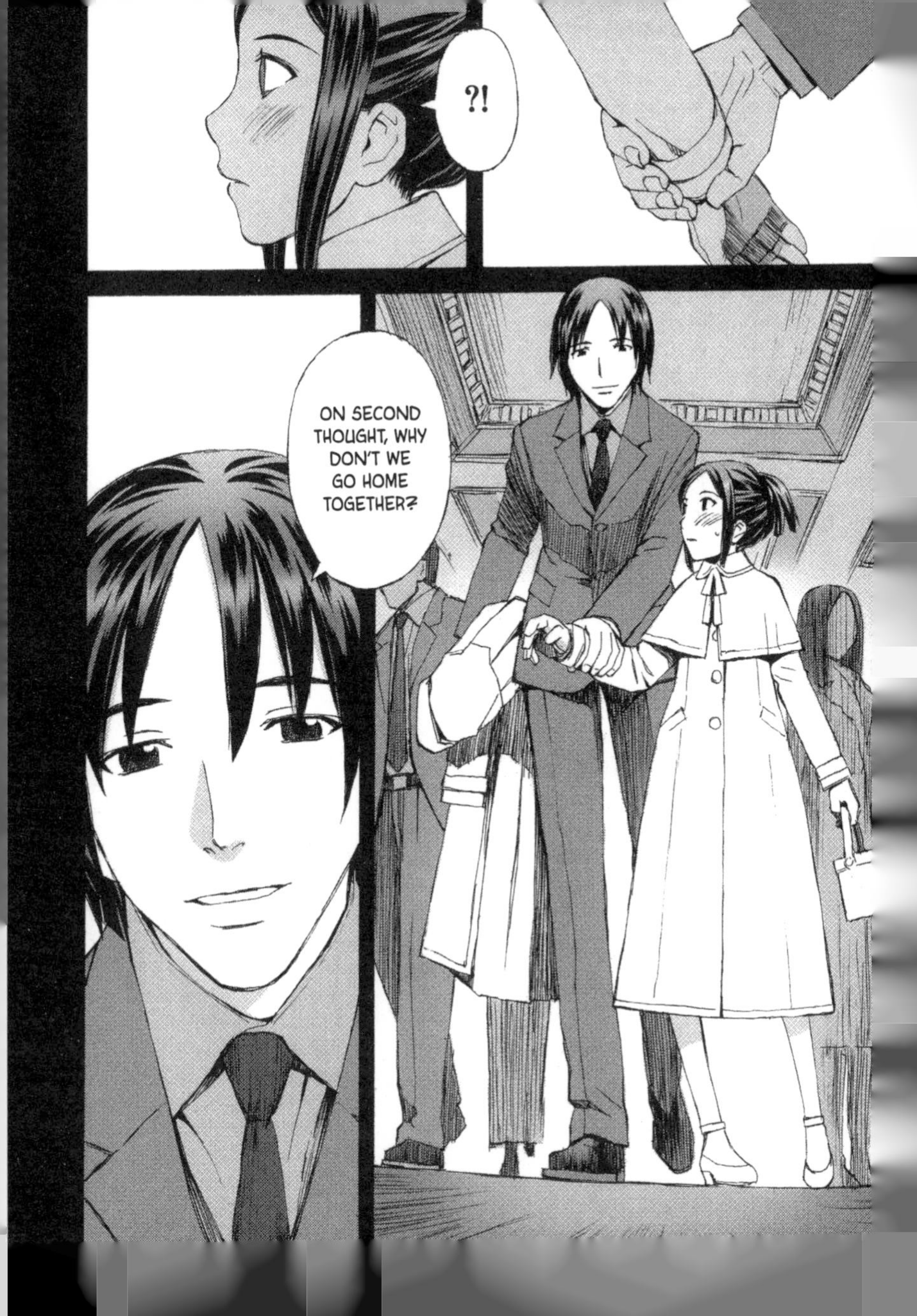
?!
ON SECOND THOUGHT, WHY DON'T WE GO HOME TOGETHER?

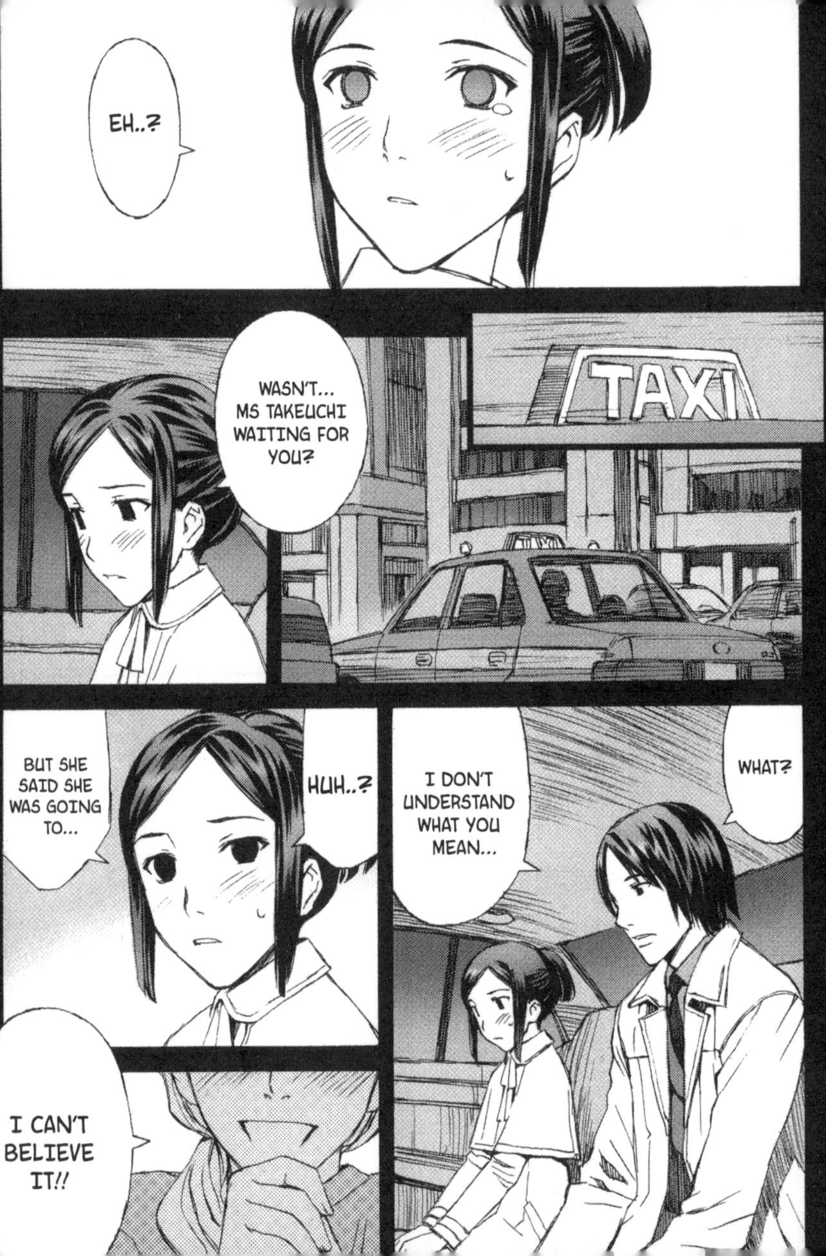
EH..?
WASN'T... MS TAKEUCHI WAITING FOR YOU?
TAXI
WHAT?
I DON'T UNDERSTAND WHAT YOU MEAN...
HUH..?
BUT SHE SAID SHE WAS GOING TO...
I CAN'T BELIEVE IT!!

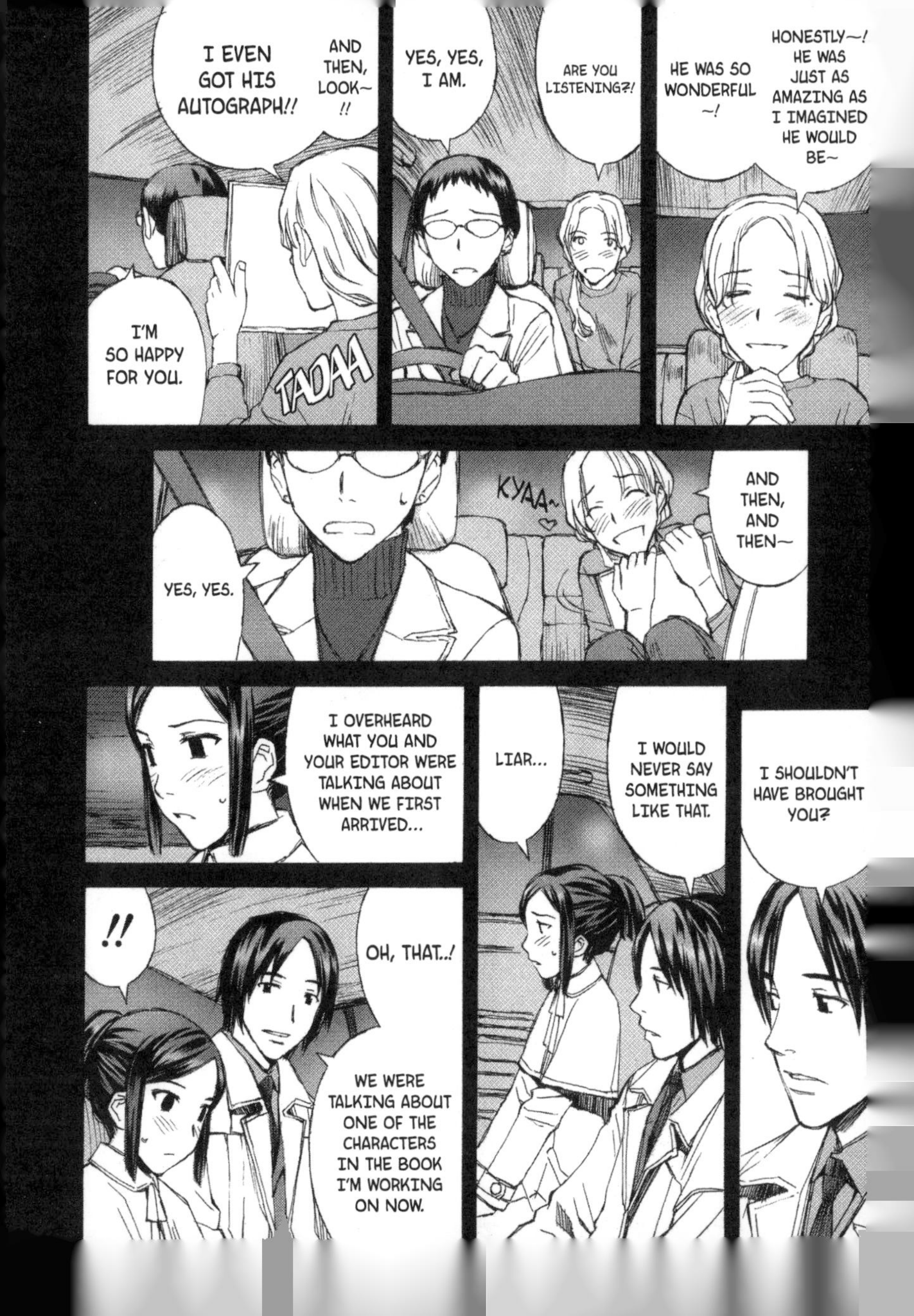
HONESTLY~! HE WAS JUST AS AMAZING AS I IMAGINED HE WOULD BE~
HE WAS SO WONDERFUL ~!
ARE YOU LISTENING?!
YES, YES, I AM.
AND THEN, LOOK~ !!
I EVEN GOT HIS AUTOGRAPH!!
TADAA
I'M SO HAPPY FOR YOU.
AND THEN, AND THEN~
KYAA~
YES, YES.
I SHOULDN'T HAVE BROUGHT YOU?
I WOULD NEVER SAY SOMETHING LIKE THAT.
LIAR...
I OVERHEARD WHAT YOU AND YOUR EDITOR WERE TALKING ABOUT WHEN WE FIRST ARRIVED...
!!
OH, THAT..!
WE WERE TALKING ABOUT ONE OF THE CHARACTERS IN THE BOOK I'M WORKING ON NOW.

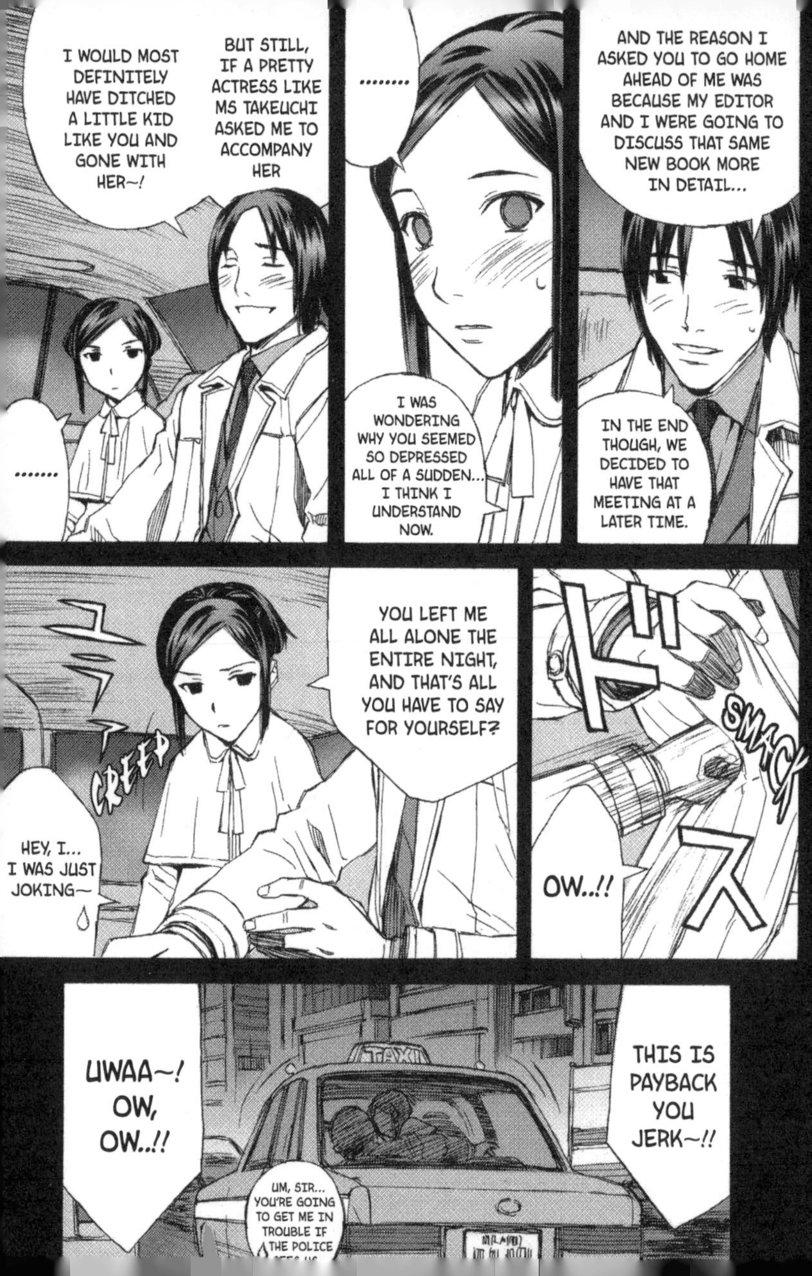
AND THE REASON I ASKED YOU TO GO HOME AHEAD OF ME WAS BECAUSE MY EDITOR AND I WERE GOING TO DISCUSS THAT SAME NEW BOOK MORE IN DETAIL...
IN THE END THOUGH, WE DECIDED TO HAVE THAT MEETING AT A LATER TIME.
....
I WAS WONDERING WHY YOU SEEMED SO DEPRESSED ALL OF A SUDDEN... I THINK I UNDERSTAND NOW.
BUT STILL, IF A PRETTY ACTRESS LIKE MS TAKEUCHI ASKED ME TO ACCOMPANY HER
I WOULD MOST DEFINITELY HAVE DITCHED A LITTLE KID LIKE YOU AND GONE WITH HER~!
....
SMACK
OW..!!
YOU LEFT ME ALL ALONE THE ENTIRE NIGHT, AND THAT'S ALL YOU HAVE TO SAY FOR YOURSELF?
CREEP
HEY, I... I WAS JUST JOKING~
THIS IS PAYBACK YOU JERK~!!
TAXI
UWAA~! OW, OW..!!
UM, SIR... YOU'RE GOING TO GET ME IN TROUBLE IF THE POLICE

Episode 9
ANOTHER FACE
彼女の秘密 – Her Secret

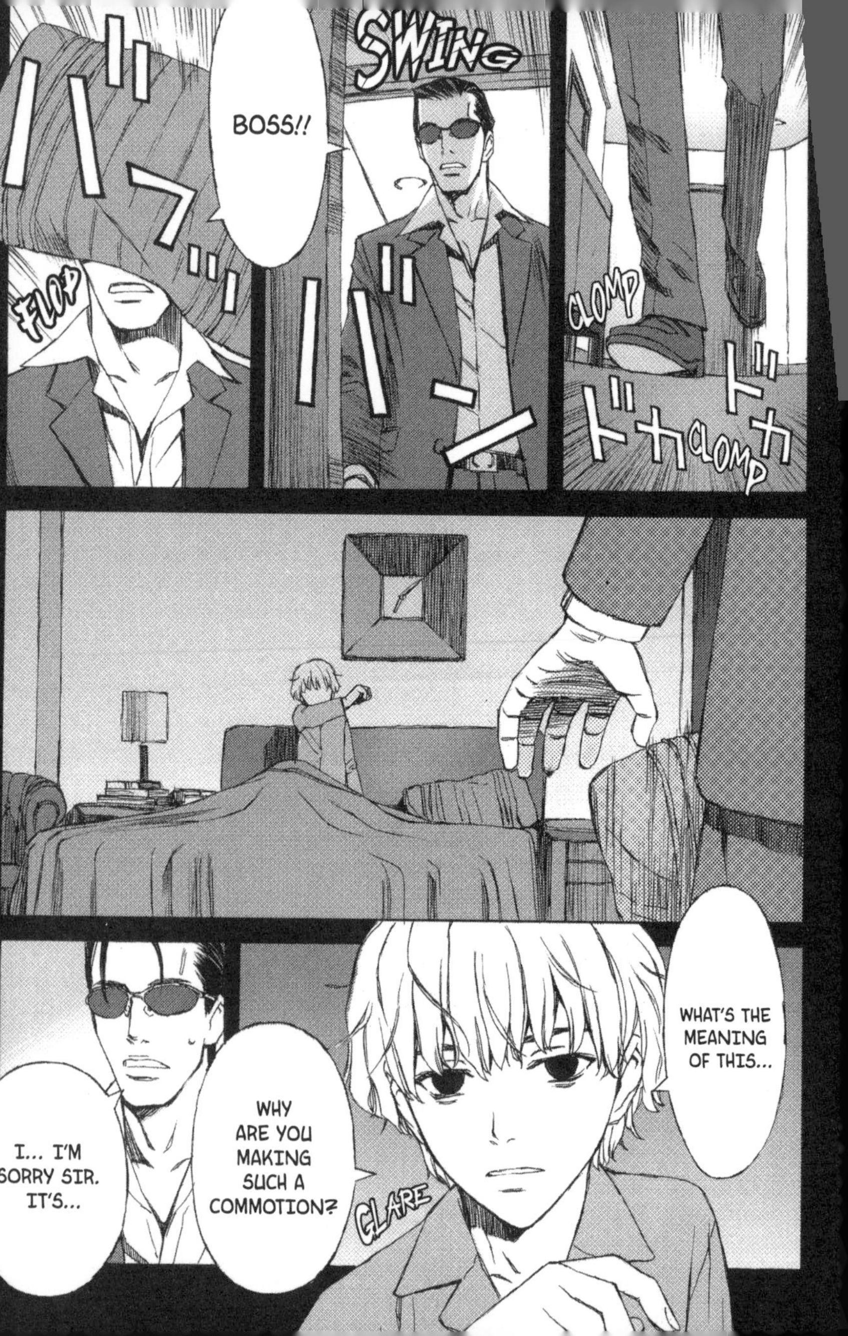
CLOMP
CLOMP
SWING
BOSS!!
FLOP
WHAT'S THE MEANING OF THIS...
GLARE
WHY ARE YOU MAKING SUCH A COMMOTION?
I... I'M SORRY SIR. IT'S...

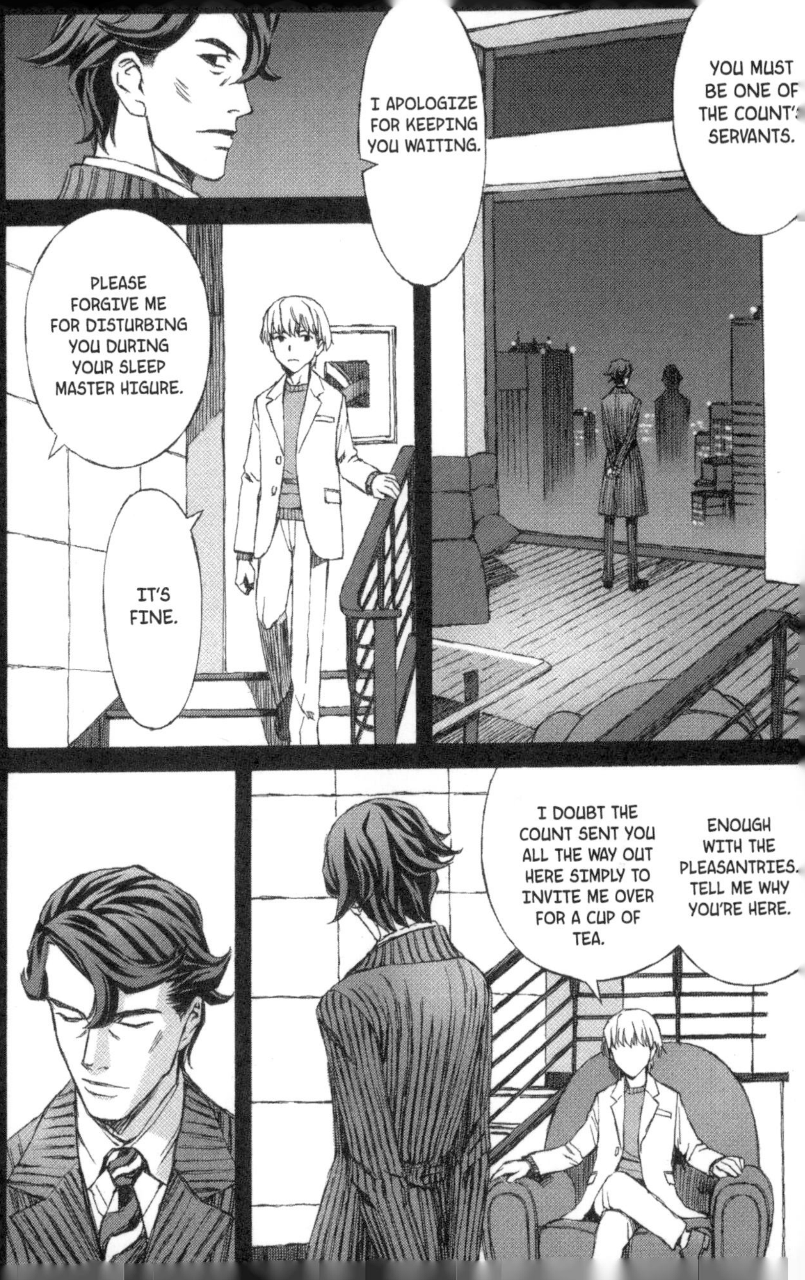
YOU MUST BE ONE OF THE COUNT'S SERVANTS.
I APOLOGIZE FOR KEEPING YOU WAITING.
PLEASE FORGIVE ME FOR DISTURBING YOU DURING YOUR SLEEP MASTER HIGURE.
IT'S FINE.
ENOUGH WITH THE PLEASANTRIES. TELL ME WHY YOU'RE HERE.
I DOUBT THE COUNT SENT YOU ALL THE WAY OUT HERE SIMPLY TO INVITE ME OVER FOR A CUP OF TEA.

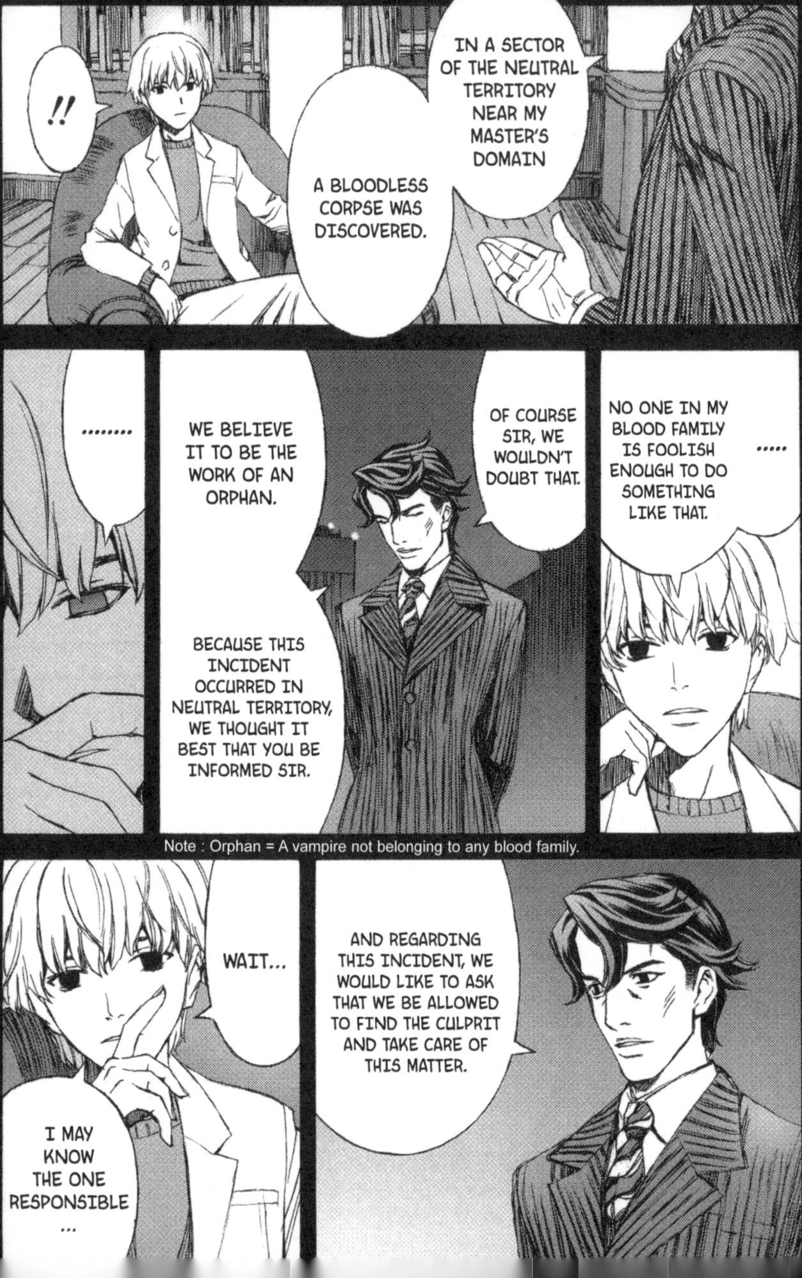
IN A SECTOR OF THE NEUTRAL TERRITORY NEAR MY MASTER'S DOMAIN
A BLOODLESS CORPSE WAS DISCOVERED.
!!
NO ONE IN MY BLOOD FAMILY IS FOOLISH ENOUGH TO DO SOMETHING LIKE THAT.
.....
OF COURSE SIR, WE WOULDN'T DOUBT THAT.
WE BELIEVE IT TO BE THE WORK OF AN ORPHAN.
BECAUSE THIS INCIDENT OCCURRED IN NEUTRAL TERRITORY, WE THOUGHT IT BEST THAT YOU BE INFORMED SIR.
....
AND REGARDING THIS INCIDENT, WE WOULD LIKE TO ASK THAT WE BE ALLOWED TO FIND THE CULPRIT AND TAKE CARE OF THIS MATTER.
WAIT...
I MAY KNOW THE ONE RESPONSIBLE ...

Note : Orphan = A vampire not belonging to any blood family.

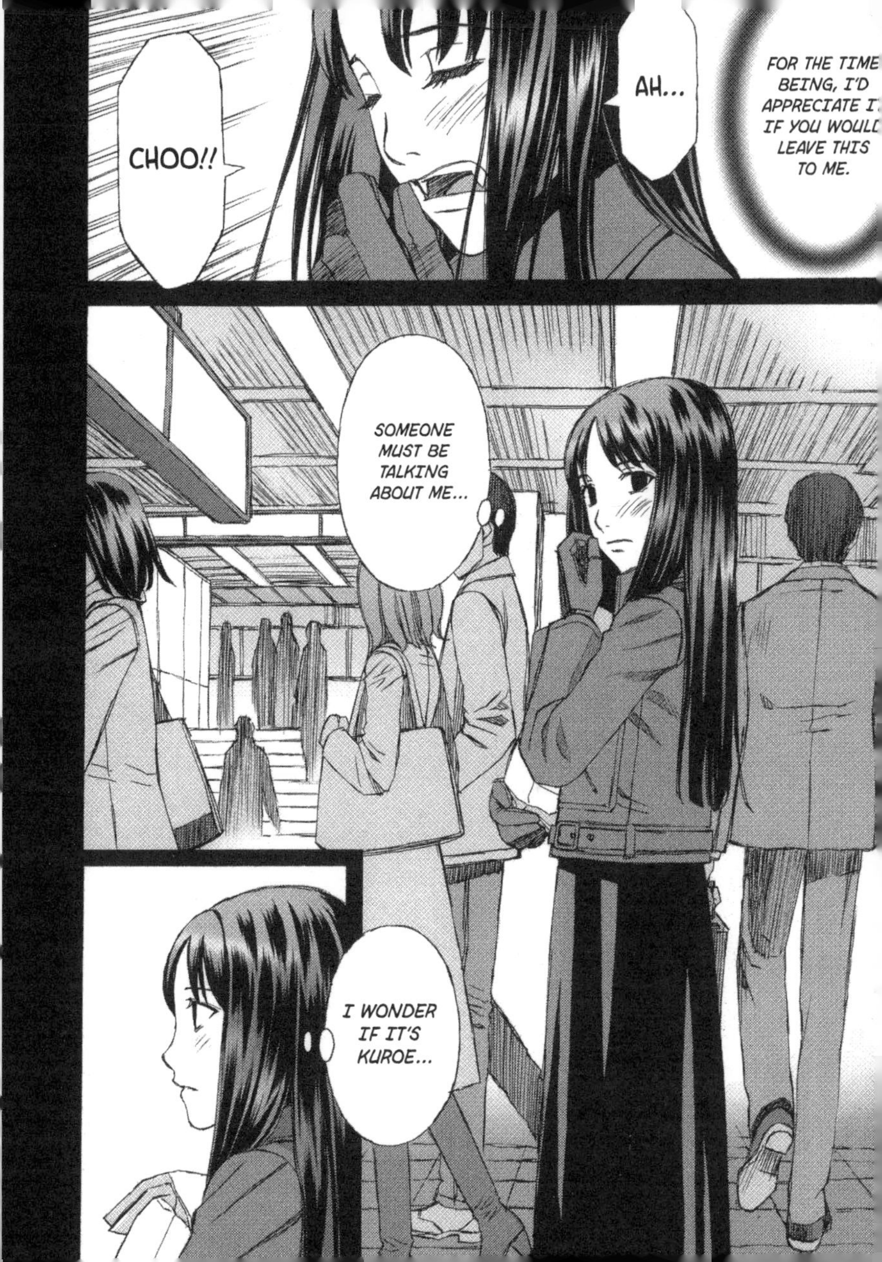
FOR THE TIME BEING, I'D APPRECIATE IT IF YOU WOULD LEAVE THIS TO ME.
AH...
CHOO!!
SOMEONE MUST BE TALKING ABOUT ME...
I WONDER IF IT'S KUROE...

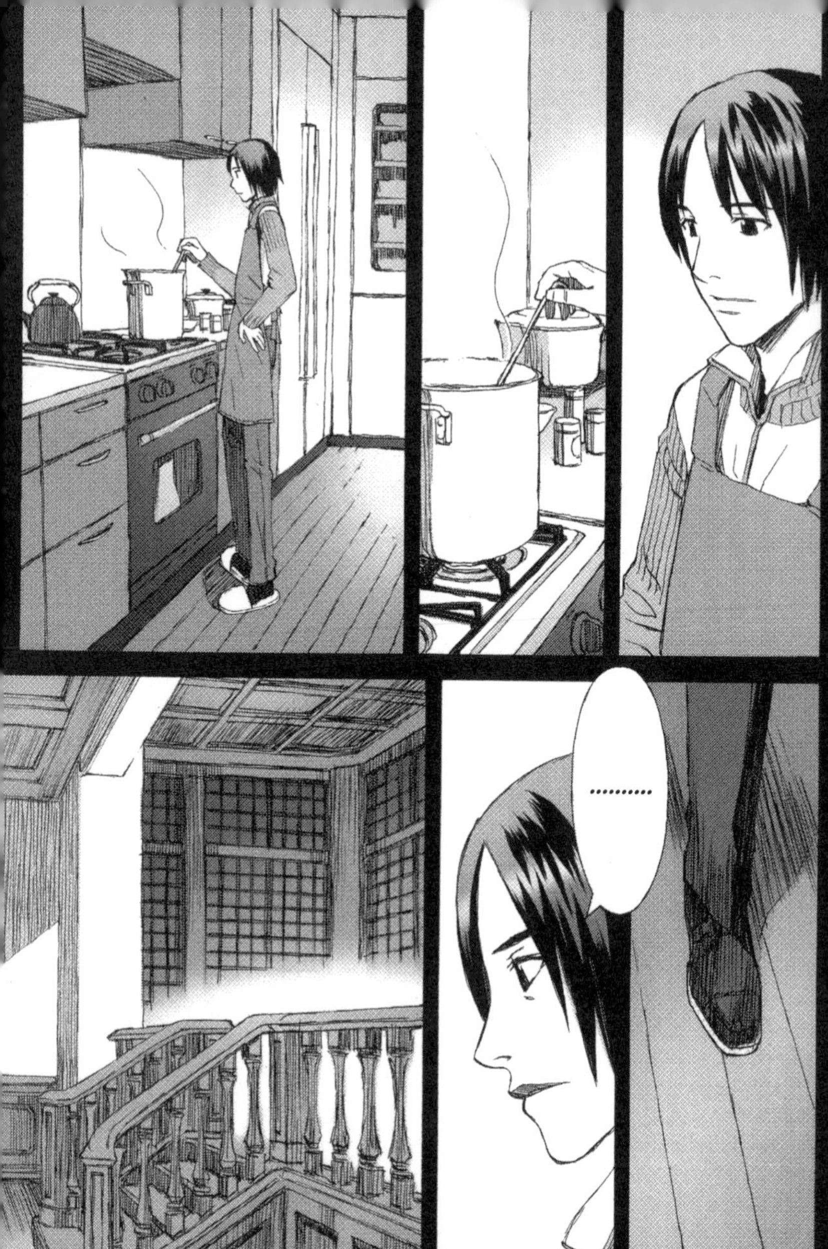
....

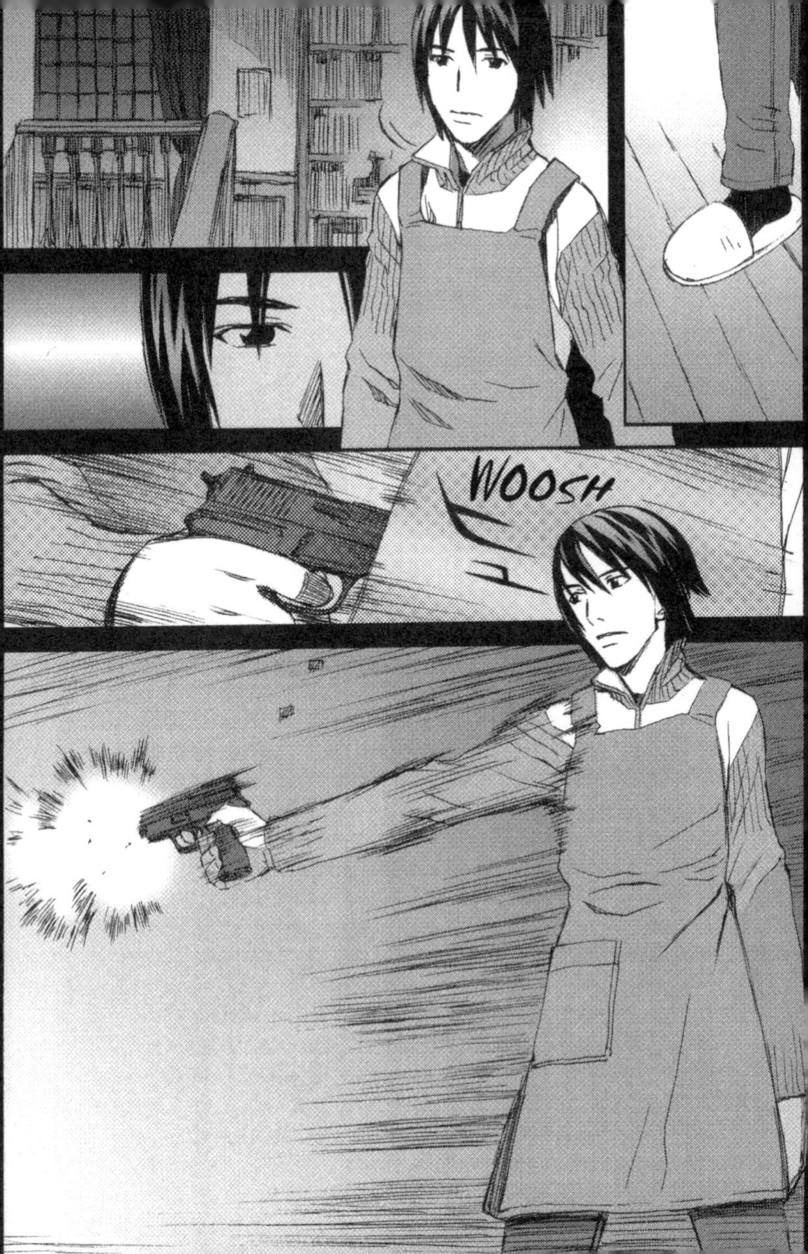
WOOSH

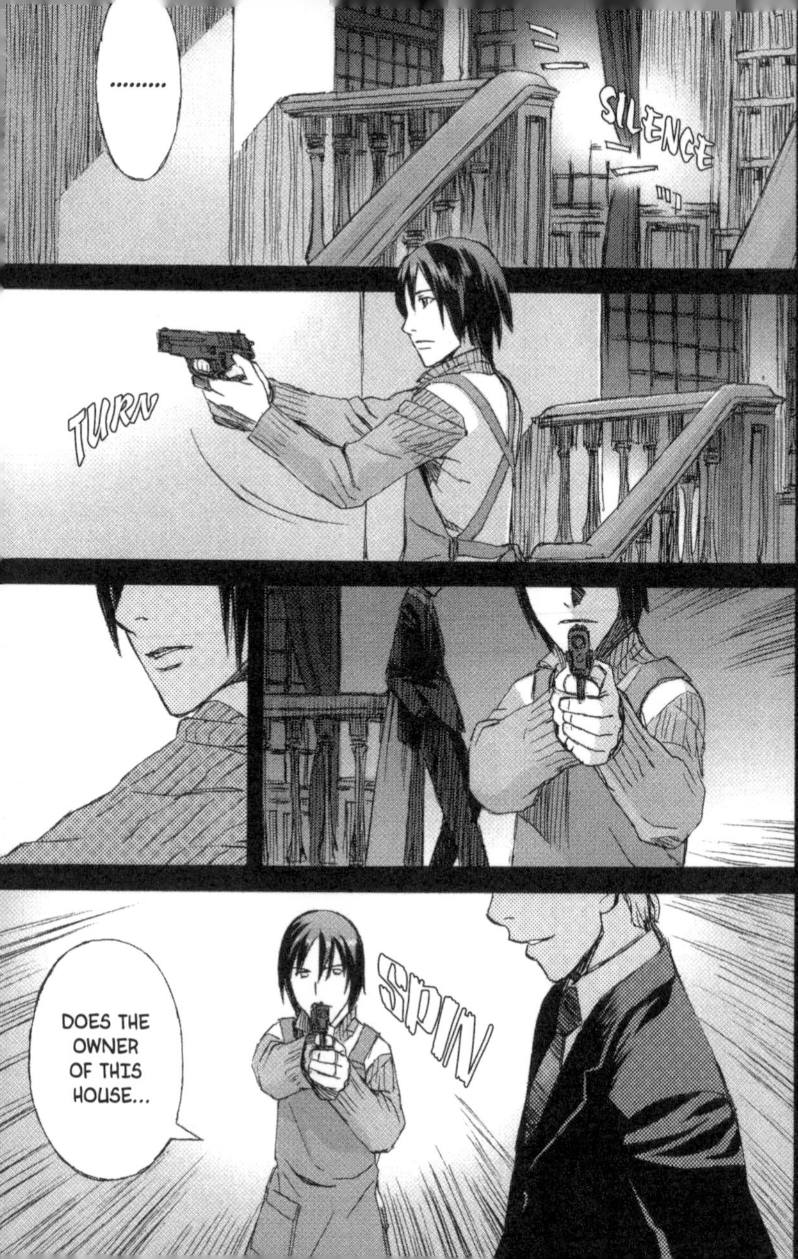
SILENCE
....
TURN
SPIN
DOES THE OWNER OF THIS HOUSE...

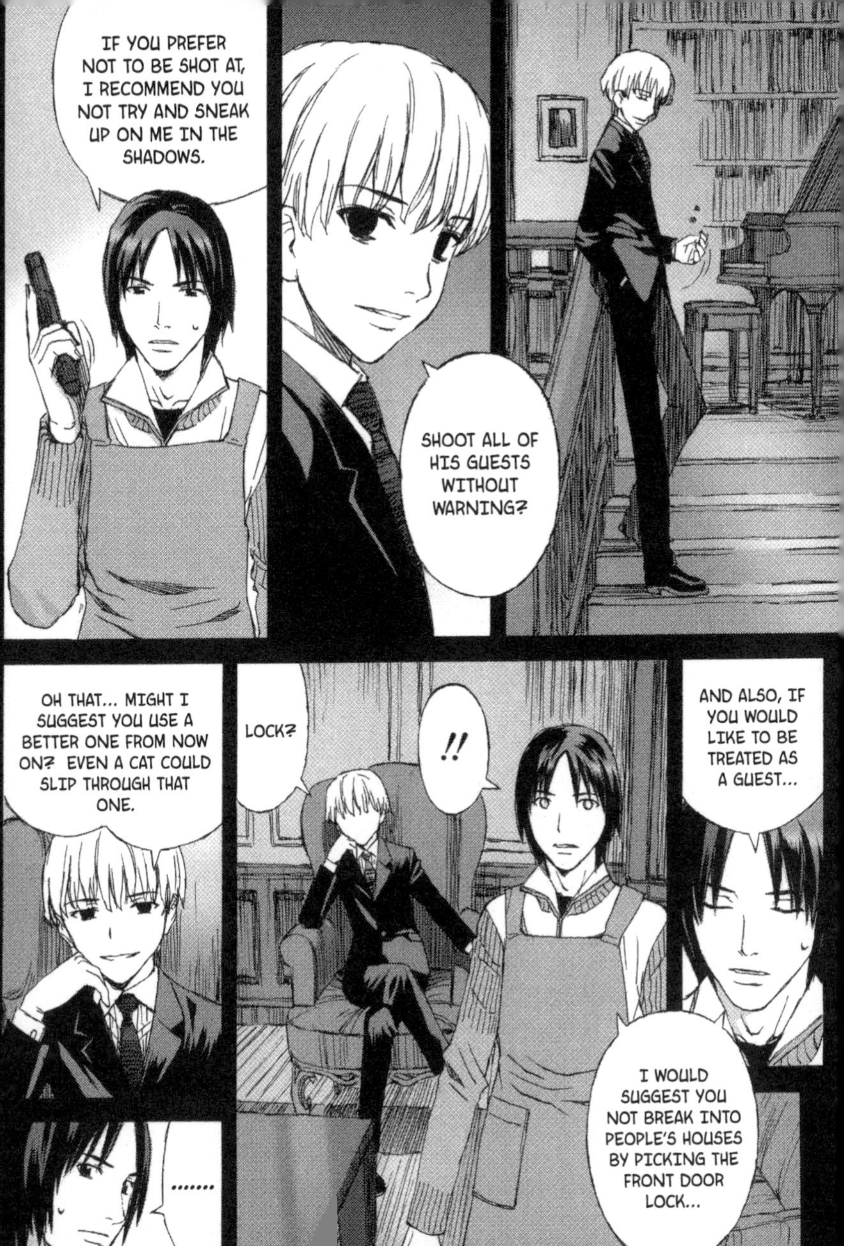
SHOOT ALL OF HIS GUESTS WITHOUT WARNING?
IF YOU PREFER NOT TO BE SHOT AT, I RECOMMEND YOU NOT TRY AND SNEAK UP ON ME IN THE SHADOWS.
AND ALSO, IF YOU WOULD LIKE TO BE TREATED AS A GUEST...
I WOULD SUGGEST YOU NOT BREAK INTO PEOPLE'S HOUSES BY PICKING THE FRONT DOOR LOCK...
!!
LOCK?
OH THAT... MIGHT I SUGGEST YOU USE A BETTER ONE FROM NOW ON? EVEN A CAT COULD SLIP THROUGH THAT ONE.
....

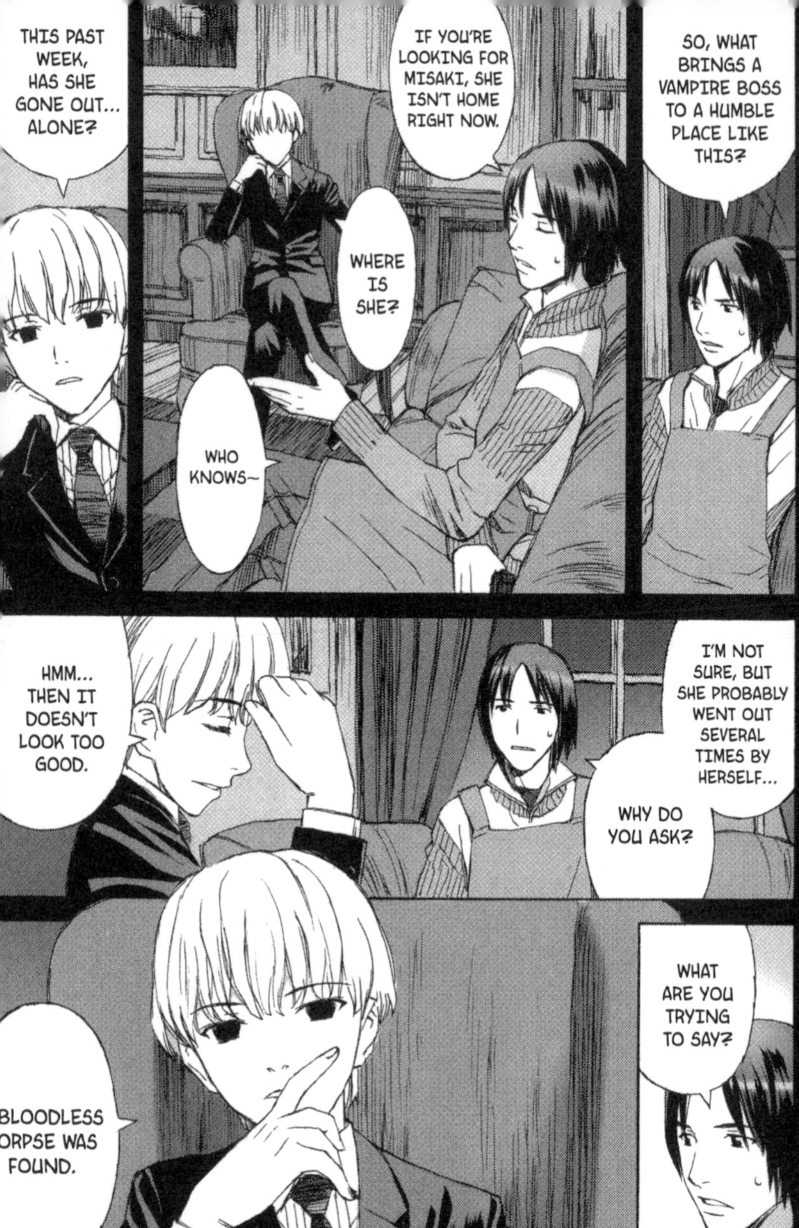
SO, WHAT BRINGS A VAMPIRE BOSS TO A HUMBLE PLACE LIKE THIS?
IF YOU'RE LOOKING FOR MISAKI, SHE ISN'T HOME RIGHT NOW.
WHERE IS SHE?
WHO KNOWS~
THIS PAST WEEK, HAS SHE GONE OUT... ALONE?
I'M NOT SURE, BUT SHE PROBABLY WENT OUT SEVERAL TIMES BY HERSELF...
WHY DO YOU ASK?
HMM... THEN IT DOESN'T LOOK TOO GOOD.
WHAT ARE YOU TRYING TO SAY?
BLOODLESS
ORPSE WAS
FOUND.

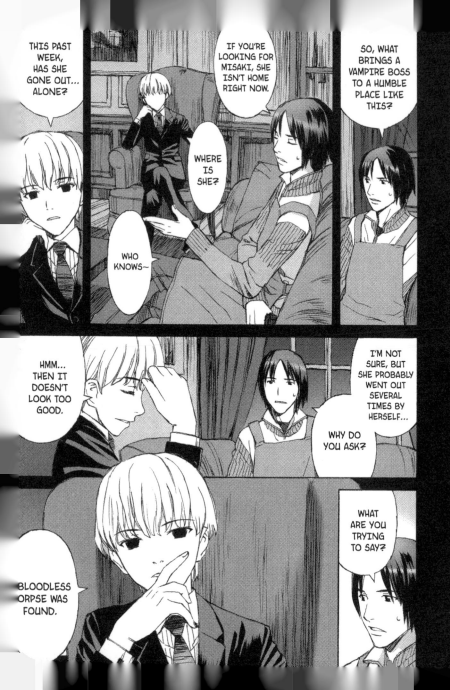

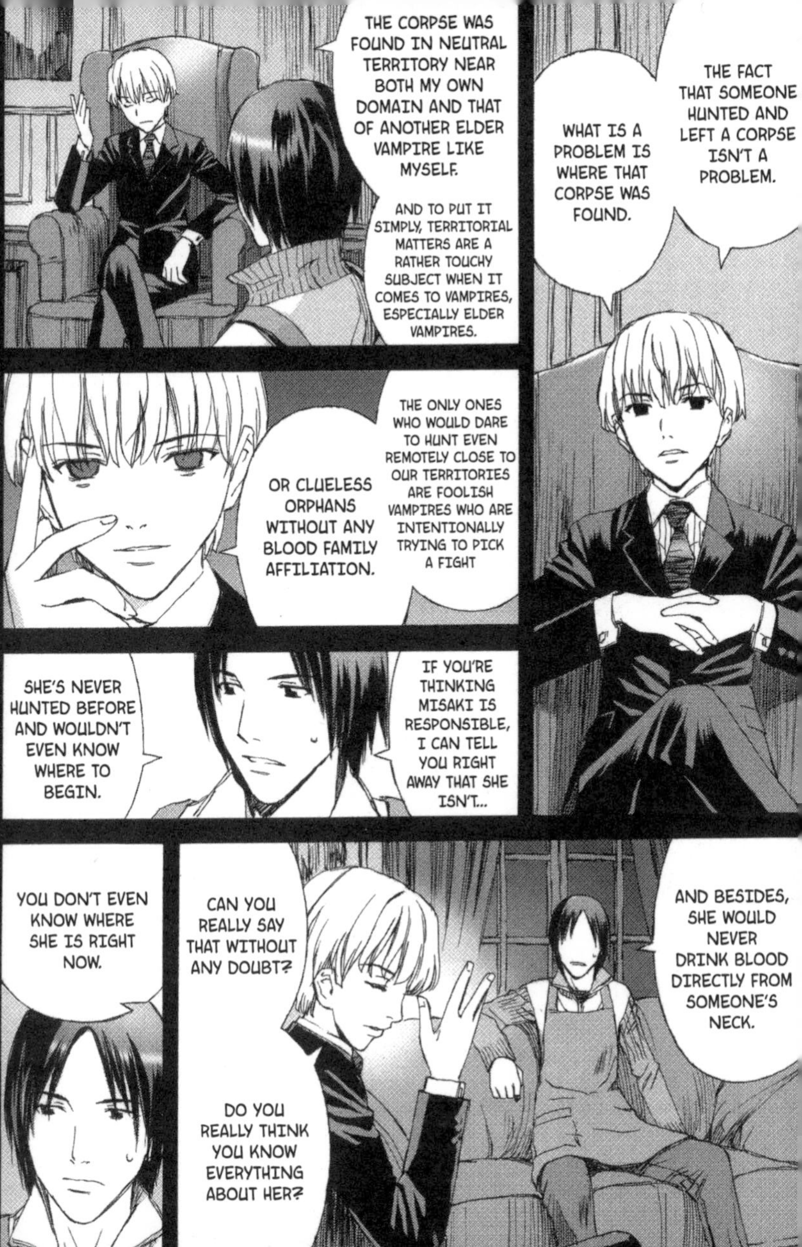
THE FACT THAT SOMEONE HUNTED AND LEFT A CORPSE ISN'T A PROBLEM.
WHAT IS A PROBLEM IS WHERE THAT CORPSE WAS FOUND.
THE CORPSE WAS FOUND IN NEUTRAL TERRITORY NEAR BOTH MY OWN DOMAIN AND THAT OF ANOTHER ELDER VAMPIRE LIKE MYSELF.
AND TO PUT IT SIMPLY, TERRITORIAL MATTERS ARE A RATHER TOUCHY SUBJECT WHEN IT COMES TO VAMPIRES, ESPECIALLY ELDER VAMPIRES.
THE ONLY ONES WHO WOULD DARE TO HUNT EVEN REMOTELY CLOSE TO OUR TERRITORIES ARE FOOLISH VAMPIRES WHO ARE INTENTIONALLY TRYING TO PICK A FIGHT
OR CLUELESS ORPHANS WITHOUT ANY BLOOD FAMILY AFFILIATION.
IF YOU'RE THINKING MISAKI IS RESPONSIBLE, I CAN TELL YOU RIGHT AWAY THAT SHE ISN'T...
SHE'S NEVER HUNTED BEFORE AND WOULDN'T EVEN KNOW WHERE TO BEGIN.
AND BESIDES, SHE WOULD NEVER DRINK BLOOD DIRECTLY FROM SOMEONE'S NECK.
CAN YOU REALLY SAY THAT WITHOUT ANY DOUBT?
DO YOU REALLY THINK YOU KNOW EVERYTHING ABOUT HER?
YOU DON'T EVEN KNOW WHERE SHE IS RIGHT NOW.

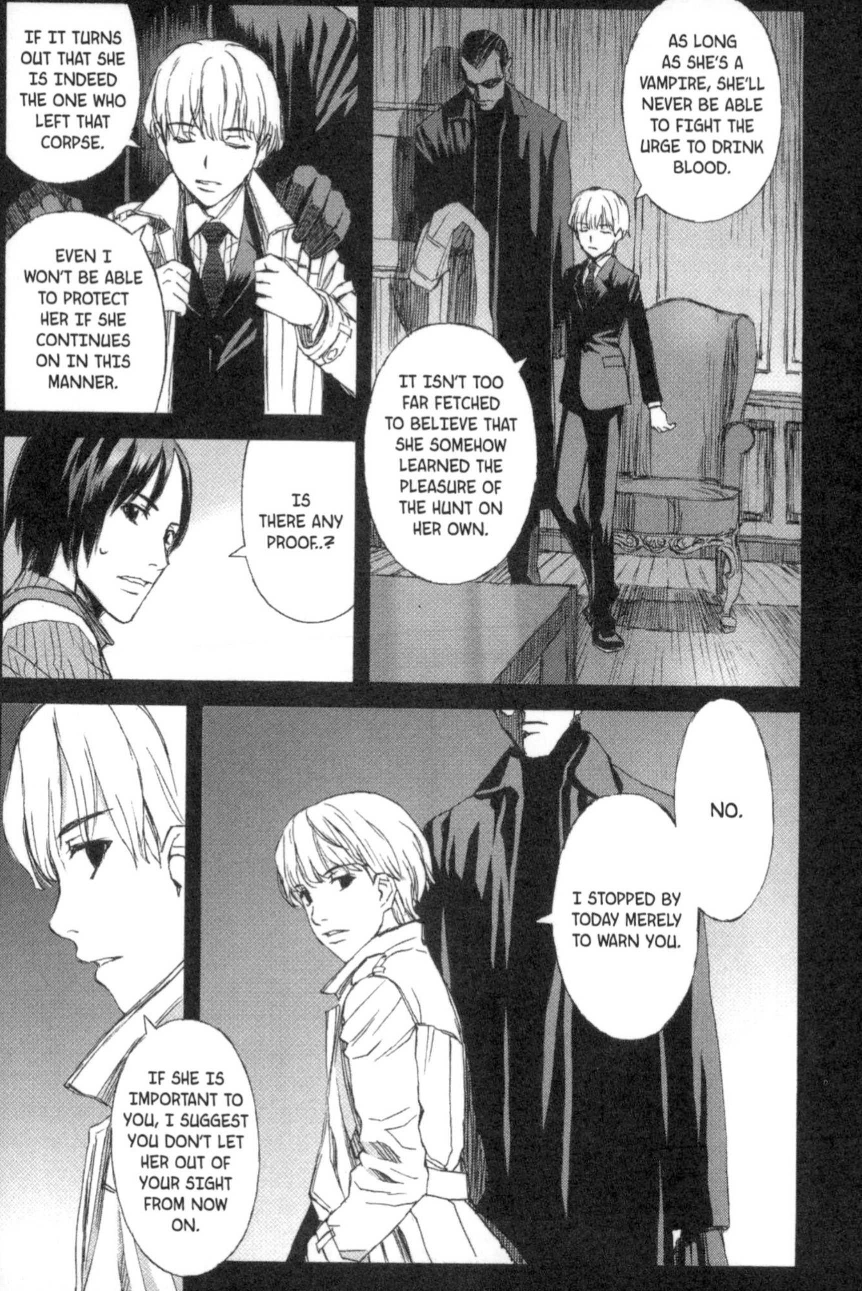
AS LONG AS SHE'S A VAMPIRE, SHE'LL NEVER BE ABLE TO FIGHT THE URGE TO DRINK BLOOD.
IT ISN'T TOO FAR FETCHED TO BELIEVE THAT SHE SOMEHOW LEARNED THE PLEASURE OF THE HUNT ON HER OWN.
IF IT TURNS OUT THAT SHE IS INDEED THE ONE WHO LEFT THAT CORPSE.
EVEN I WON'T BE ABLE TO PROTECT HER IF SHE CONTINUES ON IN THIS MANNER.
IS THERE ANY PROOF..?
NO.
I STOPPED BY TODAY MERELY TO WARN YOU.
IF SHE IS IMPORTANT TO YOU, I SUGGEST YOU DON'T LET HER OUT OF YOUR SIGHT FROM NOW ON.

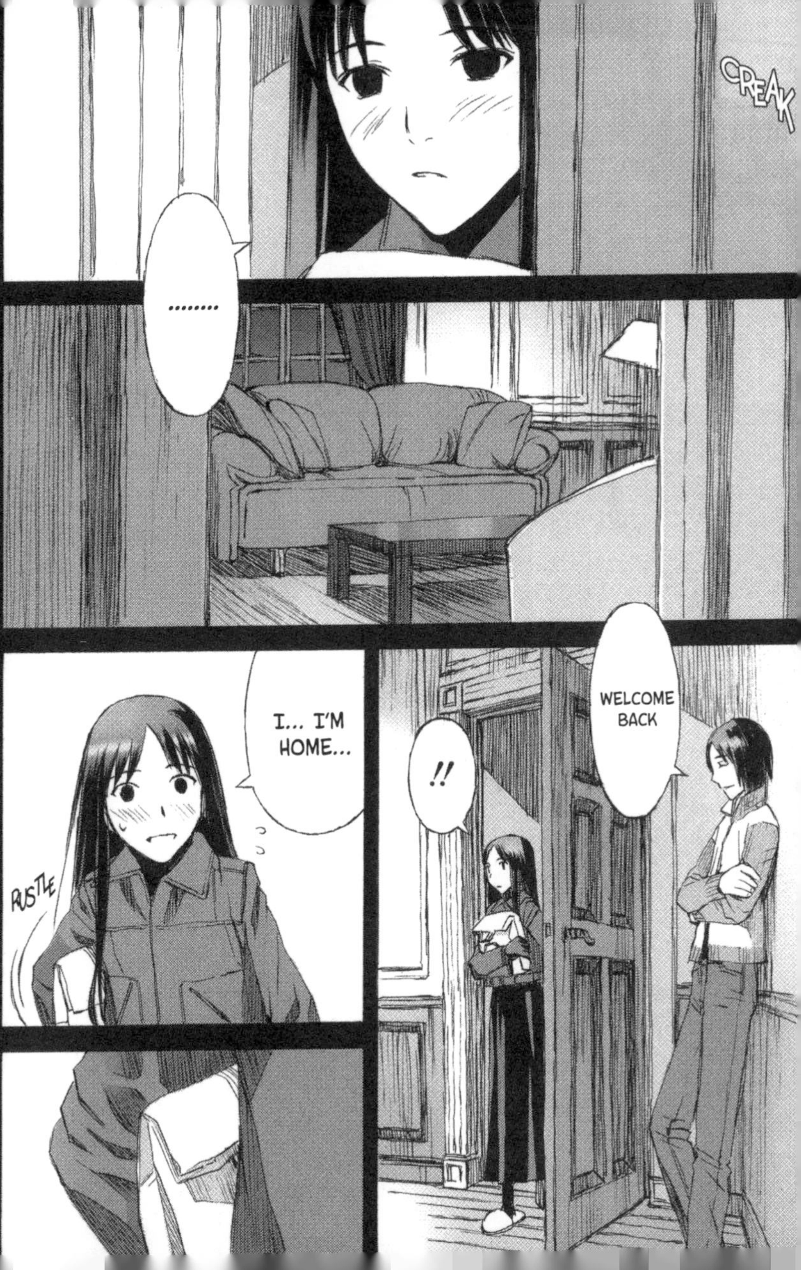
CREAK
....
WELCOME BACK
!!
I... I'M HOME...
RUSTLE

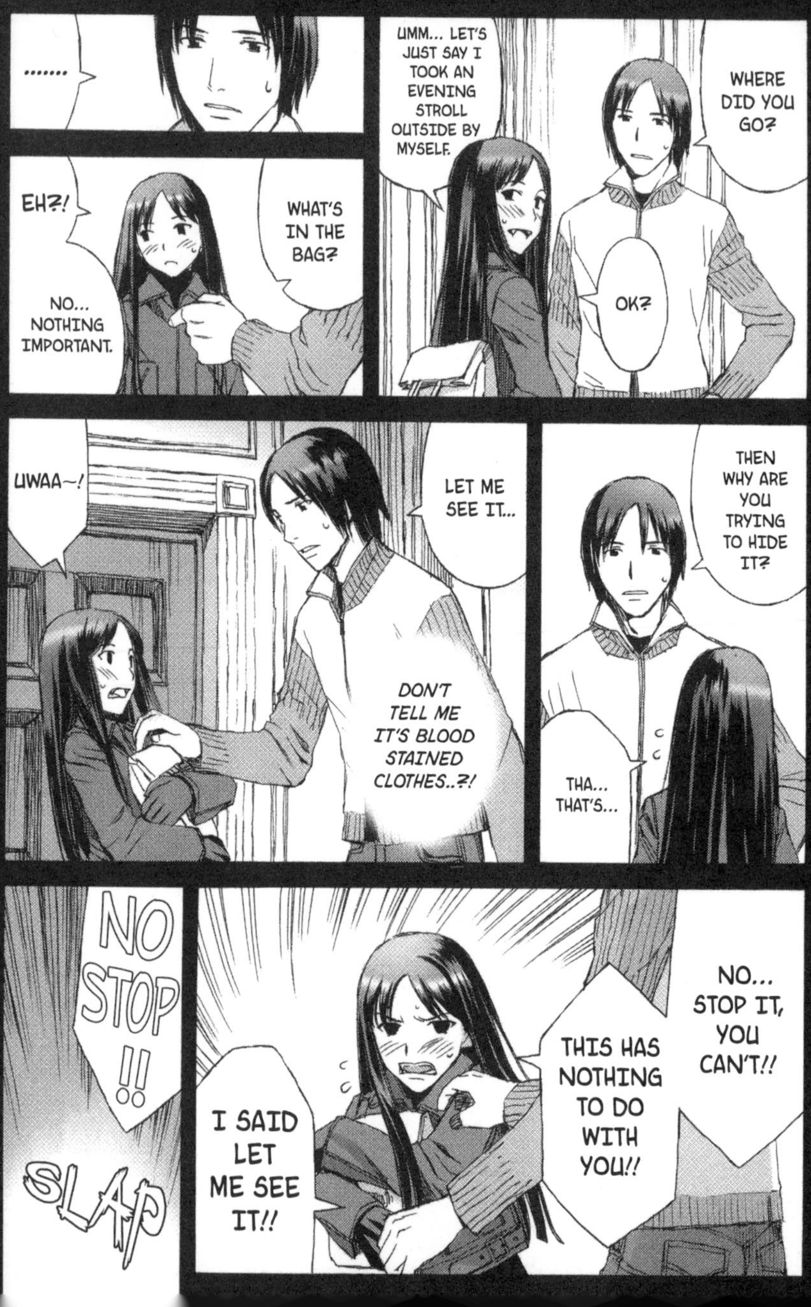
WHERE DID YOU GO?
UMM... LET'S JUST SAY I TOOK AN EVENING STROLL OUTSIDE BY MYSELF.
OK?
....
WHAT'S IN THE BAG?
EH?!
NO... NOTHING IMPORTANT.
THEN WHY ARE YOU TRYING TO HIDE IT?
THA... THAT'S...
LET ME SEE IT...
UWAA~!
DON'T TELL ME IT'S BLOOD STAINED CLOTHES..?!
NO... STOP IT, YOU CAN'T!!
THIS HAS NOTHING TO DO WITH YOU!!
I SAID LET ME SEE IT!!
NO STOP !!
SLAP

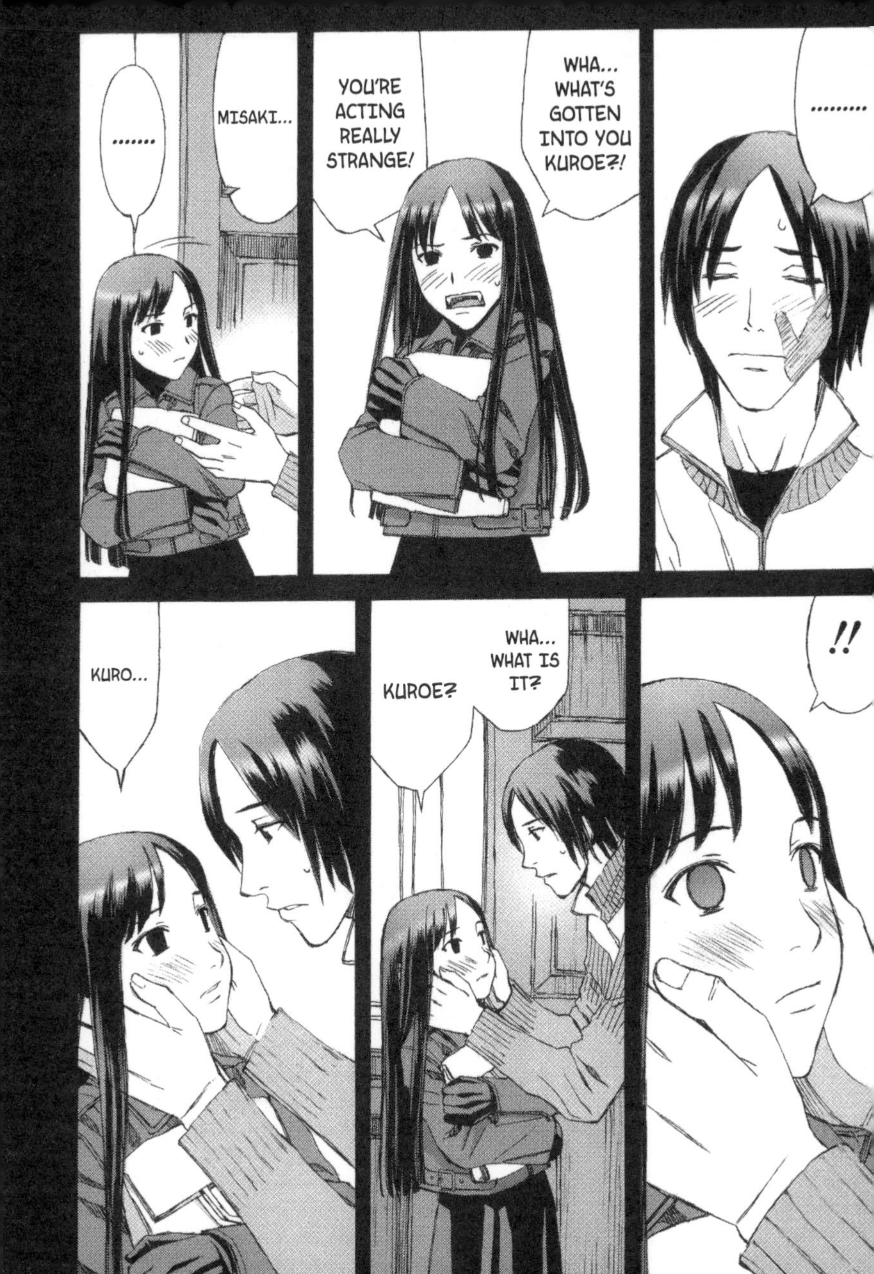
....
WHA... WHAT'S GOTTEN INTO YOU KUROE?!
YOU'RE ACTING REALLY STRANGE!
MISAKI...
....
!!
WHA... WHAT IS IT?
KUROE?
KURO...

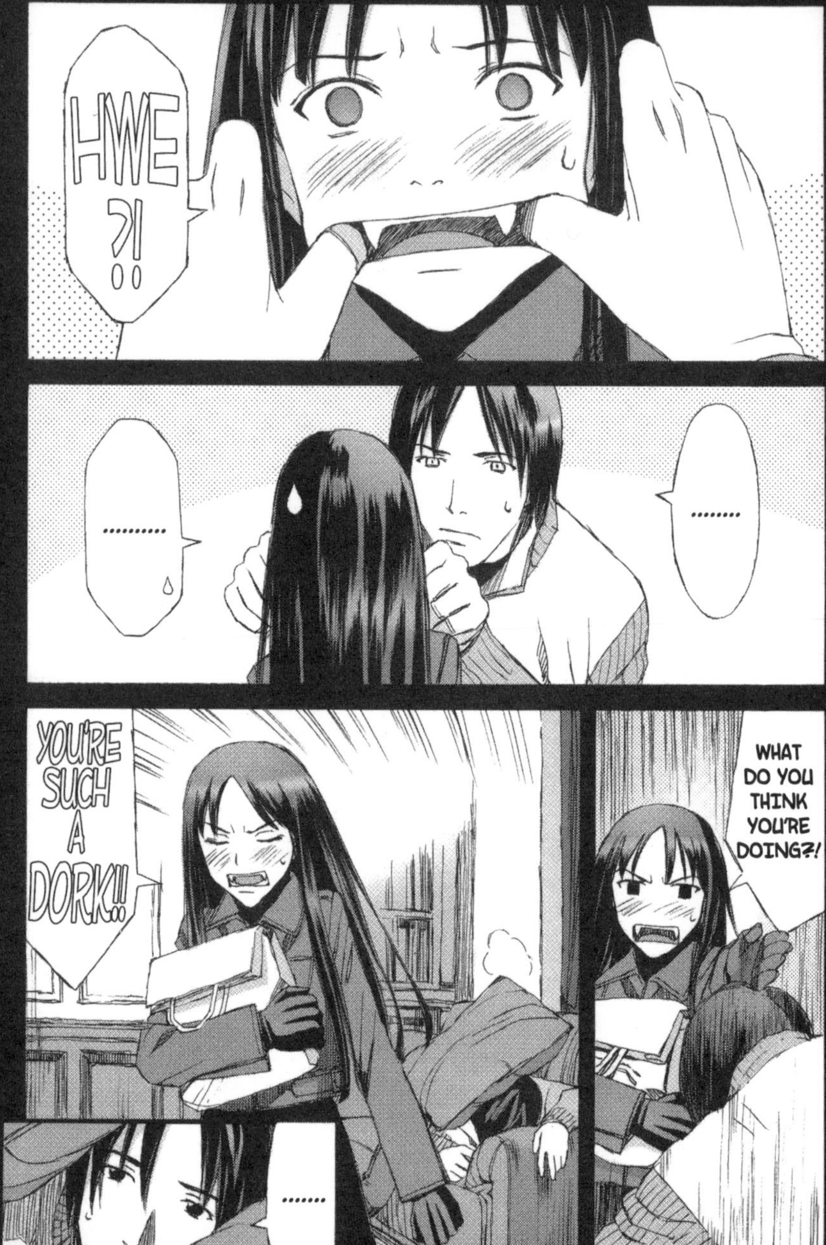
HWE?!!
....
....
WHAT DO YOU THINK YOU'RE DOING?!
YOU'RE SUCH A DORK!!
....

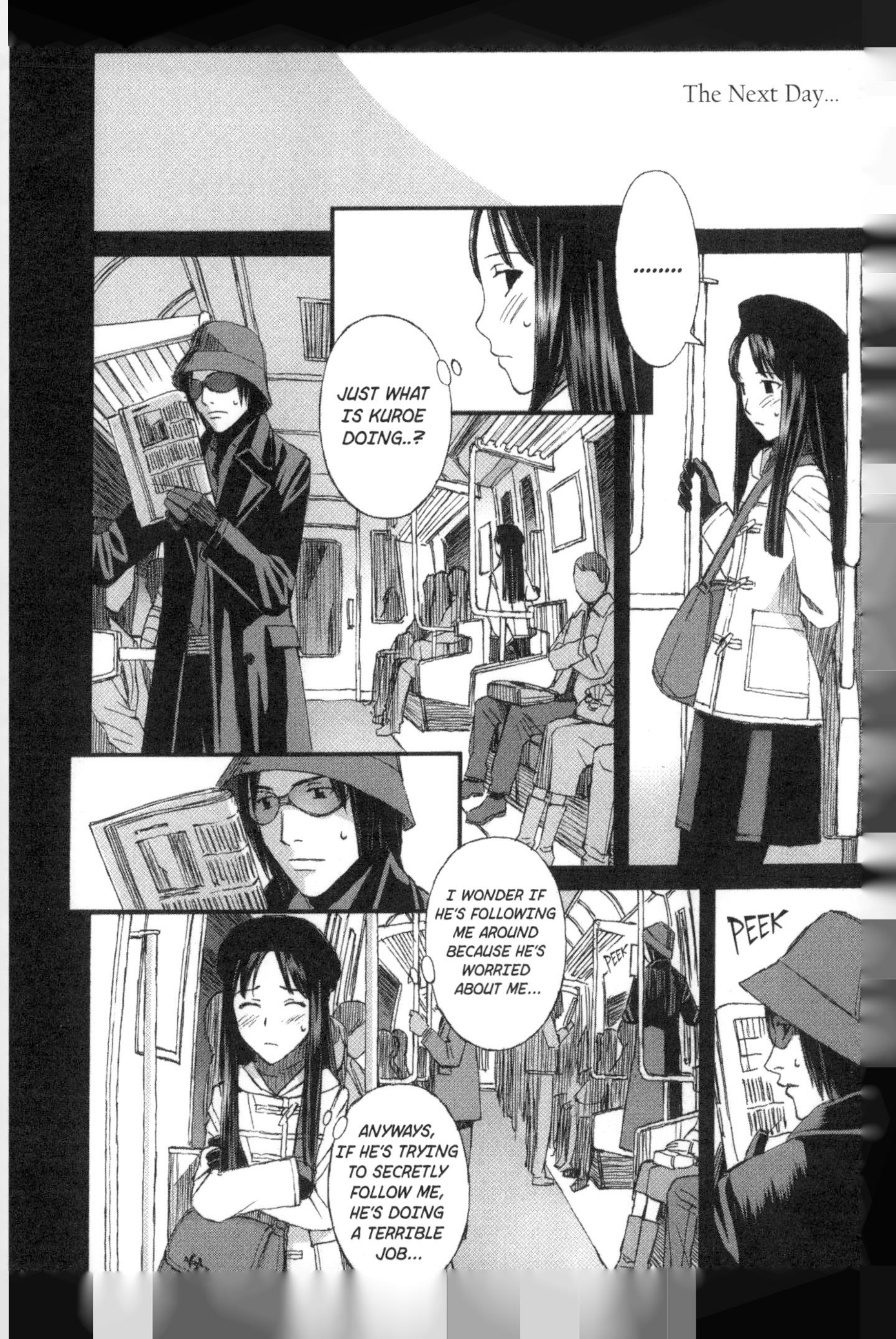
The Next Day...
....
JUST WHAT IS KUROE DOING..?
PEEK
I WONDER IF HE'S FOLLOWING ME AROUND BECAUSE HE'S WORRIED ABOUT ME...
PEEK
ANYWAYS, IF HE'S TRYING TO SECRETLY FOLLOW ME, HE'S DOING A TERRIBLE JOB...

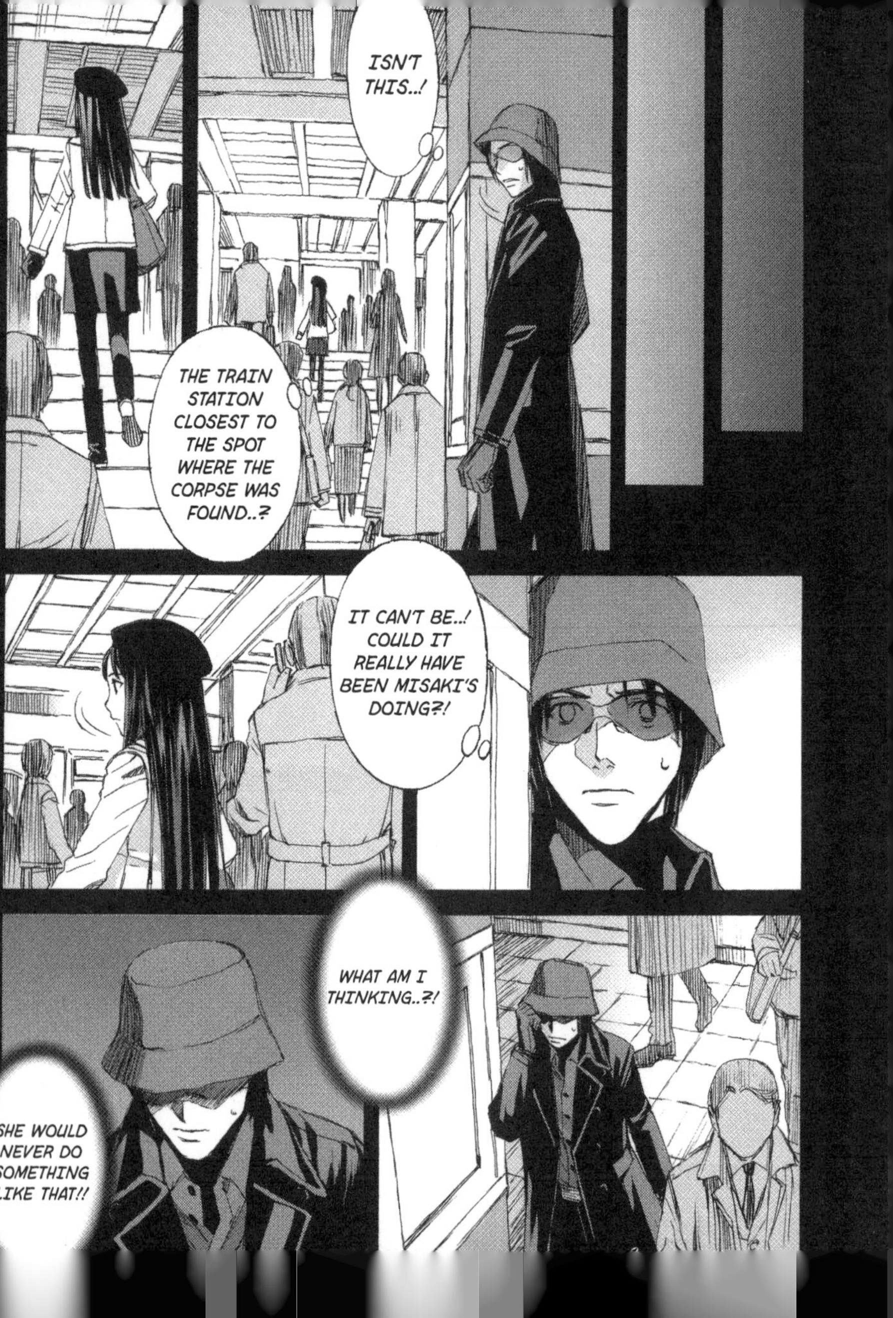
ISN'T THIS..!
THE TRAIN STATION CLOSEST TO THE SPOT WHERE THE CORPSE WAS FOUND..?
IT CAN'T BE..! COULD IT REALLY HAVE BEEN MISAKI'S DOING?!
WHAT AM I THINKING..?!
SHE WOULD NEVER DO SOMETHING LIKE THAT!!

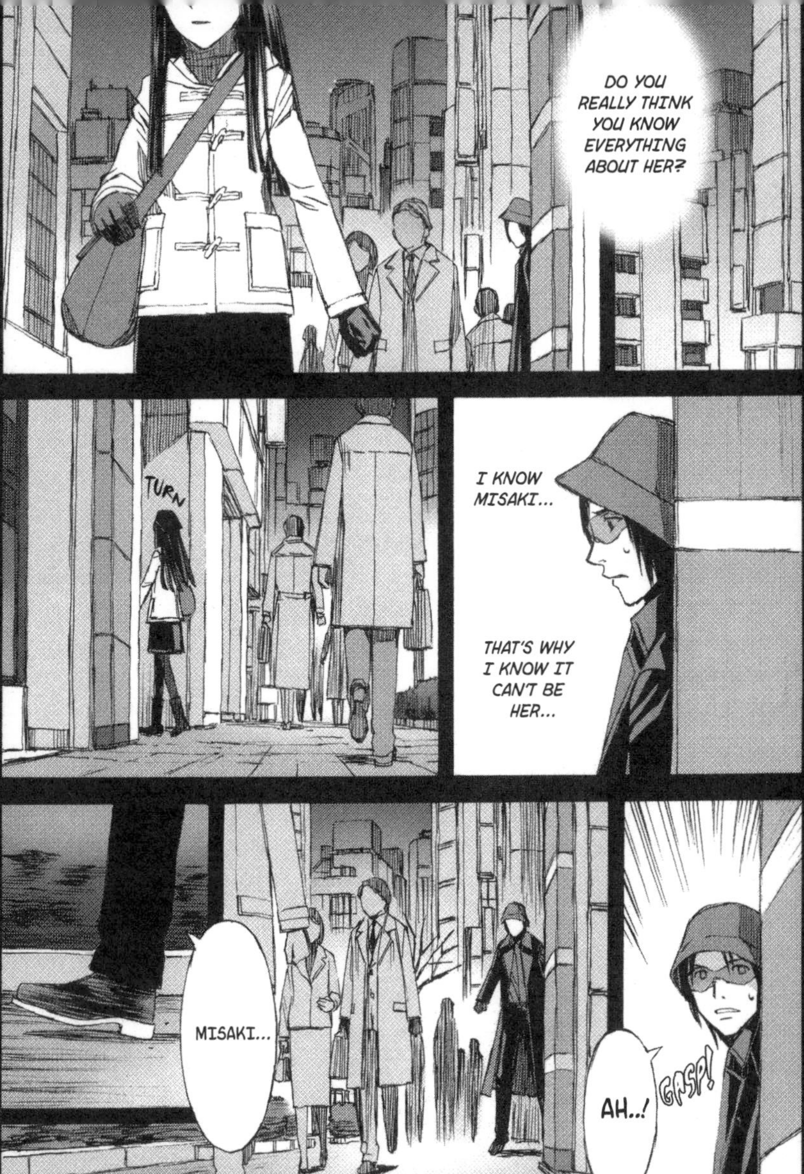
DO YOU REALLY THINK YOU KNOW EVERYTHING ABOUT HER?
I KNOW MISAKI...
THAT'S WHY I KNOW IT CAN'T BE HER...
TURN
AH..!
GASP!
MISAKI...

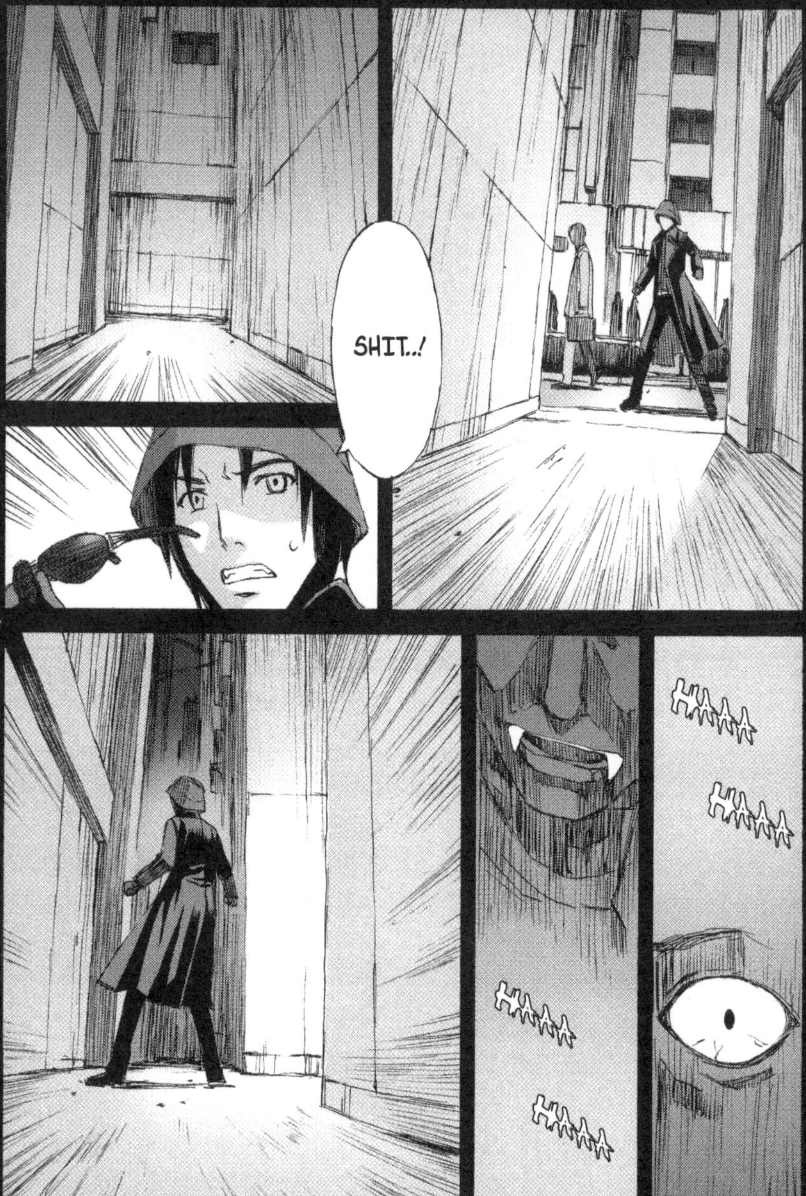
SHIT..!
HAAAA
HAAAA
HAAAA
HAAAA

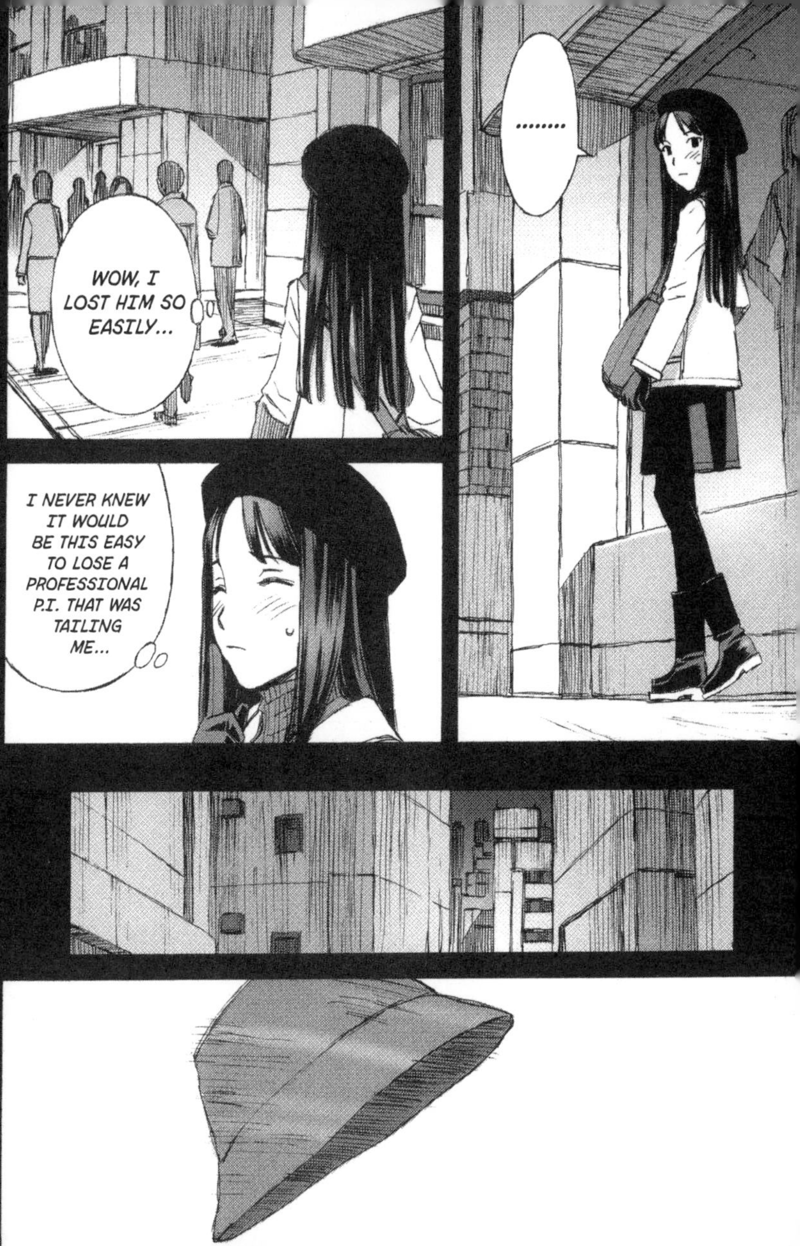
....
WOW, I LOST HIM SO EASILY...
I NEVER KNEW IT WOULD BE THIS EASY TO LOSE A PROFESSIONAL P.I. THAT WAS TAILING ME...

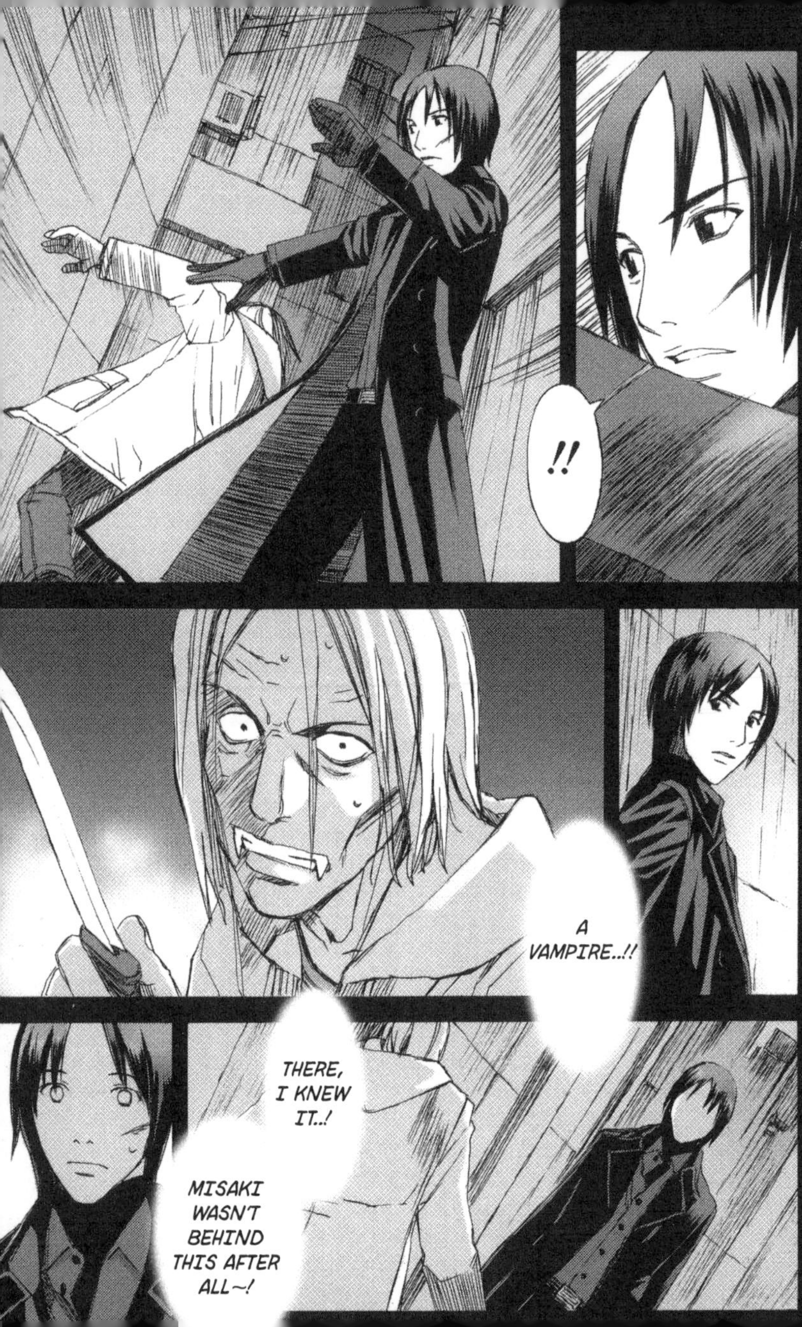
!!
A VAMPIRE..!!
THERE, I KNEW IT..!
MISAKI WASN'T BEHIND THIS AFTER ALL~!

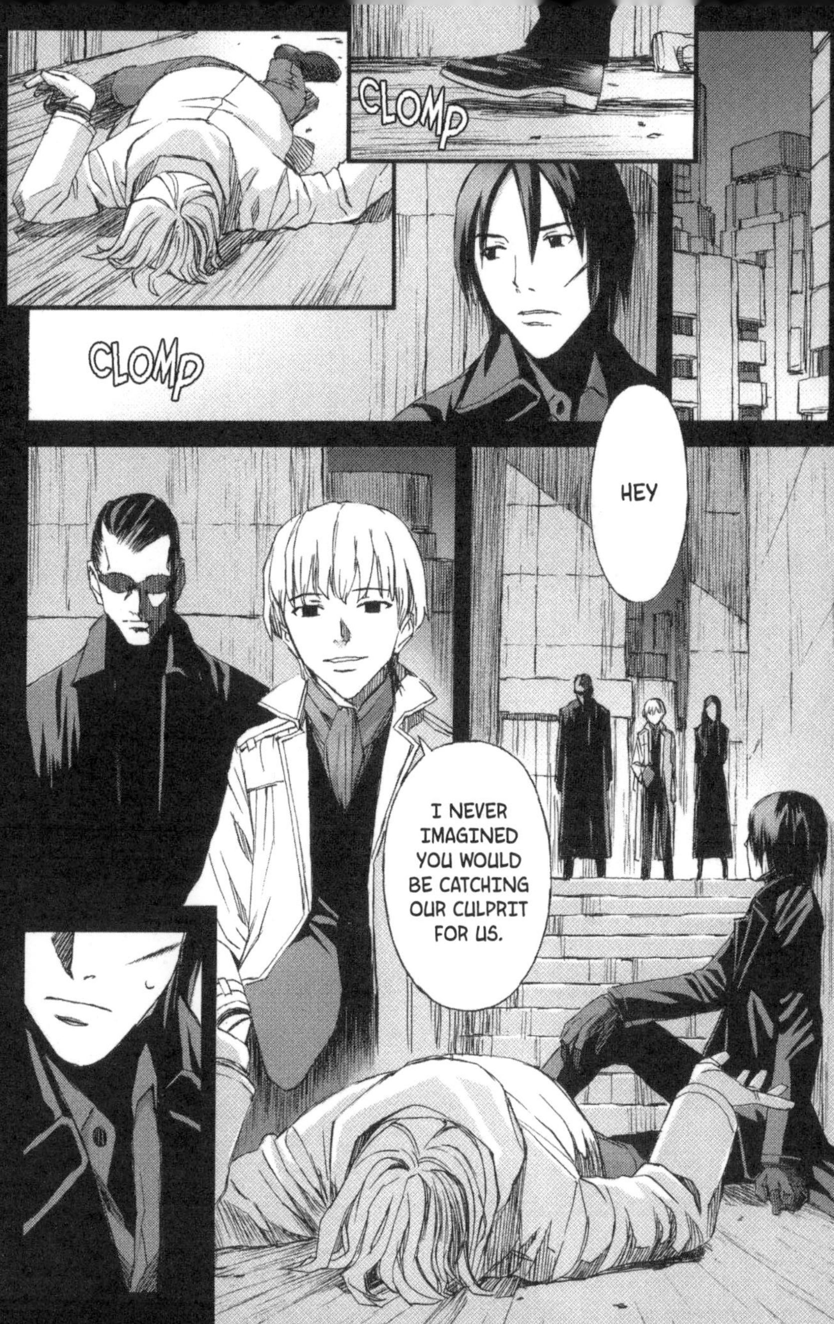
CLOMP
CLOMP
HEY
I NEVER IMAGINED YOU WOULD BE CATCHING OUR CULPRIT FOR US.

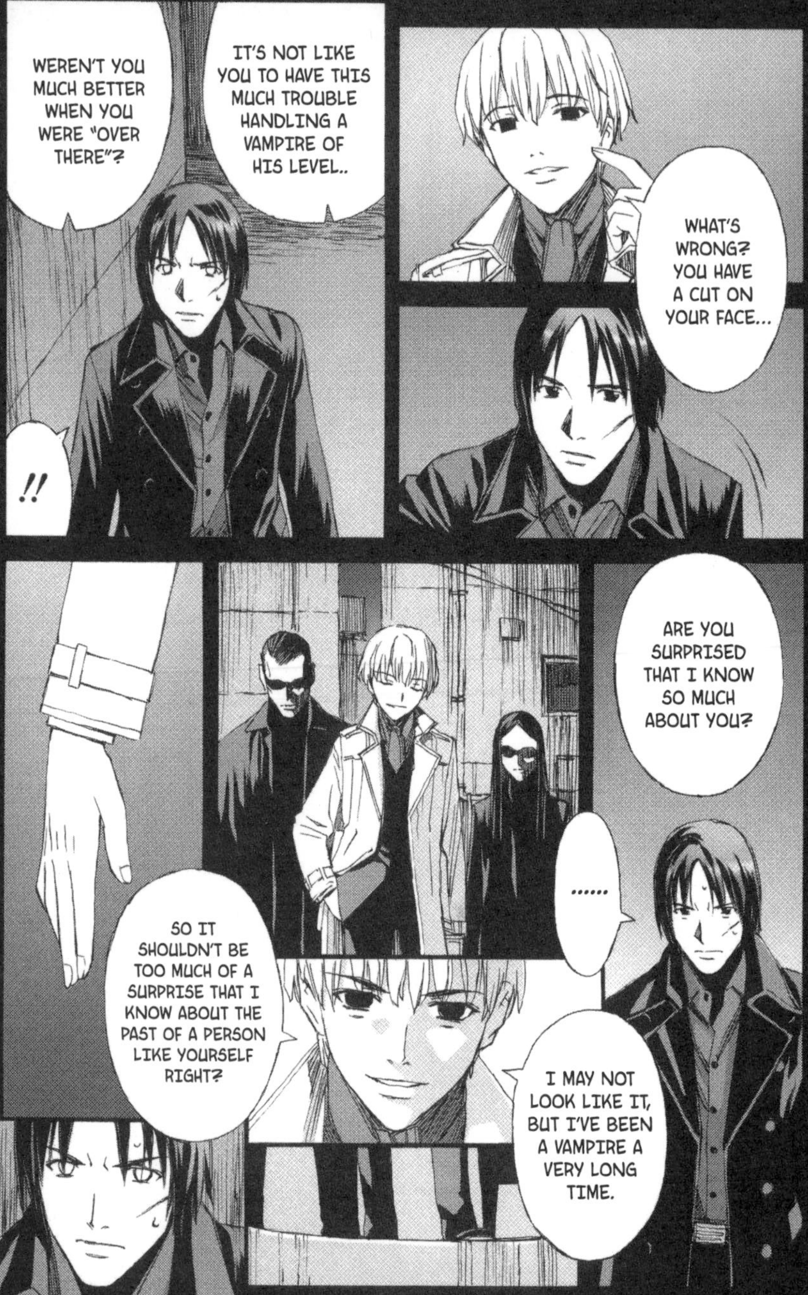
WHAT'S WRONG? YOU HAVE A CUT ON YOUR FACE...
IT'S NOT LIKE YOU TO HAVE THIS MUCH TROUBLE HANDLING A VAMPIRE OF HIS LEVEL..
WEREN'T YOU MUCH BETTER WHEN YOU WERE "OVER THERE"?
!!
ARE YOU SURPRISED THAT I KNOW SO MUCH ABOUT YOU?
......
I MAY NOT LOOK LIKE IT, BUT I'VE BEEN A VAMPIRE A VERY LONG TIME.
SO IT SHOULDN'T BE TOO MUCH OF A SURPRISE THAT I KNOW ABOUT THE PAST OF A PERSON LIKE YOURSELF RIGHT?

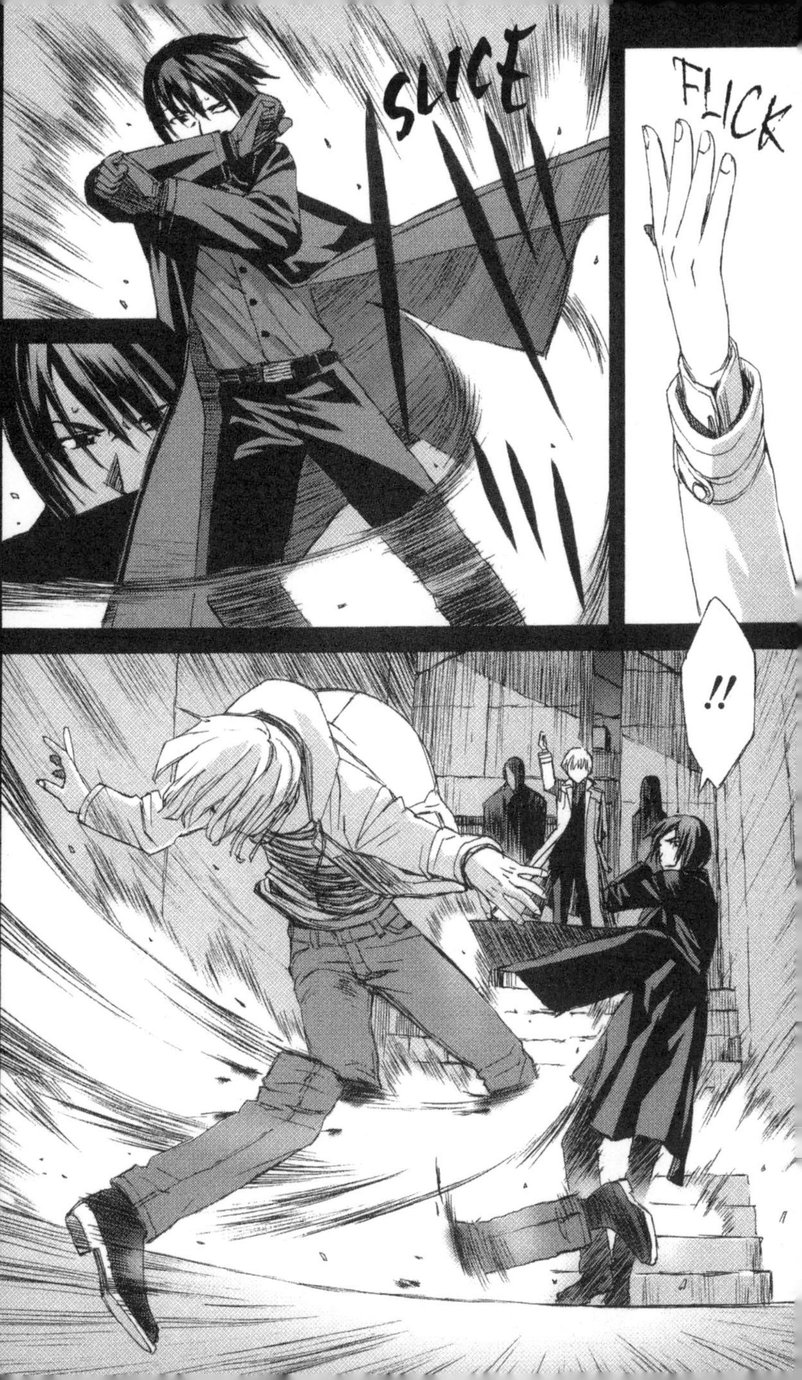
FLICK
SLICE
!!

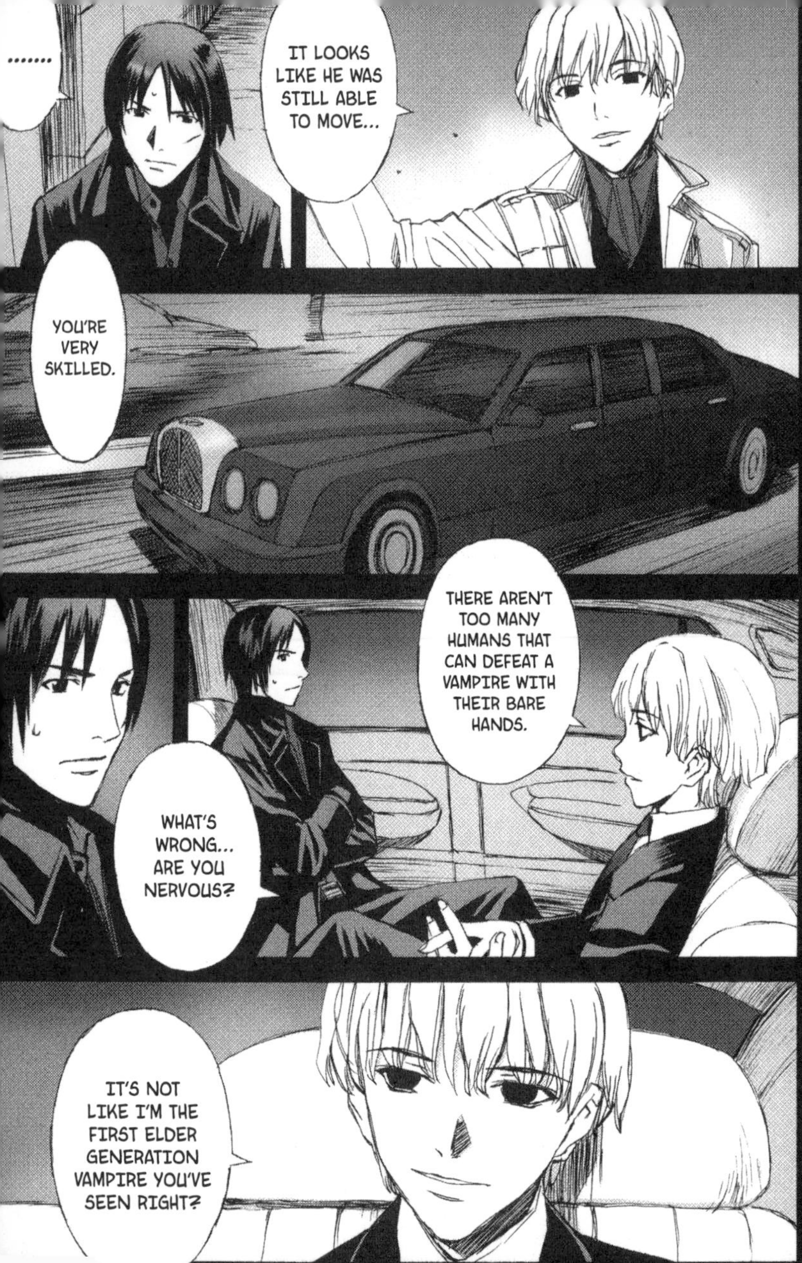
IT LOOKS LIKE HE WAS STILL ABLE TO MOVE...
....
YOU'RE VERY SKILLED.
THERE AREN'T TOO MANY HUMANS THAT CAN DEFEAT A VAMPIRE WITH THEIR BARE HANDS.
WHAT'S WRONG... ARE YOU NERVOUS?
IT'S NOT LIKE I'M THE FIRST ELDER GENERATION VAMPIRE YOU'VE SEEN RIGHT?

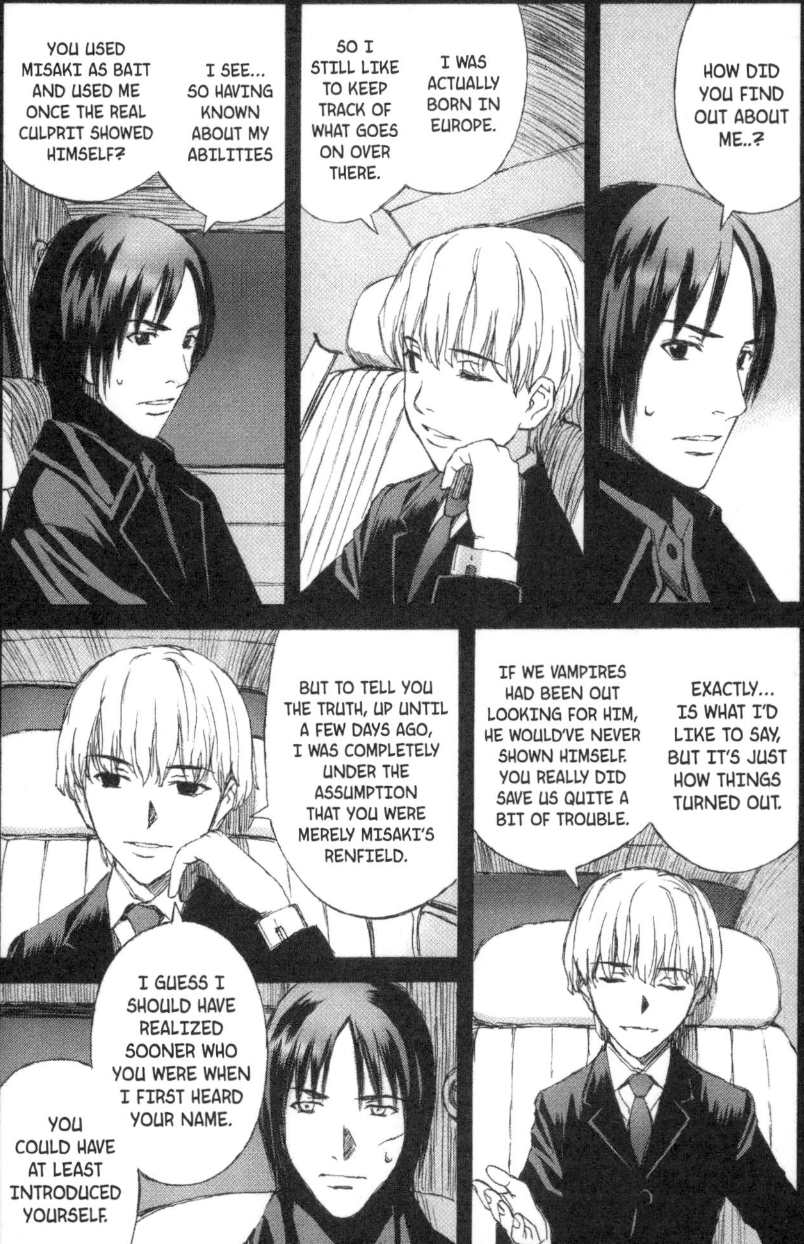
HOW DID YOU FIND OUT ABOUT ME..?
I WAS ACTUALLY BORN IN EUROPE.
SO I STILL LIKE TO KEEP TRACK OF WHAT GOES ON OVER THERE.
I SEE... SO HAVING KNOWN ABOUT MY ABILITIES
YOU USED MISAKI AS BAIT AND USED ME ONCE THE REAL CULPRIT SHOWED HIMSELF?
EXACTLY... IS WHAT I'D LIKE TO SAY, BUT IT'S JUST HOW THINGS TURNED OUT.
IF WE VAMPIRES HAD BEEN OUT LOOKING FOR HIM, HE WOULD'VE NEVER SHOWN HIMSELF. YOU REALLY DID SAVE US QUITE A BIT OF TROUBLE.
BUT TO TELL YOU THE TRUTH, UP UNTIL A FEW DAYS AGO, I WAS COMPLETELY UNDER THE ASSUMPTION THAT YOU WERE MERELY MISAKI'S RENFIELD.
I GUESS I SHOULD HAVE REALIZED SOONER WHO YOU WERE WHEN I FIRST HEARD YOUR NAME.
YOU COULD HAVE AT LEAST INTRODUCED YOURSELF.

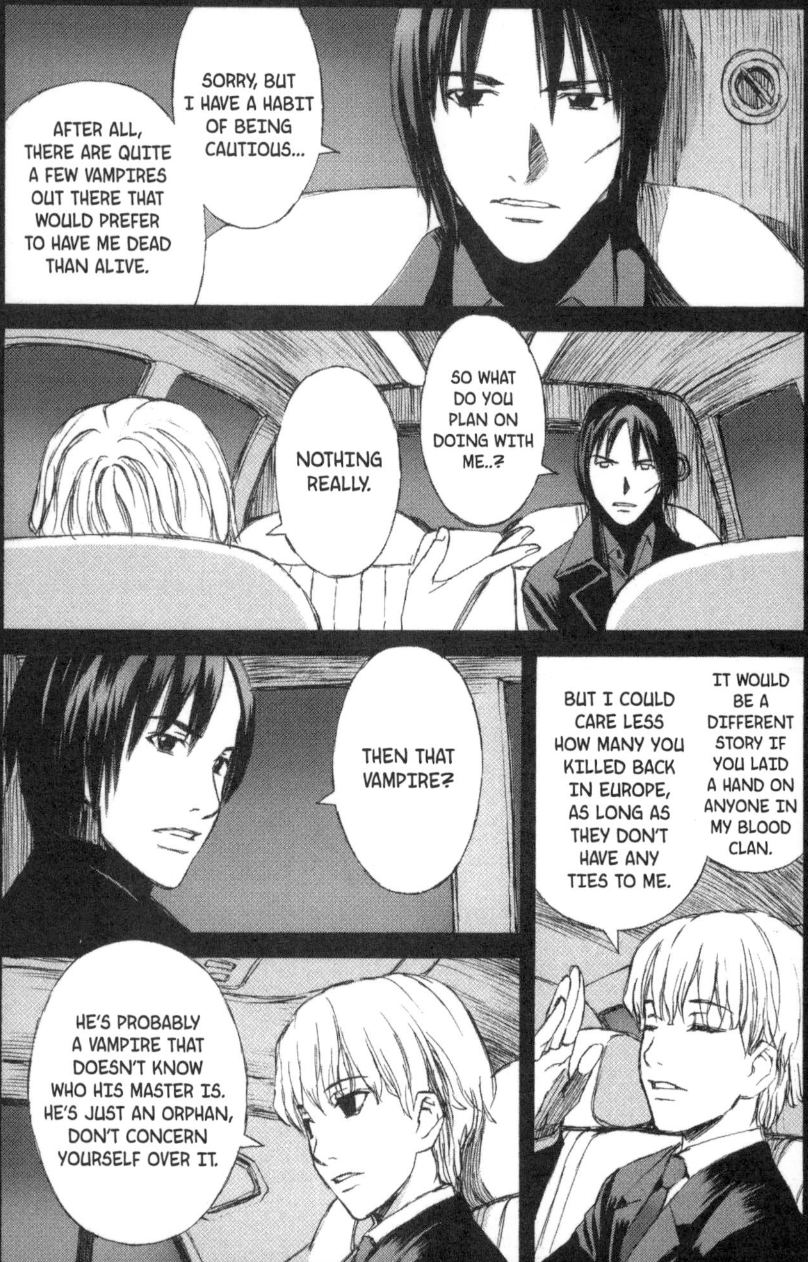
SORRY, BUT I HAVE A HABIT OF BEING CAUTIOUS...
AFTER ALL, THERE ARE QUITE A FEW VAMPIRES OUT THERE THAT WOULD PREFER TO HAVE ME DEAD THAN ALIVE.
SO WHAT DO YOU PLAN ON DOING WITH ME..?
NOTHING REALLY.
IT WOULD BE A DIFFERENT STORY IF YOU LAID A HAND ON ANYONE IN MY BLOOD CLAN.
BUT I COULD CARE LESS HOW MANY YOU KILLED BACK IN EUROPE, AS LONG AS THEY DON'T HAVE ANY TIES TO ME.
THEN THAT VAMPIRE?
HE'S PROBABLY A VAMPIRE THAT DOESN'T KNOW WHO HIS MASTER IS. HE'S JUST AN ORPHAN, DON'T CONCERN YOURSELF OVER IT.

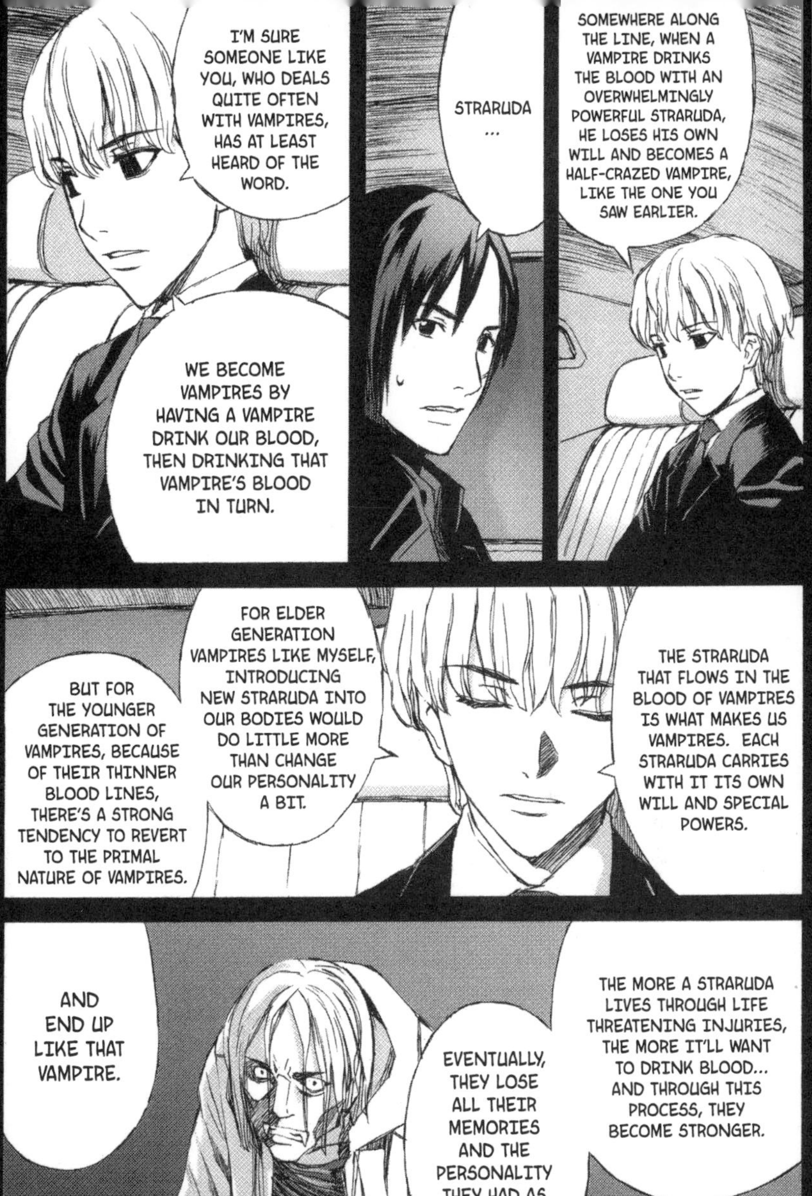
SOMEWHERE ALONG THE LINE, WHEN A VAMPIRE DRINKS THE BLOOD WITH AN OVERWHELMINGLY POWERFUL STRARUDA, HE LOSES HIS OWN WILL AND BECOMES A HALF-CRAZED VAMPIRE, LIKE THE ONE YOU SAW EARLIER.
STRARUDA ...
I'M SURE SOMEONE LIKE YOU, WHO DEALS QUITE OFTEN WITH VAMPIRES, HAS AT LEAST HEARD OF THE WORD.
WE BECOME VAMPIRES BY HAVING A VAMPIRE DRINK OUR BLOOD, THEN DRINKING THAT VAMPIRE'S BLOOD IN TURN.
THE STRARUDA THAT FLOWS IN THE BLOOD OF VAMPIRES IS WHAT MAKES US VAMPIRES. EACH STRARUDA CARRIES WITH IT ITS OWN WILL AND SPECIAL POWERS.
FOR ELDER GENERATION VAMPIRES LIKE MYSELF, INTRODUCING NEW STRARUDA INTO OUR BODIES WOULD DO LITTLE MORE THAN CHANGE OUR PERSONALITY A BIT.
BUT FOR THE YOUNGER GENERATION OF VAMPIRES, BECAUSE OF THEIR THINNER BLOOD LINES, THERE'S A STRONG TENDENCY TO REVERT TO THE PRIMAL NATURE OF VAMPIRES.
THE MORE A STRARUDA LIVES THROUGH LIFE THREATENING INJURIES, THE MORE IT'LL WANT TO DRINK BLOOD... AND THROUGH THIS PROCESS, THEY BECOME STRONGER.
EVENTUALLY, THEY LOSE ALL THEIR MEMORIES AND THE PERSONALITY THEY HAD AS A HUMAN...
AND END UP LIKE THAT VAMPIRE.

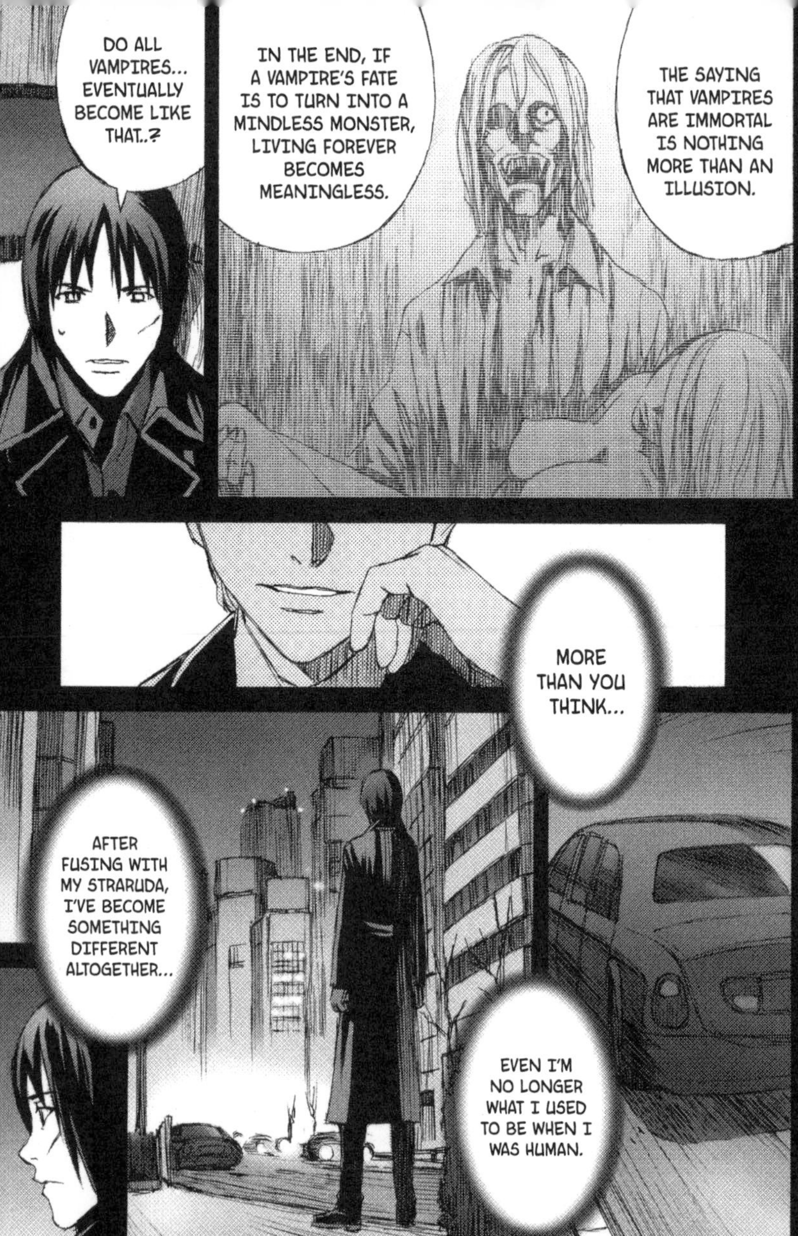
THE SAYING THAT VAMPIRES ARE IMMORTAL IS NOTHING MORE THAN AN ILLUSION.
IN THE END, IF A VAMPIRE'S FATE IS TO TURN INTO A MINDLESS MONSTER, LIVING FOREVER BECOMES MEANINGLESS.
DO ALL VAMPIRES... EVENTUALLY BECOME LIKE THAT..?
MORE THAN YOU THINK...
AFTER FUSING WITH MY STRARUDA, I'VE BECOME SOMETHING DIFFERENT ALTOGETHER...
EVEN I'M NO LONGER WHAT I USED TO BE WHEN I WAS HUMAN.

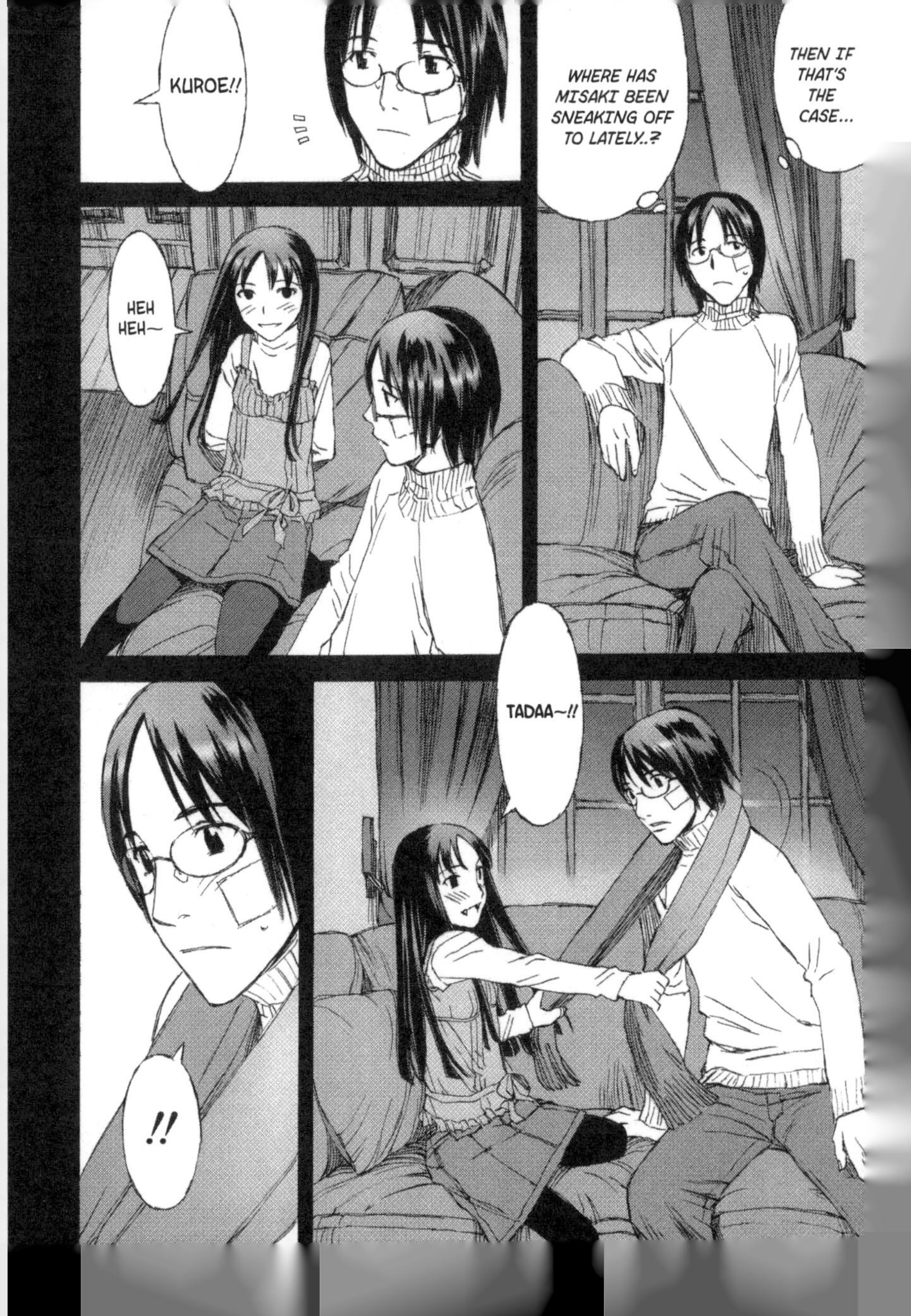
THEN IF THAT'S THE CASE...
WHERE HAS MISAKI BEEN SNEAKING OFF TO LATELY..?
KUROE!!
HEH HEH~
TADAA~!!
!!

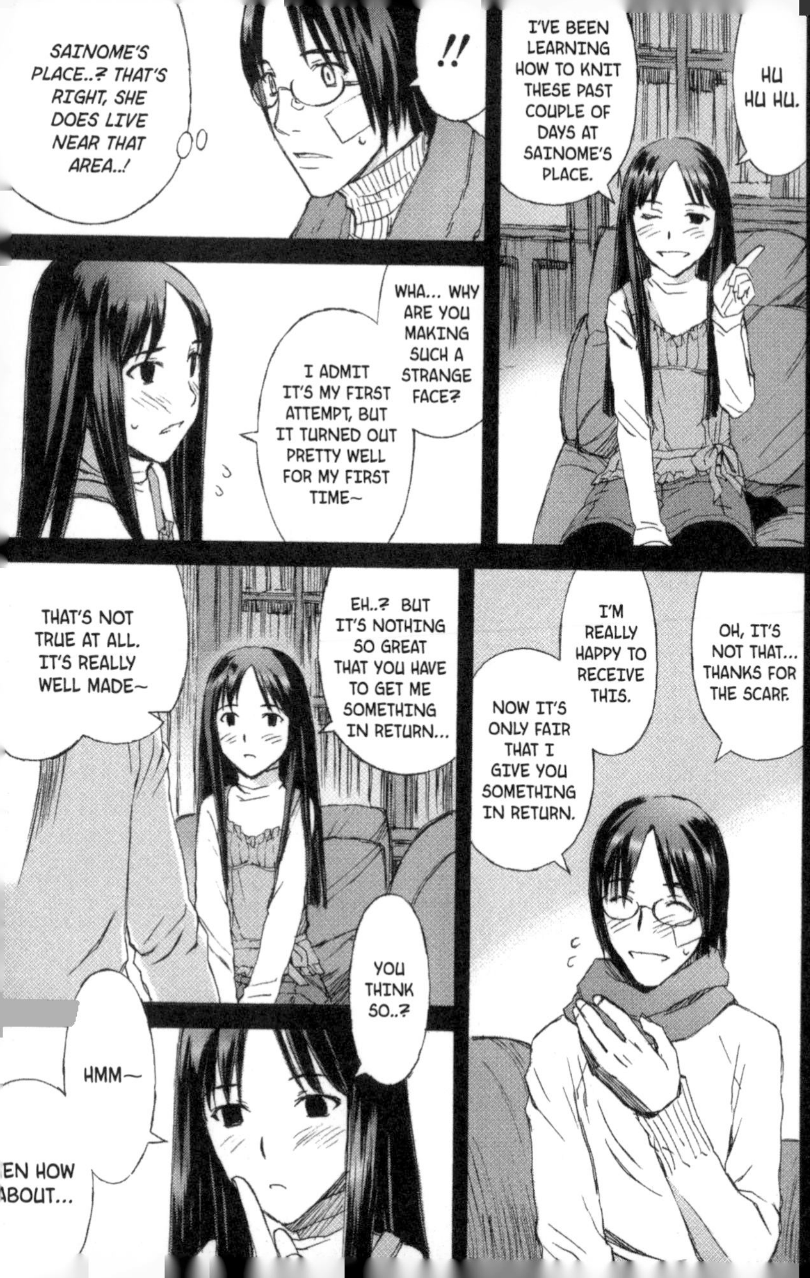
HU HU HU.
I'VE BEEN LEARNING HOW TO KNIT THESE PAST COUPLE OF DAYS AT SAINOME'S PLACE.
!!
SAINOME'S PLACE..? THAT'S RIGHT, SHE DOES LIVE NEAR THAT AREA..!
WHA... WHY ARE YOU MAKING SUCH A STRANGE FACE?
I ADMIT IT'S MY FIRST ATTEMPT, BUT IT TURNED OUT PRETTY WELL FOR MY FIRST TIME~
OH, IT'S NOT THAT... THANKS FOR THE SCARF.
I'M REALLY HAPPY TO RECEIVE THIS.
NOW IT'S ONLY FAIR THAT I GIVE YOU SOMETHING IN RETURN.
EH..? BUT IT'S NOTHING SO GREAT THAT YOU HAVE TO GET ME SOMETHING IN RETURN...
THAT'S NOT TRUE AT ALL. IT'S REALLY WELL MADE~
YOU THINK SO..?
HMM~
EN HOW ABOUT...

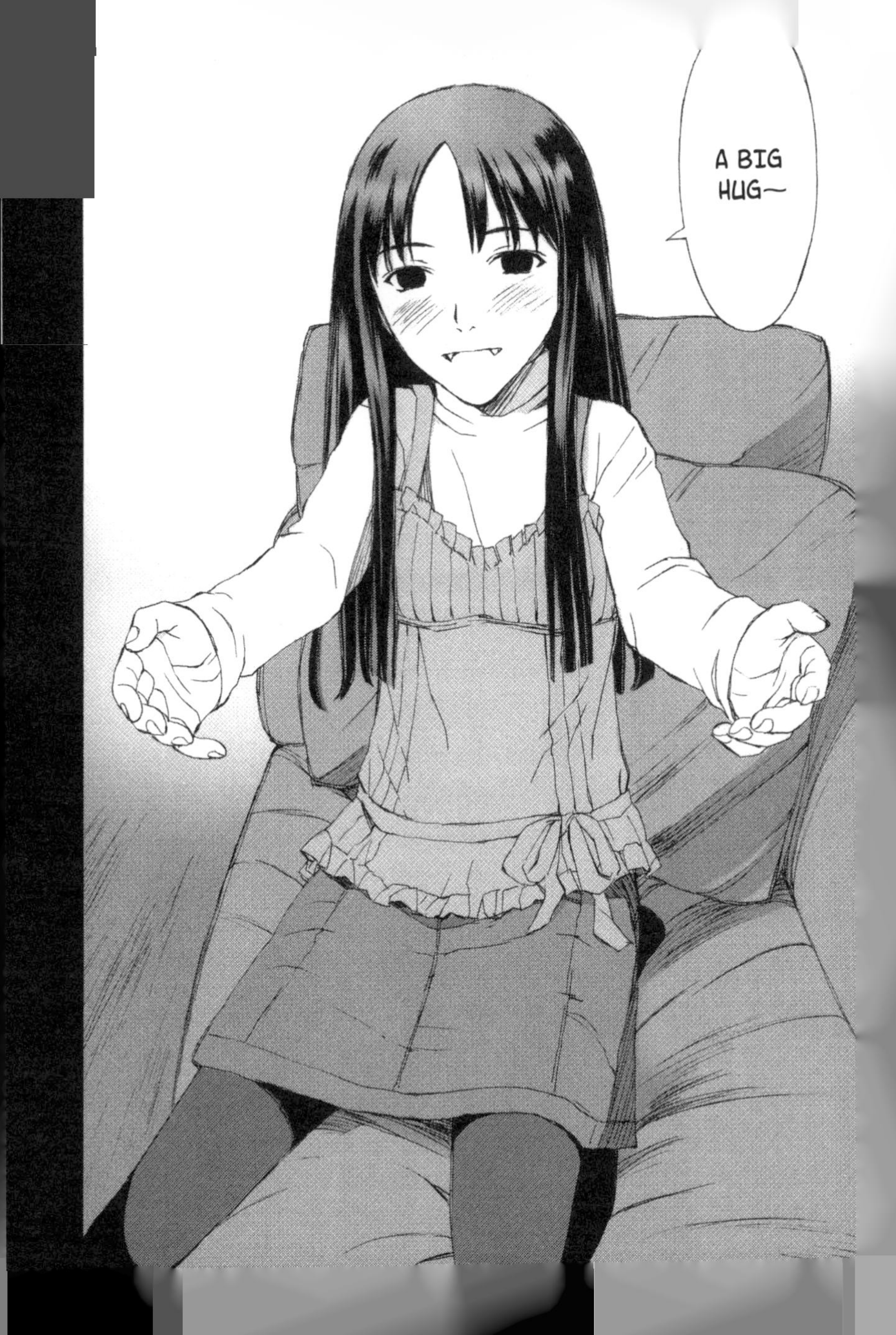
A BIG HUG~

SWEET MUSIC

心ふるわせる音楽 – Music That Soothes the Soul

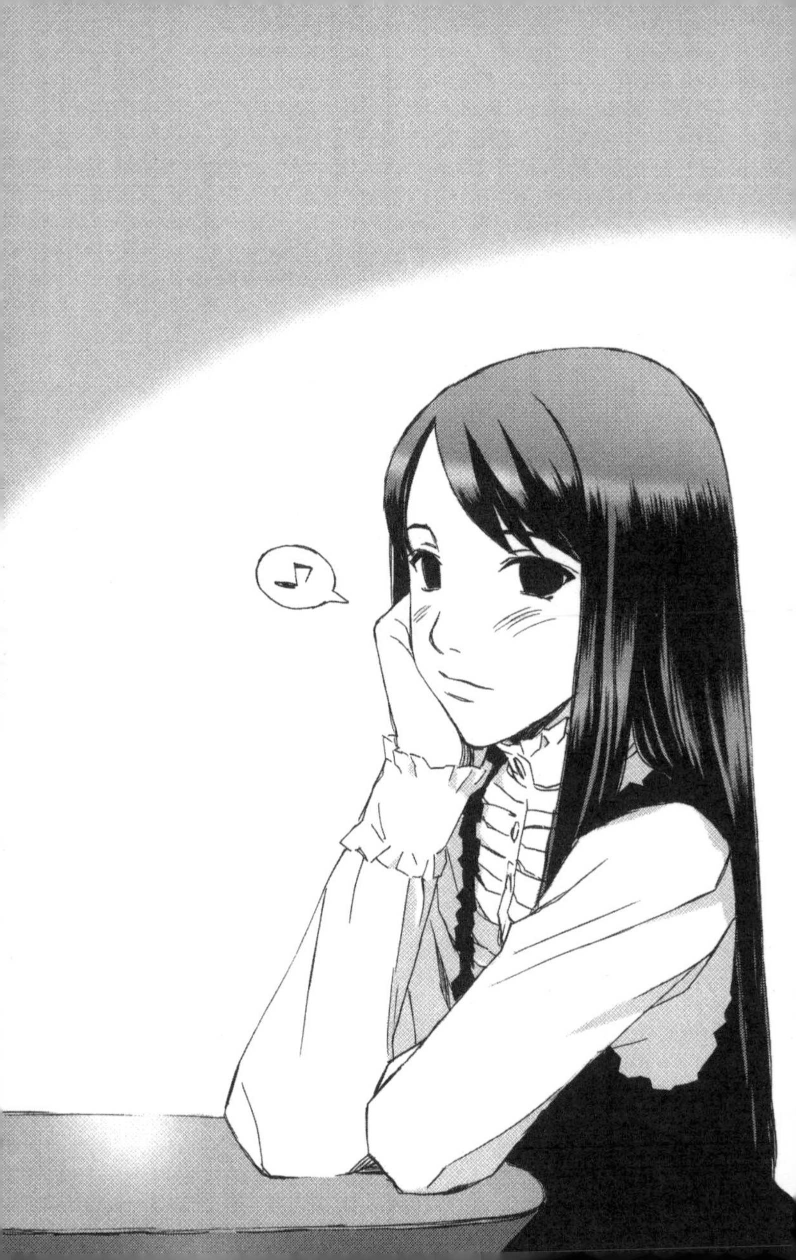

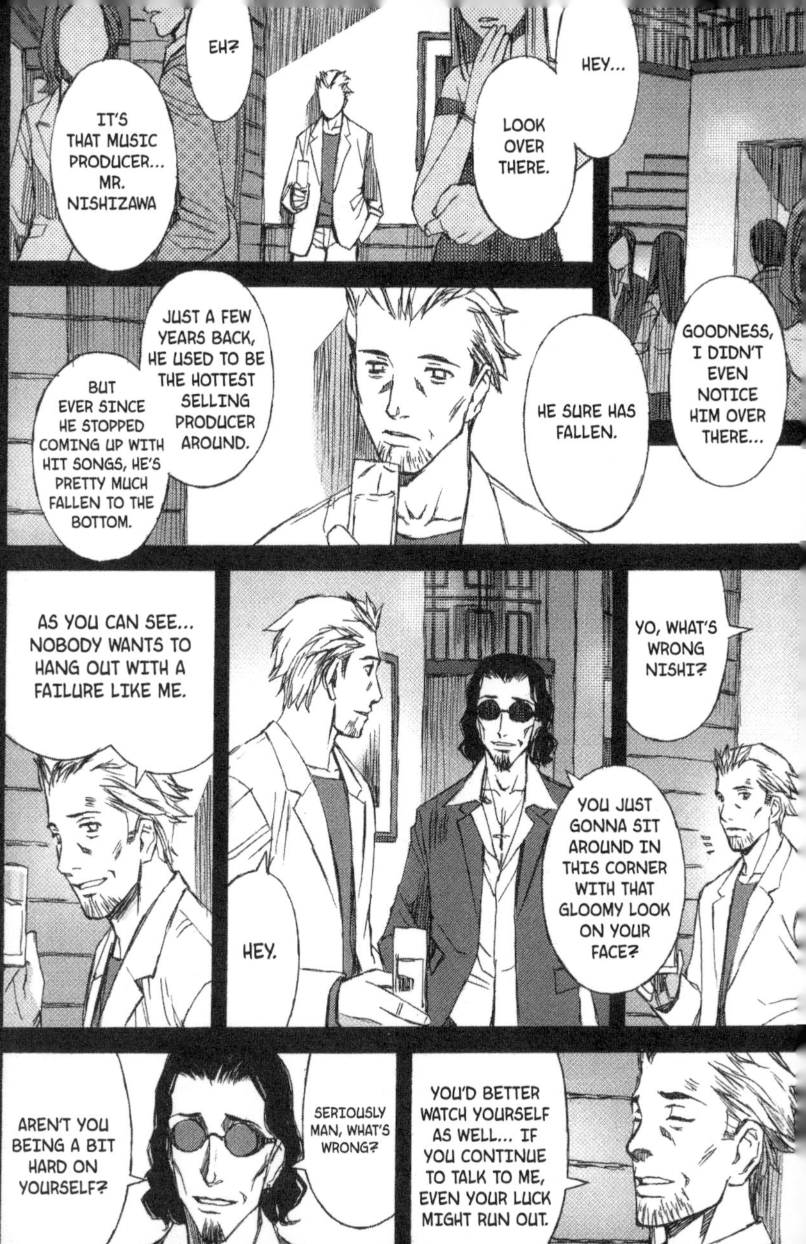
HEY...
LOOK OVER THERE.
EH?
IT'S THAT MUSIC PRODUCER... MR. NISHIZAWA
GOODNESS, I DIDN'T EVEN NOTICE HIM OVER THERE...
HE SURE HAS FALLEN.
JUST A FEW YEARS BACK, HE USED TO BE THE HOTTEST SELLING PRODUCER AROUND.
BUT EVER SINCE HE STOPPED COMING UP WITH HIT SONGS, HE'S PRETTY MUCH FALLEN TO THE BOTTOM.
YO, WHAT'S WRONG NISHI?
YOU JUST GONNA SIT AROUND IN THIS CORNER WITH THAT GLOOMY LOOK ON YOUR FACE?
HEY.
AS YOU CAN SEE... NOBODY WANTS TO HANG OUT WITH A FAILURE LIKE ME.
YOU'D BETTER WATCH YOURSELF AS WELL... IF YOU CONTINUE TO TALK TO ME, EVEN YOUR LUCK MIGHT RUN OUT.
SERIOUSLY MAN, WHAT'S WRONG?
AREN'T YOU BEING A BIT HARD ON YOURSELF?

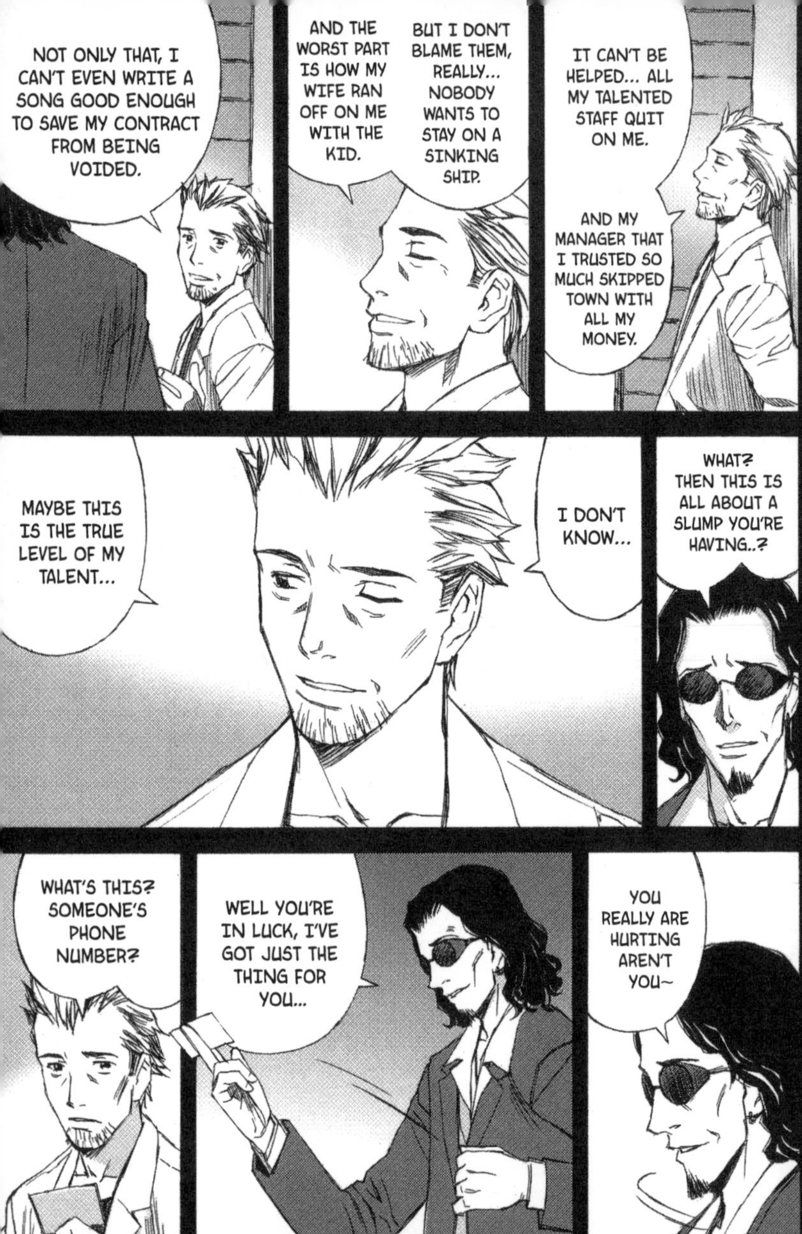
IT CAN'T BE HELPED... ALL MY TALENTED STAFF QUIT ON ME.
AND MY MANAGER THAT I TRUSTED SO MUCH SKIPPED TOWN WITH ALL MY MONEY.
BUT I DON'T BLAME THEM, REALLY... NOBODY WANTS TO STAY ON A SINKING SHIP.
AND THE WORST PART IS HOW MY WIFE RAN OFF ON ME WITH THE KID.
NOT ONLY THAT, I CAN'T EVEN WRITE A SONG GOOD ENOUGH TO SAVE MY CONTRACT FROM BEING VOIDED.
WHAT? THEN THIS IS ALL ABOUT A SLUMP YOU'RE HAVING..?
I DON'T KNOW...
MAYBE THIS IS THE TRUE LEVEL OF MY TALENT...
YOU REALLY ARE HURTING AREN'T YOU~
WELL YOU'RE IN LUCK, I'VE GOT JUST THE THING FOR YOU...
WHAT'S THIS? SOMEONE'S PHONE NUMBER?

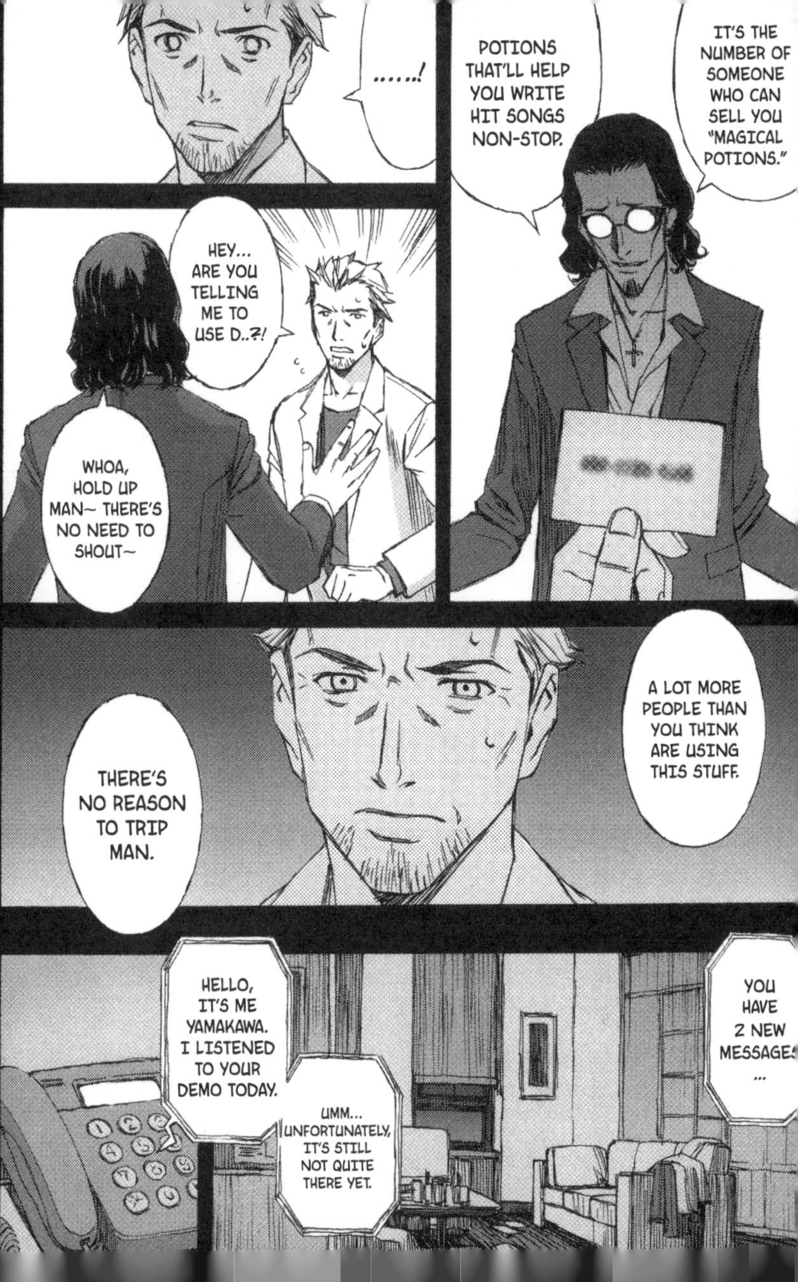
IT'S THE NUMBER OF SOMEONE WHO CAN SELL YOU "MAGICAL POTIONS."
POTIONS THAT'LL HELP YOU WRITE HIT SONGS NON-STOP.
......!
HEY... ARE YOU TELLING ME TO USE D..?!
WHOA, HOLD UP MAN~ THERE'S NO NEED TO SHOUT~
A LOT MORE PEOPLE THAN YOU THINK ARE USING THIS STUFF.
THERE'S NO REASON TO TRIP MAN.
YOU HAVE 2 NEW MESSAGES ...
HELLO, IT'S ME YAMAKAWA. I LISTENED TO YOUR DEMO TODAY.
UMM... UNFORTUNATELY, IT'S STILL NOT QUITE THERE YET.

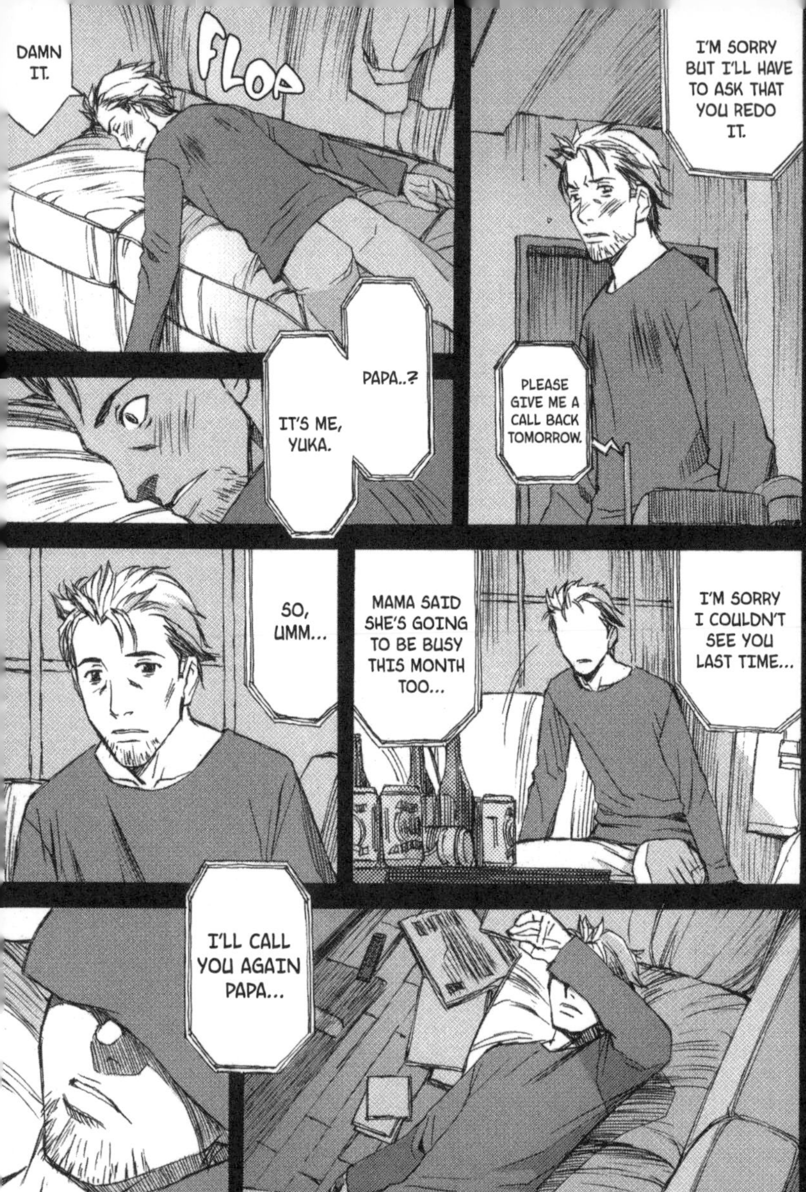
I'M SORRY BUT I'LL HAVE TO ASK THAT YOU REDO IT.
PLEASE GIVE ME A CALL BACK TOMORROW.
FLOP
DAMN IT.
PAPA..?
IT'S ME, YUKA.
I'M SORRY I COULDN'T SEE YOU LAST TIME...
MAMA SAID SHE'S GOING TO BE BUSY THIS MONTH TOO...
SO, UMM...
I'LL CALL YOU AGAIN PAPA...

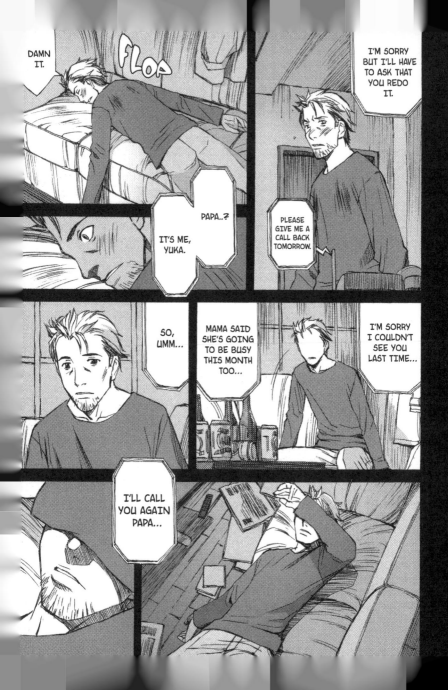

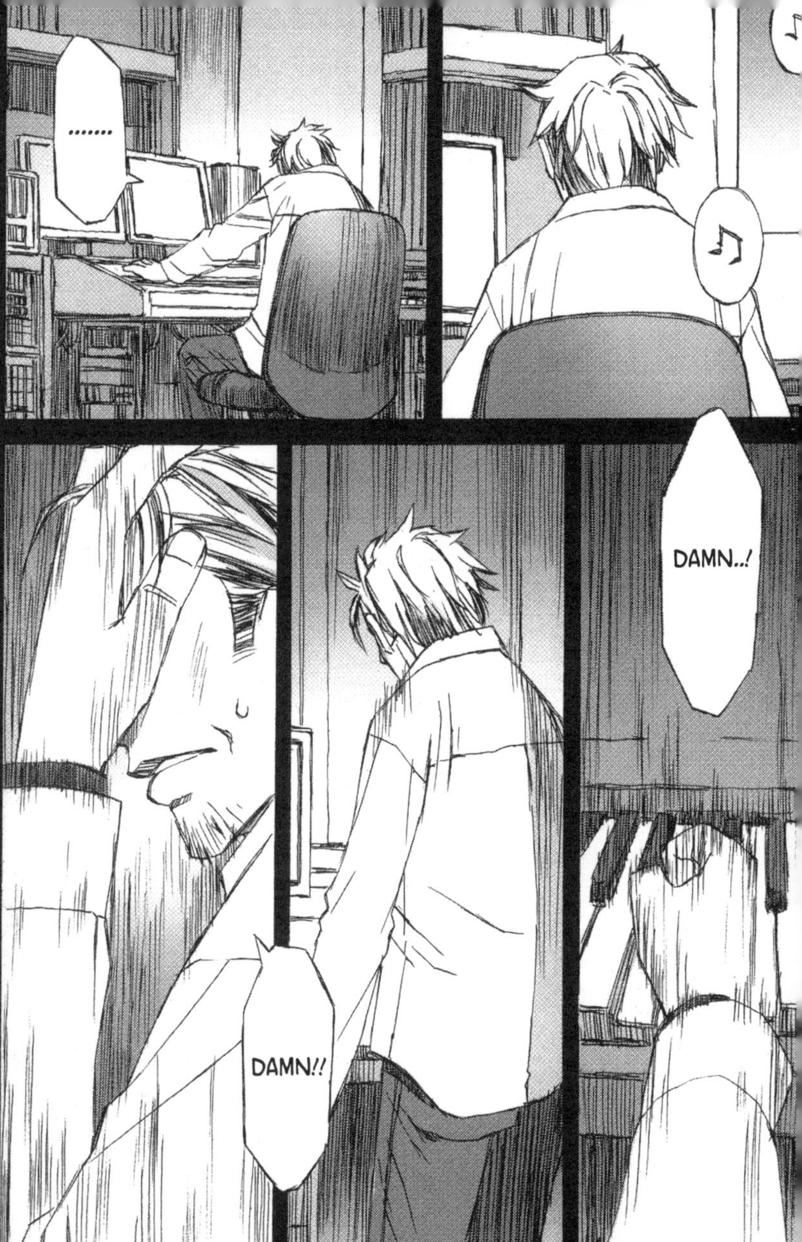
♪
♪
....
DAMN..!
DAMN!!

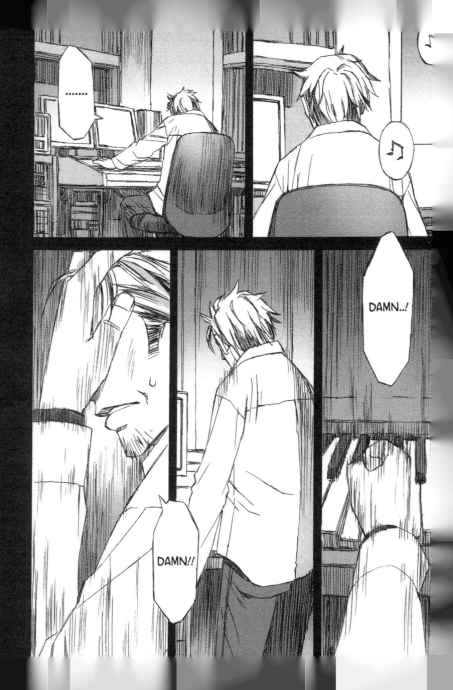

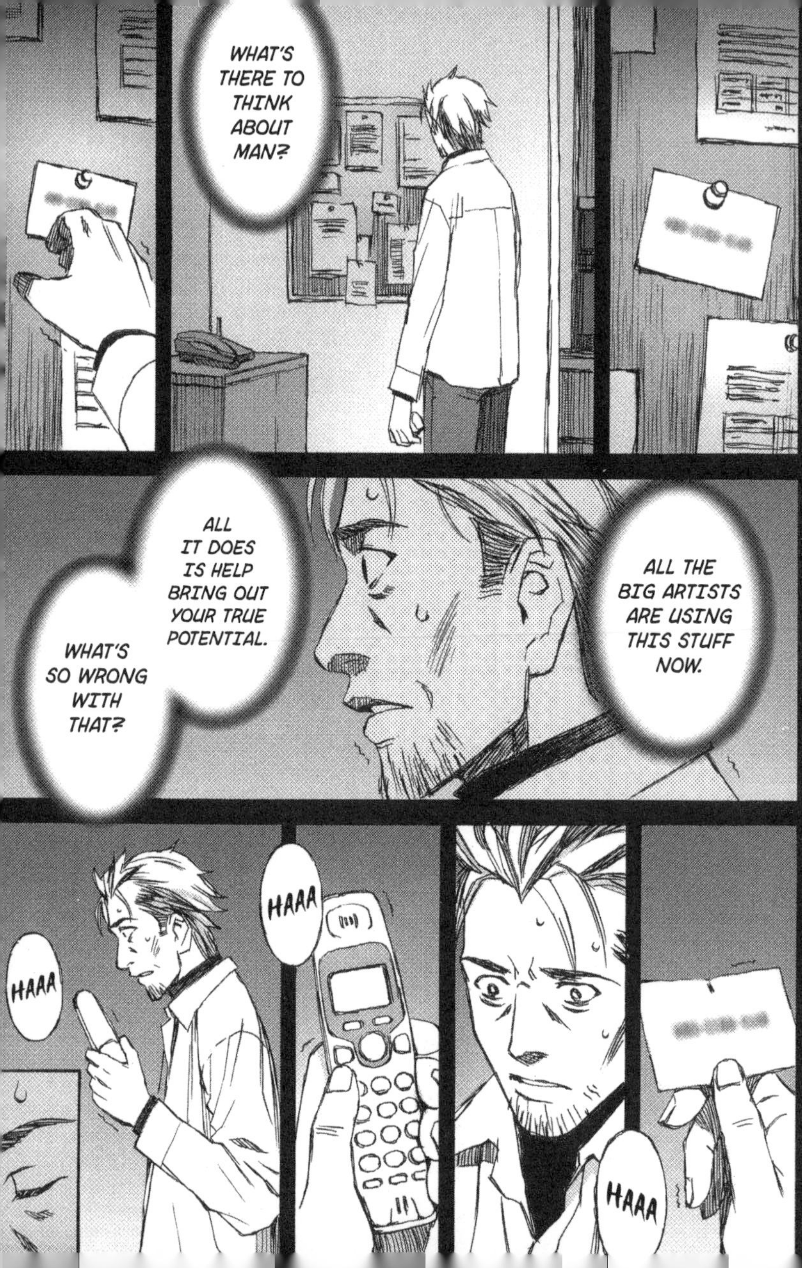
WHAT'S THERE TO THINK ABOUT MAN?
ALL THE BIG ARTISTS ARE USING THIS STUFF NOW.
ALL IT DOES IS HELP BRING OUT YOUR TRUE POTENTIAL.
WHAT'S SO WRONG WITH THAT?
HAAA
HAAA
HAAA

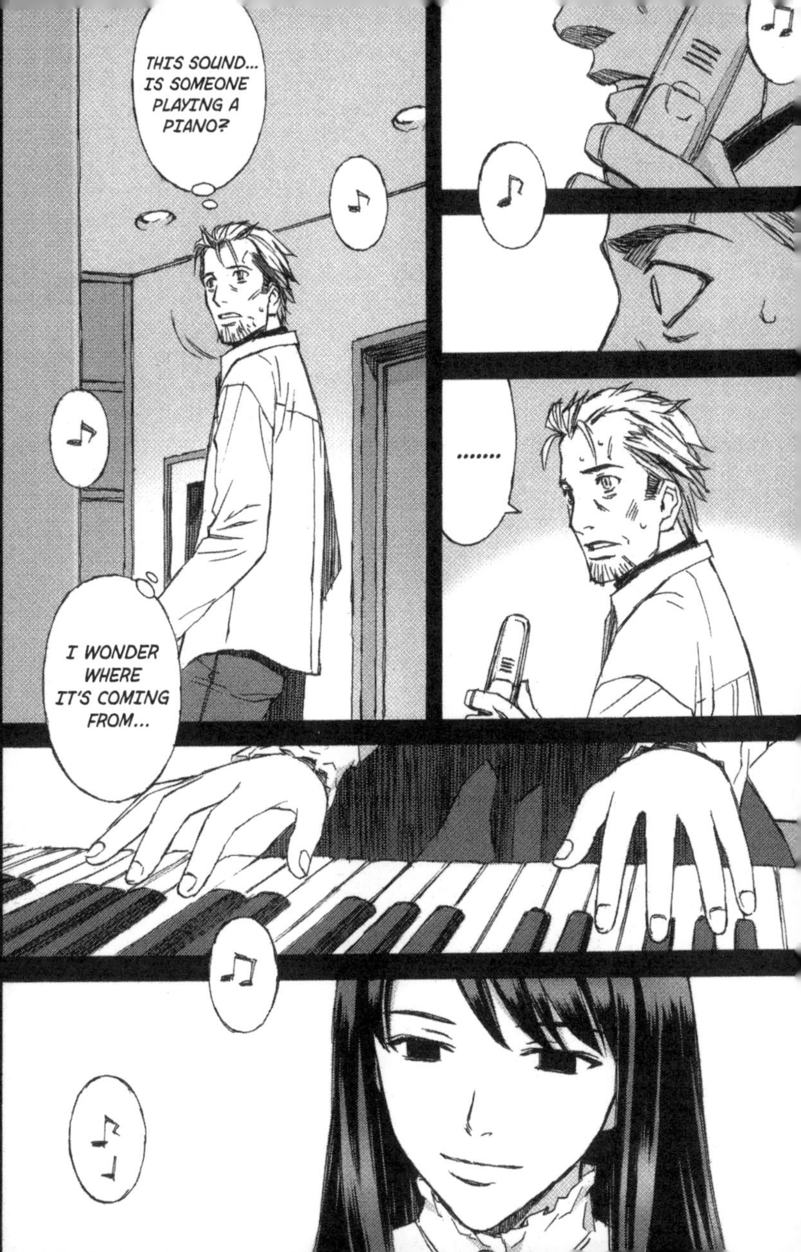
......
THIS SOUND... IS SOMEONE PLAYING A PIANO?
I WONDER WHERE IT'S COMING FROM...

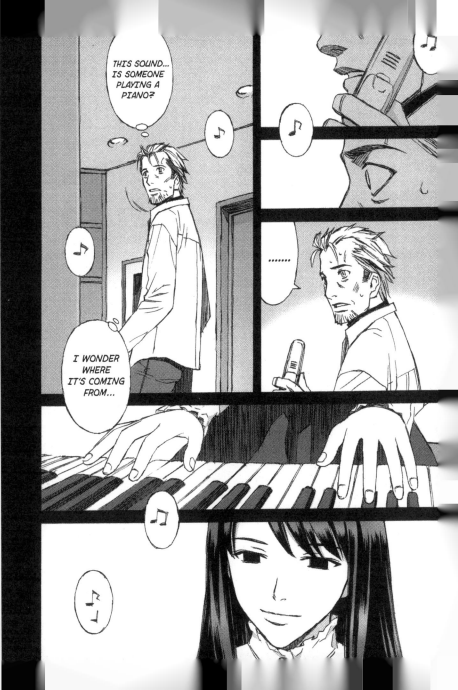

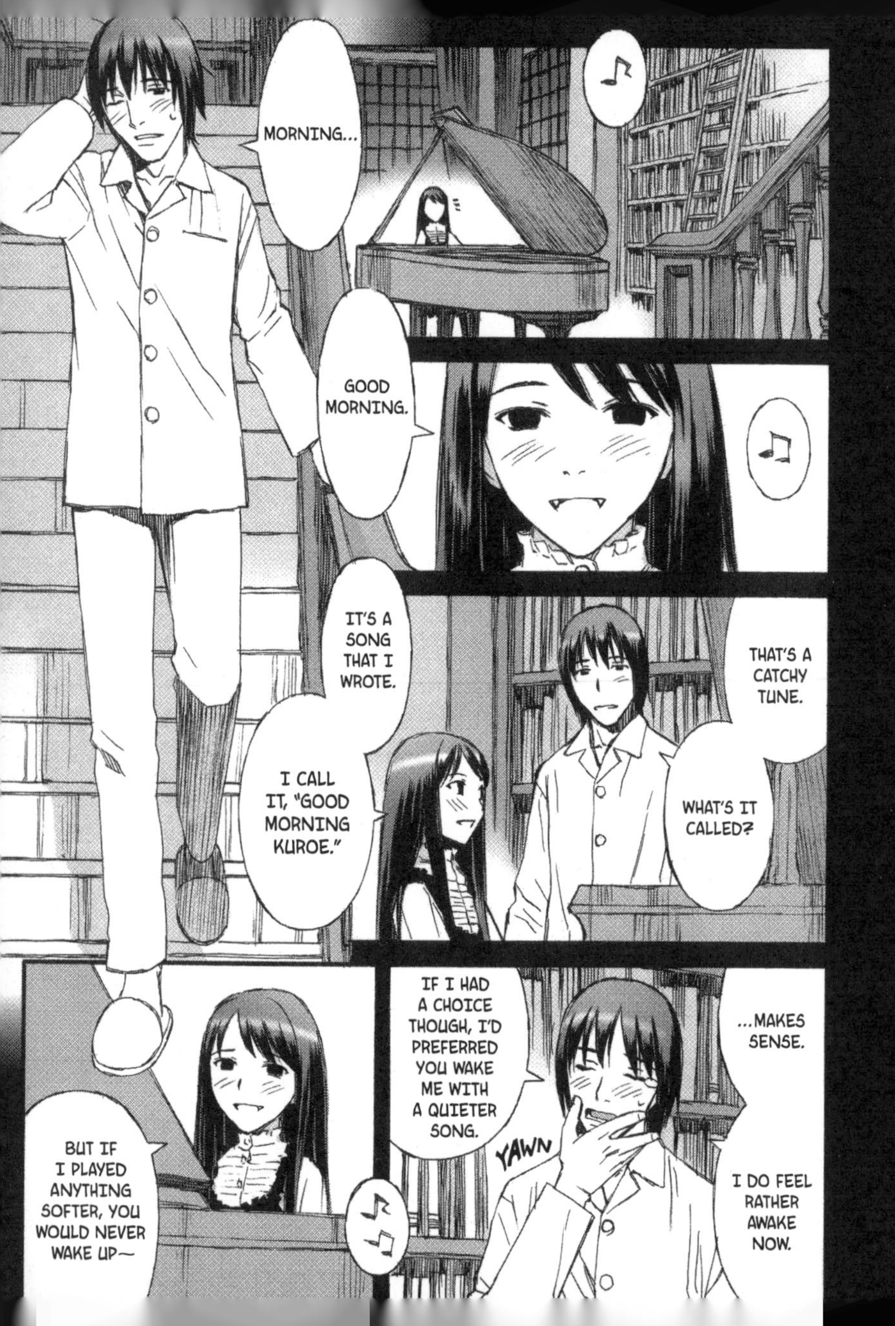
♪
MORNING...
GOOD MORNING.
♪
THAT'S A CATCHY TUNE.
IT'S A SONG THAT I WROTE.
WHAT'S IT CALLED?
I CALL IT, "GOOD MORNING KUROE."
...MAKES SENSE.
IF I HAD A CHOICE THOUGH, I'D PREFERRED YOU WAKE ME WITH A QUIETER SONG.
YAWN
I DO FEEL RATHER AWAKE NOW.
♪ ♪
BUT IF I PLAYED ANYTHING SOFTER, YOU WOULD NEVER WAKE UP~

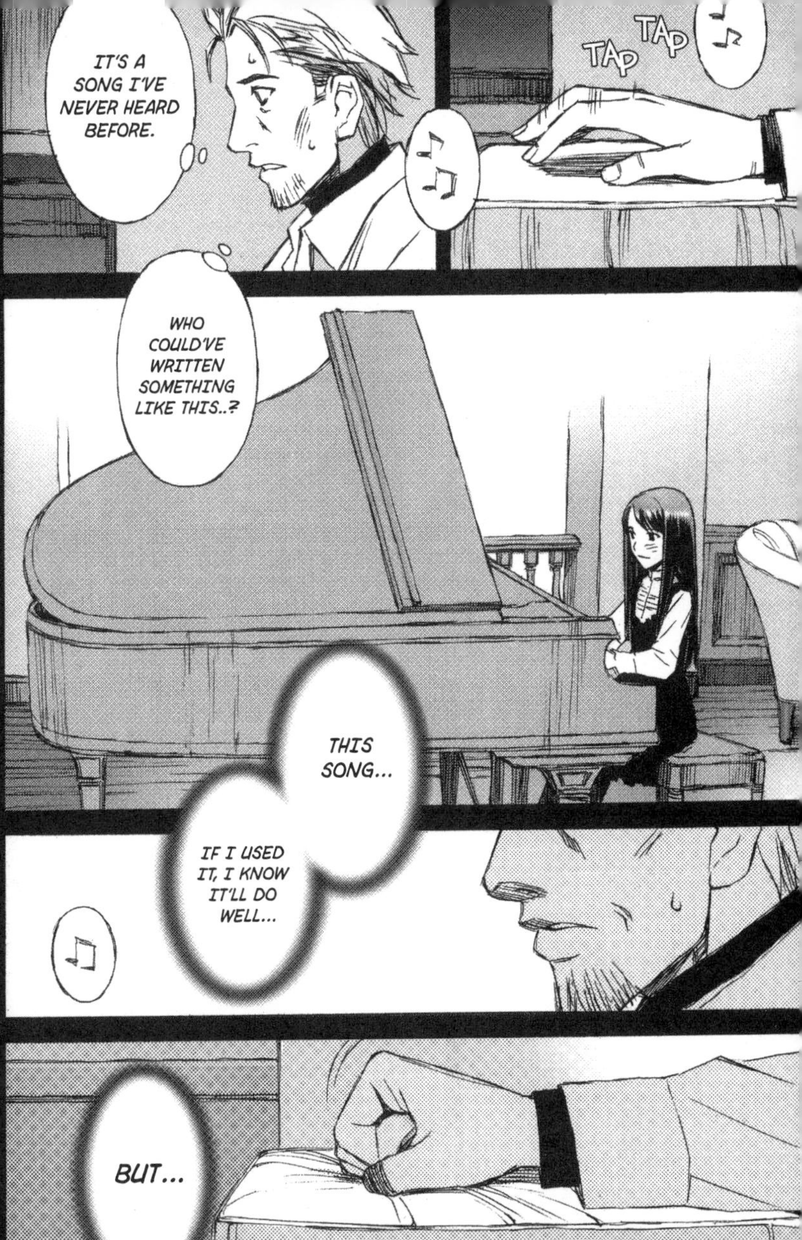
TAP TAP
IT'S A SONG I'VE NEVER HEARD BEFORE.
WHO COULD'VE WRITTEN SOMETHING LIKE THIS..?
THIS SONG...
IF I USED IT, I KNOW IT'LL DO WELL...
BUT...

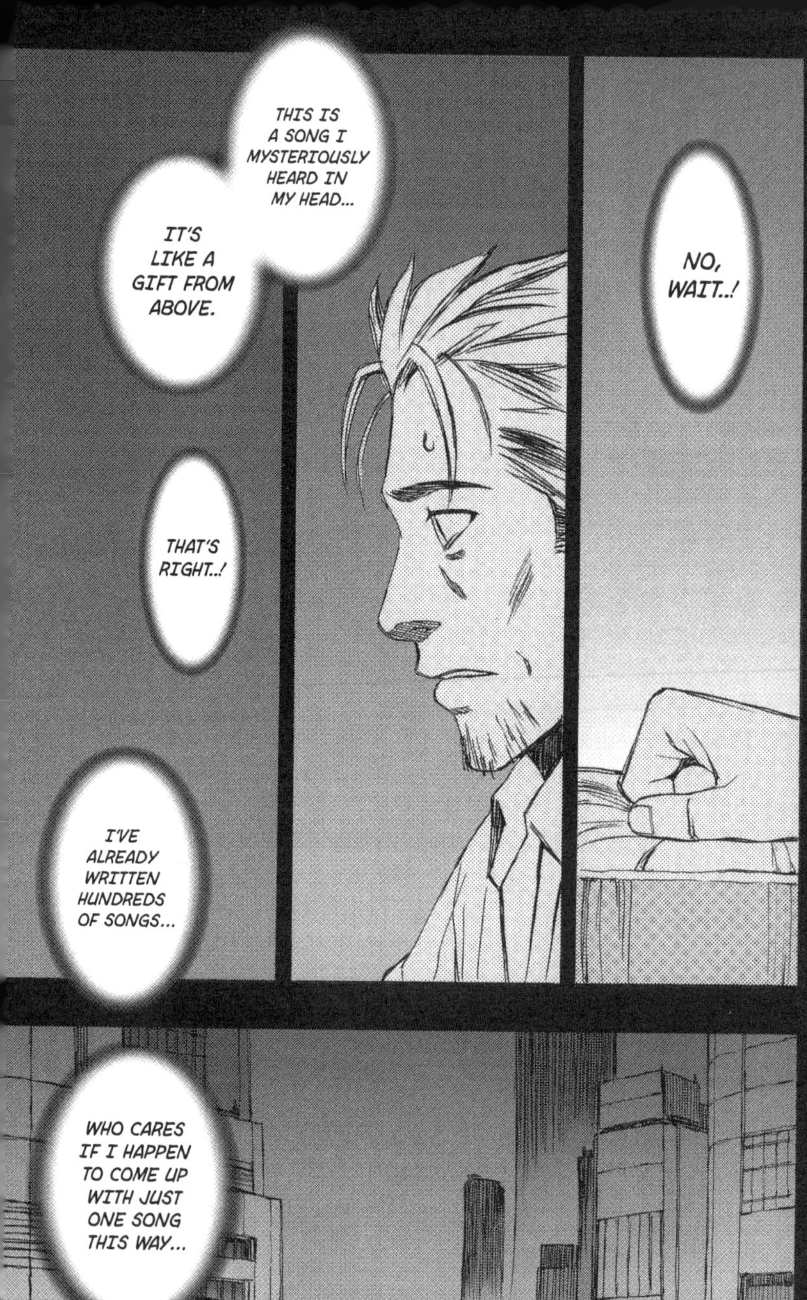
NO, WAIT..!
THIS IS A SONG I MYSTERIOUSLY HEARD IN MY HEAD...
IT'S LIKE A GIFT FROM ABOVE.
THAT'S RIGHT..!
I'VE ALREADY WRITTEN HUNDREDS OF SONGS...
WHO CARES IF I HAPPEN TO COME UP WITH JUST ONE SONG THIS WAY...

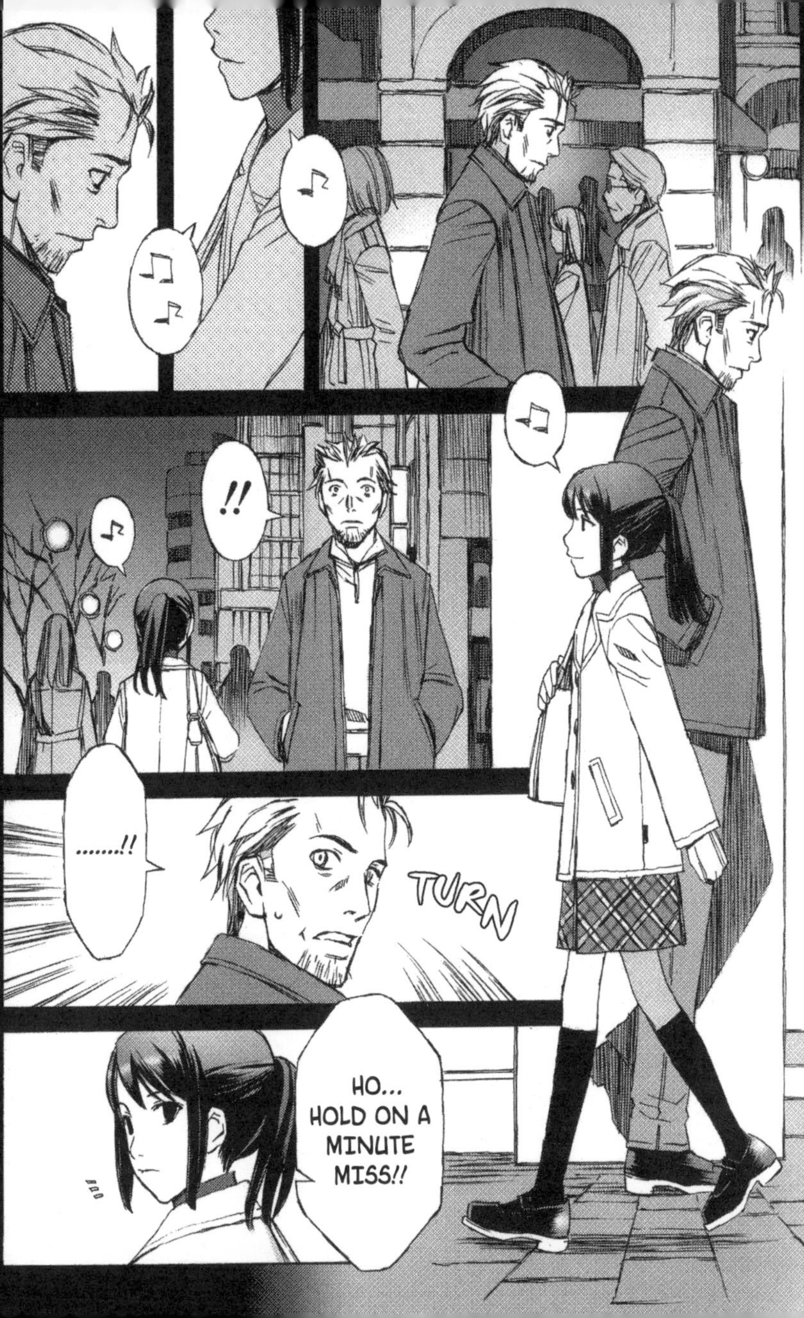
!!
........!!
TURN
HO... HOLD ON A MINUTE MISS!!

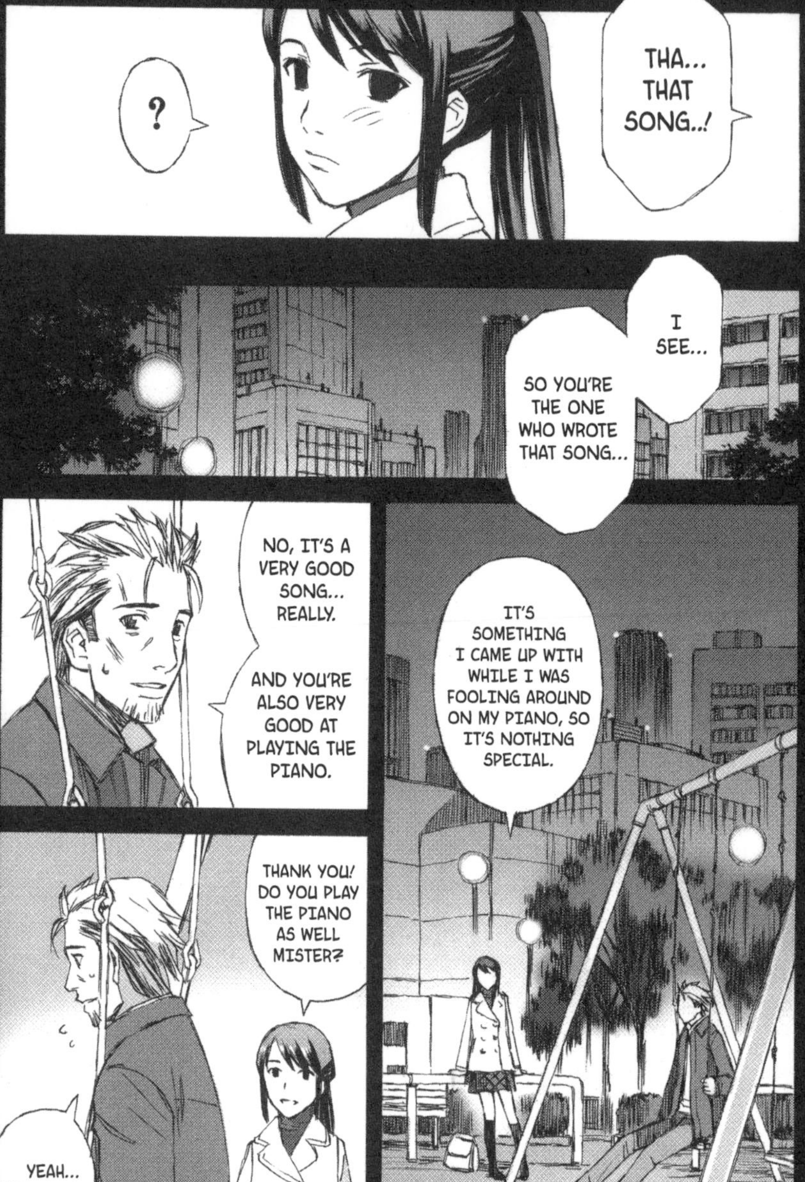
THA... THAT SONG..!
?
I SEE...
SO YOU'RE THE ONE WHO WROTE THAT SONG...
IT'S SOMETHING I CAME UP WITH WHILE I WAS FOOLING AROUND ON MY PIANO, SO IT'S NOTHING SPECIAL.
NO, IT'S A VERY GOOD SONG... REALLY.
AND YOU'RE ALSO VERY GOOD AT PLAYING THE PIANO.
THANK YOU! DO YOU PLAY THE PIANO AS WELL MISTER?
YEAH... YOU COULD SAY THAT...

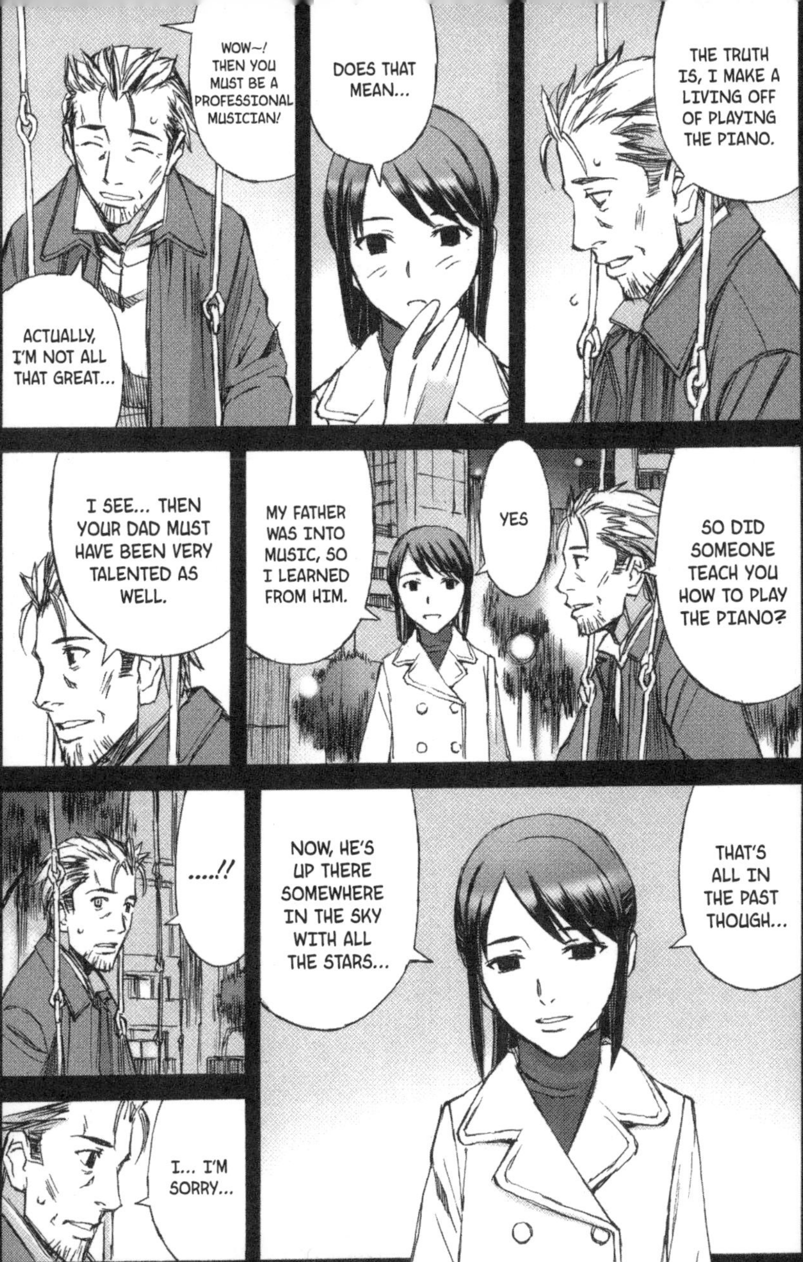
THE TRUTH IS, I MAKE A LIVING OFF OF PLAYING THE PIANO.
DOES THAT MEAN...
WOW~! THEN YOU MUST BE A PROFESSIONAL MUSICIAN!
ACTUALLY, I'M NOT ALL THAT GREAT...
SO DID SOMEONE TEACH YOU HOW TO PLAY THE PIANO?
YES
MY FATHER WAS INTO MUSIC, SO I LEARNED FROM HIM.
I SEE... THEN YOUR DAD MUST HAVE BEEN VERY TALENTED AS WELL.
THAT'S ALL IN THE PAST THOUGH...
NOW, HE'S UP THERE SOMEWHERE IN THE SKY WITH ALL THE STARS...
.....!!
I... I'M SORRY...

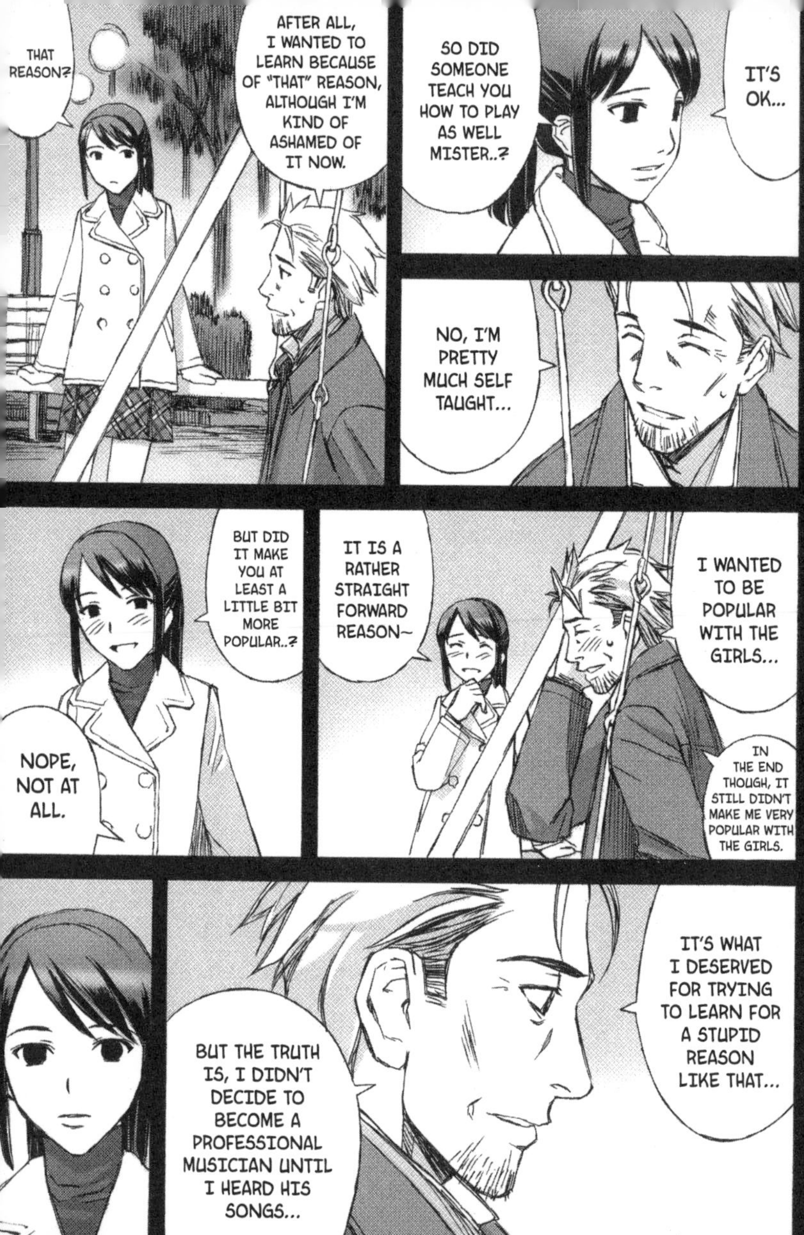
IT'S OK...
SO DID SOMEONE TEACH YOU HOW TO PLAY AS WELL MISTER..?
NO, I'M PRETTY MUCH SELF TAUGHT...
AFTER ALL, I WANTED TO LEARN BECAUSE OF "THAT" REASON, ALTHOUGH I'M KIND OF ASHAMED OF IT NOW.
THAT REASON?
I WANTED TO BE POPULAR WITH THE GIRLS...
IT IS A RATHER STRAIGHT FORWARD REASON~
IN THE END THOUGH, IT STILL DIDN'T MAKE ME VERY POPULAR WITH THE GIRLS.
BUT DID IT MAKE YOU AT LEAST A LITTLE BIT MORE POPULAR..?
NOPE, NOT AT ALL.
IT'S WHAT I DESERVED FOR TRYING TO LEARN FOR A STUPID REASON LIKE THAT...
BUT THE TRUTH IS, I DIDN'T DECIDE TO BECOME A PROFESSIONAL MUSICIAN UNTIL I HEARD HIS SONGS...

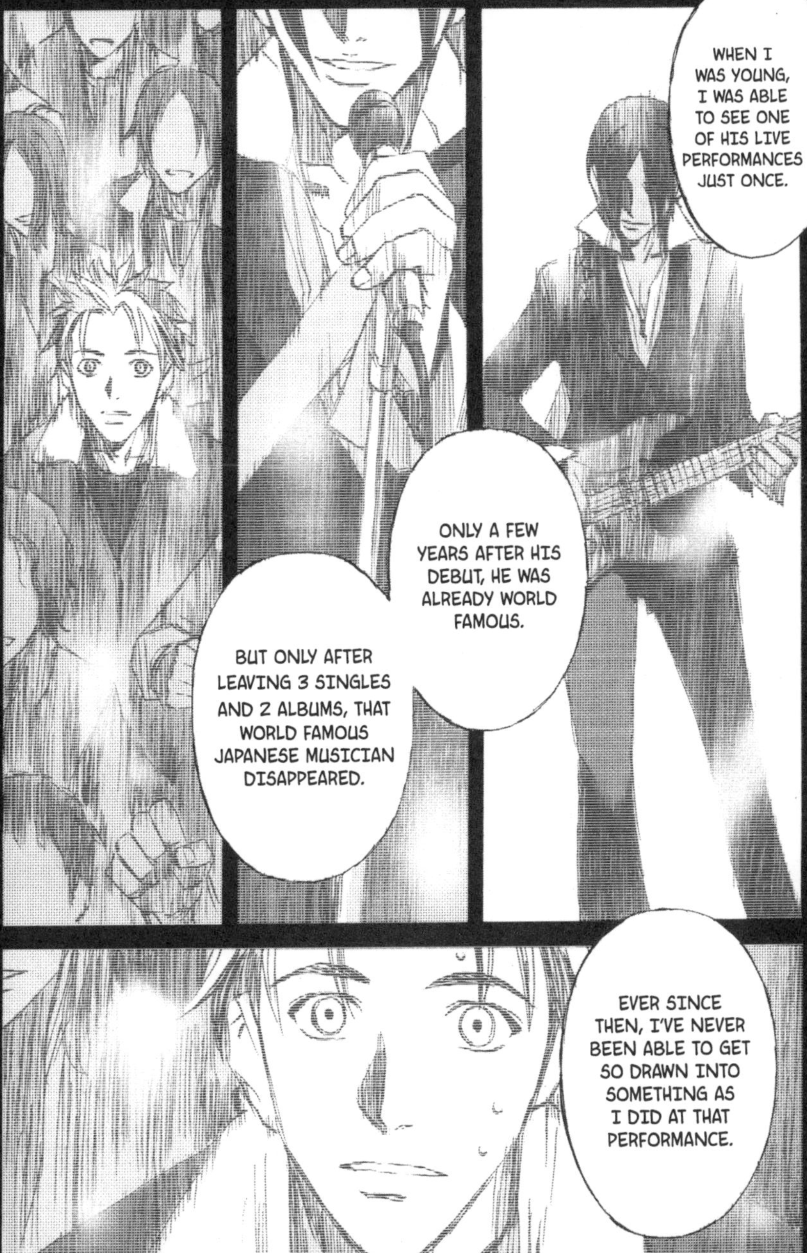
WHEN I WAS YOUNG, I WAS ABLE TO SEE ONE OF HIS LIVE PERFORMANCES JUST ONCE.
ONLY A FEW YEARS AFTER HIS DEBUT, HE WAS ALREADY WORLD FAMOUS.
BUT ONLY AFTER LEAVING 3 SINGLES AND 2 ALBUMS, THAT WORLD FAMOUS JAPANESE MUSICIAN DISAPPEARED.
EVER SINCE THEN, I'VE NEVER BEEN ABLE TO GET SO DRAWN INTO SOMETHING AS I DID AT THAT PERFORMANCE.

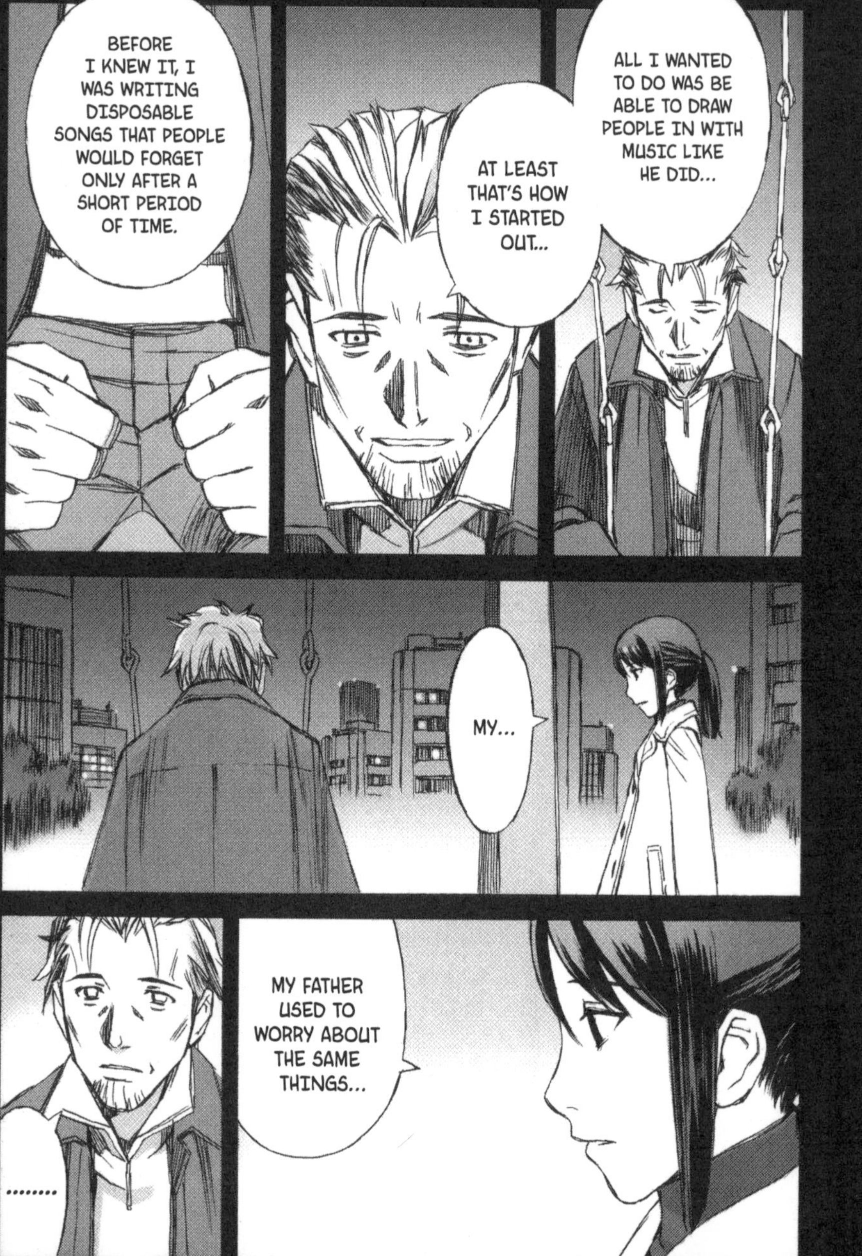
ALL I WANTED TO DO WAS BE ABLE TO DRAW PEOPLE IN WITH MUSIC LIKE HE DID...
AT LEAST THAT'S HOW I STARTED OUT...
BEFORE I KNEW IT, I WAS WRITING DISPOSABLE SONGS THAT PEOPLE WOULD FORGET ONLY AFTER A SHORT PERIOD OF TIME.
MY...
MY FATHER USED TO WORRY ABOUT THE SAME THINGS...
....

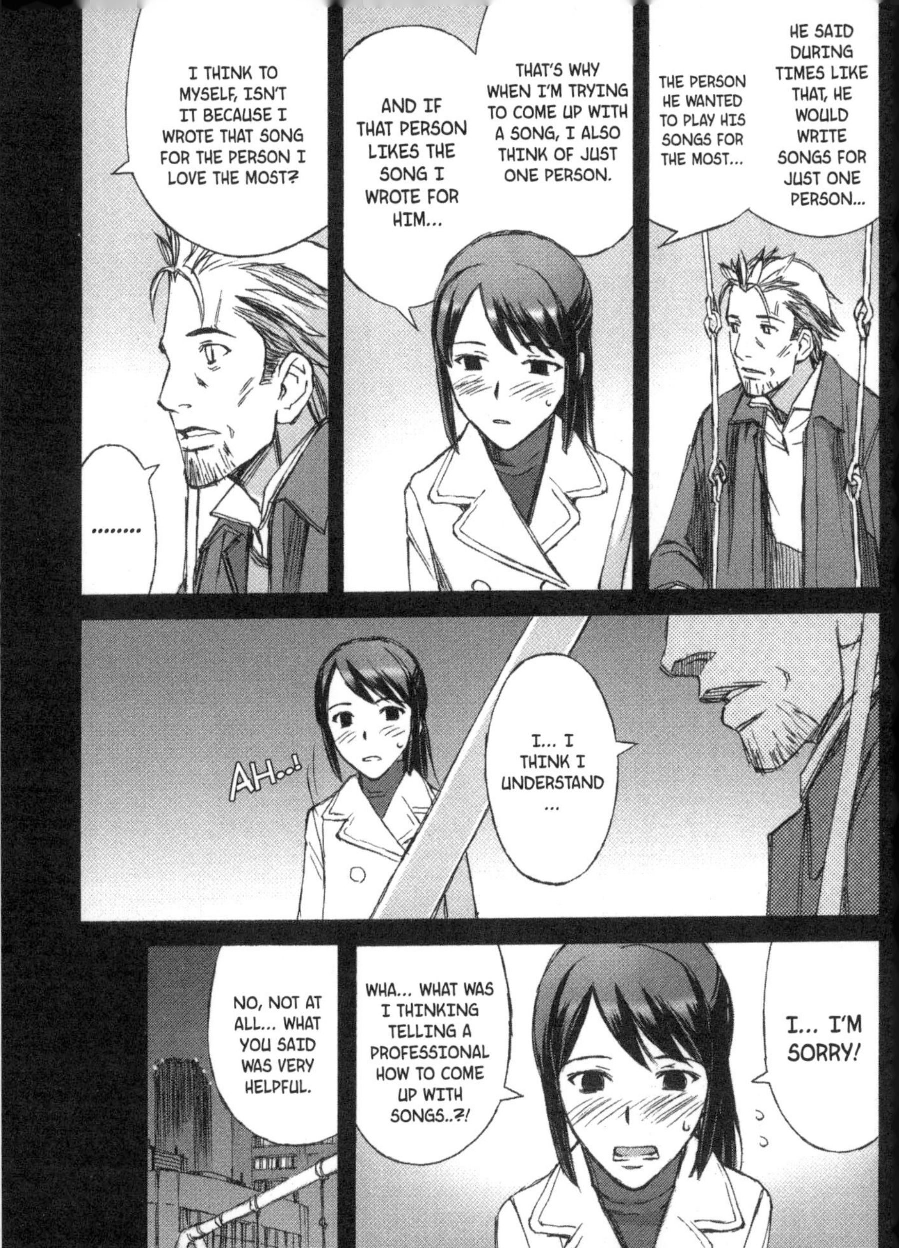
HE SAID DURING TIMES LIKE THAT, HE WOULD WRITE SONGS FOR JUST ONE PERSON...
THE PERSON HE WANTED TO PLAY HIS SONGS FOR THE MOST...
THAT'S WHY WHEN I'M TRYING TO COME UP WITH A SONG, I ALSO THINK OF JUST ONE PERSON.
AND IF THAT PERSON LIKES THE SONG I WROTE FOR HIM...
I THINK TO MYSELF, ISN'T IT BECAUSE I WROTE THAT SONG FOR THE PERSON I LOVE THE MOST?
....
I... I THINK I UNDERSTAND ...
AH..!
I... I'M SORRY!
WHA... WHAT WAS I THINKING TELLING A PROFESSIONAL HOW TO COME UP WITH SONGS..?!
NO, NOT AT ALL... WHAT YOU SAID WAS VERY HELPFUL.

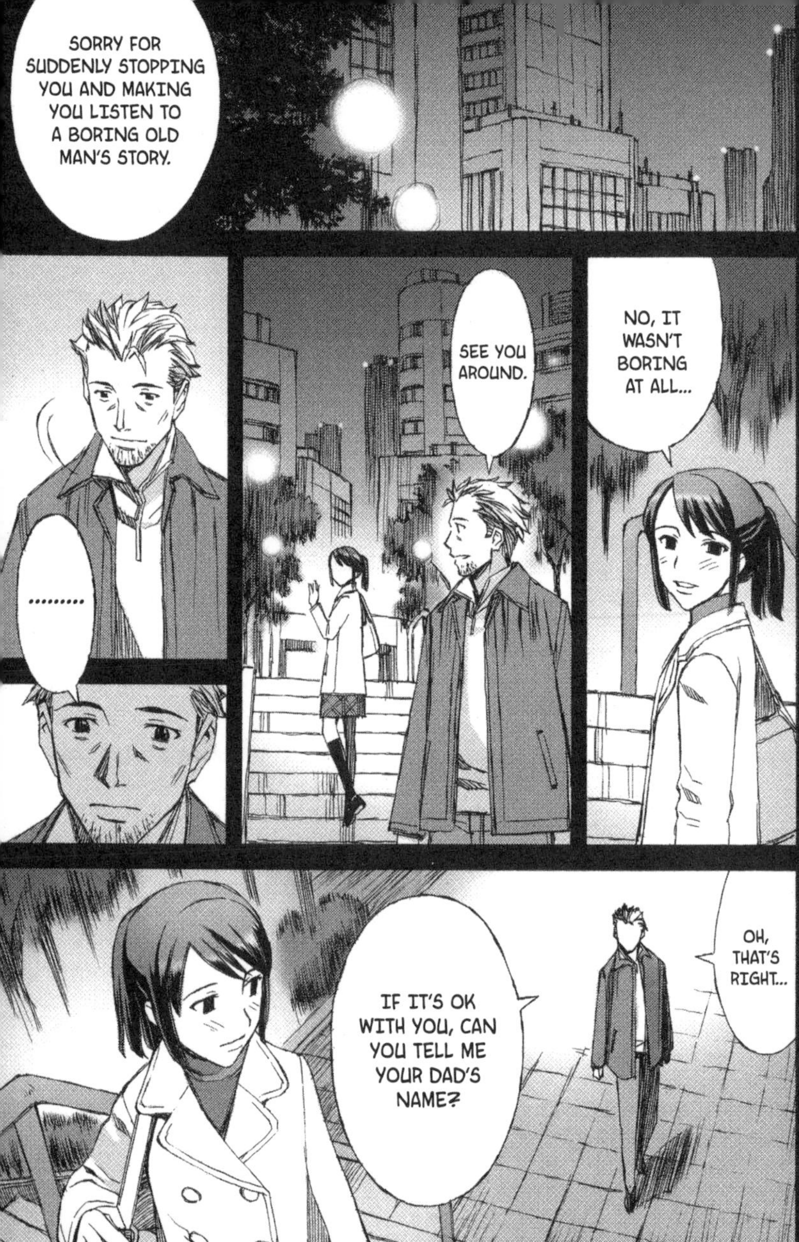
SORRY FOR SUDDENLY STOPPING YOU AND MAKING YOU LISTEN TO A BORING OLD MAN'S STORY.
NO, IT WASN'T BORING AT ALL...
SEE YOU AROUND.
....
OH, THAT'S RIGHT...
IF IT'S OK WITH YOU, CAN YOU TELL ME YOUR DAD'S NAME?

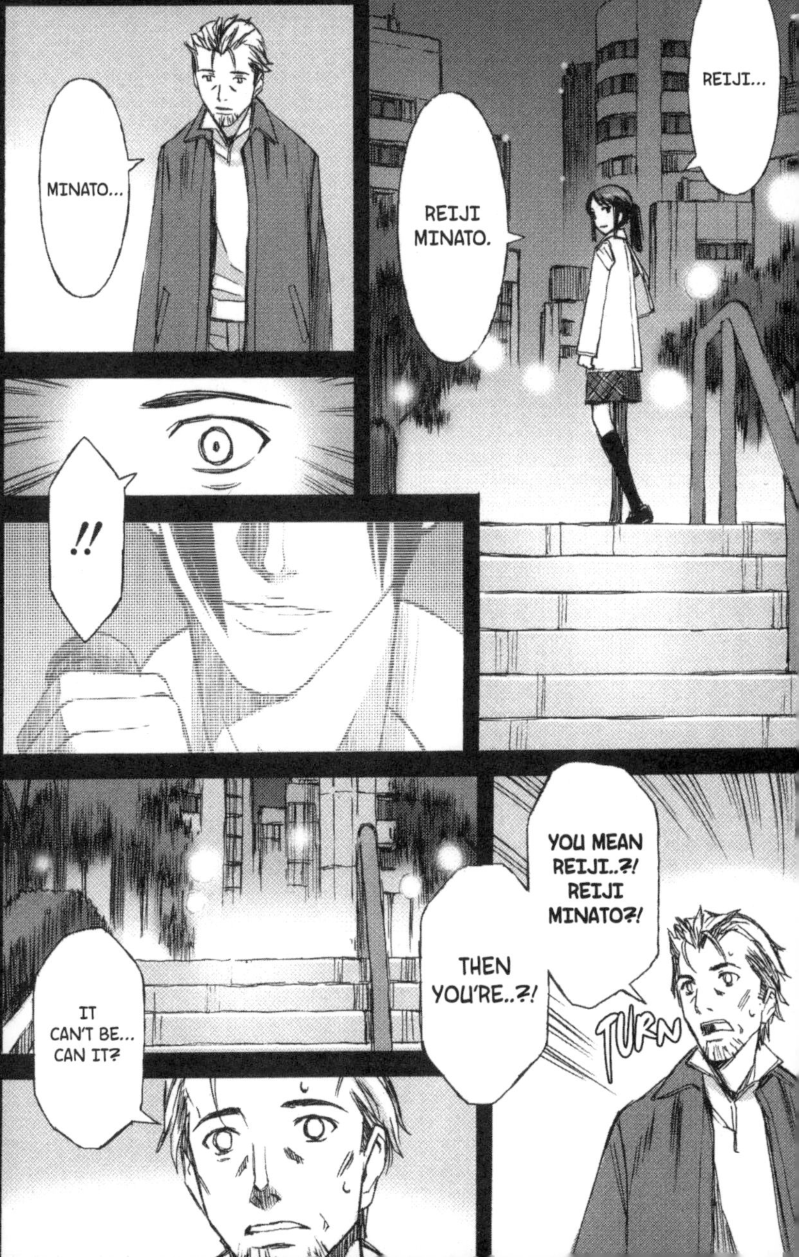
REIJI...
REIJI MINATO.
MINATO...
!!
YOU MEAN REIJI..?! REIJI MINATO?!
TURN
THEN YOU'RE..?!
IT CAN'T BE... CAN IT?

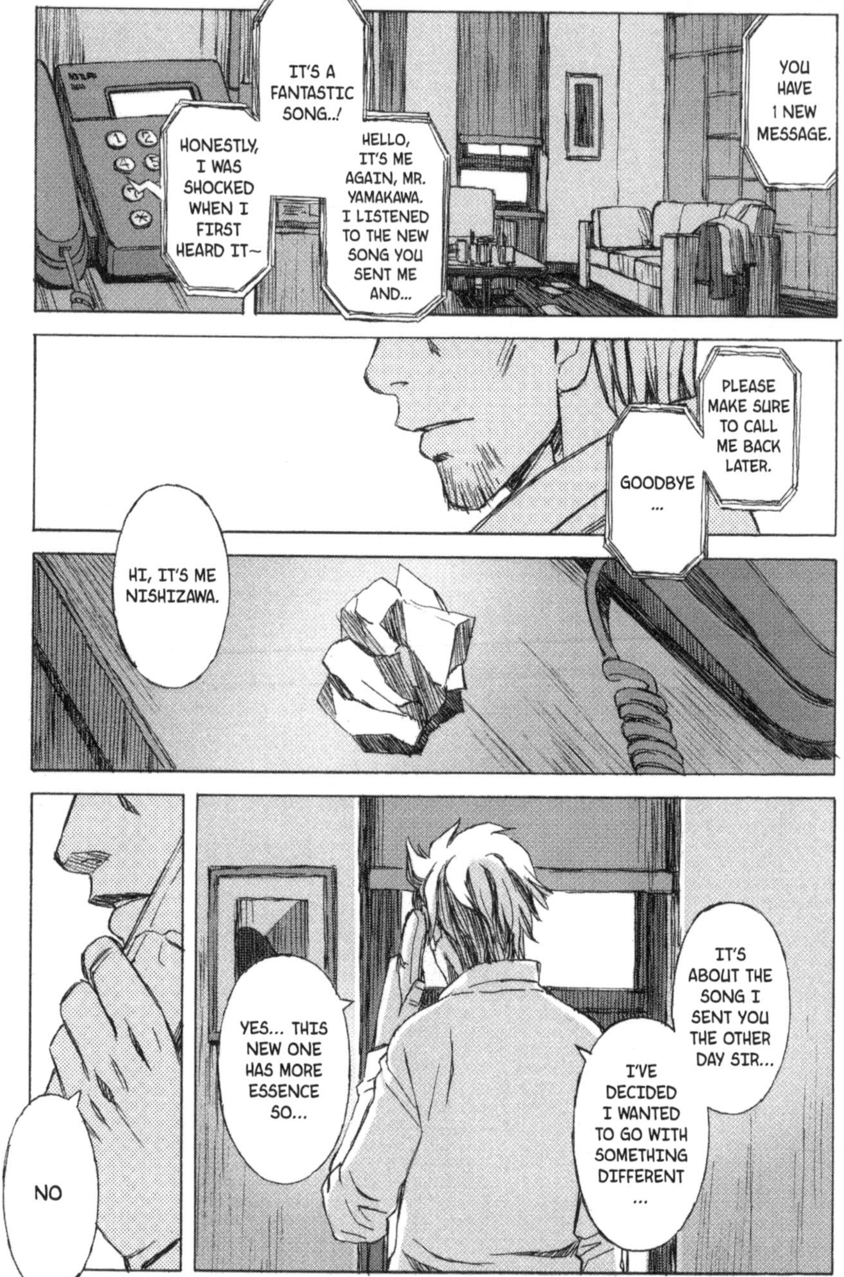
YOU HAVE 1 NEW MESSAGE.
HELLO, IT'S ME AGAIN, MR. YAMAKAWA. I LISTENED TO THE NEW SONG YOU SENT ME AND...
IT'S A FANTASTIC SONG..!
HONESTLY, I WAS SHOCKED WHEN I FIRST HEARD IT~
PLEASE MAKE SURE TO CALL ME BACK LATER.
GOODBYE ...
HI, IT'S ME NISHIZAWA.
IT'S ABOUT THE SONG I SENT YOU THE OTHER DAY SIR...
I'VE DECIDED I WANTED TO GO WITH SOMETHING DIFFERENT ...
YES... THIS NEW ONE HAS MORE ESSENCE SO...
NO

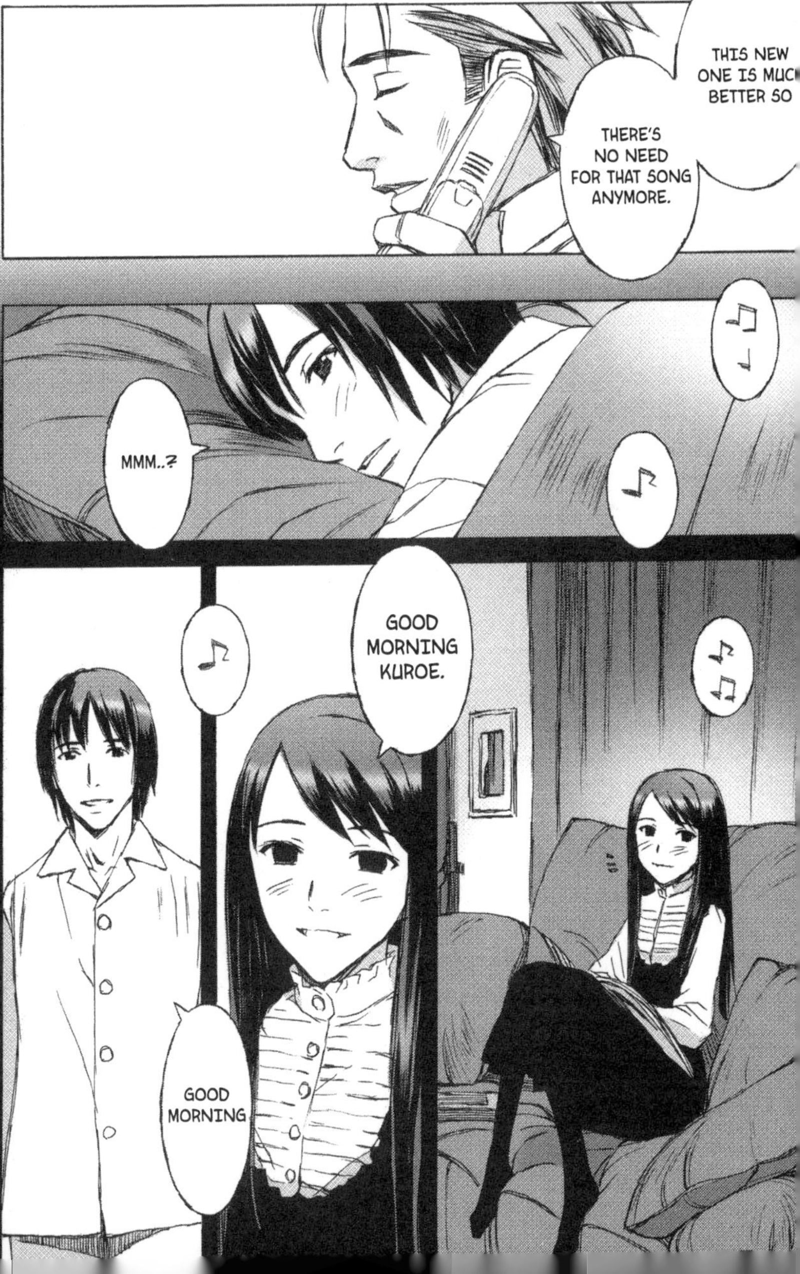
THIS NEW ONE IS MUC BETTER SO
THERE'S NO NEED FOR THAT SONG ANYMORE.
MMM..?
GOOD MORNING KUROE.
GOOD MORNING

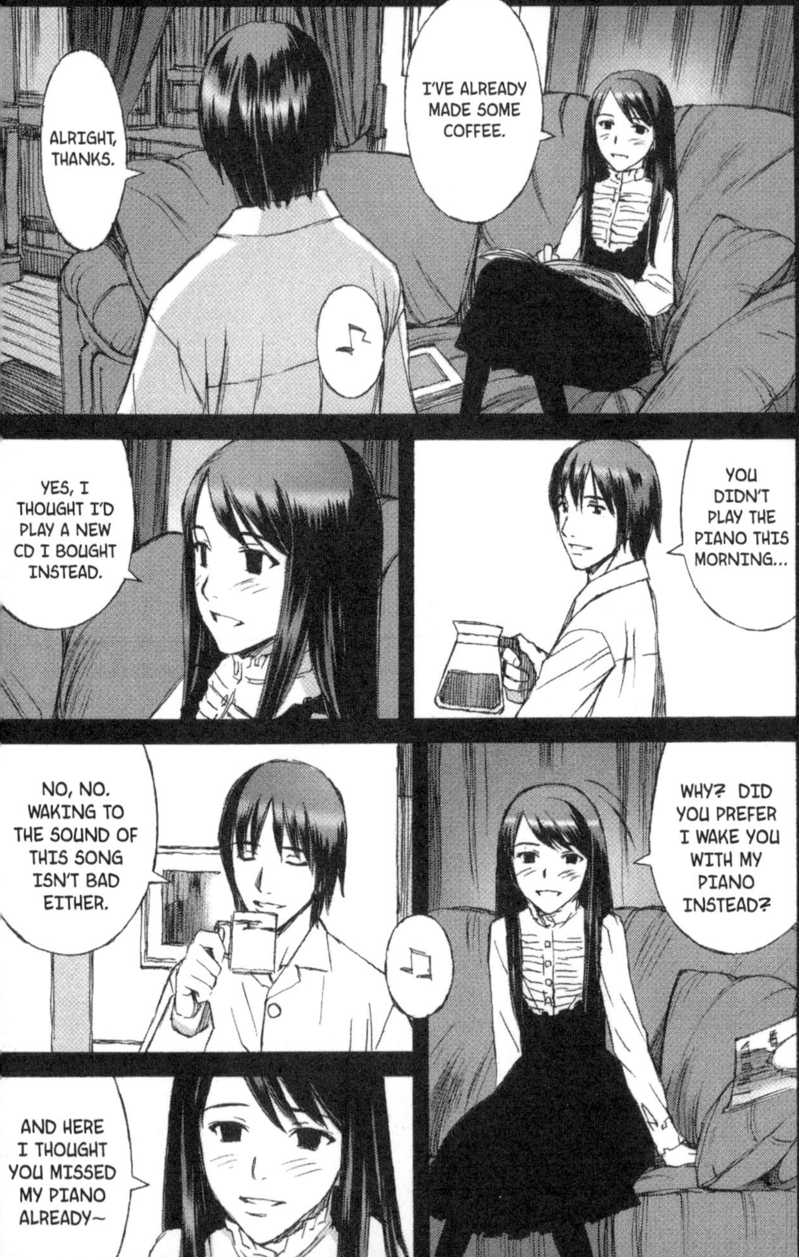
I'VE ALREADY MADE SOME COFFEE.
ALRIGHT, THANKS.
YOU DIDN'T PLAY THE PIANO THIS MORNING...
YES, I THOUGHT I'D PLAY A NEW CD I BOUGHT INSTEAD.
WHY? DID YOU PREFER I WAKE YOU WITH MY PIANO INSTEAD?
NO, NO. WAKING TO THE SOUND OF THIS SONG ISN'T BAD EITHER.
AND HERE I THOUGHT YOU MISSED MY PIANO ALREADY~

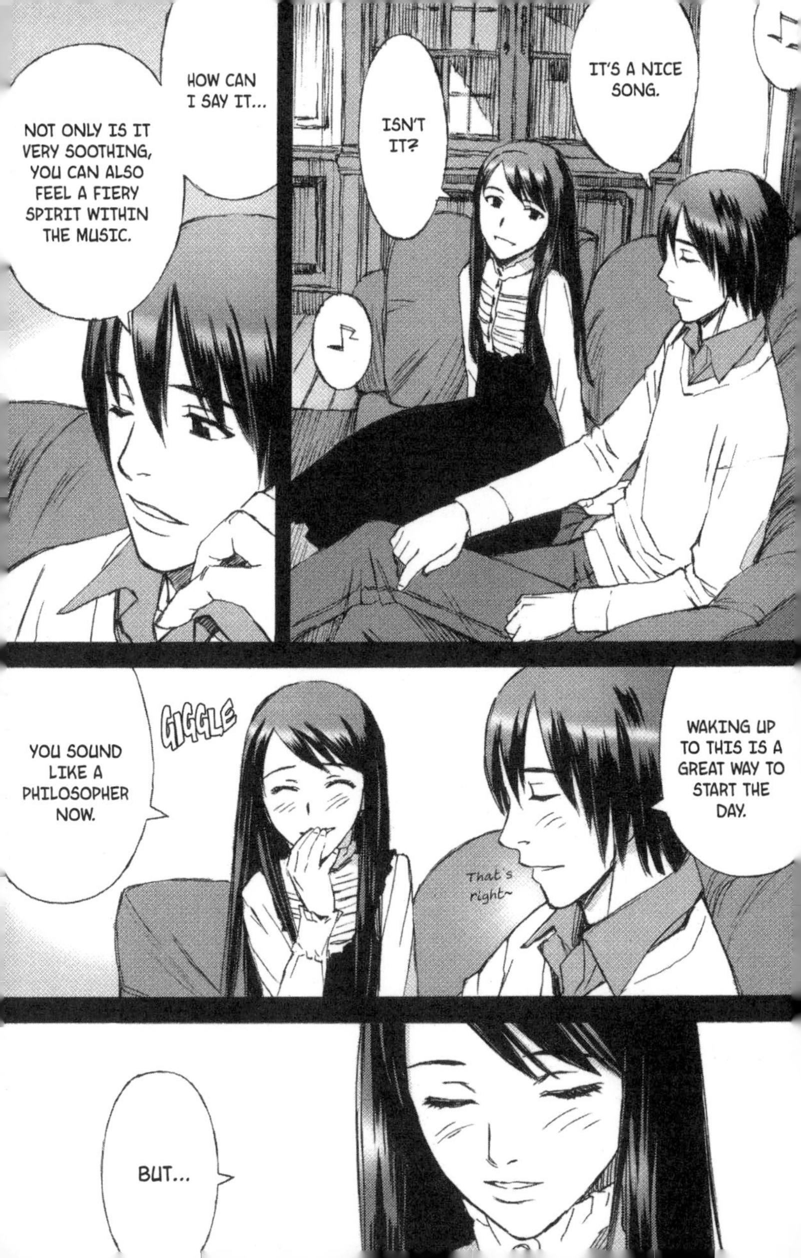
IT'S A NICE SONG.
ISN'T IT?
HOW CAN I SAY IT...
NOT ONLY IS IT VERY SOOTHING, YOU CAN ALSO FEEL A FIERY SPIRIT WITHIN THE MUSIC.
WAKING UP TO THIS IS A GREAT WAY TO START THE DAY.
That's right~
GIGGLE
YOU SOUND LIKE A PHILOSOPHER NOW.
BUT...

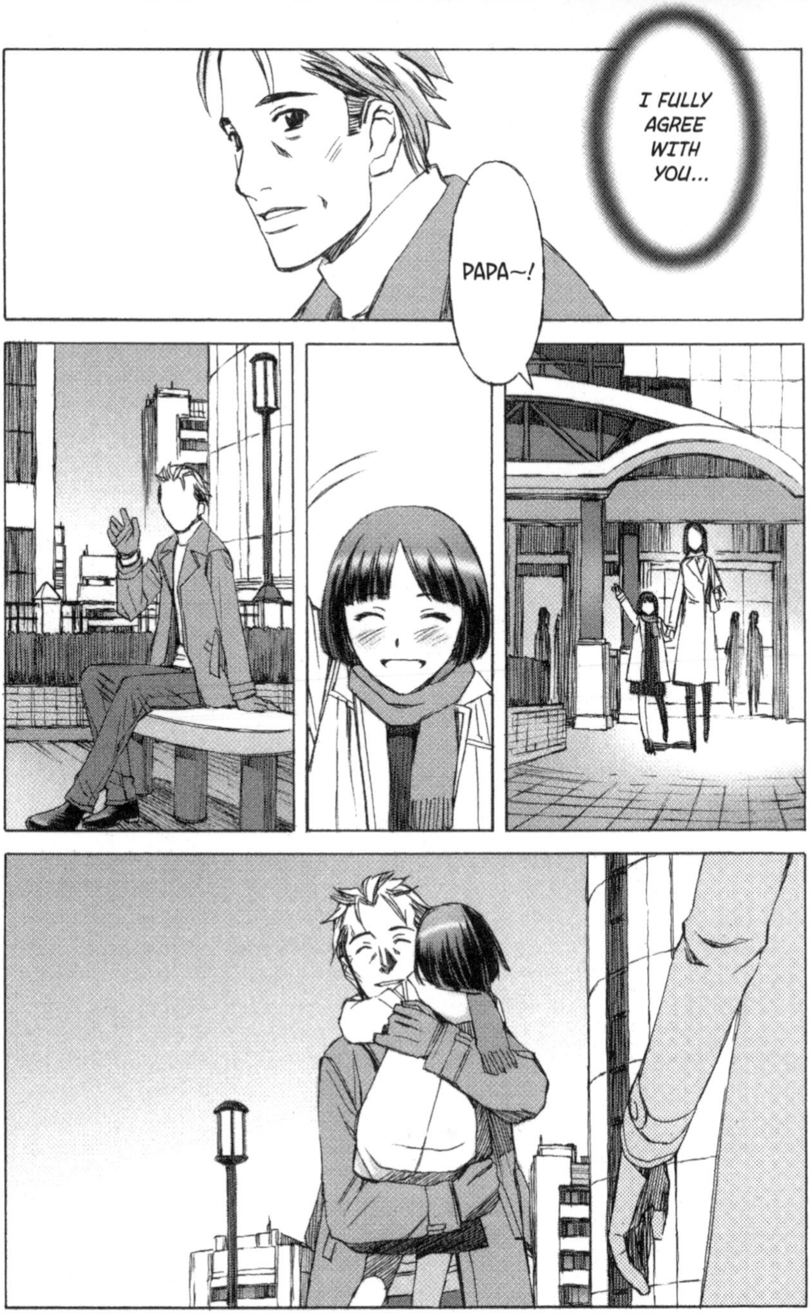
I FULLY AGREE WITH YOU...
PAPA~!

VALENTINE NIGHT

チョコレート失踪事件 – The Missing Chocolate Incident

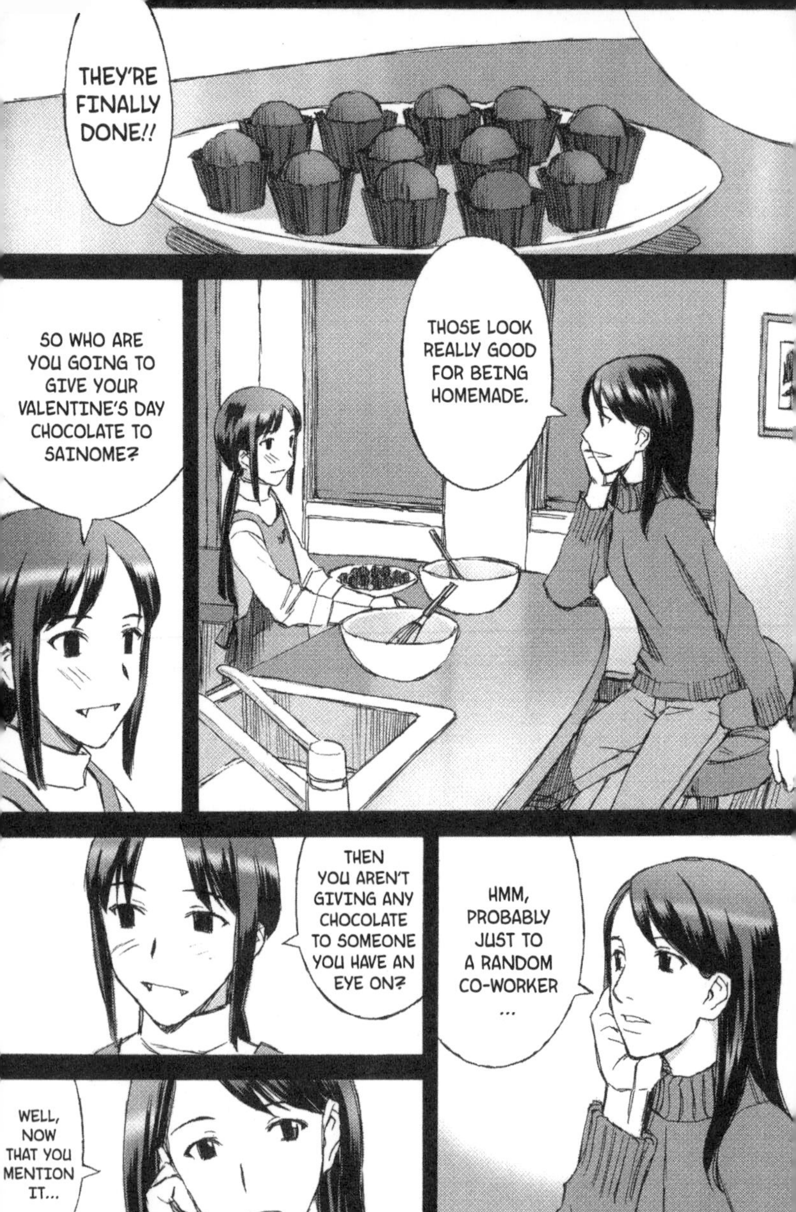
THEY'RE FINALLY DONE!!
THOSE LOOK REALLY GOOD FOR BEING HOMEMADE.
SO WHO ARE YOU GOING TO GIVE YOUR VALENTINE'S DAY CHOCOLATE TO SAINOME?
HMM, PROBABLY JUST TO A RANDOM CO-WORKER ...
THEN YOU AREN'T GIVING ANY CHOCOLATE TO SOMEONE YOU HAVE AN EYE ON?
WELL, NOW THAT YOU MENTION IT...

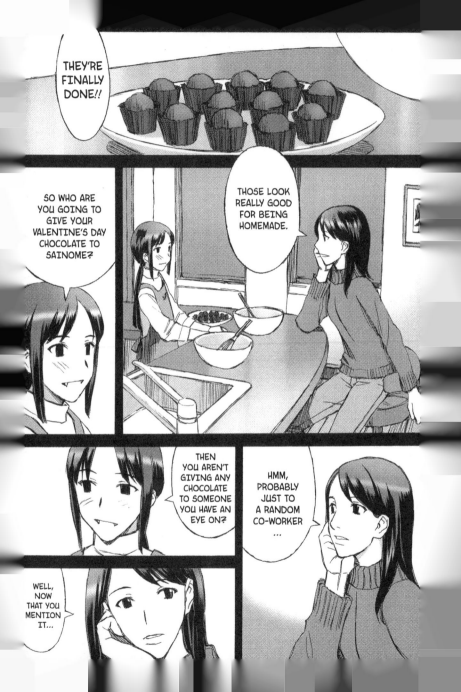

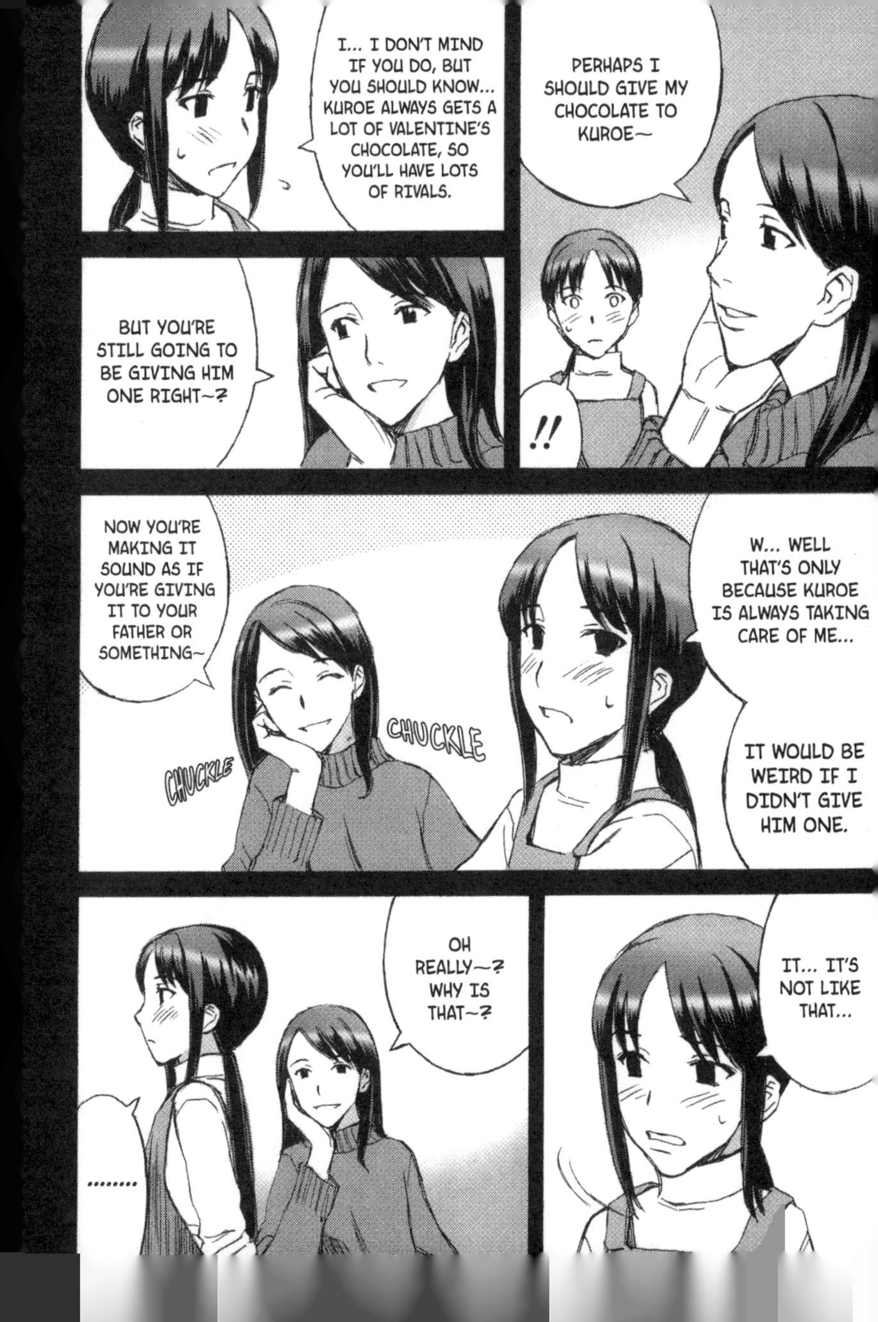
PERHAPS I SHOULD GIVE MY CHOCOLATE TO KUROE~
!!
I... I DON'T MIND IF YOU DO, BUT YOU SHOULD KNOW... KUROE ALWAYS GETS A LOT OF VALENTINE'S CHOCOLATE, SO YOU'LL HAVE LOTS OF RIVALS.
BUT YOU'RE STILL GOING TO BE GIVING HIM ONE RIGHT~?
W... WELL THAT'S ONLY BECAUSE KUROE IS ALWAYS TAKING CARE OF ME...
IT WOULD BE WEIRD IF I DIDN'T GIVE HIM ONE.
NOW YOU'RE MAKING IT SOUND AS IF YOU'RE GIVING IT TO YOUR FATHER OR SOMETHING~
CHUCKLE
CHUCKLE
IT... IT'S NOT LIKE THAT...
OH REALLY~? WHY IS THAT~?
....

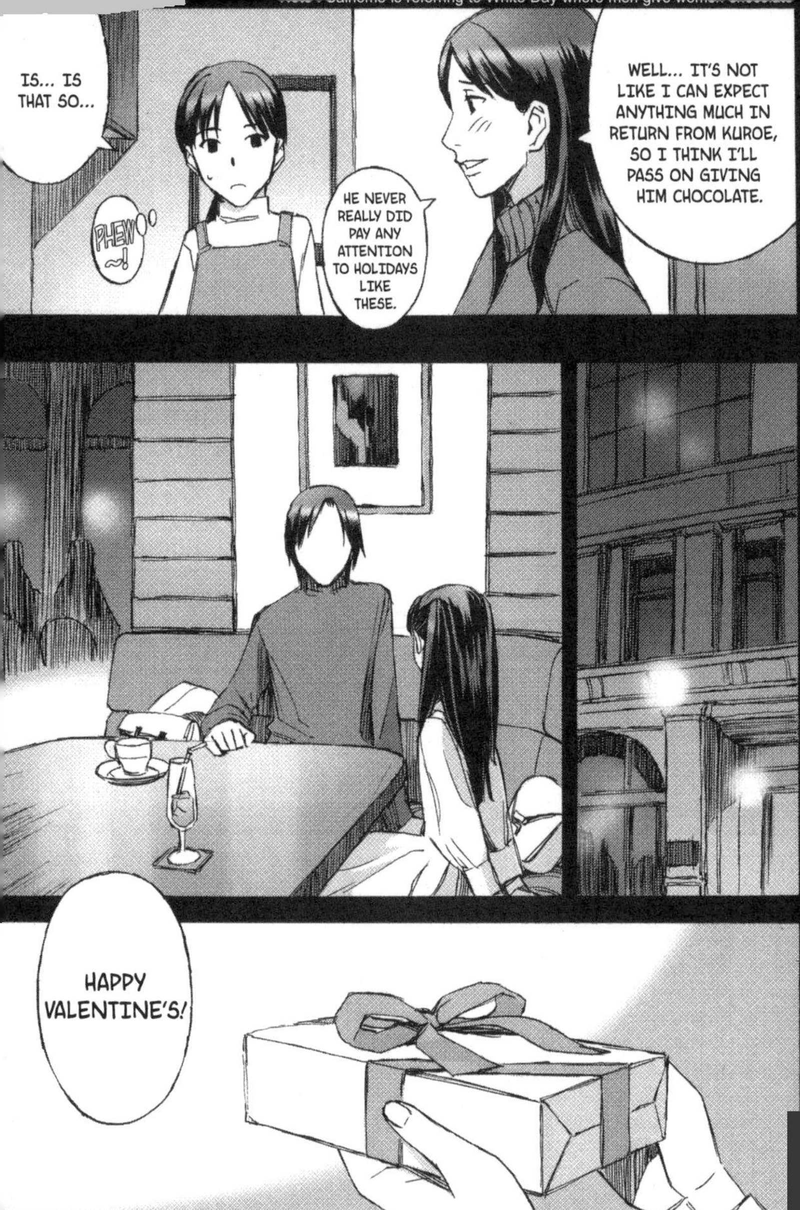
WELL... IT'S NOT LIKE I CAN EXPECT ANYTHING MUCH IN RETURN FROM KUROE, SO I THINK I'LL PASS ON GIVING HIM CHOCOLATE.
HE NEVER REALLY DID PAY ANY ATTENTION TO HOLIDAYS LIKE THESE.
IS... IS THAT SO...
PHEW~!
HAPPY VALENTINE'S!

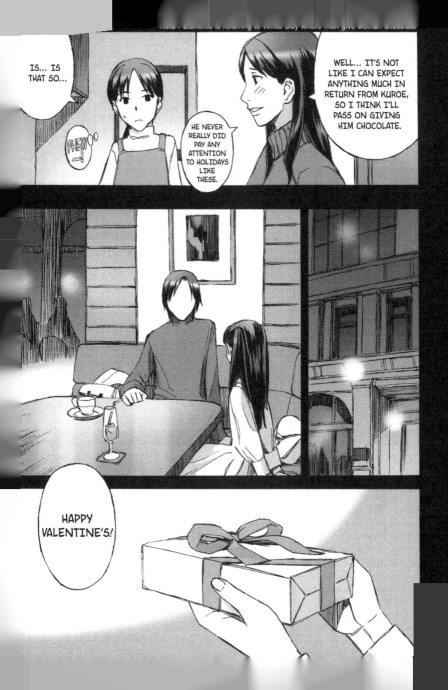

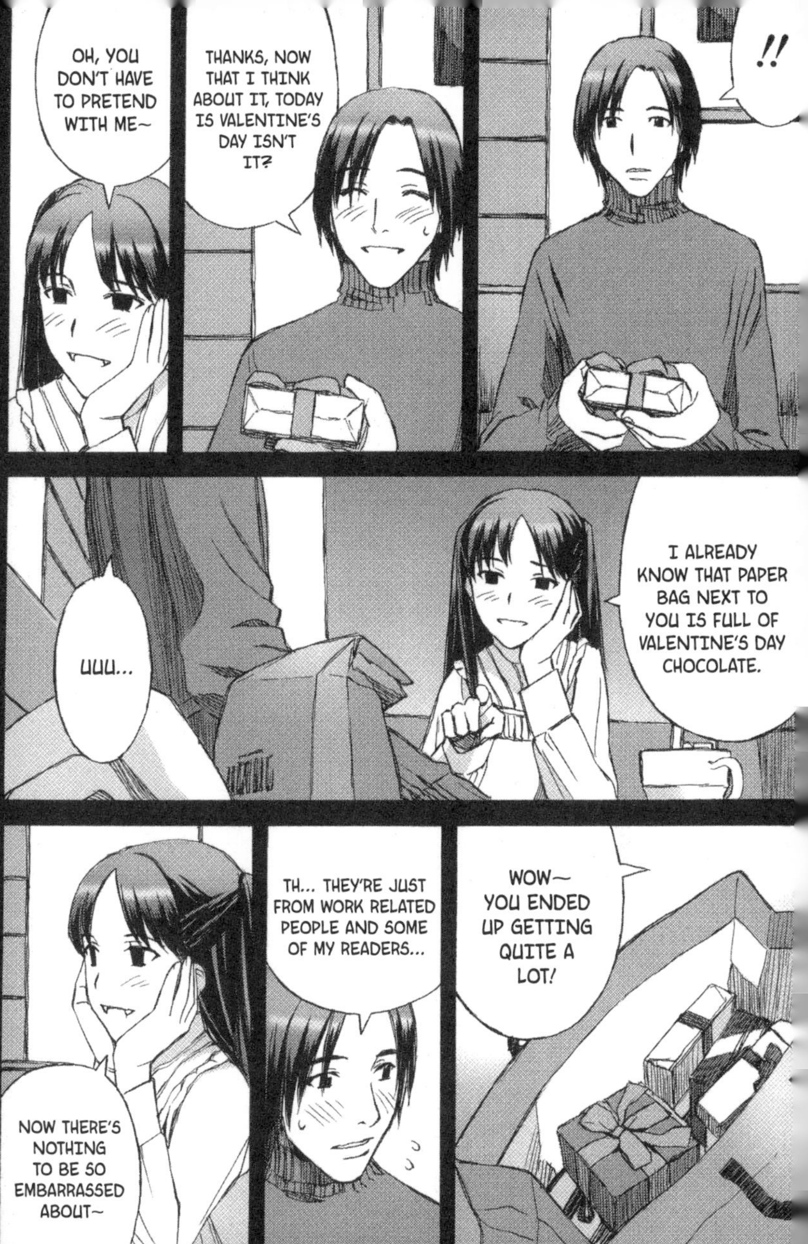
!!
THANKS, NOW THAT I THINK ABOUT IT, TODAY IS VALENTINE'S DAY ISN'T IT?
OH, YOU DON'T HAVE TO PRETEND WITH ME~
I ALREADY KNOW THAT PAPER BAG NEXT TO YOU IS FULL OF VALENTINE'S DAY CHOCOLATE.
UUU...
WOW~ YOU ENDED UP GETTING QUITE A LOT!
TH... THEY'RE JUST FROM WORK RELATED PEOPLE AND SOME OF MY READERS...
NOW THERE'S NOTHING TO BE SO EMBARRASSED ABOUT~

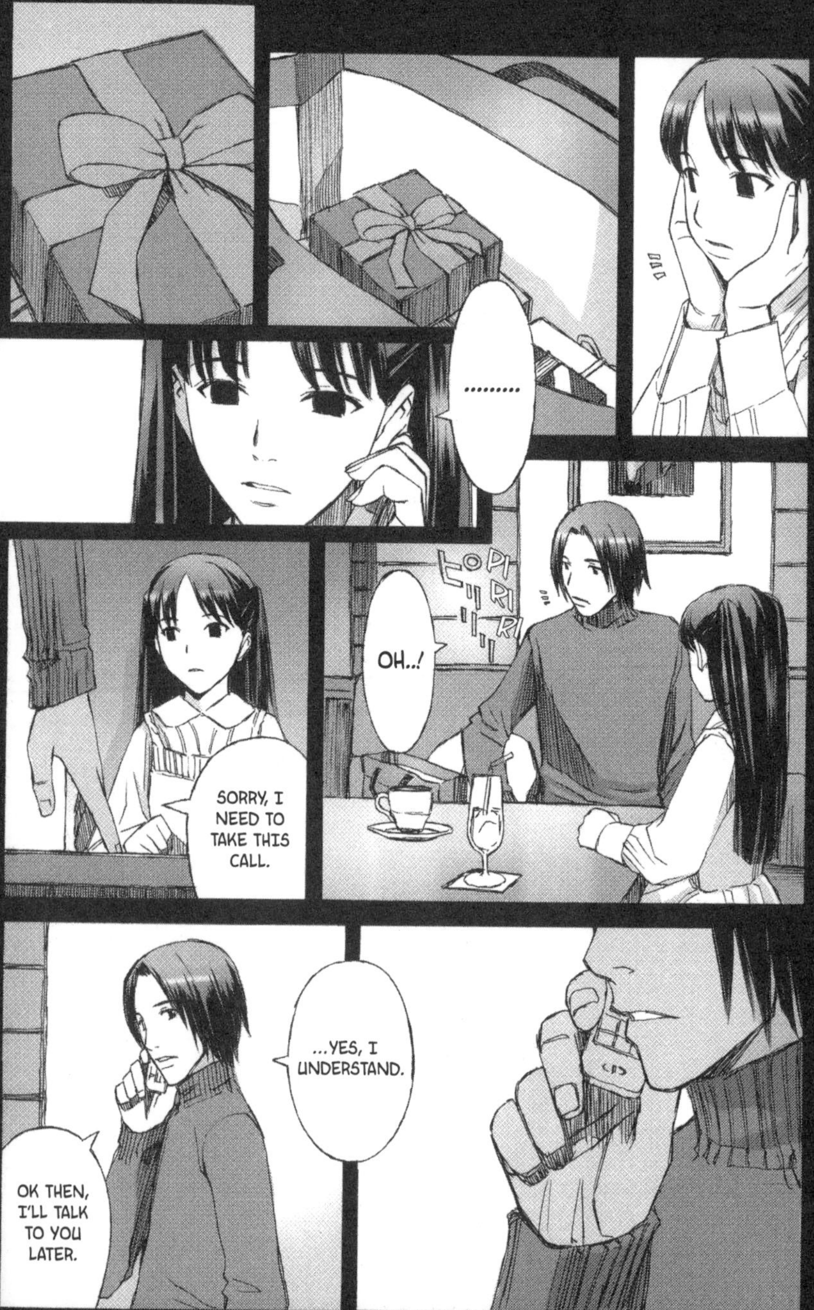
....
PI RI RI
OH..!
SORRY, I NEED TO TAKE THIS CALL.
...YES, I UNDERSTAND.
OK THEN, I'LL TALK TO YOU LATER.

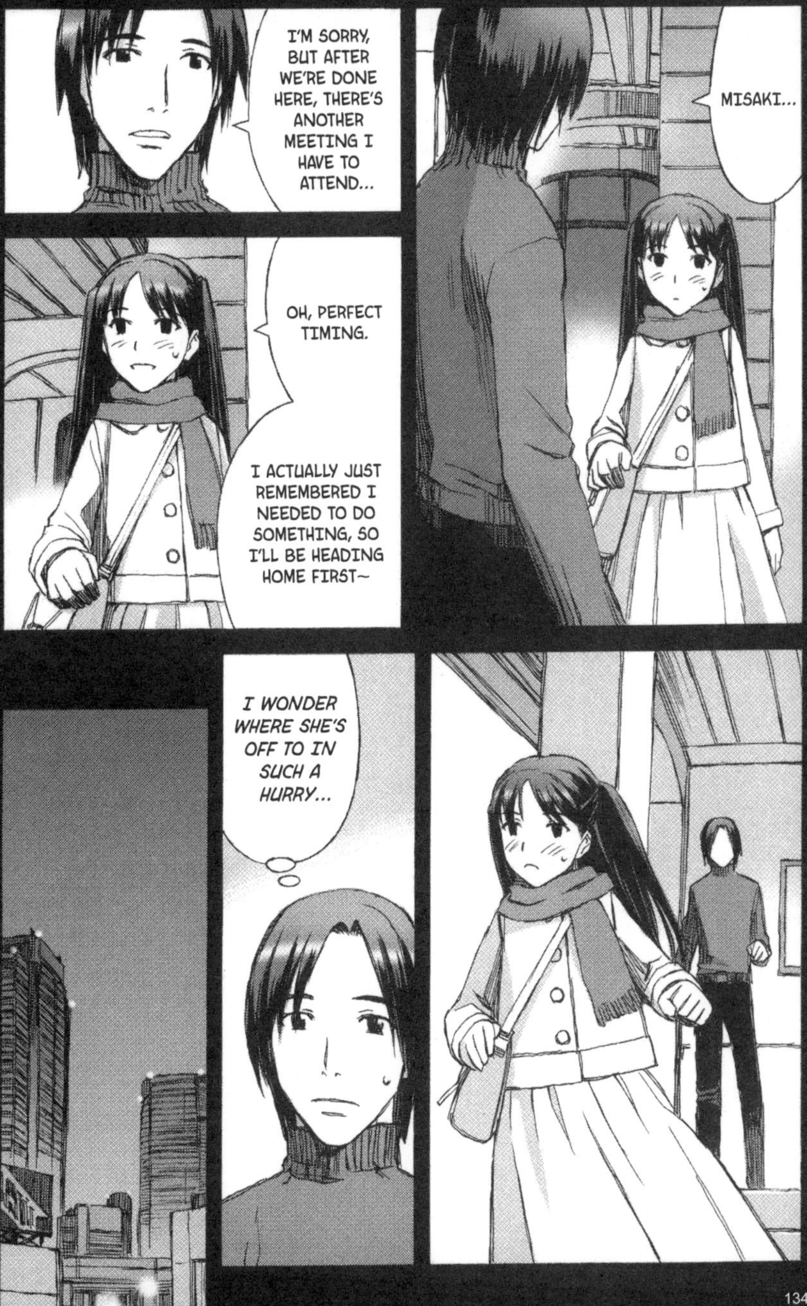
MISAKI...
I'M SORRY, BUT AFTER WE'RE DONE HERE, THERE'S ANOTHER MEETING I HAVE TO ATTEND...
OH, PERFECT TIMING.
I ACTUALLY JUST REMEMBERED I NEEDED TO DO SOMETHING, SO I'LL BE HEADING HOME FIRST~
I WONDER WHERE SHE'S OFF TO IN SUCH A HURRY...

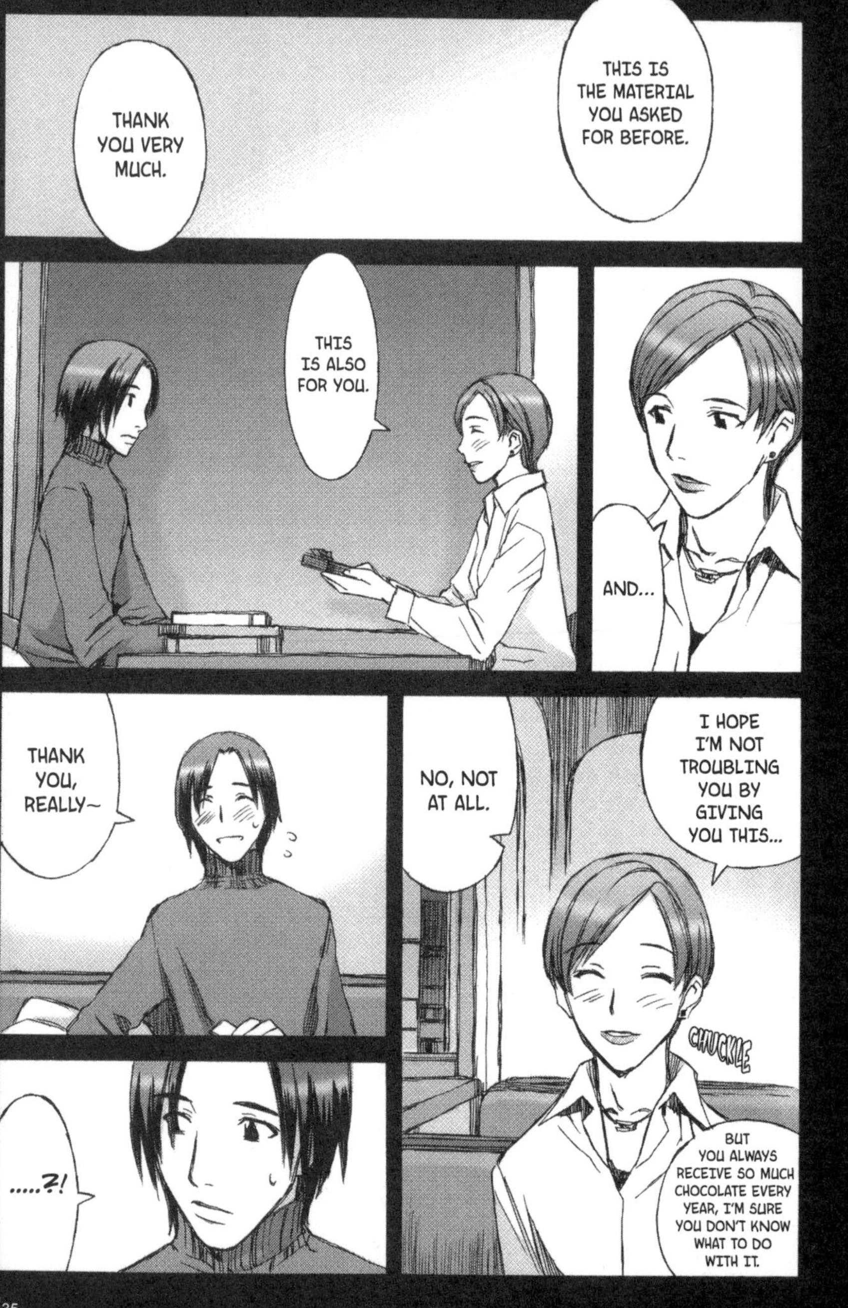
THIS IS THE MATERIAL YOU ASKED FOR BEFORE.
THANK YOU VERY MUCH.
AND...
THIS IS ALSO FOR YOU.
I HOPE I'M NOT TROUBLING YOU BY GIVING YOU THIS...
NO, NOT AT ALL.
CHUCKLE
BUT YOU ALWAYS RECEIVE SO MUCH CHOCOLATE EVERY YEAR, I'M SURE YOU DON'T KNOW WHAT TO DO WITH IT.
THANK YOU, REALLY~
.....?!

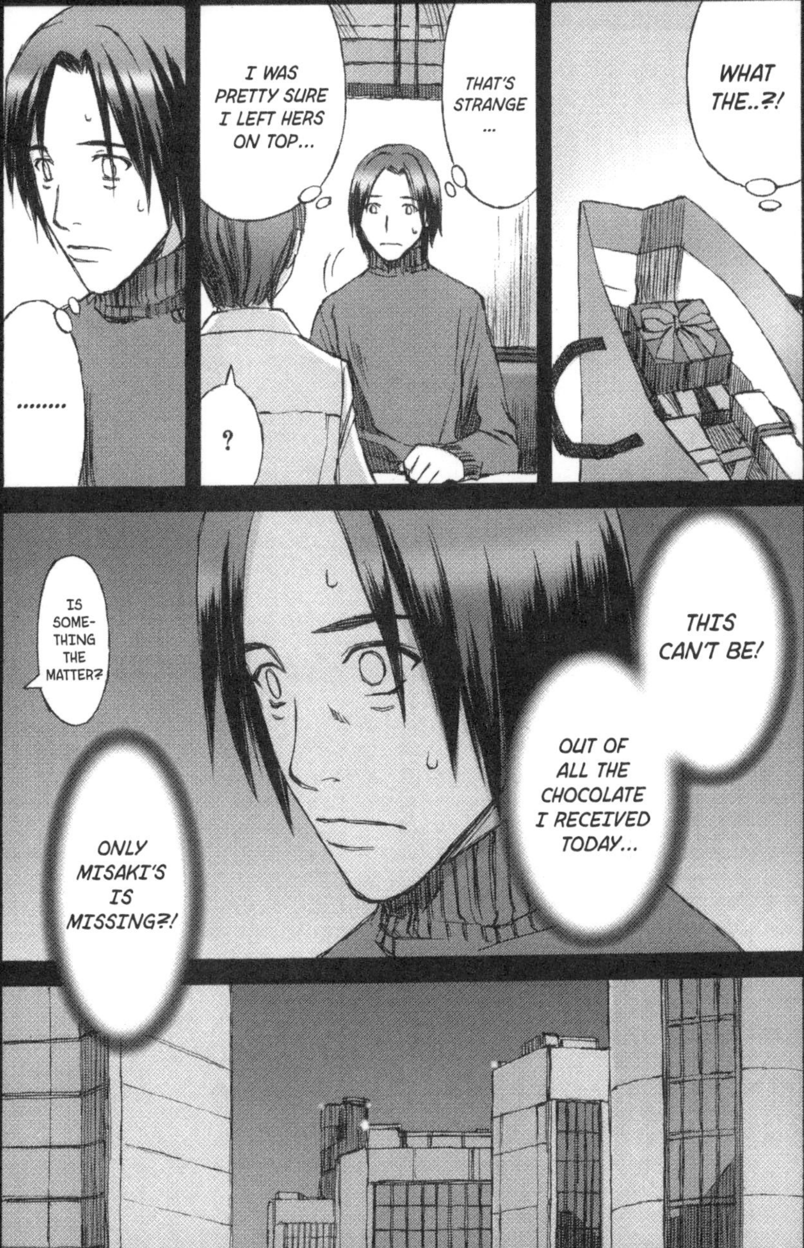
WHAT THE..?!
THAT'S STRANGE ...
I WAS PRETTY SURE I LEFT HERS ON TOP...
?
....
THIS CAN'T BE!
OUT OF ALL THE CHOCOLATE I RECEIVED TODAY...
IS SOME-THING THE MATTER?
ONLY MISAKI'S IS MISSING?!

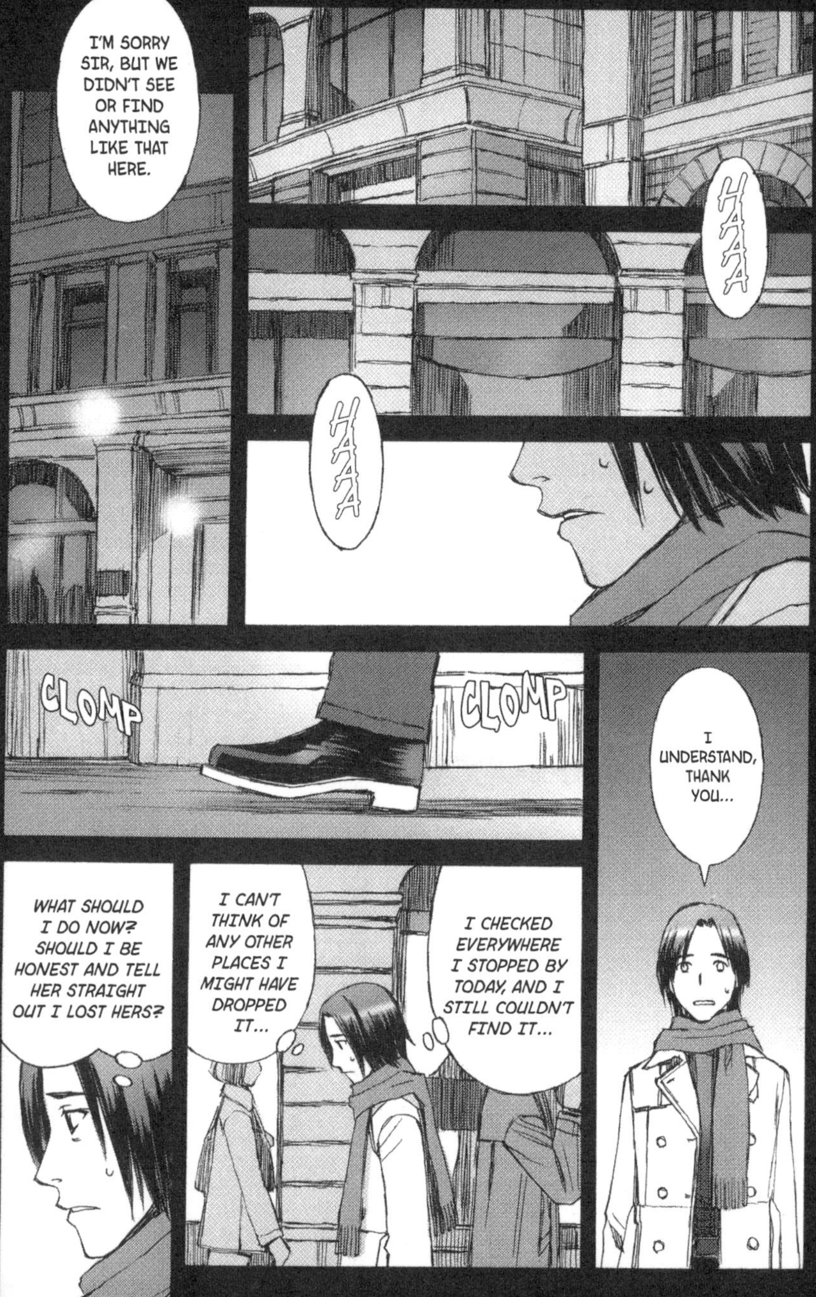
HAAA
HAAA
I'M SORRY SIR, BUT WE DIDN'T SEE OR FIND ANYTHING LIKE THAT HERE.
I UNDERSTAND, THANK YOU...
CLOMP
CLOMP
I CHECKED EVERYWHERE I STOPPED BY TODAY, AND I STILL COULDN'T FIND IT...
I CAN'T THINK OF ANY OTHER PLACES I MIGHT HAVE DROPPED IT...
WHAT SHOULD I DO NOW? SHOULD I BE HONEST AND TELL HER STRAIGHT OUT I LOST HERS?

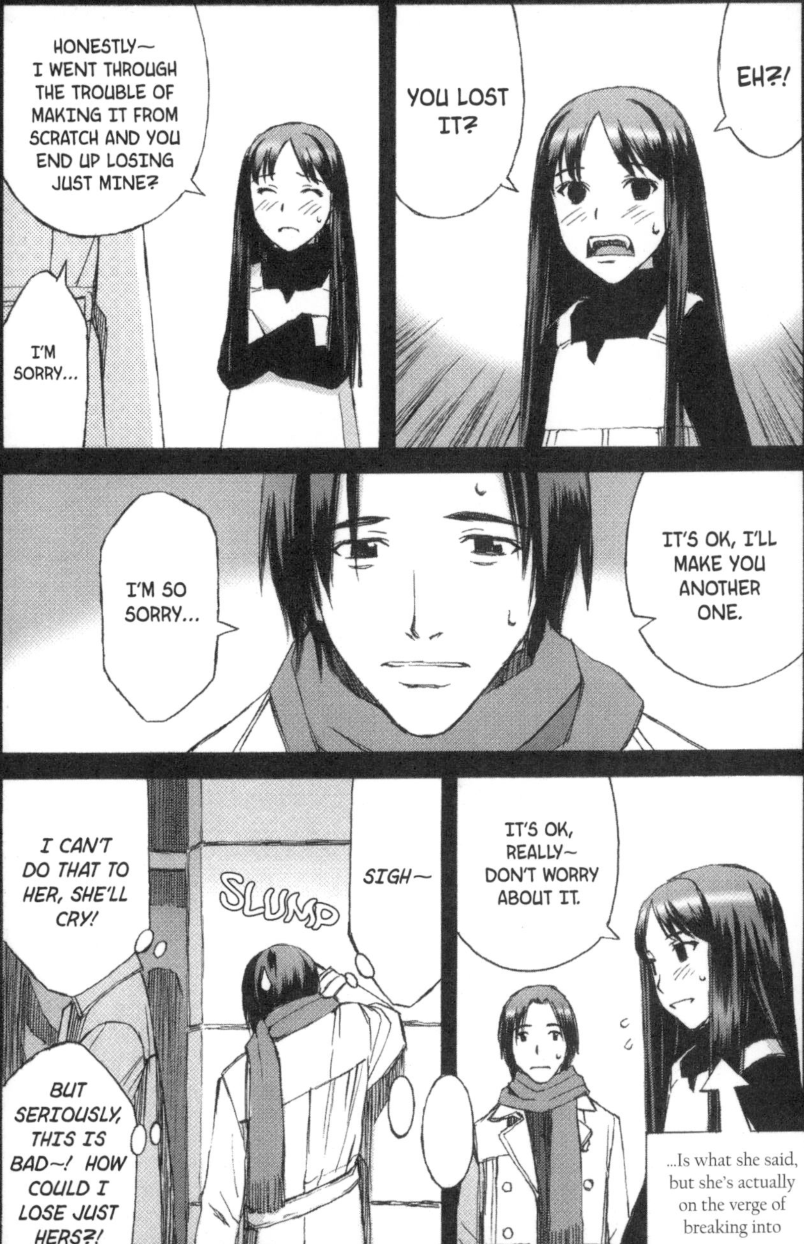
EH?!
YOU LOST IT?
HONESTLY~ I WENT THROUGH THE TROUBLE OF MAKING IT FROM SCRATCH AND YOU END UP LOSING JUST MINE?
I'M SORRY...
IT'S OK, I'LL MAKE YOU ANOTHER ONE.
I'M SO SORRY...
IT'S OK, REALLY~ DON'T WORRY ABOUT IT.
...Is what she said, but she's actually on the verge of breaking into tears.
SIGH~
SLUMP
I CAN'T DO THAT TO HER, SHE'LL CRY!
BUT SERIOUSLY, THIS IS BAD~! HOW COULD I LOSE JUST HERS?!

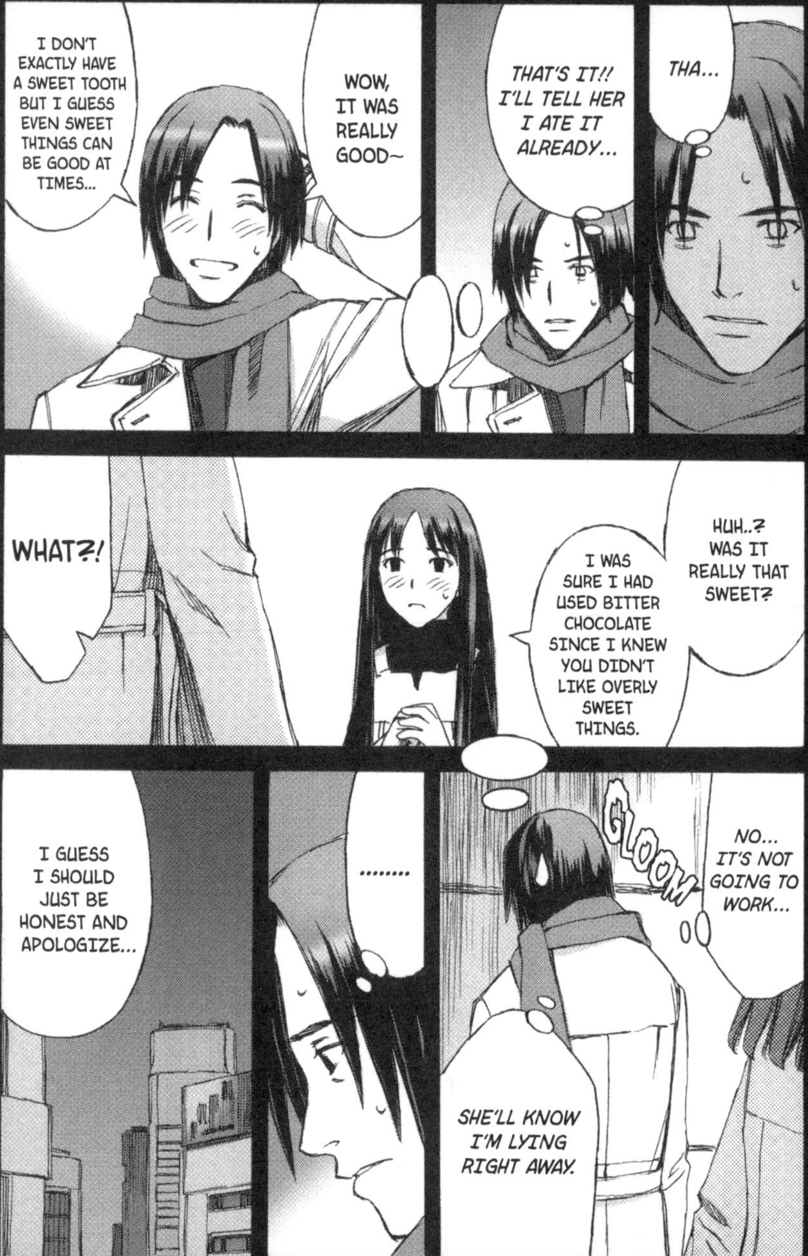
THA...
THAT'S IT!! I'LL TELL HER I ATE IT ALREADY...
WOW, IT WAS REALLY GOOD~
I DON'T EXACTLY HAVE A SWEET TOOTH BUT I GUESS EVEN SWEET THINGS CAN BE GOOD AT TIMES...
HUH..? WAS IT REALLY THAT SWEET?
I WAS SURE I HAD USED BITTER CHOCOLATE SINCE I KNEW YOU DIDN'T LIKE OVERLY SWEET THINGS.
WHAT?!
NO... IT'S NOT GOING TO WORK...
GLOOM
SHE'LL KNOW I'M LYING RIGHT AWAY.
....
I GUESS I SHOULD JUST BE HONEST AND APOLOGIZE...

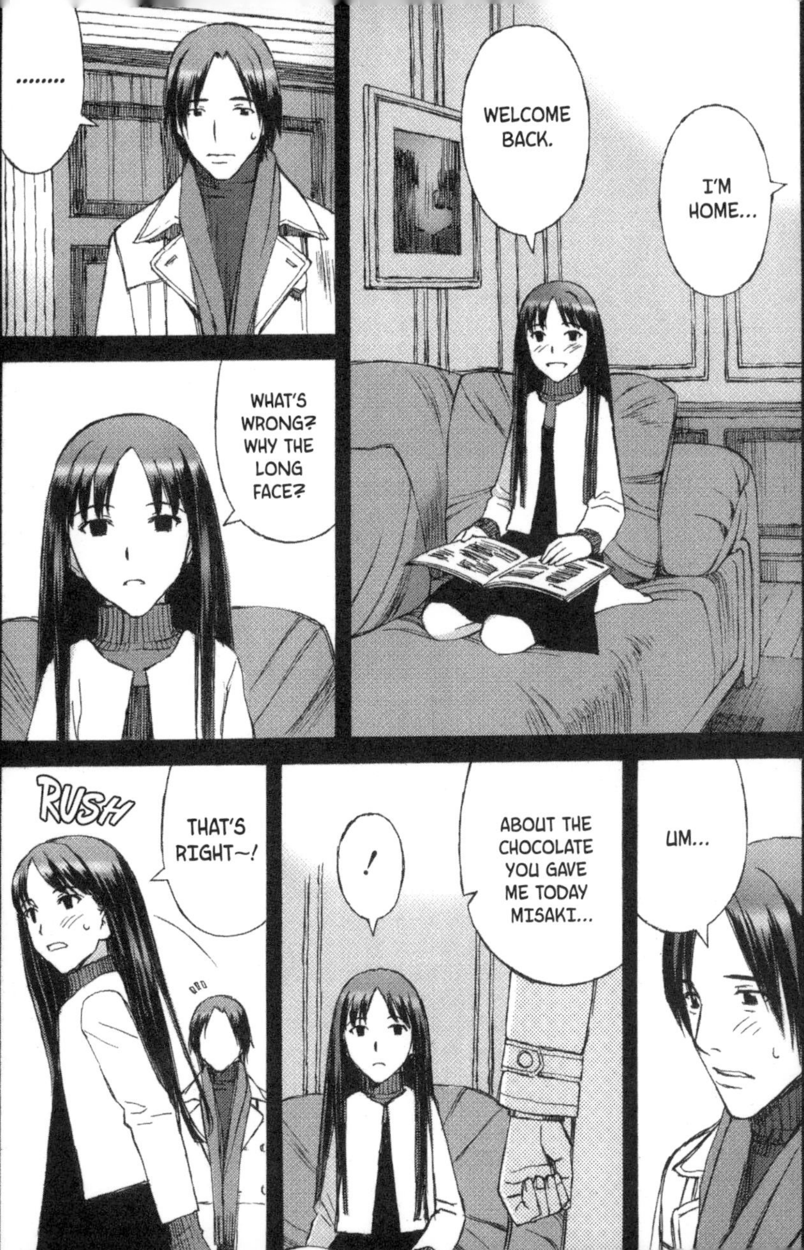
I'M HOME...
WELCOME BACK.
....
WHAT'S WRONG? WHY THE LONG FACE?
UM...
ABOUT THE CHOCOLATE YOU GAVE ME TODAY MISAKI...
!
THAT'S RIGHT~!
RUSH

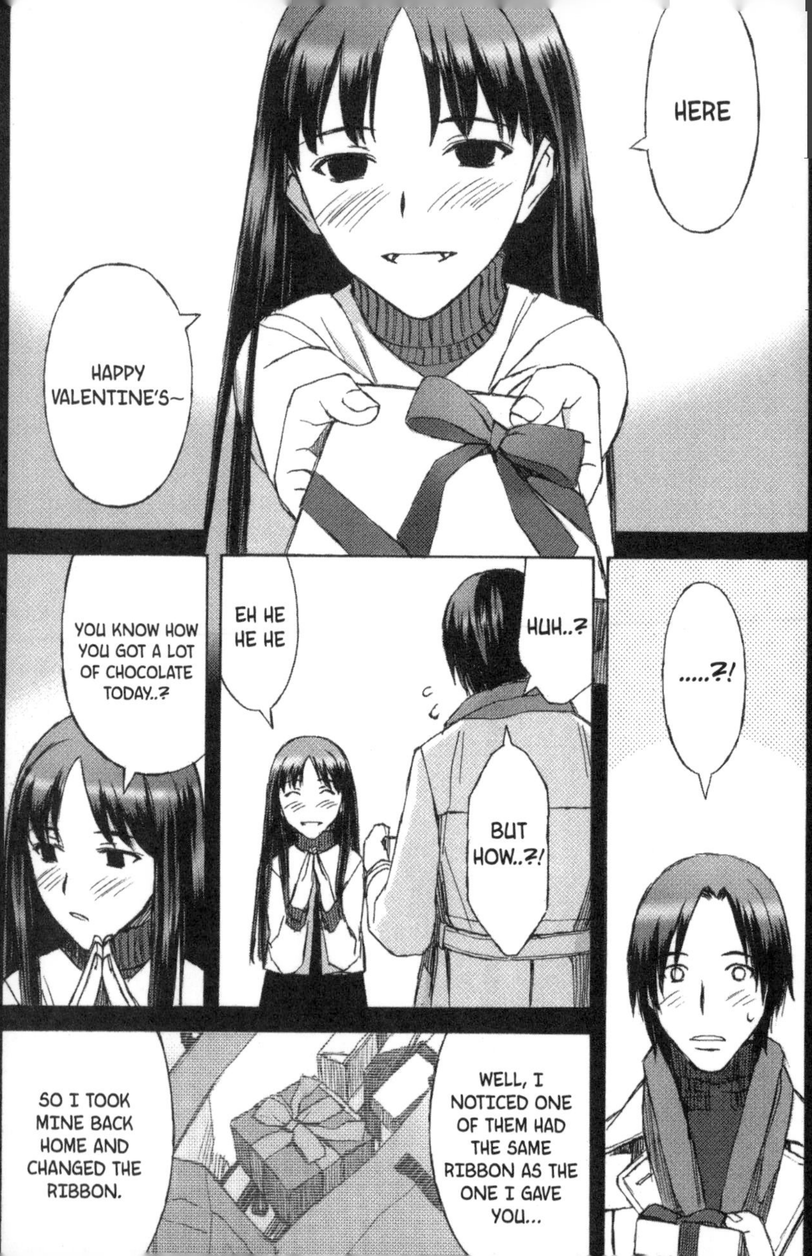
HERE
HAPPY VALENTINE'S~
.....?!
HUH..?
BUT HOW..?!
EH HE HE HE
YOU KNOW HOW YOU GOT A LOT OF CHOCOLATE TODAY..?
WELL, I NOTICED ONE OF THEM HAD THE SAME RIBBON AS THE ONE I GAVE YOU...
SO I TOOK MINE BACK HOME AND CHANGED THE RIBBON.

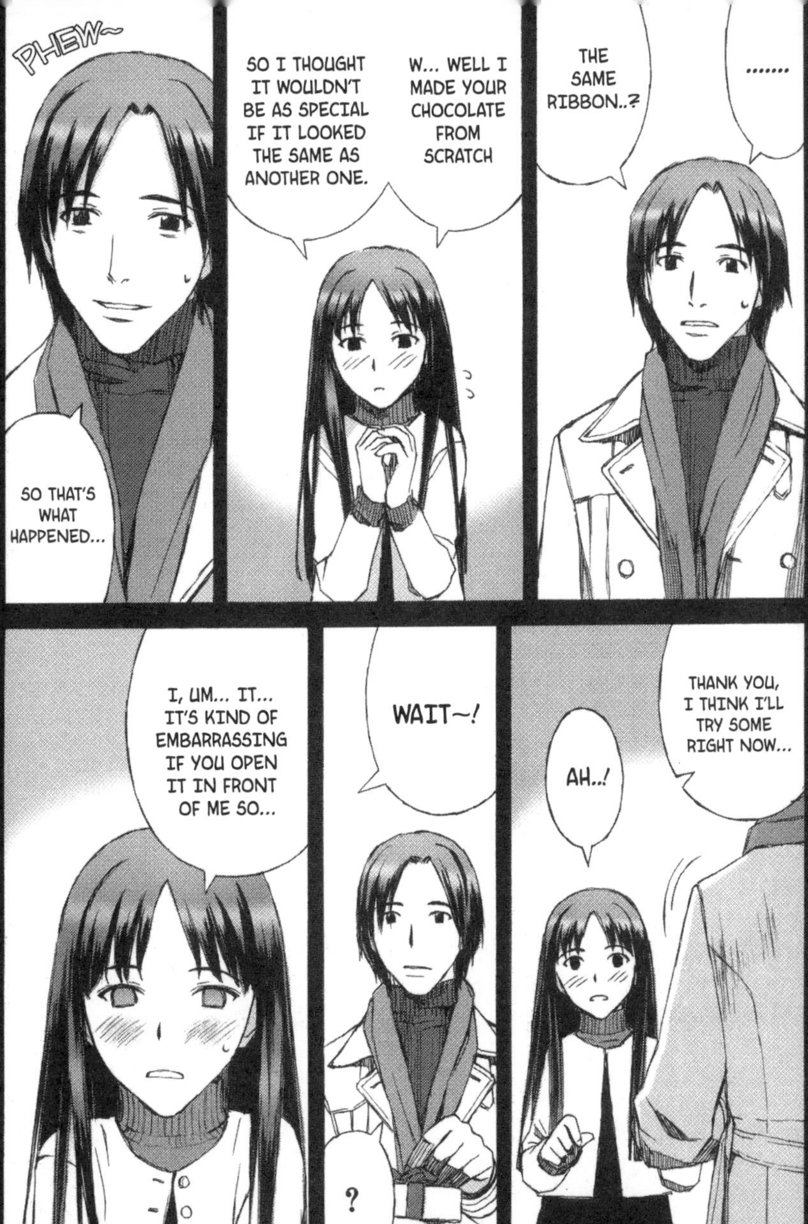
....
THE SAME RIBBON..?
W... WELL I MADE YOUR CHOCOLATE FROM SCRATCH
SO I THOUGHT IT WOULDN'T BE AS SPECIAL IF IT LOOKED THE SAME AS ANOTHER ONE.
PHEW~
SO THAT'S WHAT HAPPENED...
THANK YOU, I THINK I'LL TRY SOME RIGHT NOW...
AH..!
WAIT~!
?
I, UM... IT... IT'S KIND OF EMBARRASSING IF YOU OPEN IT IN FRONT OF ME SO...

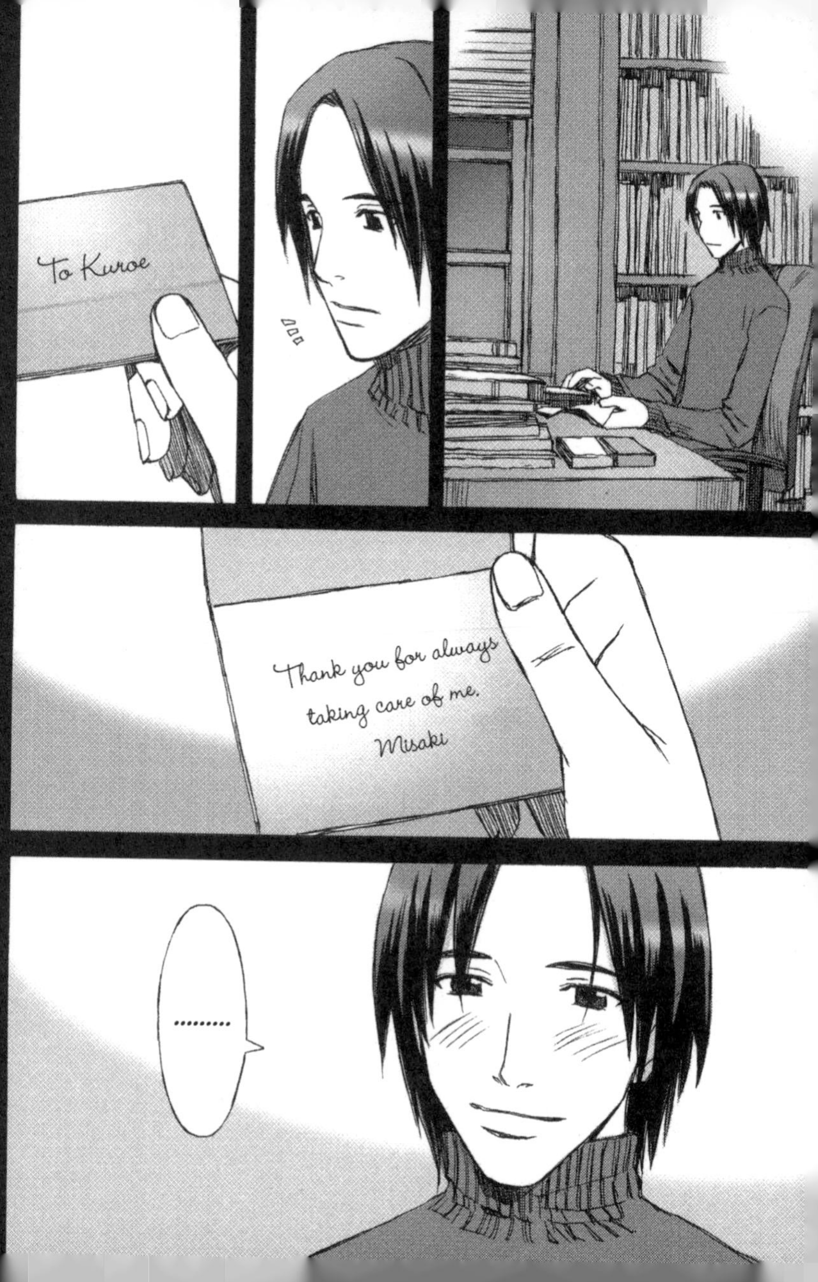
To Kuroe
Thank you for always taking care of me. Misaki
....

Episode 12
WHY CRY? part 1
真紅の剣 – The Crimson Sword

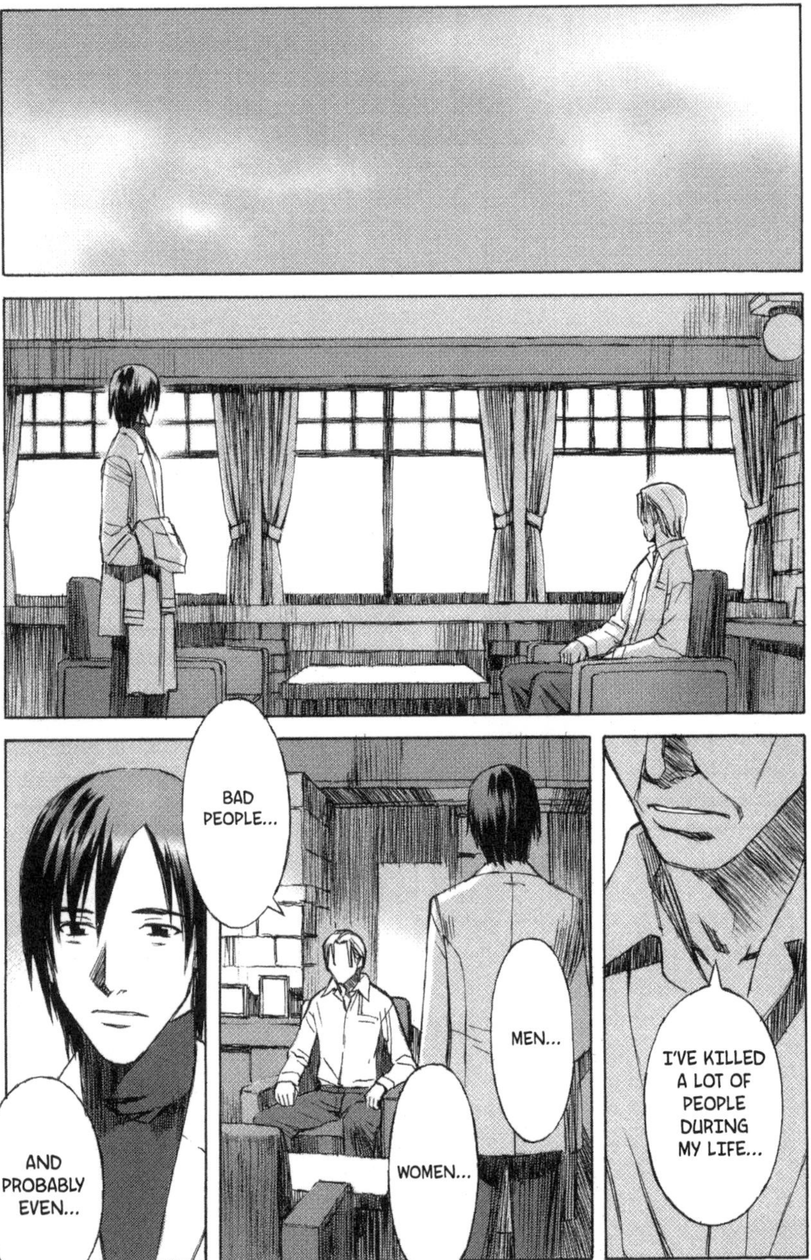
I'VE KILLED A LOT OF PEOPLE DURING MY LIFE...
MEN...
WOMEN...
BAD PEOPLE...
AND PROBABLY EVEN...

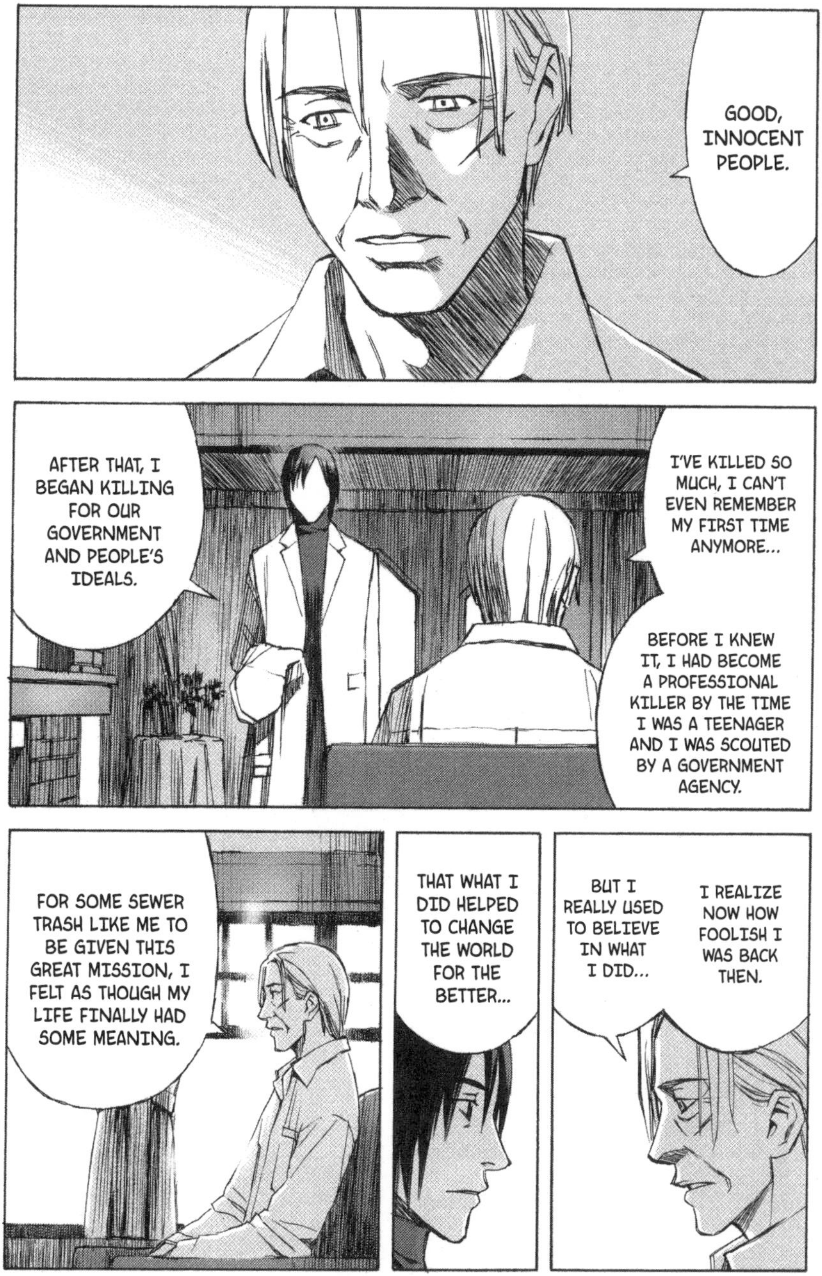
GOOD, INNOCENT PEOPLE.
I'VE KILLED SO MUCH, I CAN'T EVEN REMEMBER MY FIRST TIME ANYMORE...
BEFORE I KNEW IT, I HAD BECOME A PROFESSIONAL KILLER BY THE TIME I WAS A TEENAGER AND I WAS SCOUTED BY A GOVERNMENT AGENCY.
AFTER THAT, I BEGAN KILLING FOR OUR GOVERNMENT AND PEOPLE'S IDEALS.
I REALIZE NOW HOW FOOLISH I WAS BACK THEN.
BUT I REALLY USED TO BELIEVE IN WHAT I DID...
THAT WHAT I DID HELPED TO CHANGE THE WORLD FOR THE BETTER...
FOR SOME SEWER TRASH LIKE ME TO BE GIVEN THIS GREAT MISSION, I FELT AS THOUGH MY LIFE FINALLY HAD SOME MEANING.

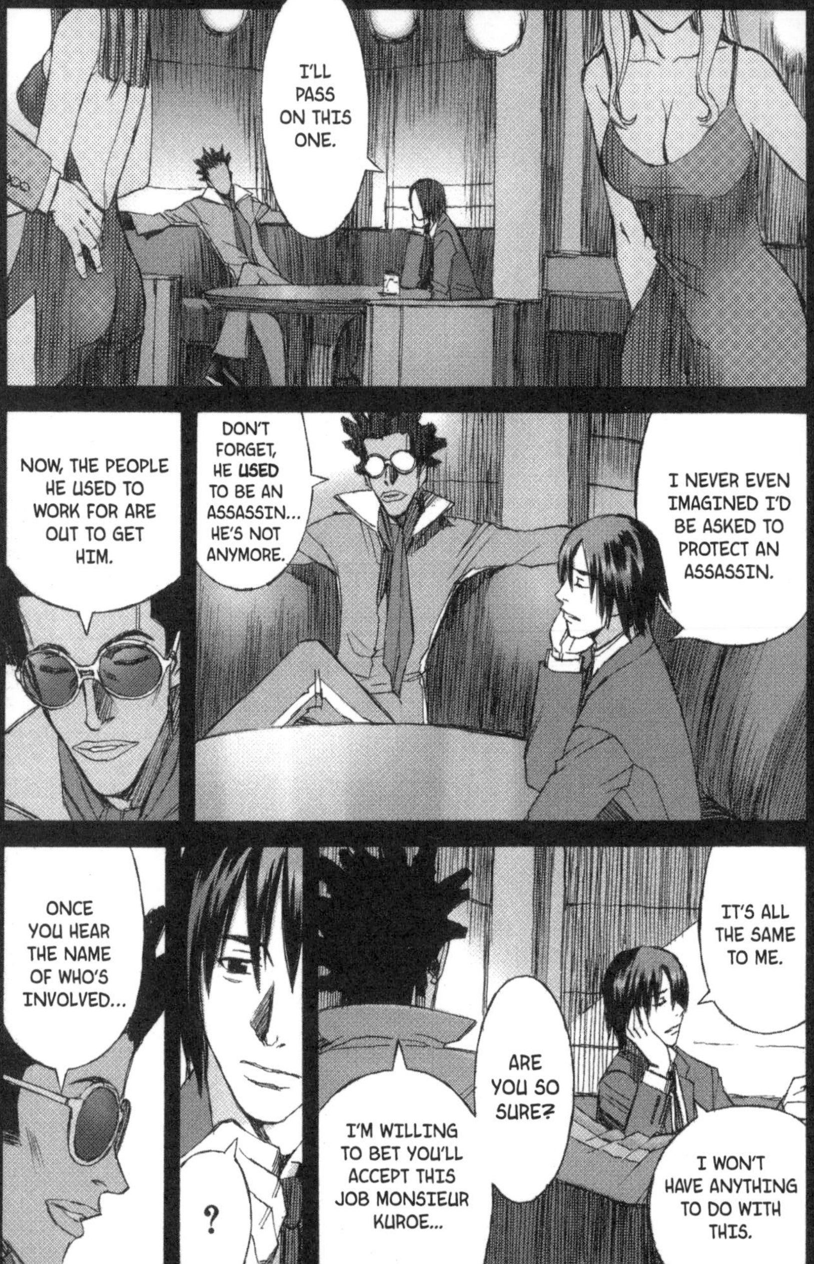
I'LL PASS ON THIS ONE.
I NEVER EVEN IMAGINED I'D BE ASKED TO PROTECT AN ASSASSIN.
DON'T FORGET, HE **USED** TO BE AN ASSASSIN... HE'S NOT ANYMORE.
NOW, THE PEOPLE HE USED TO WORK FOR ARE OUT TO GET HIM.
IT'S ALL THE SAME TO ME.
ARE YOU SO SURE?
I WON'T HAVE ANYTHING TO DO WITH THIS.
I'M WILLING TO BET YOU'LL ACCEPT THIS JOB MONSIEUR KUROE...
?
ONCE YOU HEAR THE NAME OF WHO'S INVOLVED...

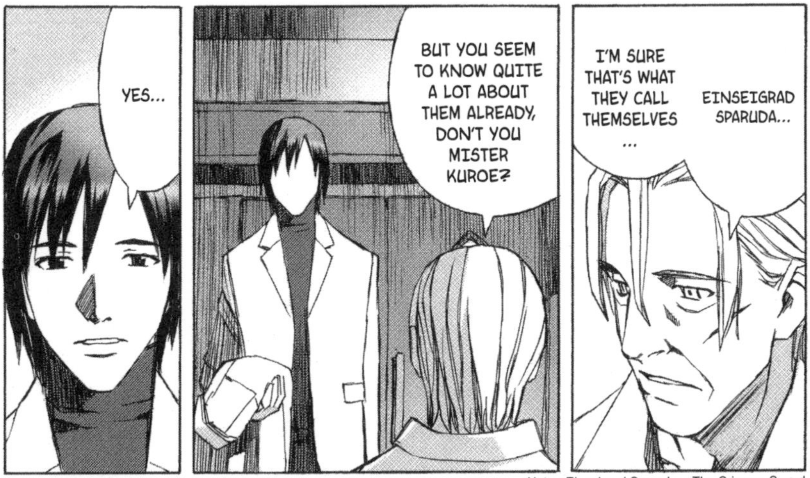
EINSEIGRAD SPARUDA...
I'M SURE THAT'S WHAT THEY CALL THEMSELVES ...
BUT YOU SEEM TO KNOW QUITE A LOT ABOUT THEM ALREADY, DON'T YOU MISTER KUROE?
YES...

Note : Einseigrad Sparuda = The Crimson Sword

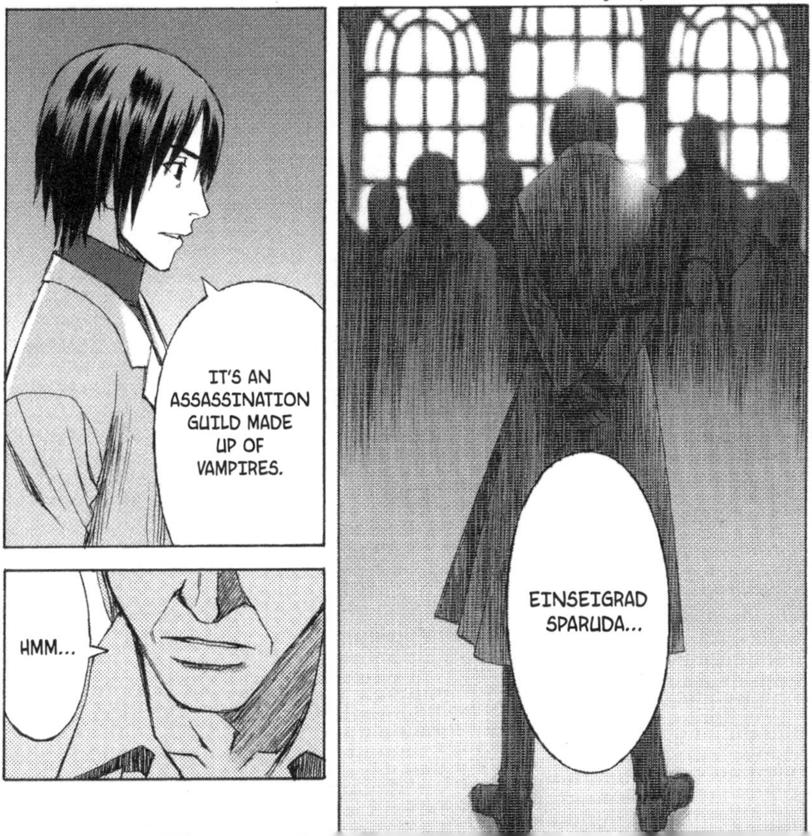
EINSEIGRAD SPARUDA...
IT'S AN ASSASSINATION GUILD MADE UP OF VAMPIRES.
HMM...

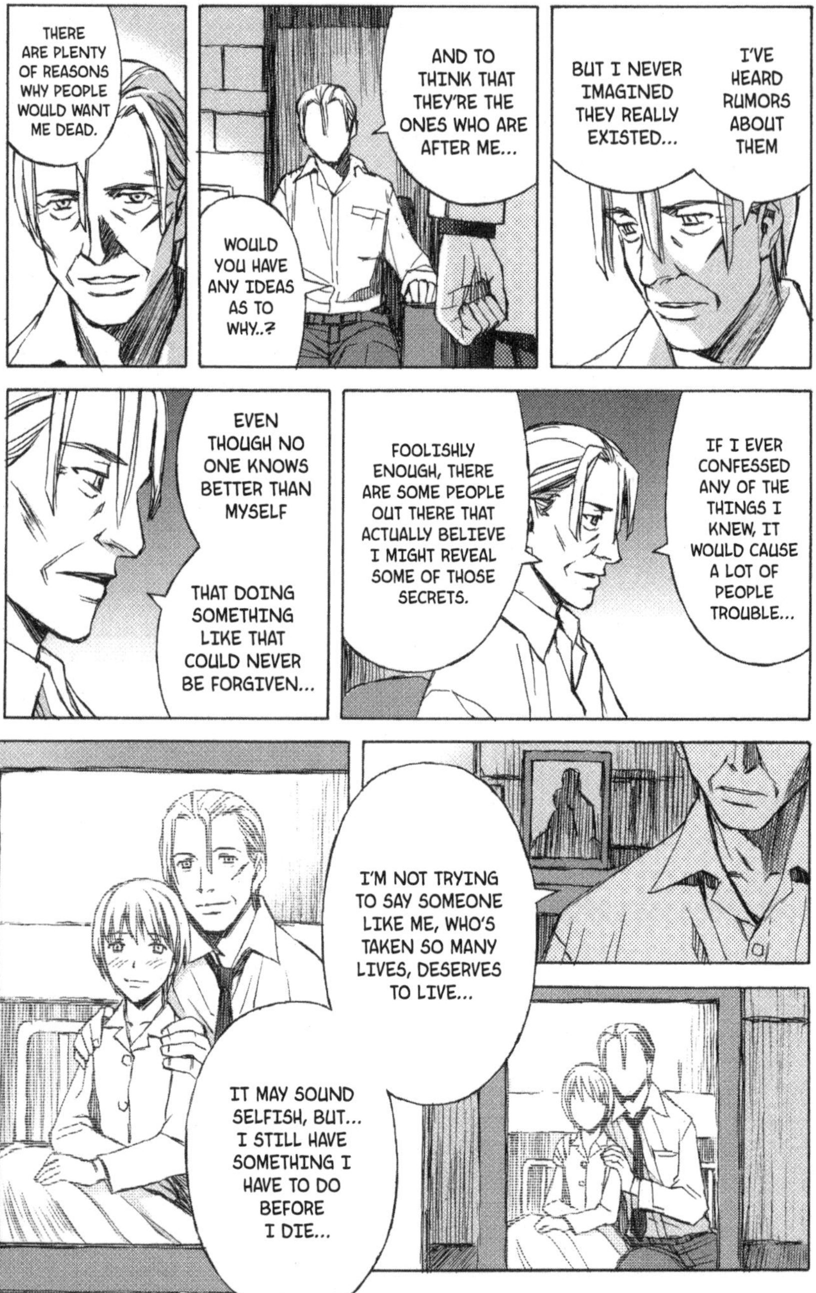
I'VE HEARD RUMORS ABOUT THEM
BUT I NEVER IMAGINED THEY REALLY EXISTED...
AND TO THINK THAT THEY'RE THE ONES WHO ARE AFTER ME...
WOULD YOU HAVE ANY IDEAS AS TO WHY..?
THERE ARE PLENTY OF REASONS WHY PEOPLE WOULD WANT ME DEAD.
IF I EVER CONFESSED ANY OF THE THINGS I KNEW, IT WOULD CAUSE A LOT OF PEOPLE TROUBLE...
FOOLISHLY ENOUGH, THERE ARE SOME PEOPLE OUT THERE THAT ACTUALLY BELIEVE I MIGHT REVEAL SOME OF THOSE SECRETS.
EVEN THOUGH NO ONE KNOWS BETTER THAN MYSELF
THAT DOING SOMETHING LIKE THAT COULD NEVER BE FORGIVEN...
I'M NOT TRYING TO SAY SOMEONE LIKE ME, WHO'S TAKEN SO MANY LIVES, DESERVES TO LIVE...
IT MAY SOUND SELFISH, BUT... I STILL HAVE SOMETHING I HAVE TO DO BEFORE I DIE...

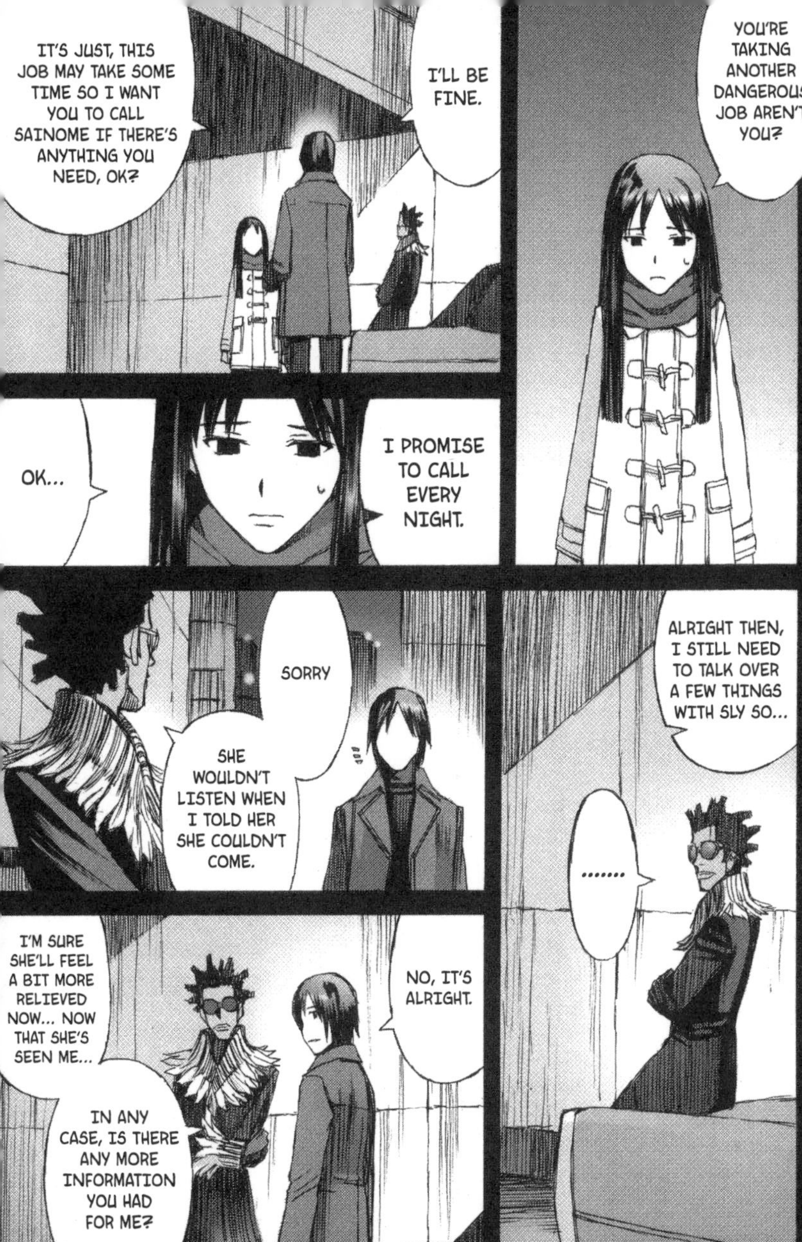
YOU'RE TAKING ANOTHER DANGEROUS JOB AREN'T YOU?
I'LL BE FINE.
IT'S JUST, THIS JOB MAY TAKE SOME TIME SO I WANT YOU TO CALL SAINOME IF THERE'S ANYTHING YOU NEED, OK?
I PROMISE TO CALL EVERY NIGHT.
OK...
ALRIGHT THEN, I STILL NEED TO TALK OVER A FEW THINGS WITH SLY SO...
....
SORRY
SHE WOULDN'T LISTEN WHEN I TOLD HER SHE COULDN'T COME.
NO, IT'S ALRIGHT.
I'M SURE SHE'LL FEEL A BIT MORE RELIEVED NOW... NOW THAT SHE'S SEEN ME...
IN ANY CASE, IS THERE ANY MORE INFORMATION YOU HAD FOR ME?

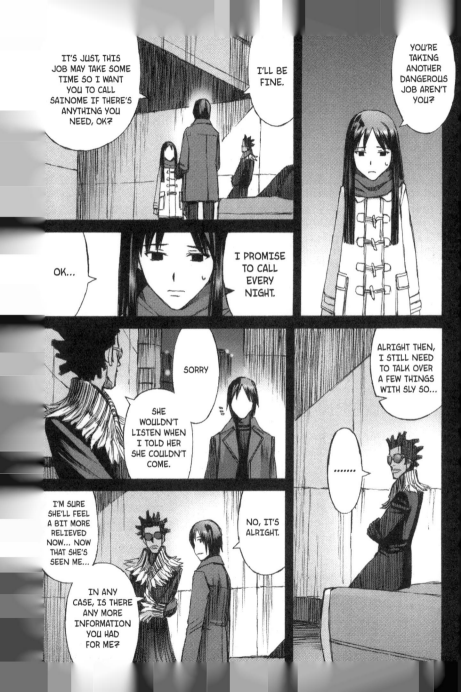

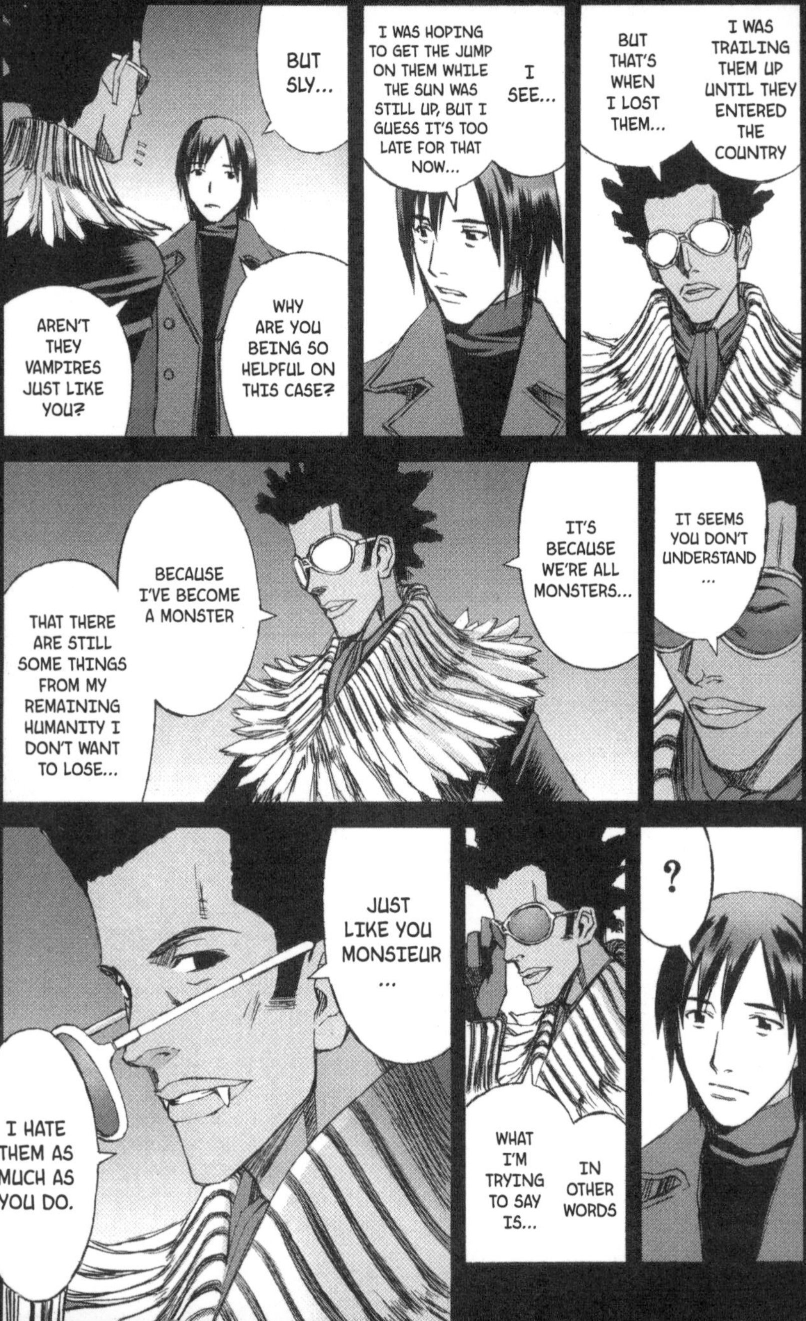
I WAS TRAILING THEM UP UNTIL THEY ENTERED THE COUNTRY
BUT THAT'S WHEN I LOST THEM...
I SEE...
I WAS HOPING TO GET THE JUMP ON THEM WHILE THE SUN WAS STILL UP, BUT I GUESS IT'S TOO LATE FOR THAT NOW...
BUT SLY...
WHY ARE YOU BEING SO HELPFUL ON THIS CASE?
AREN'T THEY VAMPIRES JUST LIKE YOU?
IT SEEMS YOU DON'T UNDERSTAND ...
IT'S BECAUSE WE'RE ALL MONSTERS...
BECAUSE I'VE BECOME A MONSTER
THAT THERE ARE STILL SOME THINGS FROM MY REMAINING HUMANITY I DON'T WANT TO LOSE...
?
IN OTHER WORDS
WHAT I'M TRYING TO SAY IS...
JUST LIKE YOU MONSIEUR ...
I HATE THEM AS MUCH AS YOU DO.

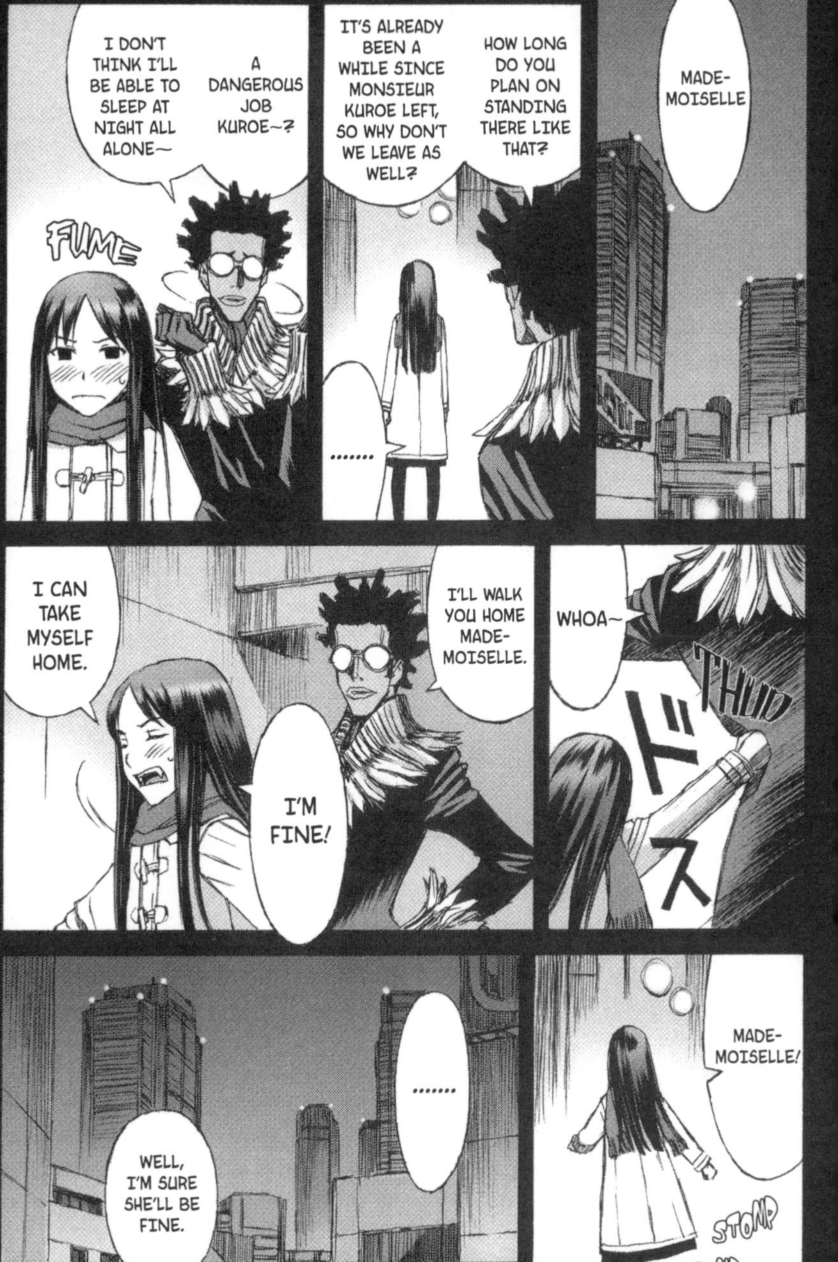
MADE-MOISELLE
HOW LONG DO YOU PLAN ON STANDING THERE LIKE THAT?
IT'S ALREADY BEEN A WHILE SINCE MONSIEUR KUROE LEFT, SO WHY DON'T WE LEAVE AS WELL?
....
A DANGEROUS JOB KUROE~?
I DON'T THINK I'LL BE ABLE TO SLEEP AT NIGHT ALL ALONE~
FUME
WHOA~
THUD
ドス
I'LL WALK YOU HOME MADE-MOISELLE.
I'M FINE!
I CAN TAKE MYSELF HOME.
MADE-MOISELLE!
STOMP
STOMP
....
WELL, I'M SURE SHE'LL BE FINE.

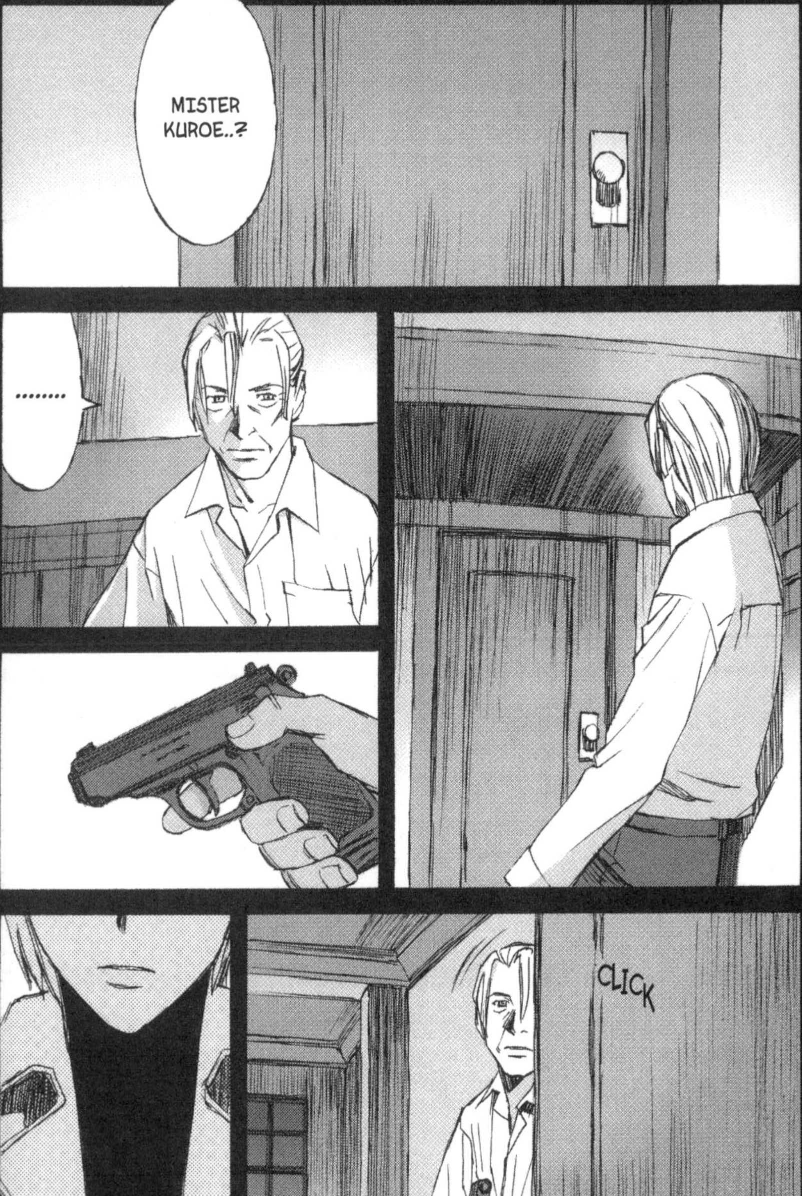
MISTER KUROE..?
....
CLICK

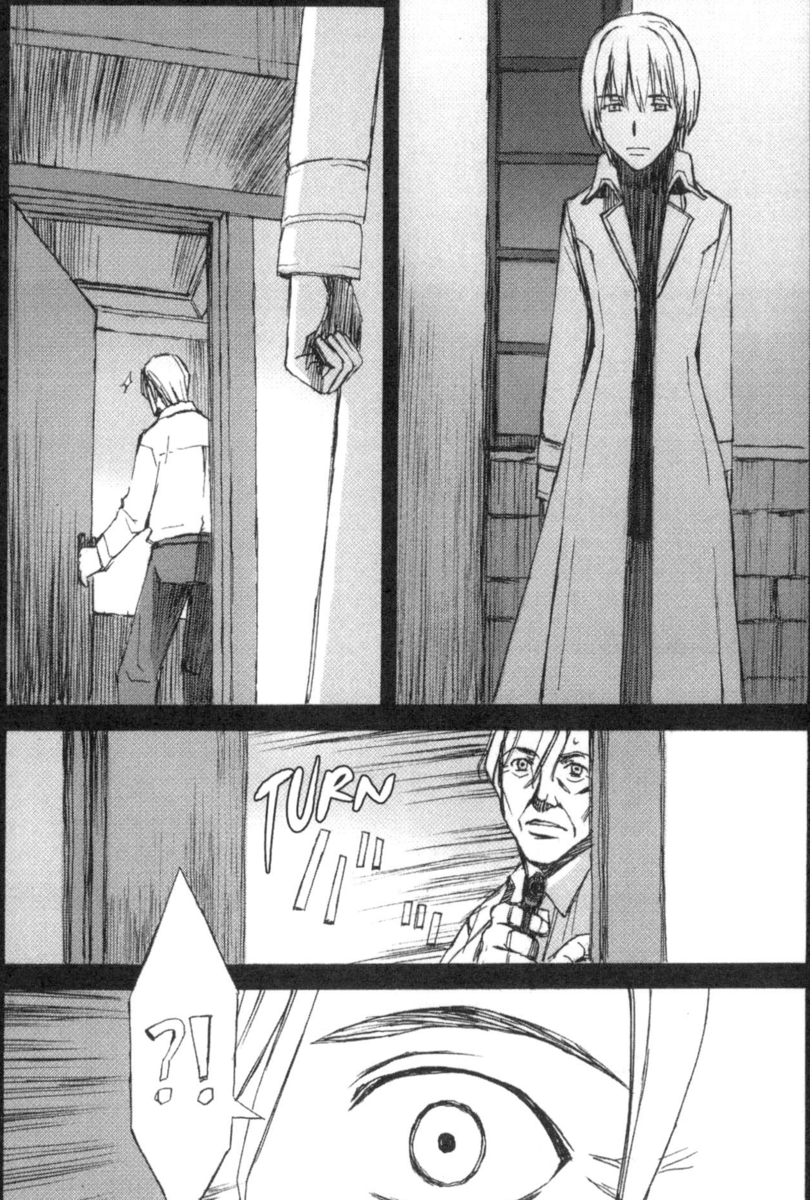
TURN
?!

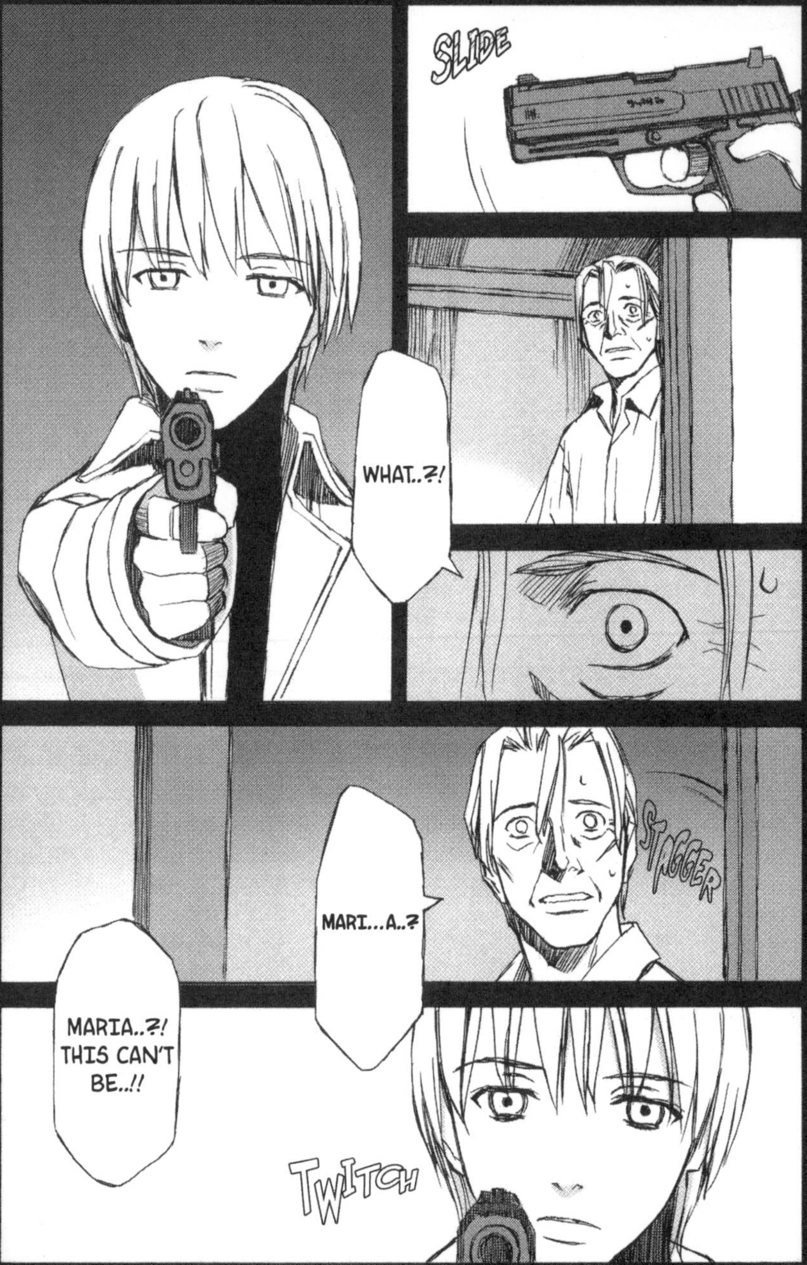
SLIDE
WHAT..?!
STAGGER
MARI...A..?
MARIA..?! THIS CAN'T BE..!!
TWITCH

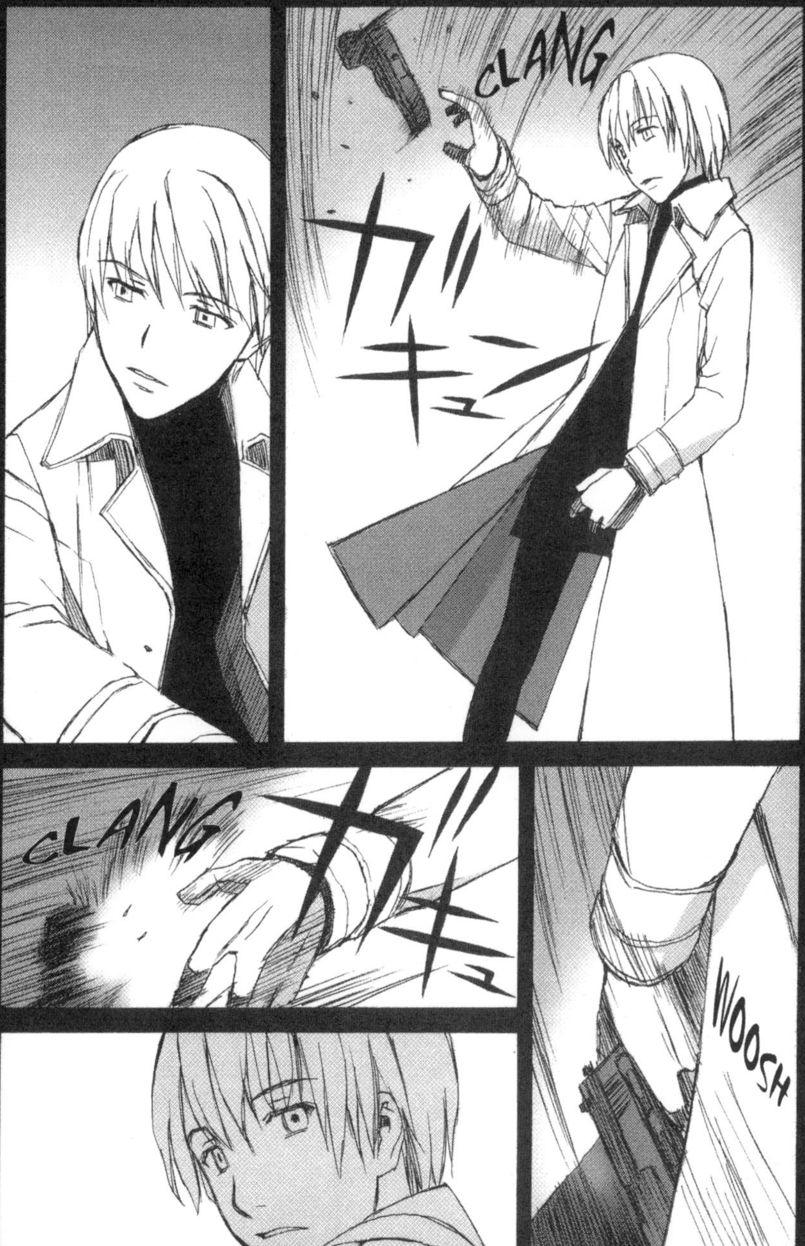
CLANG
カキュン
WOOSH
CLANG
カキュ

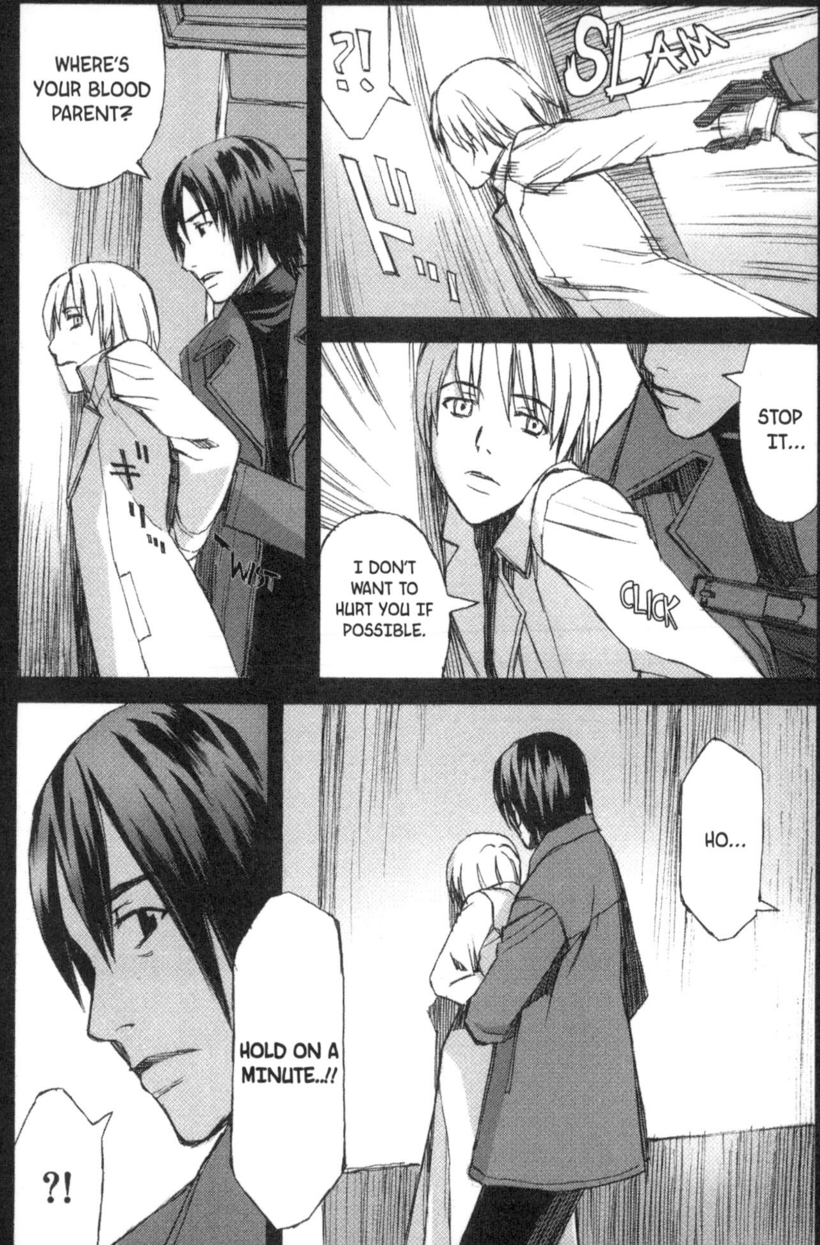
?!
SLAM
STOP IT...
I DON'T WANT TO HURT YOU IF POSSIBLE.
CLICK
WHERE'S YOUR BLOOD PARENT?
TWIST
HO...
HOLD ON A MINUTE..!!
?!

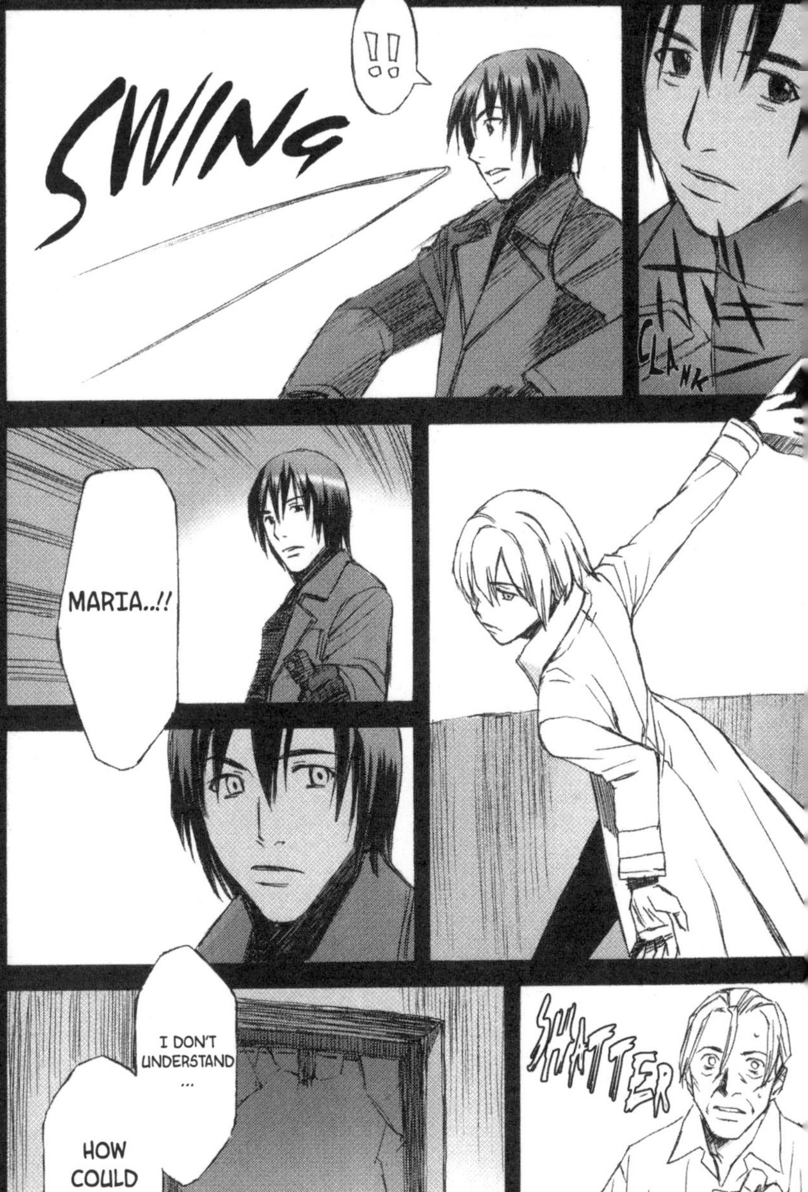
CLANK
!!
SWING
MARIA..!!
SHATTER
I DON'T UNDERSTAND ...
HOW COULD THIS BE..?

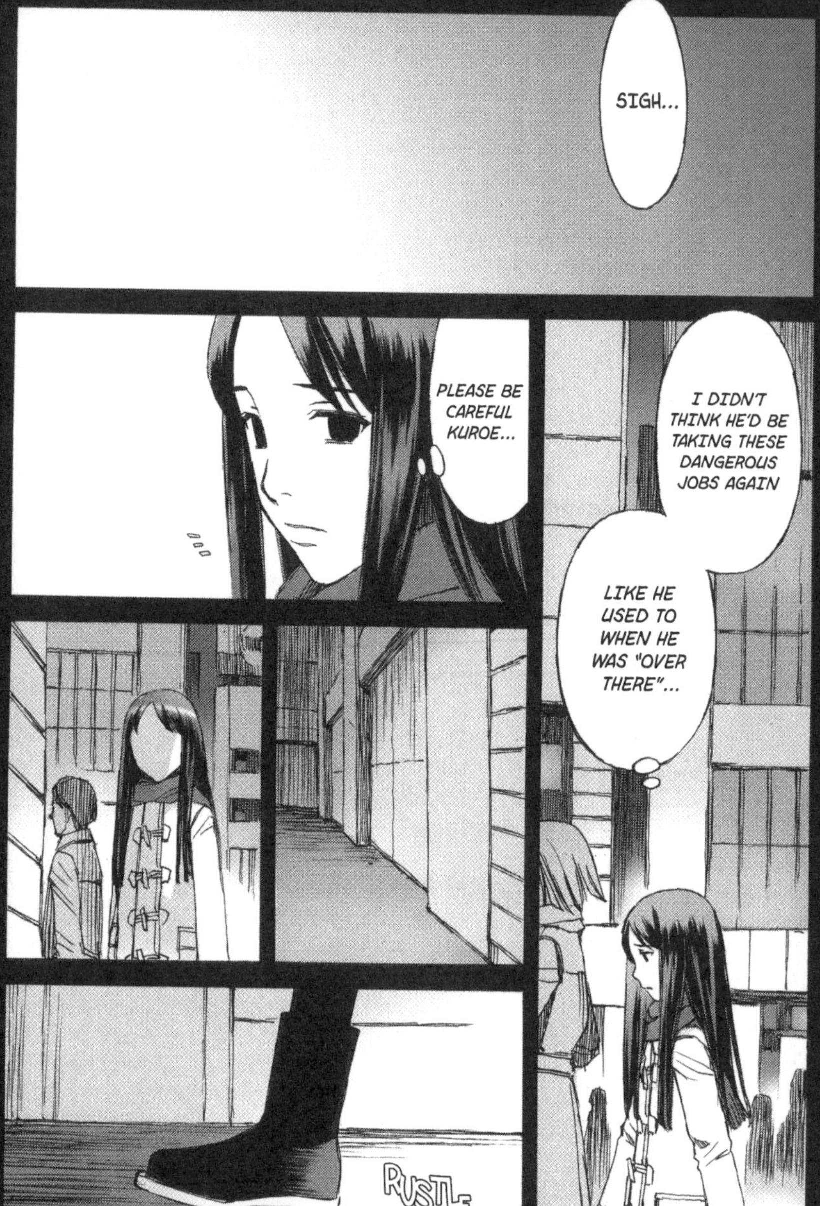

SIGH...
I DIDN'T THINK HE'D BE TAKING THESE DANGEROUS JOBS AGAIN
LIKE HE USED TO WHEN HE WAS "OVER THERE"...
PLEASE BE CAREFUL KUROE...
RUSTLE

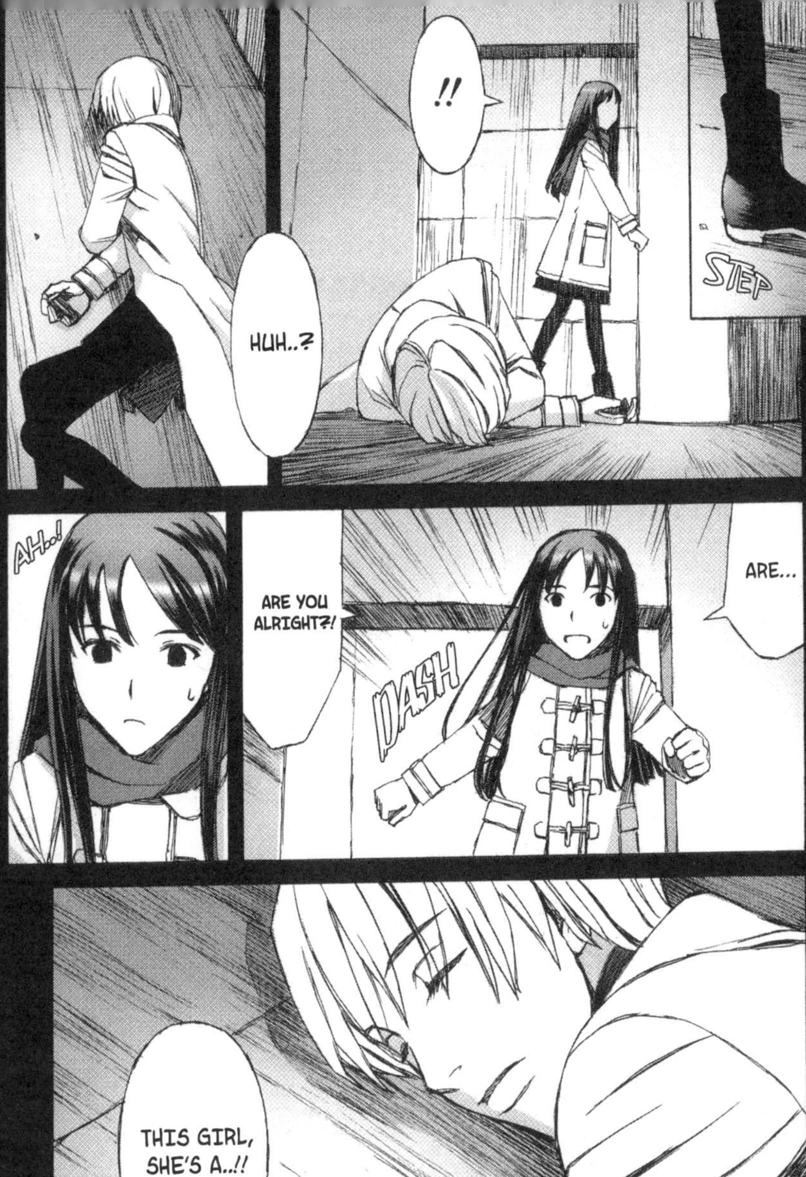
STEP
!!
HUH..?
ARE...
ARE YOU ALRIGHT?!
DASH
AH..!
THIS GIRL, SHE'S A..!!

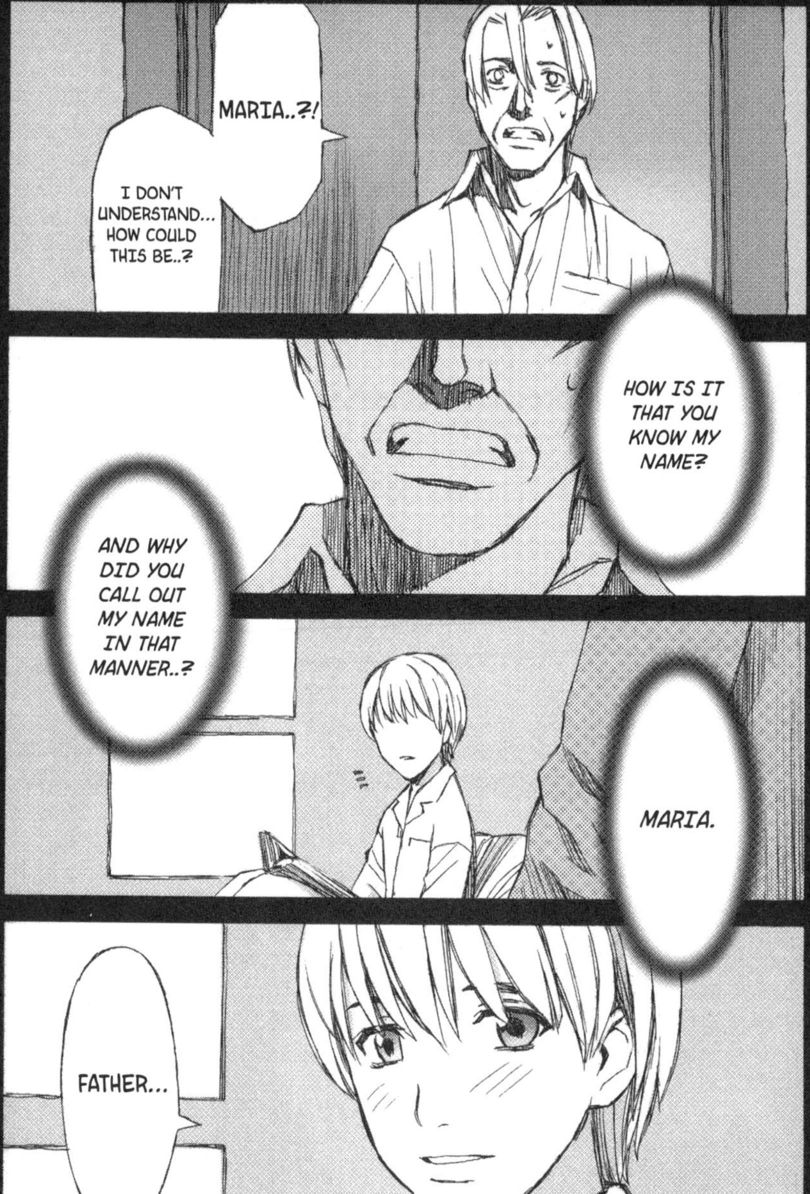
MARIA..?!
I DON'T UNDERSTAND... HOW COULD THIS BE..?
HOW IS IT THAT YOU KNOW MY NAME?
AND WHY DID YOU CALL OUT MY NAME IN THAT MANNER..?
MARIA.
FATHER...

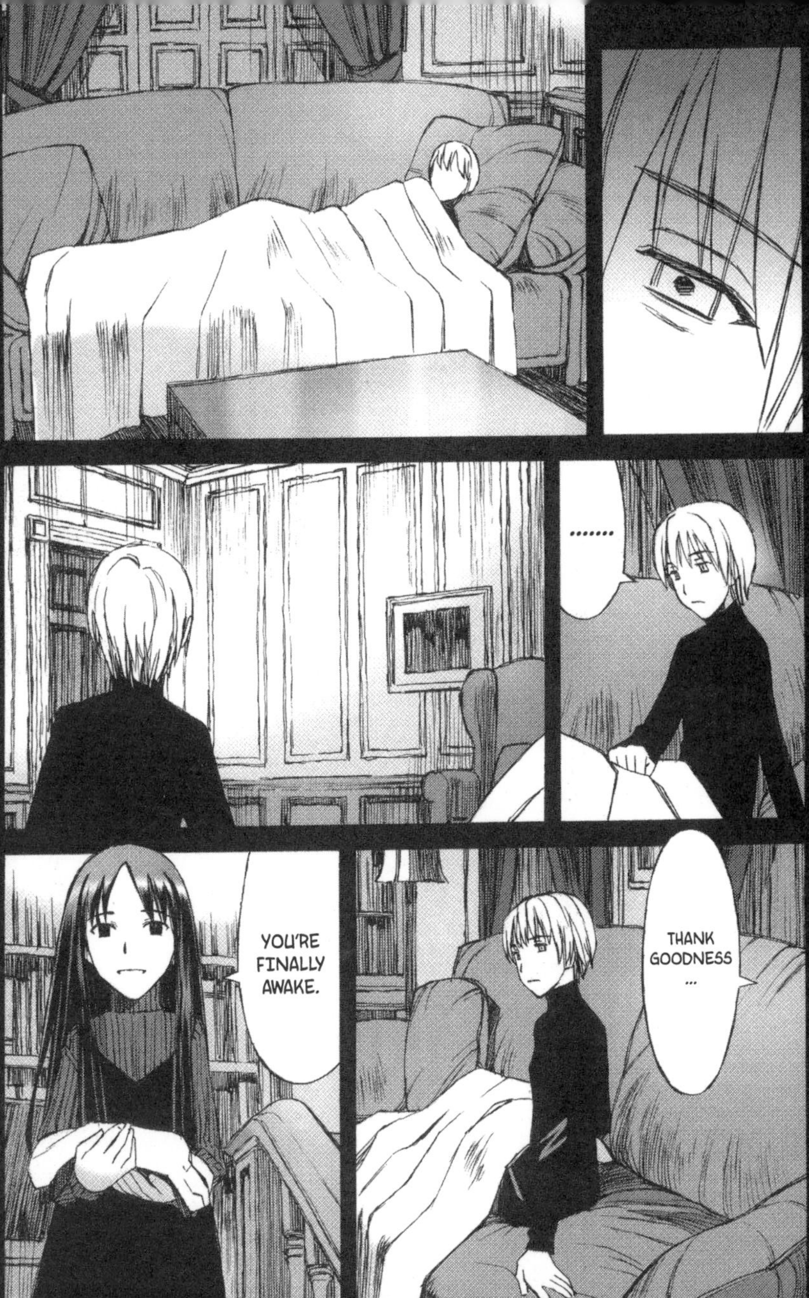
....
THANK GOODNESS ...
YOU'RE FINALLY AWAKE.

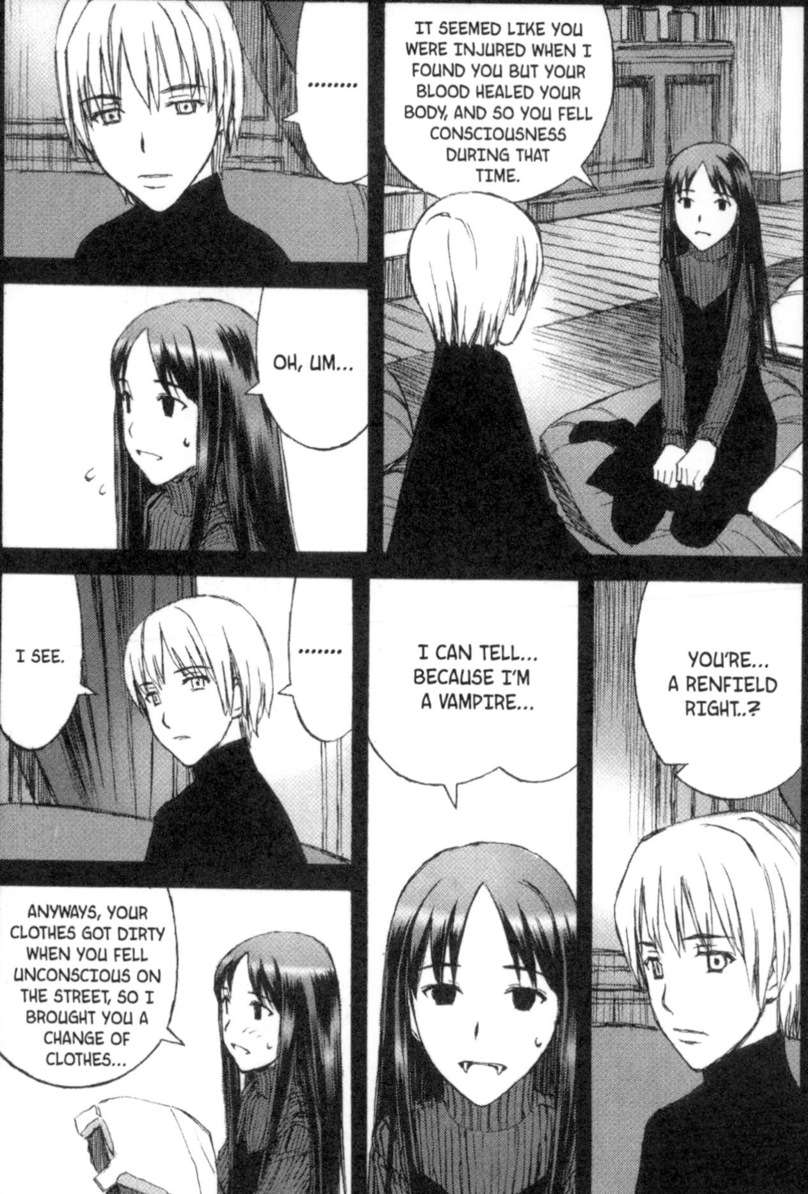
IT SEEMED LIKE YOU WERE INJURED WHEN I FOUND YOU BUT YOUR BLOOD HEALED YOUR BODY, AND SO YOU FELL CONSCIOUSNESS DURING THAT TIME.
....
OH, UM...
YOU'RE... A RENFIELD RIGHT..?
I CAN TELL... BECAUSE I'M A VAMPIRE...
....
I SEE.
ANYWAYS, YOUR CLOTHES GOT DIRTY WHEN YOU FELL UNCONSCIOUS ON THE STREET, SO I BROUGHT YOU A CHANGE OF CLOTHES...

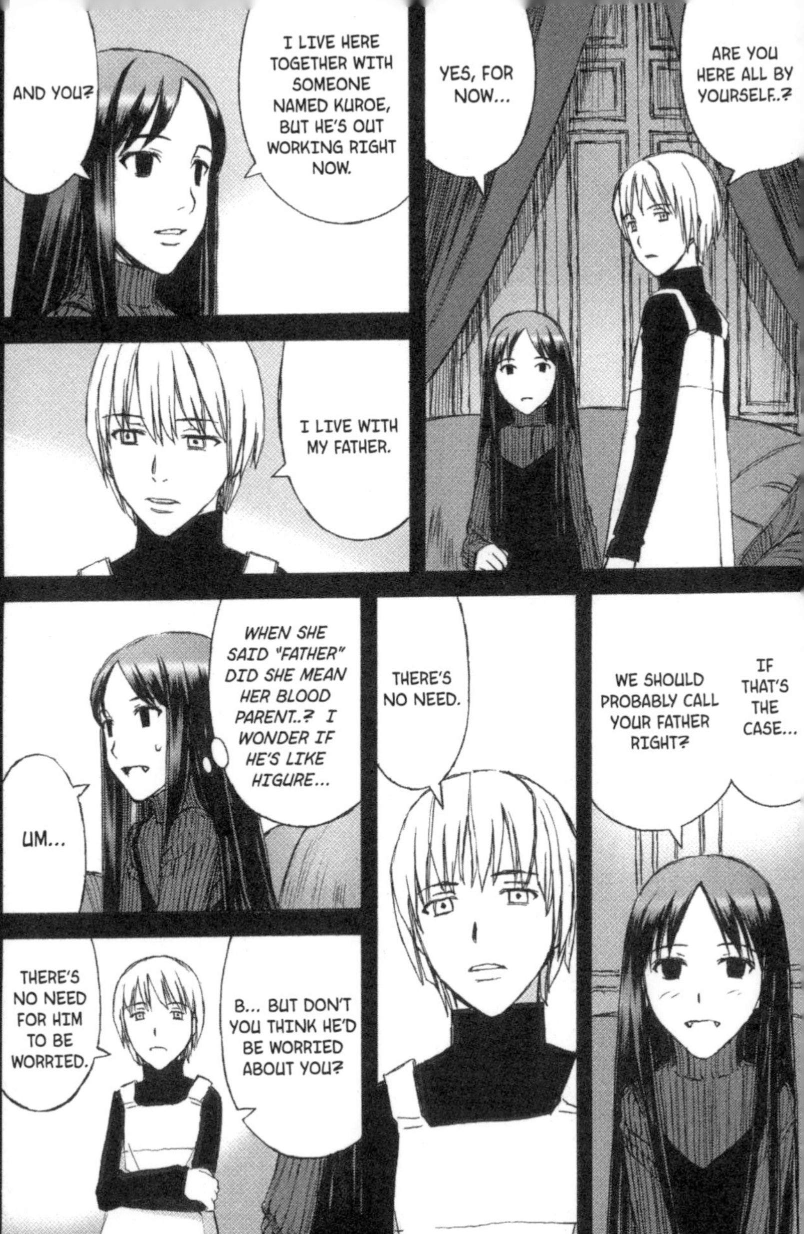
ARE YOU HERE ALL BY YOURSELF..?
YES, FOR NOW...
I LIVE HERE TOGETHER WITH SOMEONE NAMED KUROE, BUT HE'S OUT WORKING RIGHT NOW.
AND YOU?
I LIVE WITH MY FATHER.
IF THAT'S THE CASE...
WE SHOULD PROBABLY CALL YOUR FATHER RIGHT?
THERE'S NO NEED.
WHEN SHE SAID "FATHER" DID SHE MEAN HER BLOOD PARENT..? I WONDER IF HE'S LIKE HIGURE...
UM...
B... BUT DON'T YOU THINK HE'D BE WORRIED ABOUT YOU?
THERE'S NO NEED FOR HIM TO BE WORRIED.

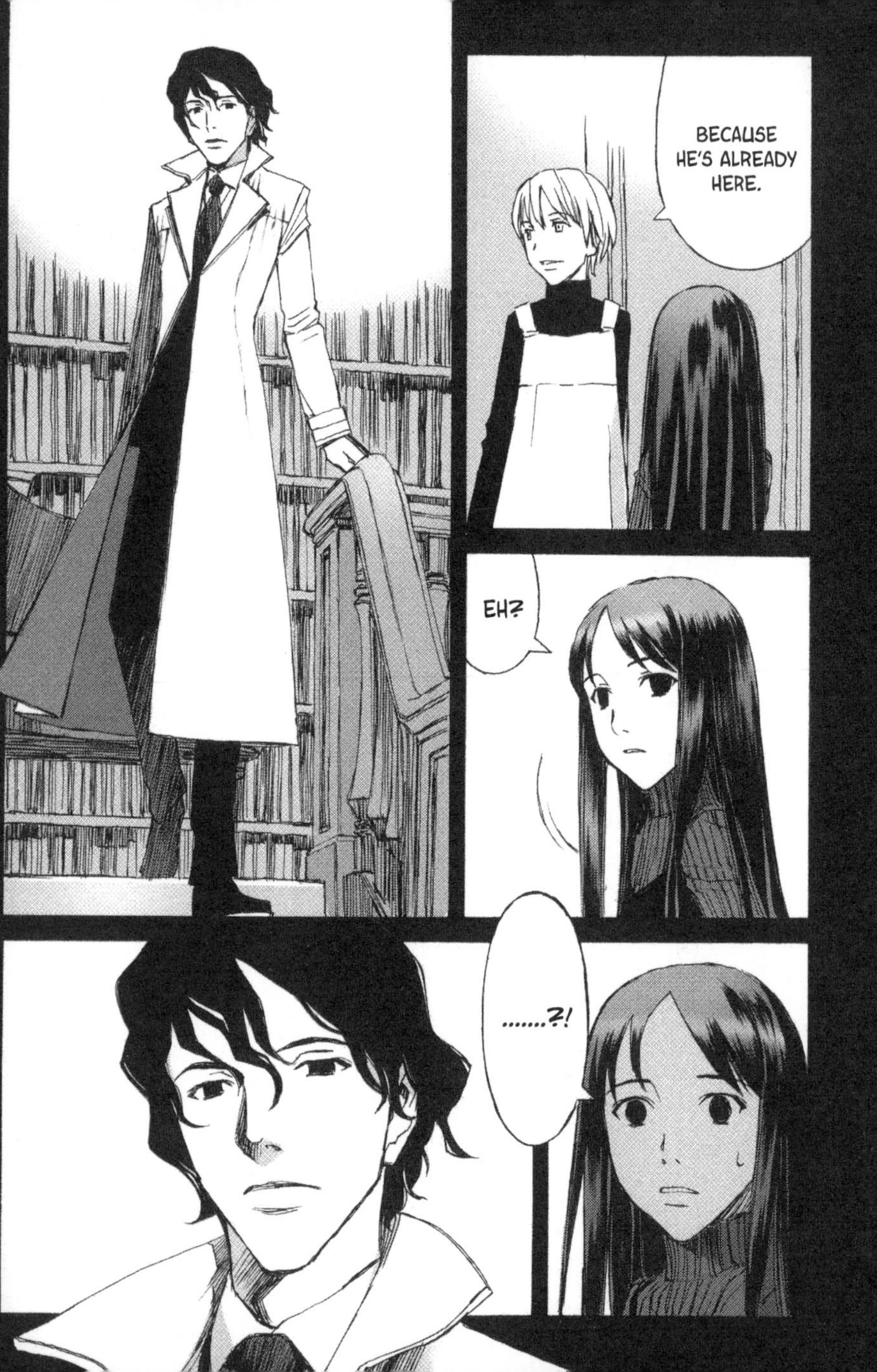
BECAUSE HE'S ALREADY HERE.
EH?
.......?!

Episode 13
WHY CRY? part 2

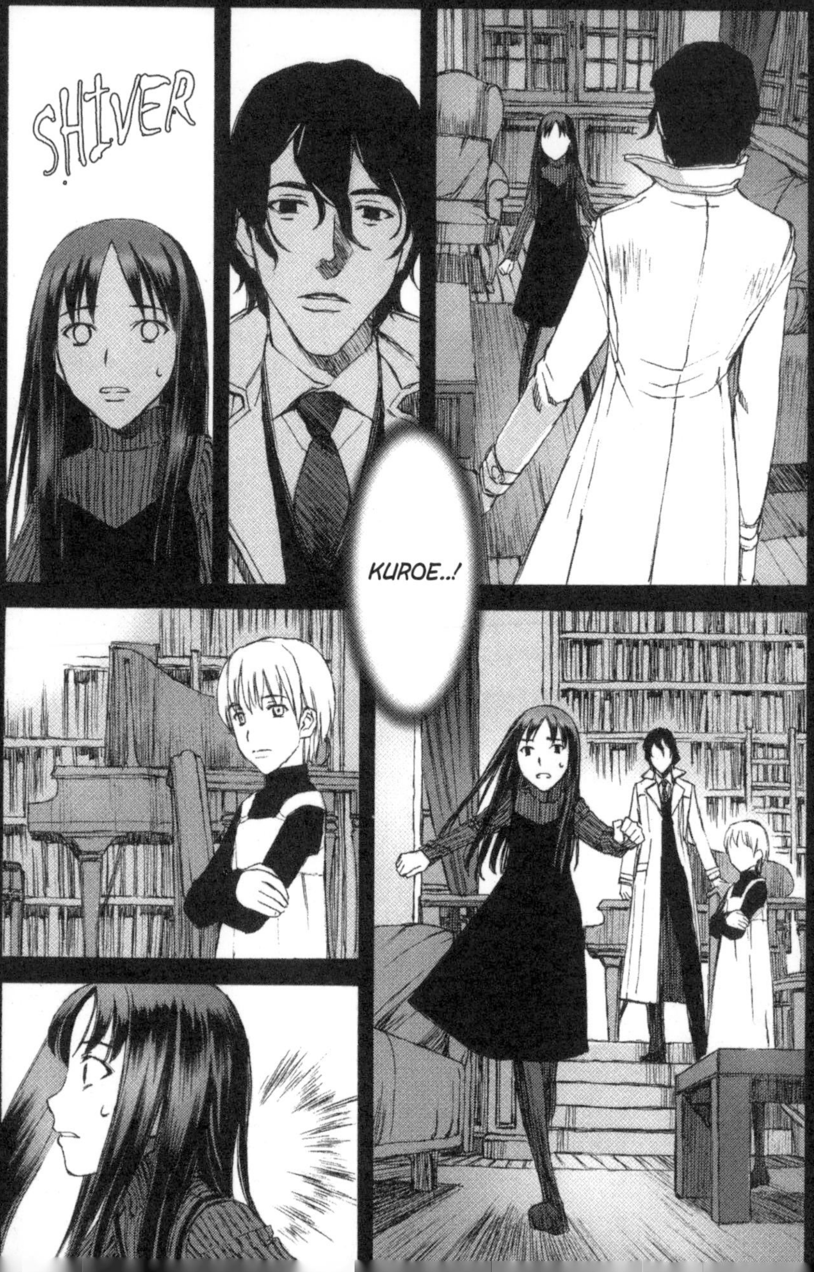
SHIVER
KUROE..!

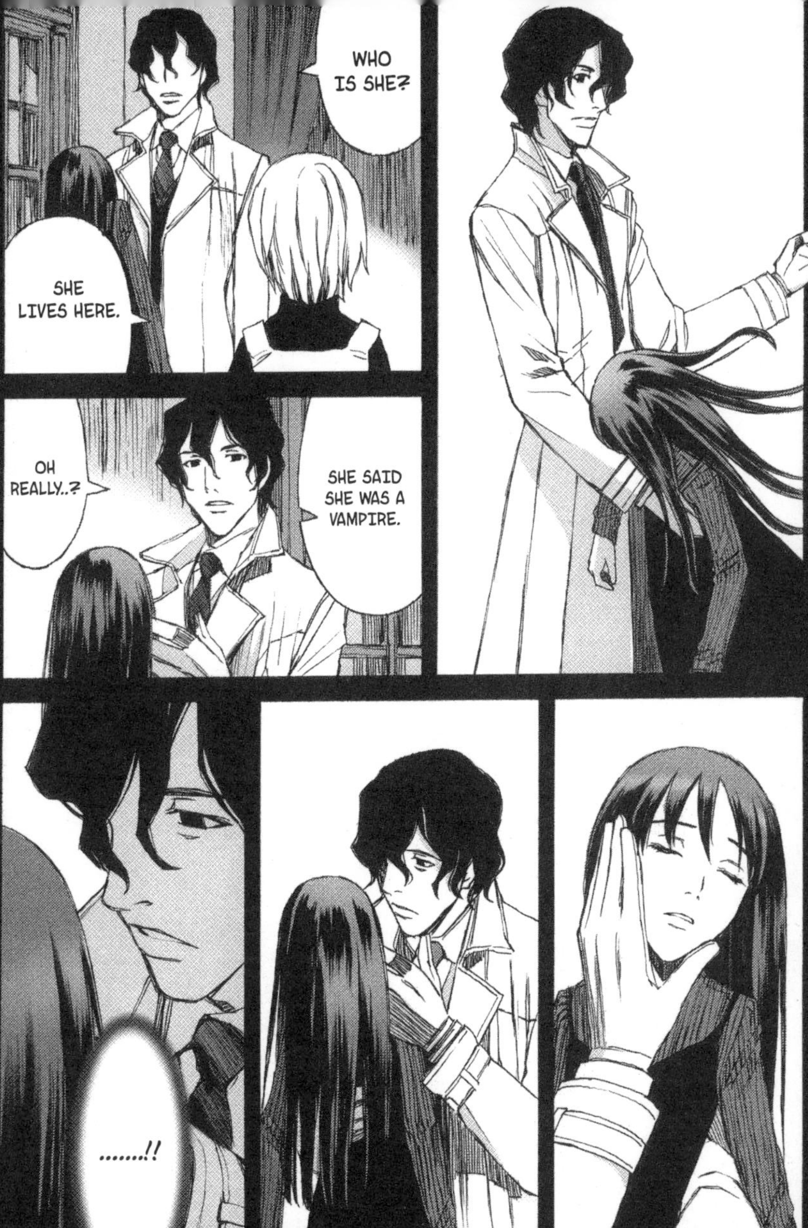
WHO IS SHE?
SHE LIVES HERE.
SHE SAID SHE WAS A VAMPIRE.
OH REALLY..?
........!!

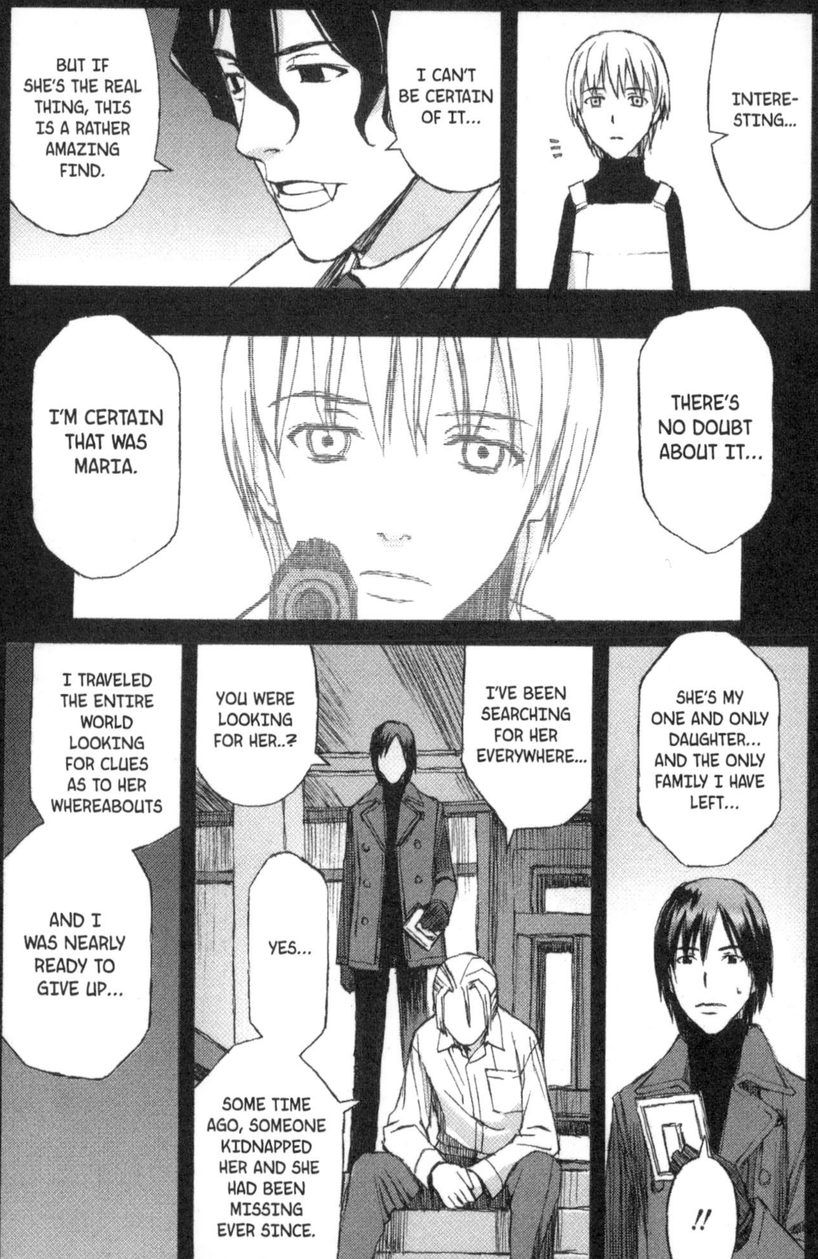
INTERE-STING...
I CAN'T BE CERTAIN OF IT...
BUT IF SHE'S THE REAL THING, THIS IS A RATHER AMAZING FIND.
THERE'S NO DOUBT ABOUT IT...
I'M CERTAIN THAT WAS MARIA.
SHE'S MY ONE AND ONLY DAUGHTER... AND THE ONLY FAMILY I HAVE LEFT...
!!
I'VE BEEN SEARCHING FOR HER EVERYWHERE...
YOU WERE LOOKING FOR HER..?
YES...
SOME TIME AGO, SOMEONE KIDNAPPED HER AND SHE HAD BEEN MISSING EVER SINCE.
I TRAVELED THE ENTIRE WORLD LOOKING FOR CLUES AS TO HER WHEREABOUTS
AND I WAS NEARLY READY TO GIVE UP...

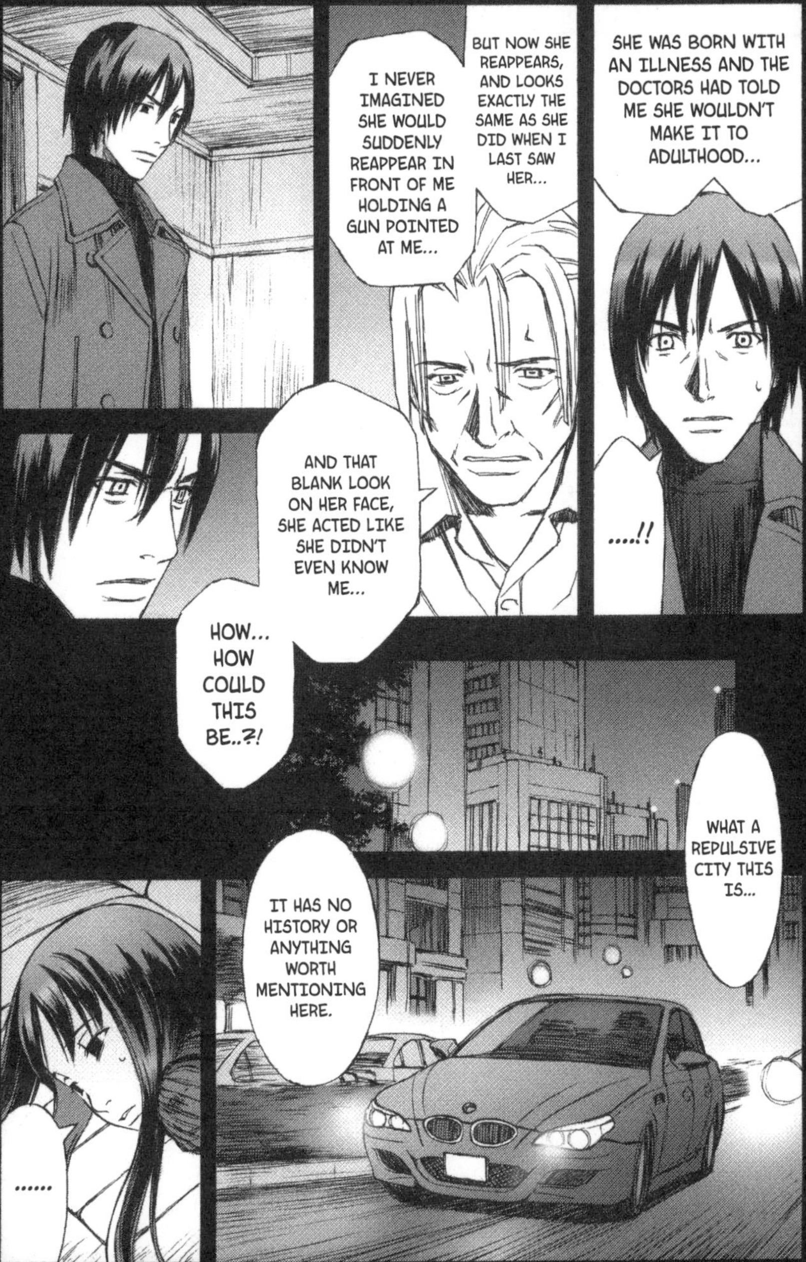
SHE WAS BORN WITH AN ILLNESS AND THE DOCTORS HAD TOLD ME SHE WOULDN'T MAKE IT TO ADULTHOOD...
....!!
BUT NOW SHE REAPPEARS, AND LOOKS EXACTLY THE SAME AS SHE DID WHEN I LAST SAW HER...
I NEVER IMAGINED SHE WOULD SUDDENLY REAPPEAR IN FRONT OF ME HOLDING A GUN POINTED AT ME...
AND THAT BLANK LOOK ON HER FACE, SHE ACTED LIKE SHE DIDN'T EVEN KNOW ME...
HOW... HOW COULD THIS BE..?!
WHAT A REPULSIVE CITY THIS IS...
IT HAS NO HISTORY OR ANYTHING WORTH MENTIONING HERE.
......

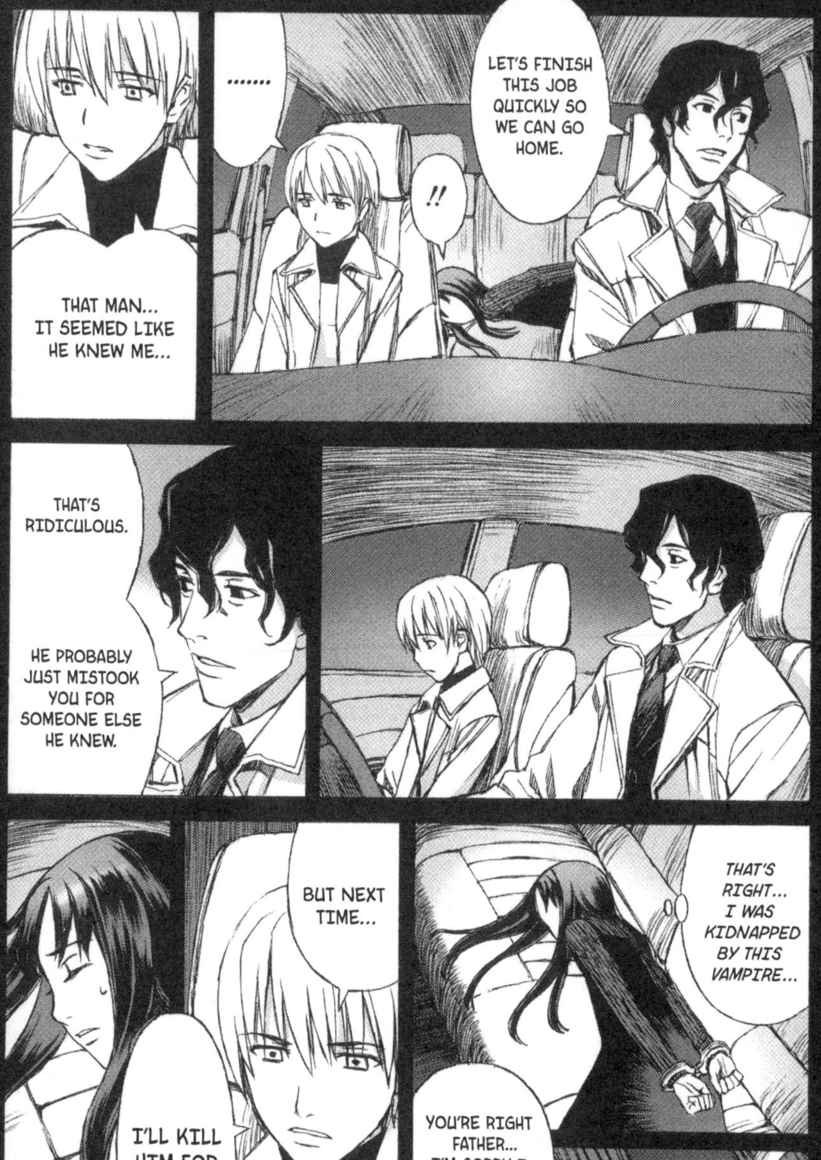
LET'S FINISH THIS JOB QUICKLY SO WE CAN GO HOME.
!!
....
THAT MAN... IT SEEMED LIKE HE KNEW ME...
THAT'S RIDICULOUS.
HE PROBABLY JUST MISTOOK YOU FOR SOMEONE ELSE HE KNEW.
THAT'S RIGHT... I WAS KIDNAPPED BY THIS VAMPIRE...
YOU'RE RIGHT FATHER... I'M SORRY I COULDN'T DO IT RIGHT THE FIRST TIME...
BUT NEXT TIME...
I'LL KILL HIM FOR SURE.

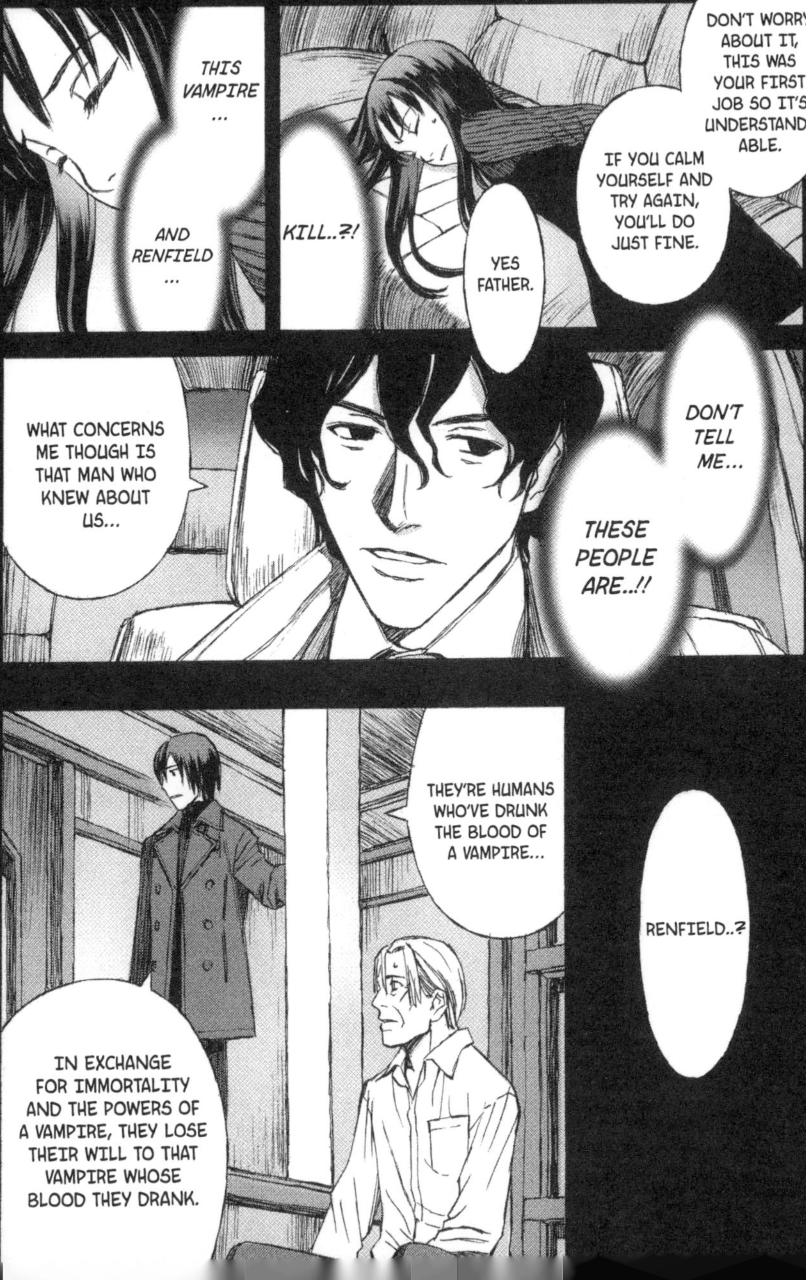
DON'T WORRY ABOUT IT, THIS WAS YOUR FIRST JOB SO IT'S UNDERSTANDABLE.
IF YOU CALM YOURSELF AND TRY AGAIN, YOU'LL DO JUST FINE.
YES FATHER.
KILL..?!
THIS VAMPIRE ...
AND RENFIELD ...
WHAT CONCERNS ME THOUGH IS THAT MAN WHO KNEW ABOUT US...
DON'T TELL ME...
THESE PEOPLE ARE..!!
RENFIELD..?
THEY'RE HUMANS WHO'VE DRUNK THE BLOOD OF A VAMPIRE...
IN EXCHANGE FOR IMMORTALITY AND THE POWERS OF A VAMPIRE, THEY LOSE THEIR WILL TO THAT VAMPIRE WHOSE BLOOD THEY DRANK.

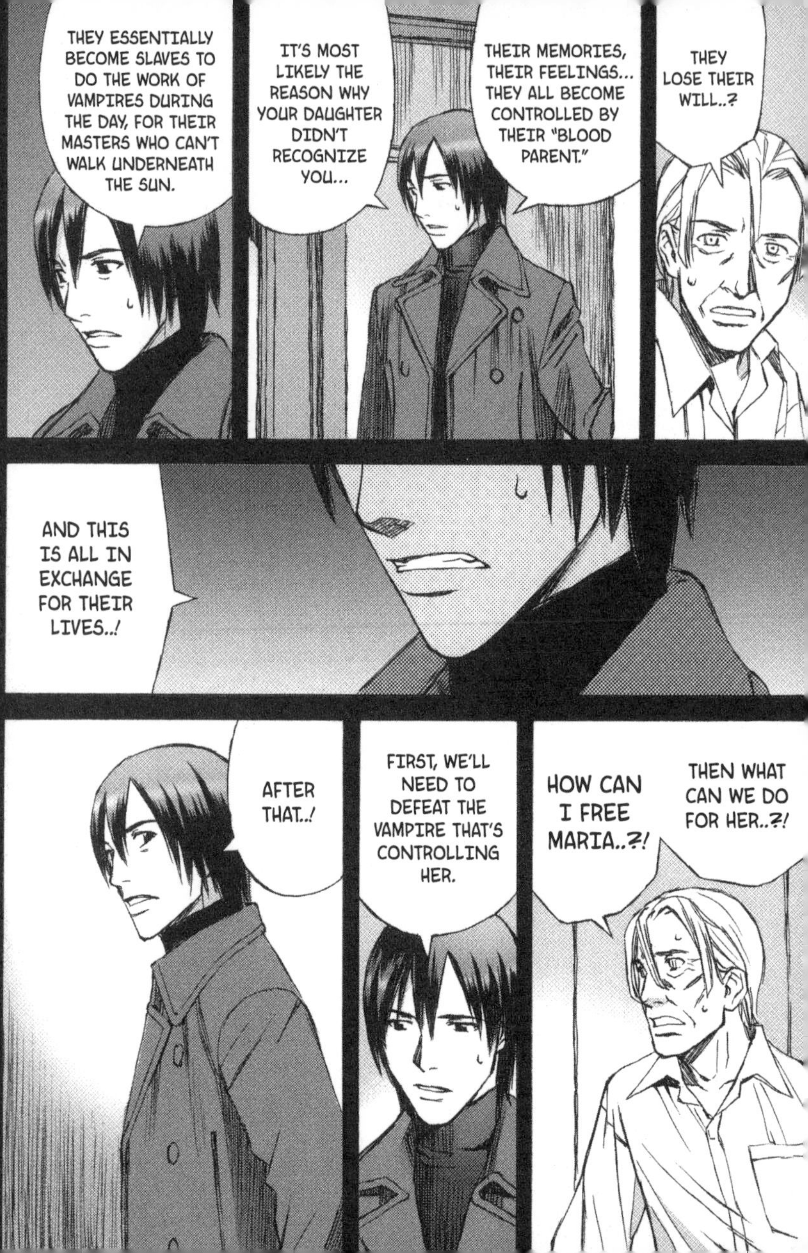
THEY LOSE THEIR WILL..?
THEIR MEMORIES, THEIR FEELINGS... THEY ALL BECOME CONTROLLED BY THEIR "BLOOD PARENT."
IT'S MOST LIKELY THE REASON WHY YOUR DAUGHTER DIDN'T RECOGNIZE YOU...
THEY ESSENTIALLY BECOME SLAVES TO DO THE WORK OF VAMPIRES DURING THE DAY, FOR THEIR MASTERS WHO CAN'T WALK UNDERNEATH THE SUN.
AND THIS IS ALL IN EXCHANGE FOR THEIR LIVES..!
THEN WHAT CAN WE DO FOR HER..?!
HOW CAN I FREE MARIA..?!
FIRST, WE'LL NEED TO DEFEAT THE VAMPIRE THAT'S CONTROLLING HER.
AFTER THAT..!

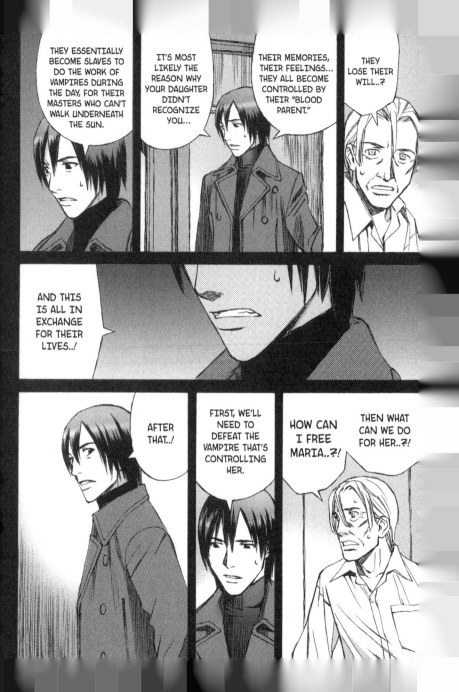

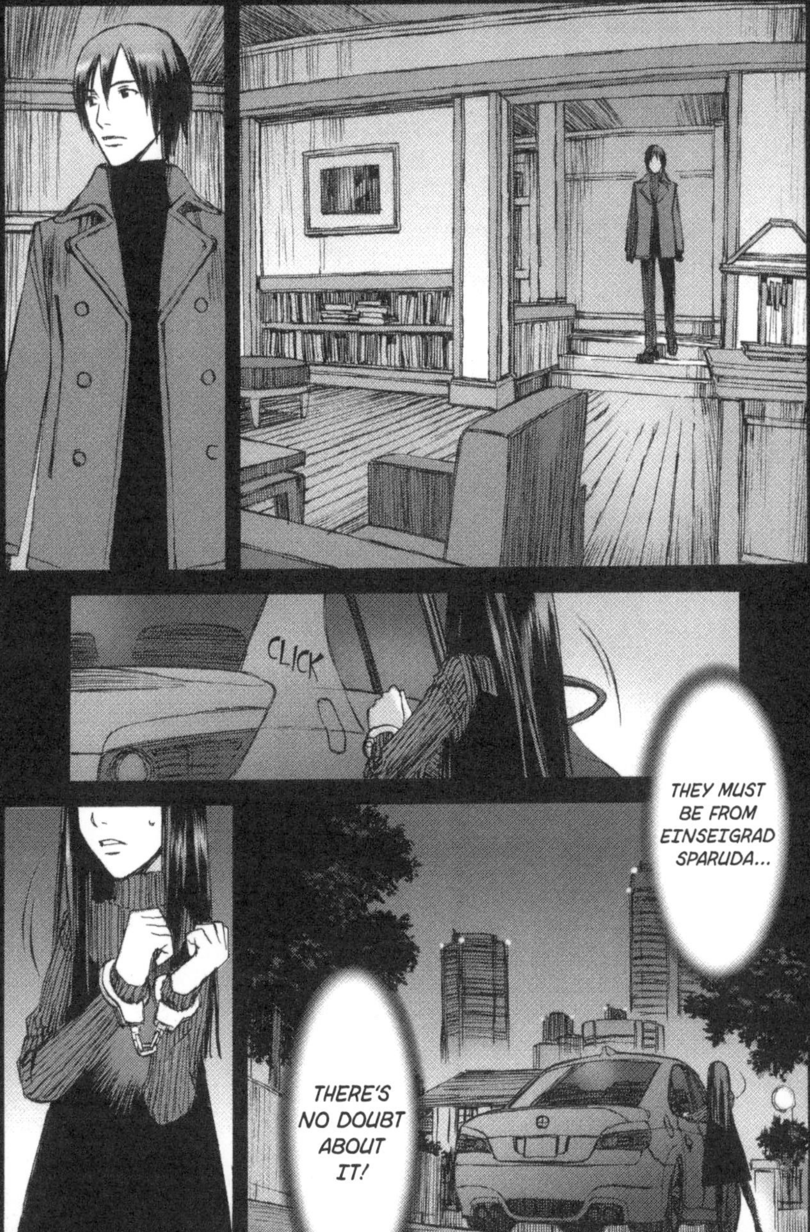
CLICK
THEY MUST BE FROM EINSEIGRAD SPARUDA...
THERE'S NO DOUBT ABOUT IT!

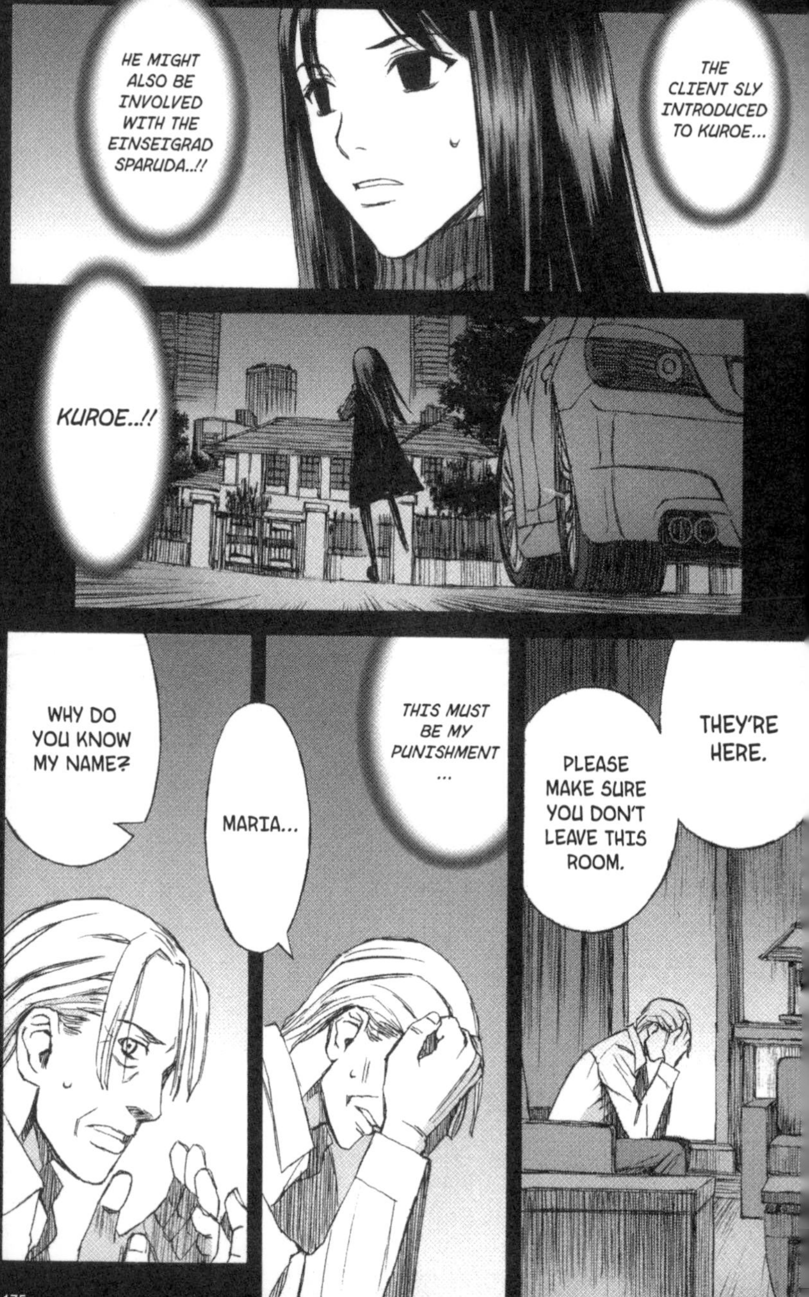
THE CLIENT SLY INTRODUCED TO KUROE...
HE MIGHT ALSO BE INVOLVED WITH THE EINSEIGRAD SPARUDA..!!
KUROE..!!
THEY'RE HERE.
PLEASE MAKE SURE YOU DON'T LEAVE THIS ROOM.
THIS MUST BE MY PUNISHMENT ...
MARIA...
WHY DO YOU KNOW MY NAME?

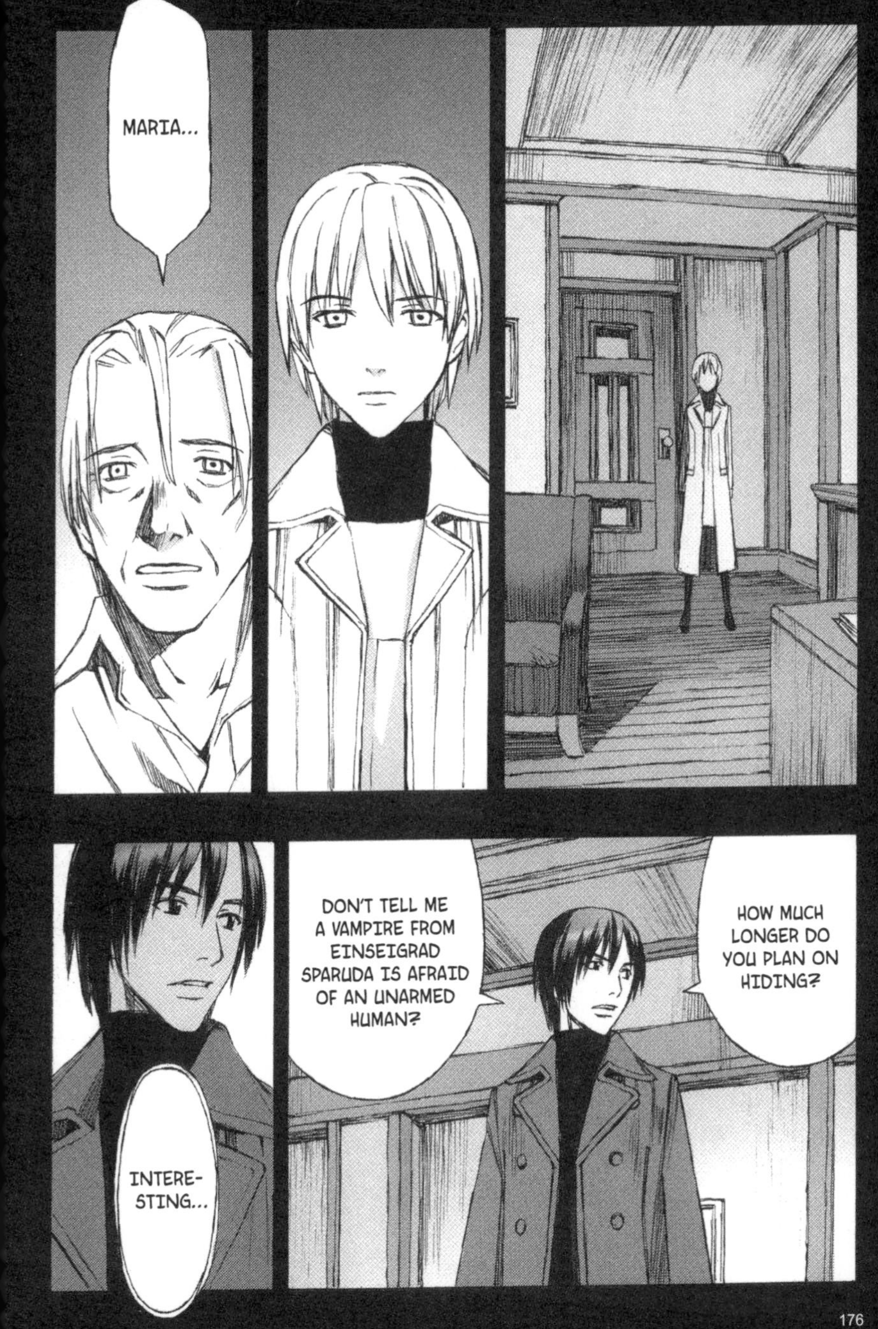
MARIA...
HOW MUCH LONGER DO YOU PLAN ON HIDING?
DON'T TELL ME A VAMPIRE FROM EINSEIGRAD SPARUDA IS AFRAID OF AN UNARMED HUMAN?
INTERE-STING...

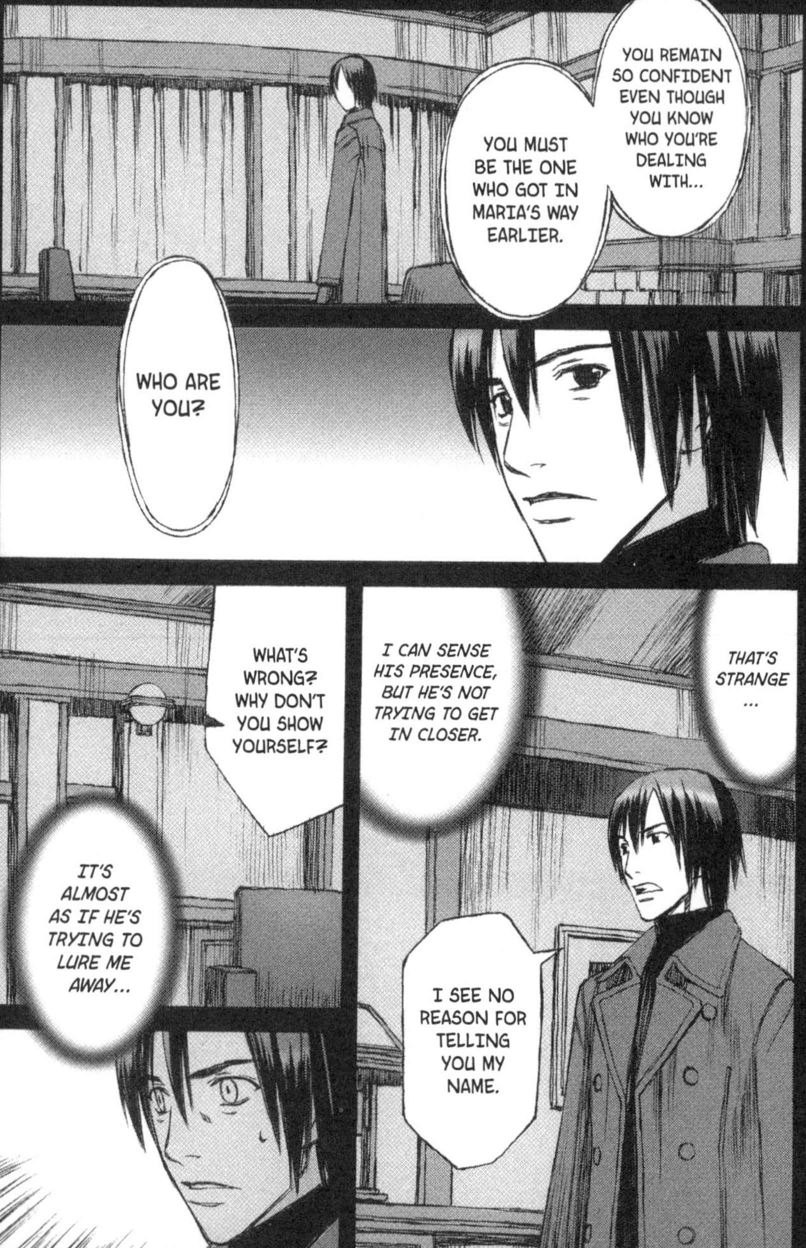
YOU REMAIN SO CONFIDENT EVEN THOUGH YOU KNOW WHO YOU'RE DEALING WITH...
YOU MUST BE THE ONE WHO GOT IN MARIA'S WAY EARLIER.
WHO ARE YOU?
THAT'S STRANGE...
I CAN SENSE HIS PRESENCE, BUT HE'S NOT TRYING TO GET IN CLOSER.
I SEE NO REASON FOR TELLING YOU MY NAME.
WHAT'S WRONG? WHY DON'T YOU SHOW YOURSELF?
IT'S ALMOST AS IF HE'S TRYING TO LURE ME AWAY...

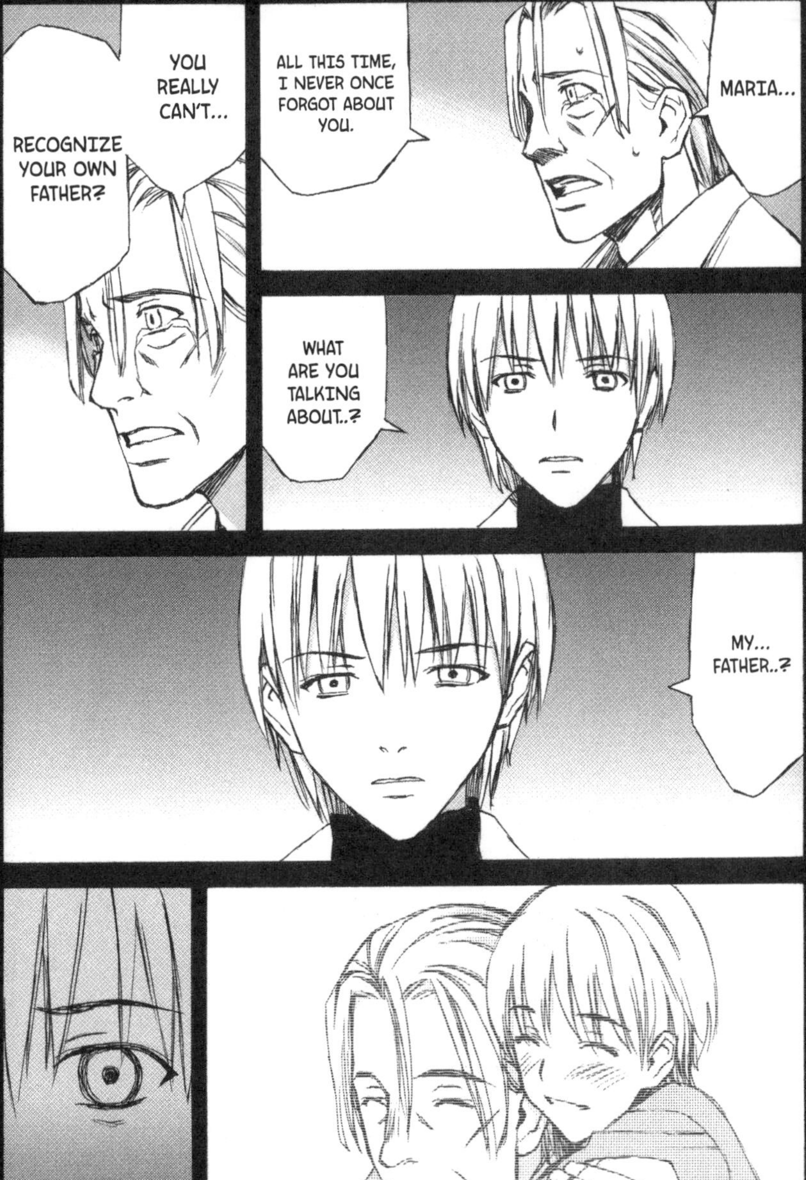
MARIA...
ALL THIS TIME, I NEVER ONCE FORGOT ABOUT YOU.
WHAT ARE YOU TALKING ABOUT..?
YOU REALLY CAN'T...
RECOGNIZE YOUR OWN FATHER?
MY... FATHER..?

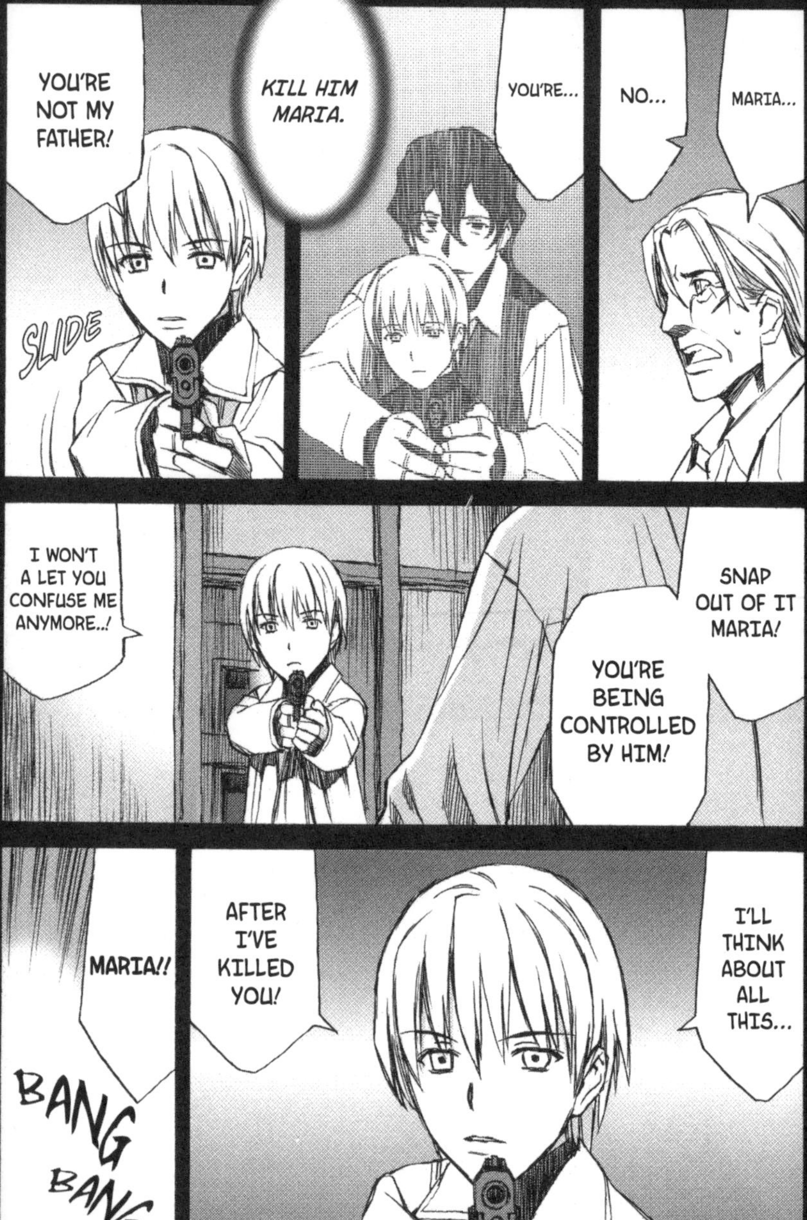
MARIA...
NO...
YOU'RE...
KILL HIM MARIA.
YOU'RE NOT MY FATHER!
SLIDE
SNAP OUT OF IT MARIA!
YOU'RE BEING CONTROLLED BY HIM!
I WON'T A LET YOU CONFUSE ME ANYMORE..!
I'LL THINK ABOUT ALL THIS...
AFTER I'VE KILLED YOU!
MARIA!!
BANG
BANG

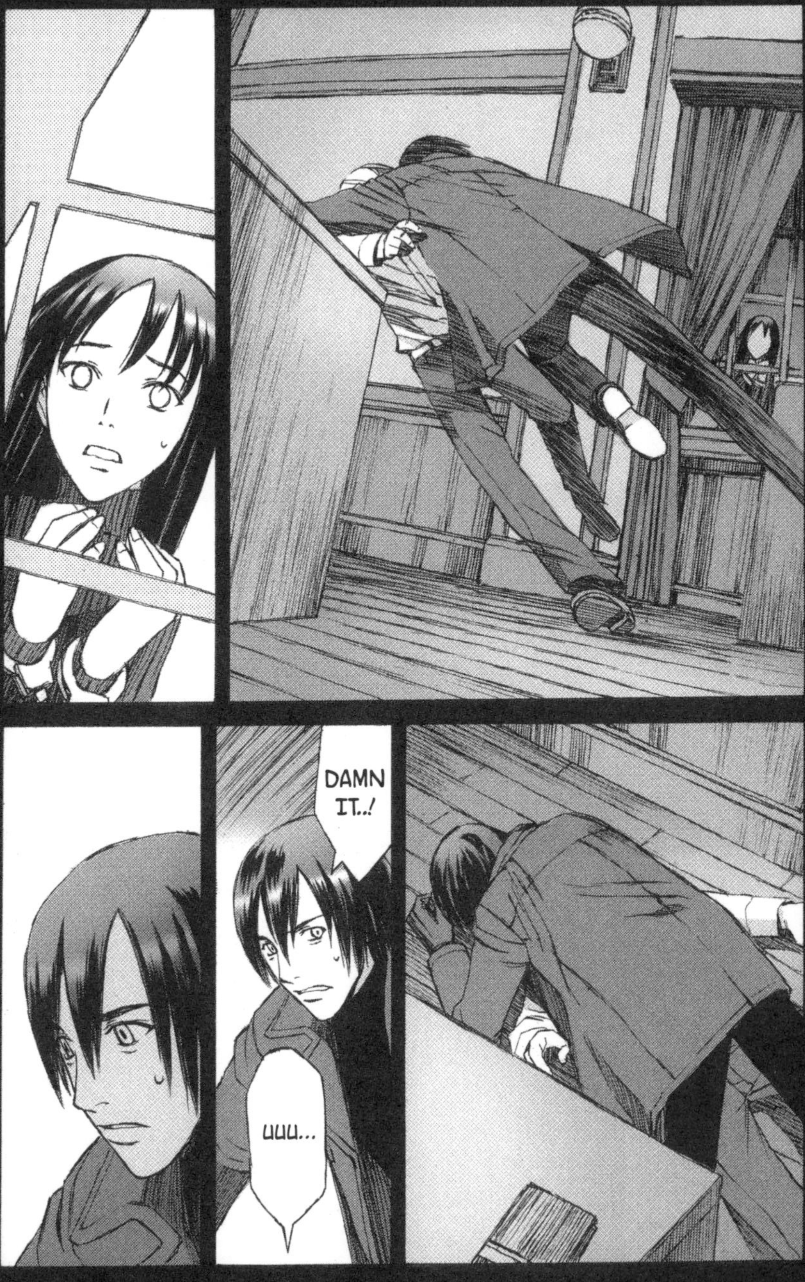
DAMN IT..!
uuu...

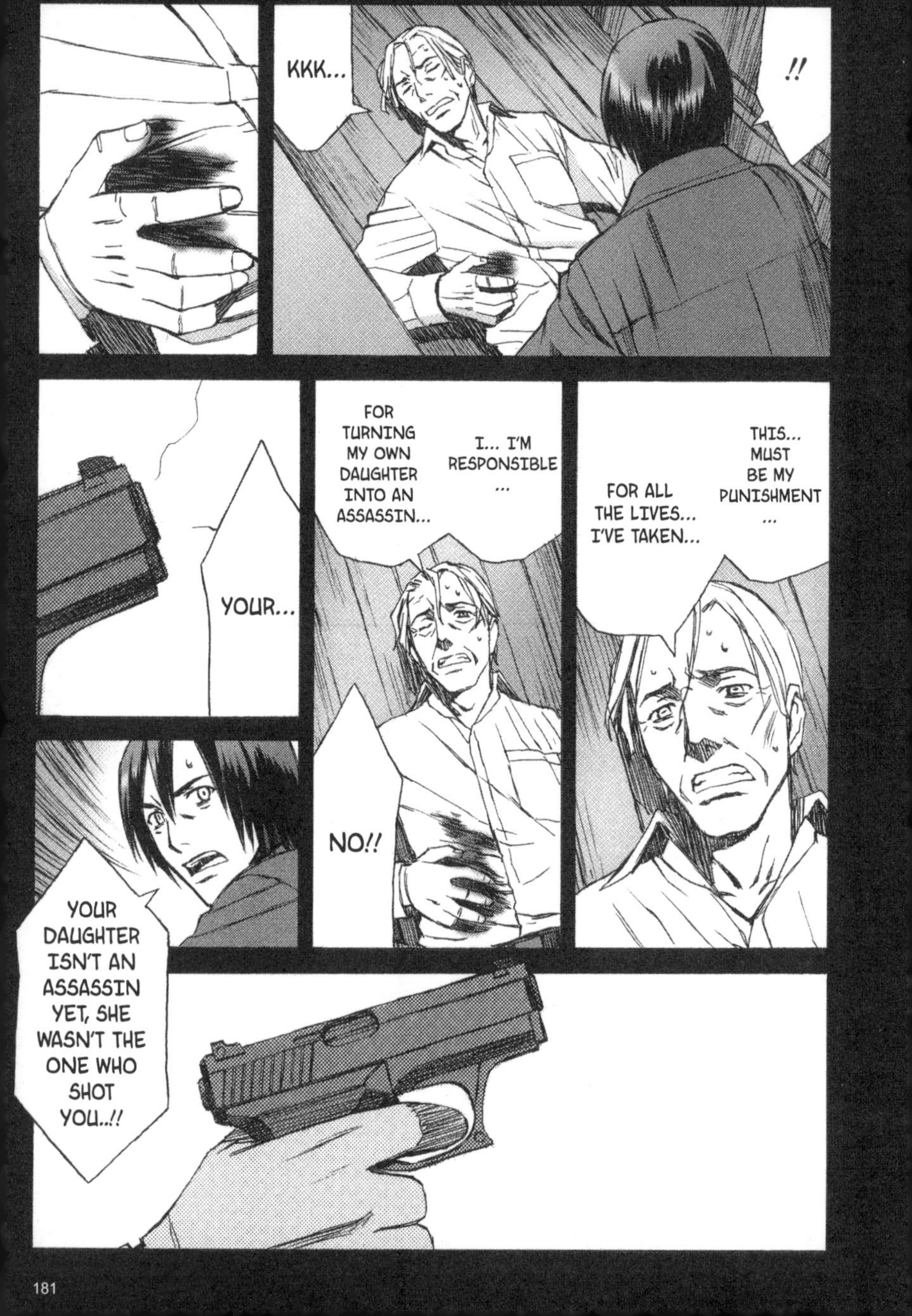
!!
KKK...
THIS... MUST BE MY PUNISHMENT...
FOR ALL THE LIVES... I'VE TAKEN...
I... I'M RESPONSIBLE...
FOR TURNING MY OWN DAUGHTER INTO AN ASSASSIN...
NO!!
YOUR...
YOUR DAUGHTER ISN'T AN ASSASSIN YET, SHE WASN'T THE ONE WHO SHOT YOU..!!

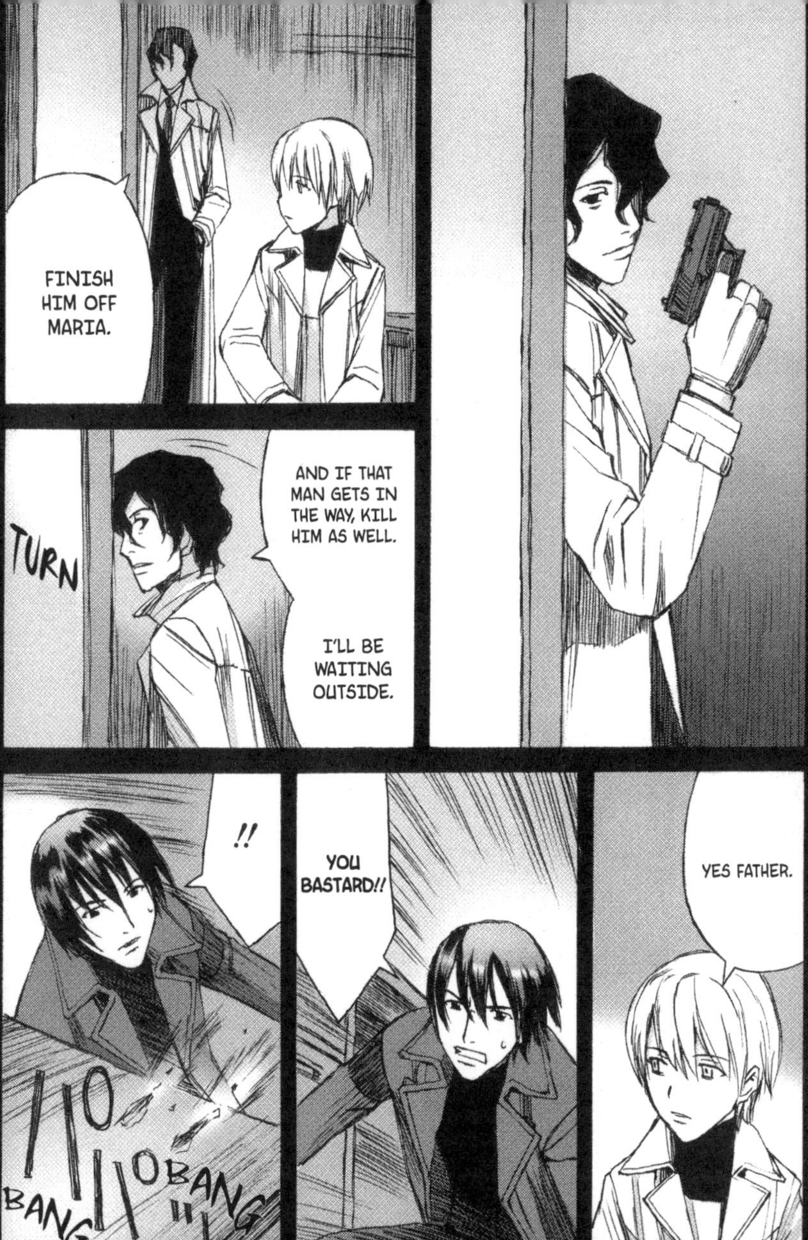
FINISH HIM OFF MARIA.
AND IF THAT MAN GETS IN THE WAY, KILL HIM AS WELL.
TURN
I'LL BE WAITING OUTSIDE.
YES FATHER.
YOU BASTARD!!
!!
BANG
BANG

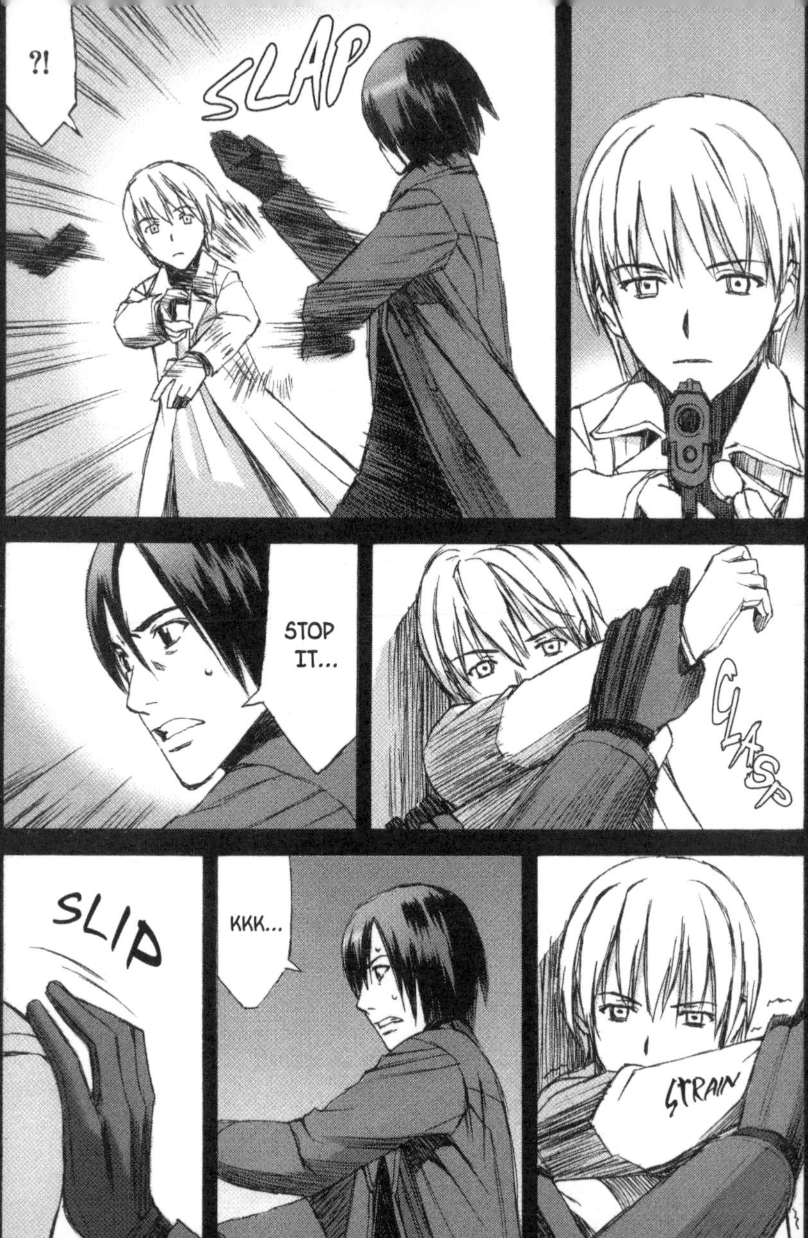
SLAP
?!
CLASP
STOP IT...
STRAIN
KKK...
SLIP

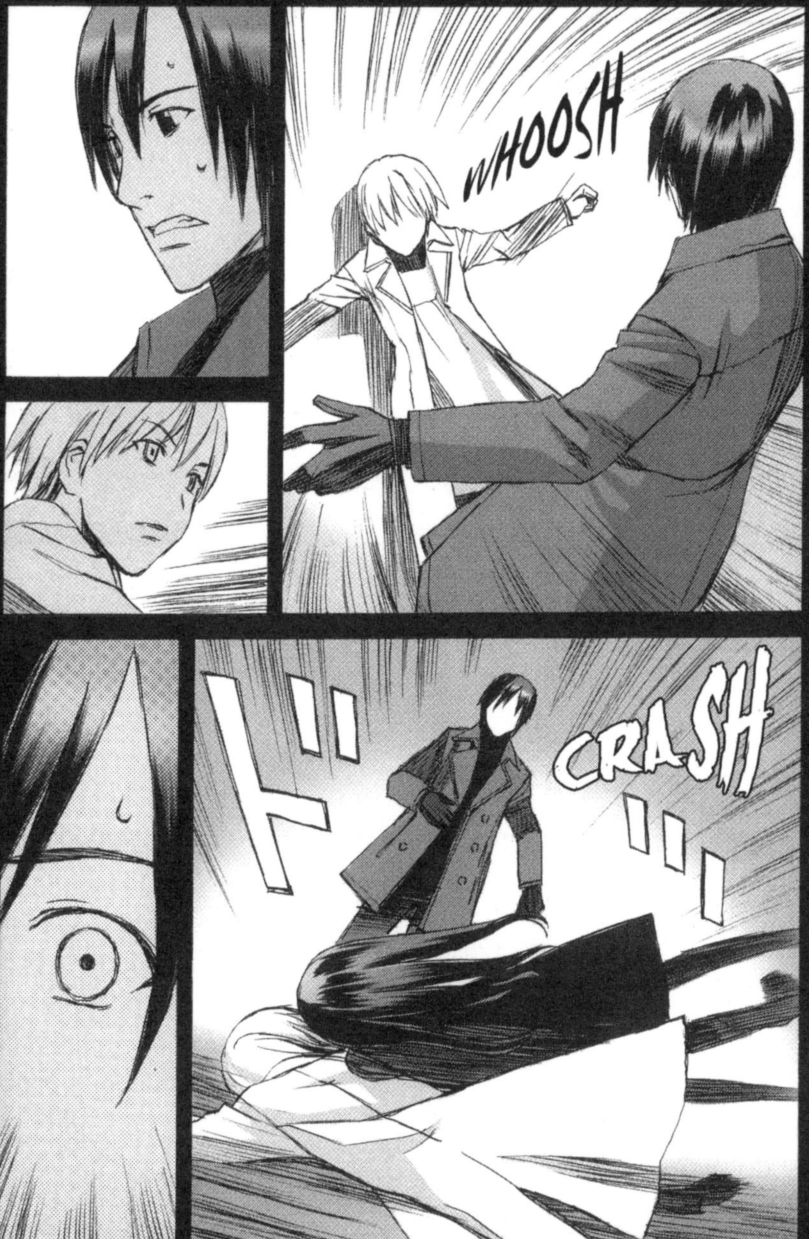
WHOOSH
CRASH
ドッ

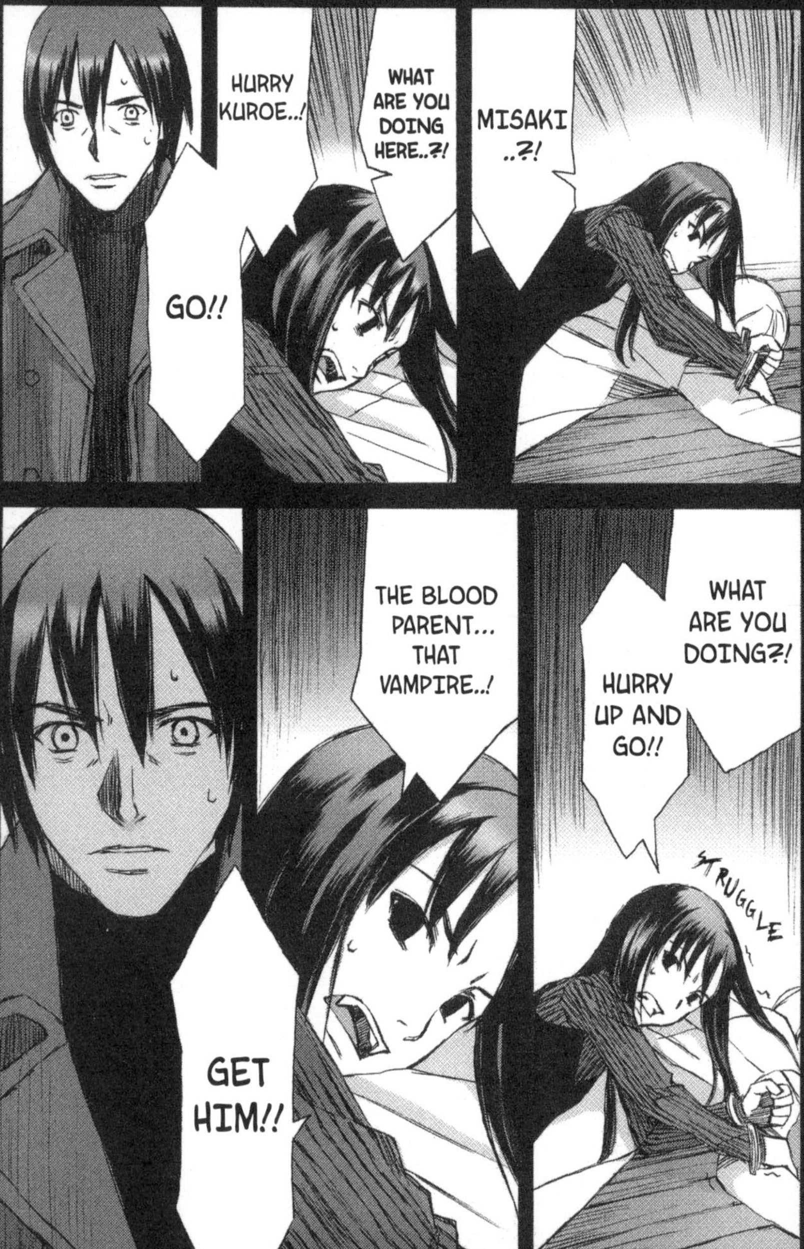
MISAKI ..?!
WHAT ARE YOU DOING HERE..?!
HURRY KUROE..!
GO!!
WHAT ARE YOU DOING?!
HURRY UP AND GO!!
STRUGGLE
THE BLOOD PARENT... THAT VAMPIRE..!
GET HIM!!

Episode 14
WHY CRY? part 3

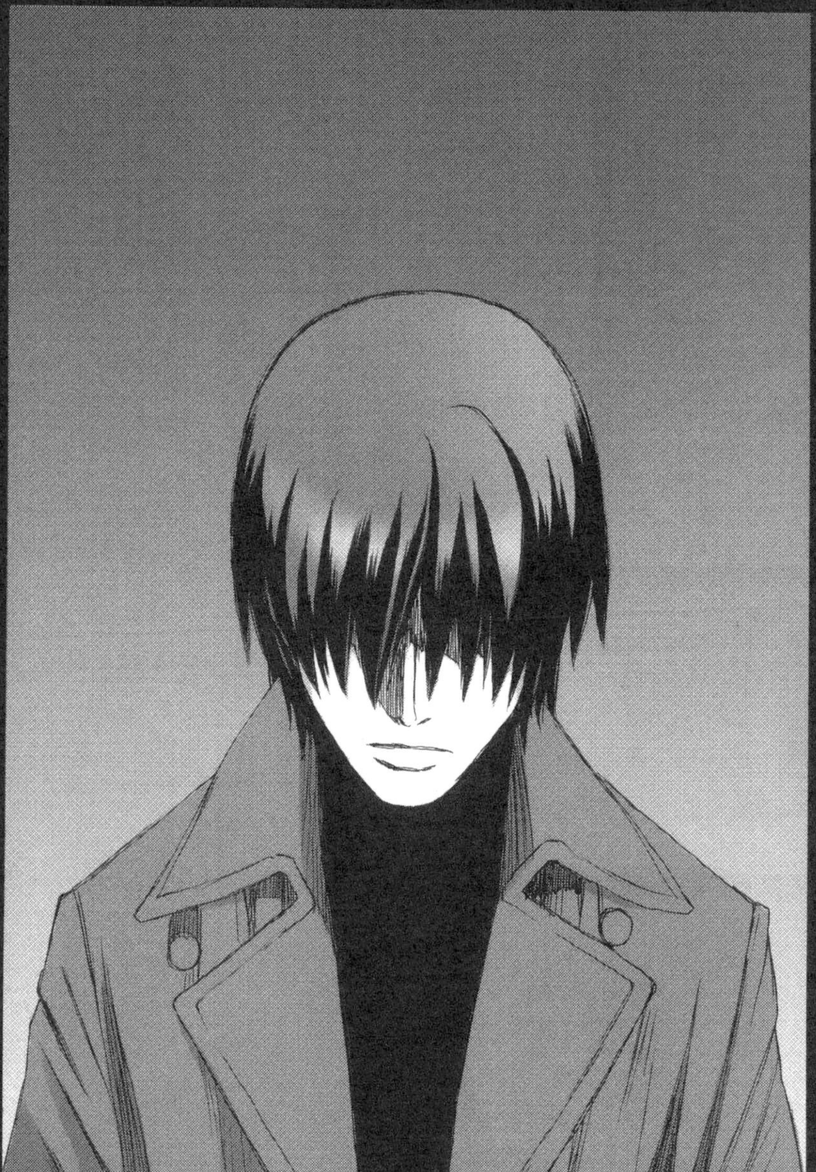

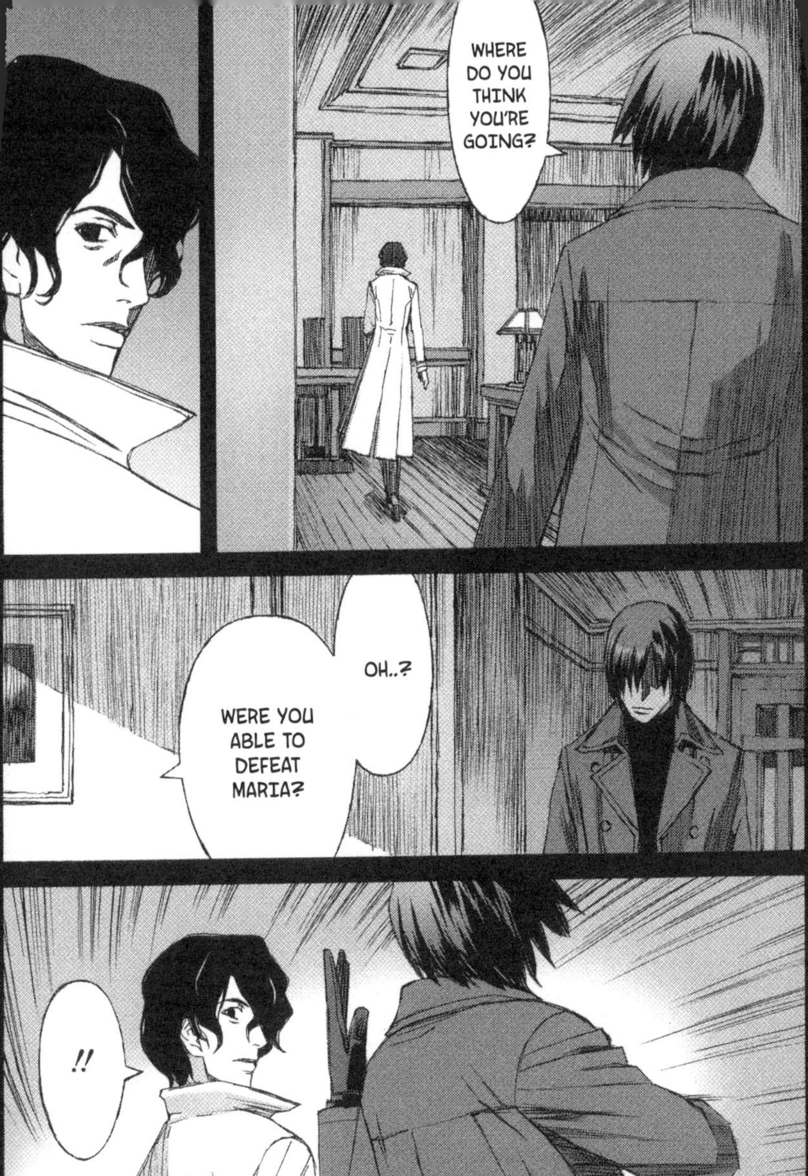
WHERE DO YOU THINK YOU'RE GOING?
OH..?
WERE YOU ABLE TO DEFEAT MARIA?
!!

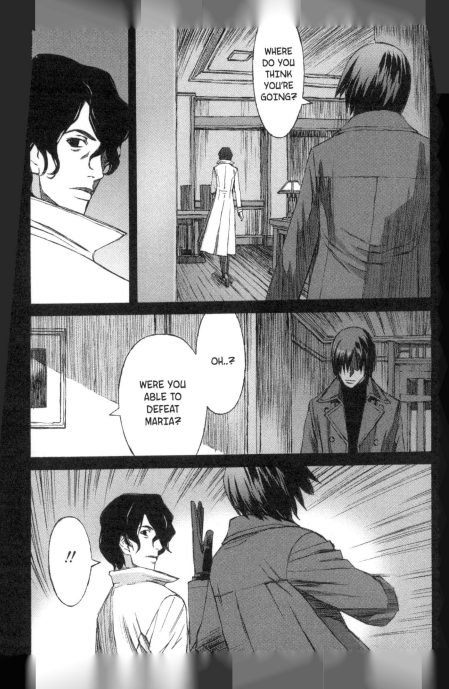

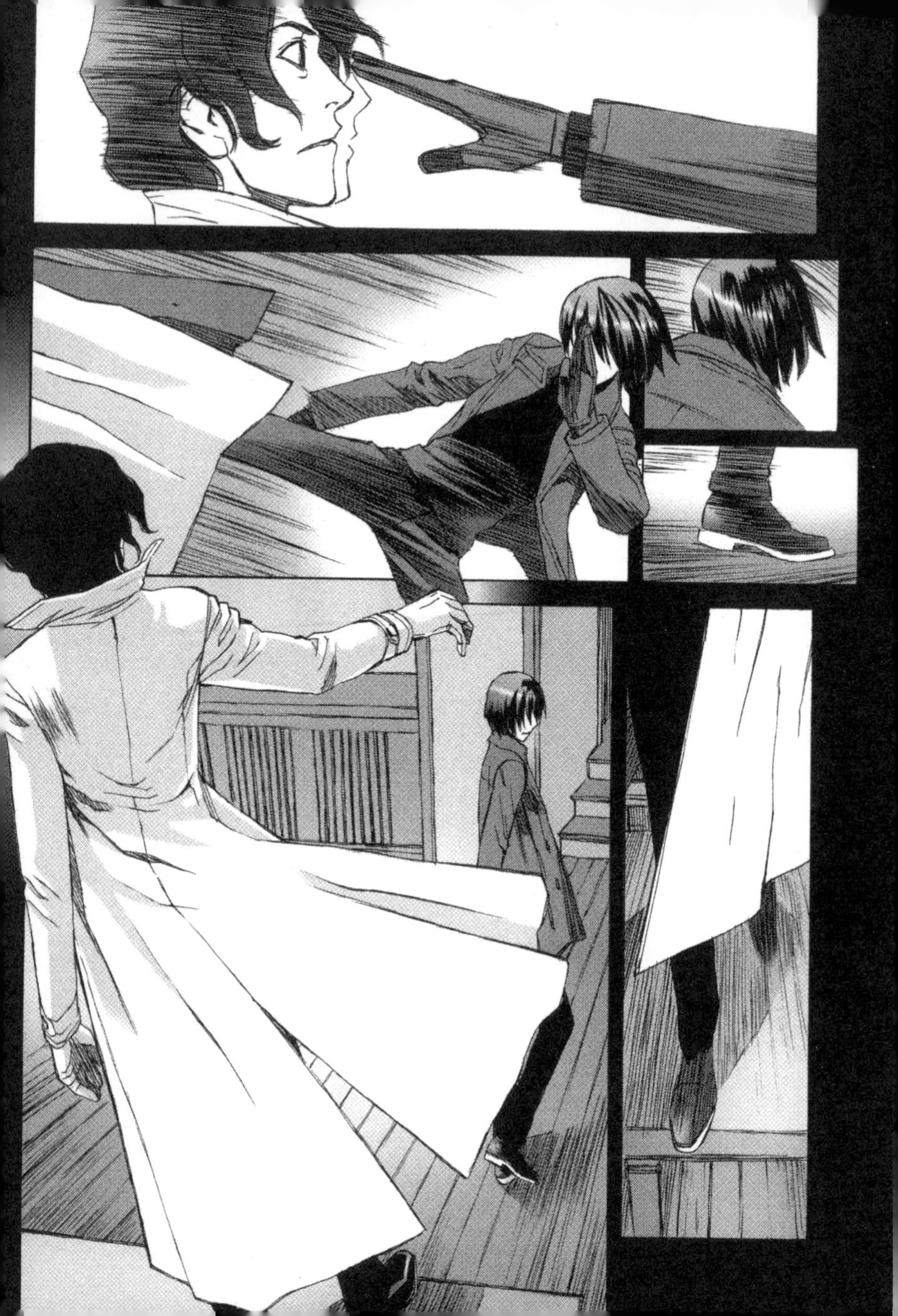

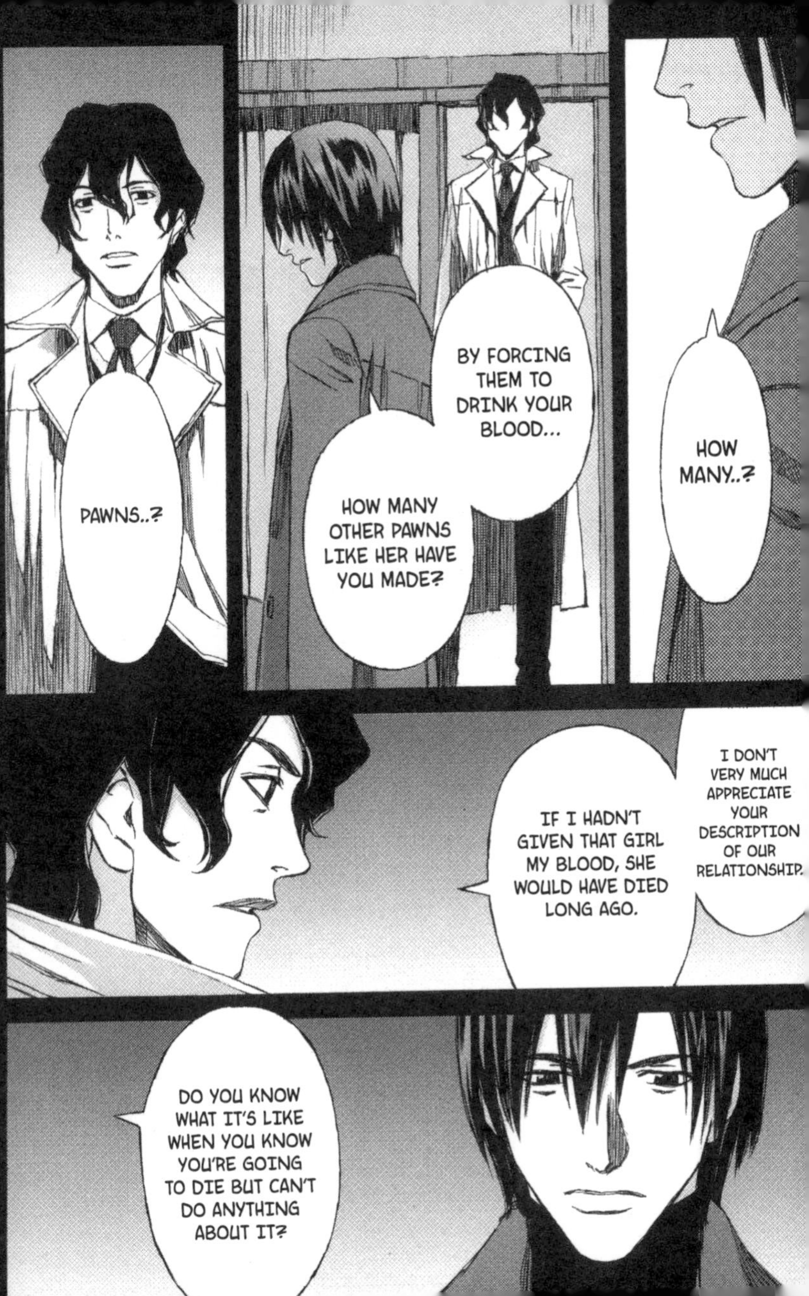
HOW MANY..?
BY FORCING THEM TO DRINK YOUR BLOOD...
HOW MANY OTHER PAWNS LIKE HER HAVE YOU MADE?
PAWNS..?
I DON'T VERY MUCH APPRECIATE YOUR DESCRIPTION OF OUR RELATIONSHIP.
IF I HADN'T GIVEN THAT GIRL MY BLOOD, SHE WOULD HAVE DIED LONG AGO.
DO YOU KNOW WHAT IT'S LIKE WHEN YOU KNOW YOU'RE GOING TO DIE BUT CAN'T DO ANYTHING ABOUT IT?

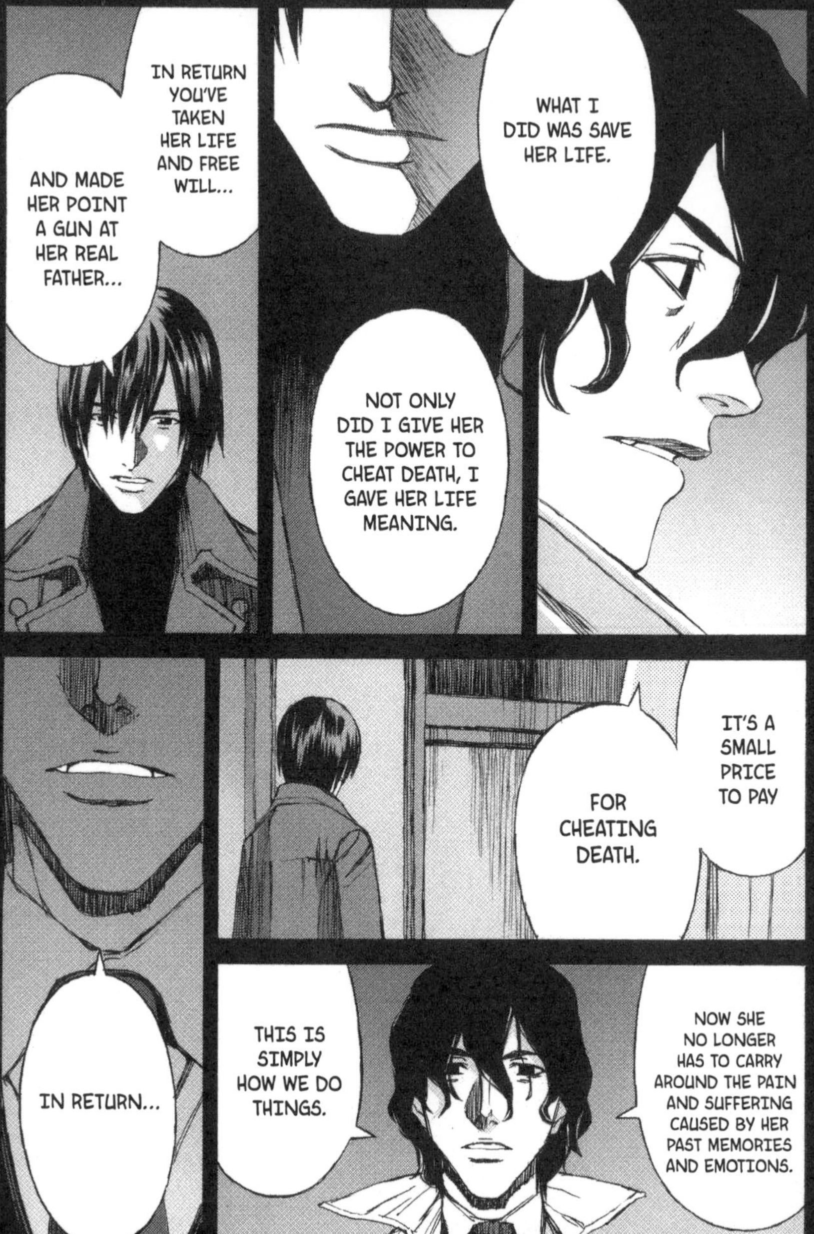
WHAT I DID WAS SAVE HER LIFE.
NOT ONLY DID I GIVE HER THE POWER TO CHEAT DEATH, I GAVE HER LIFE MEANING.
IN RETURN YOU'VE TAKEN HER LIFE AND FREE WILL...
AND MADE HER POINT A GUN AT HER REAL FATHER...
IT'S A SMALL PRICE TO PAY
FOR CHEATING DEATH.
NOW SHE NO LONGER HAS TO CARRY AROUND THE PAIN AND SUFFERING CAUSED BY HER PAST MEMORIES AND EMOTIONS.
THIS IS SIMPLY HOW WE DO THINGS.
IN RETURN...

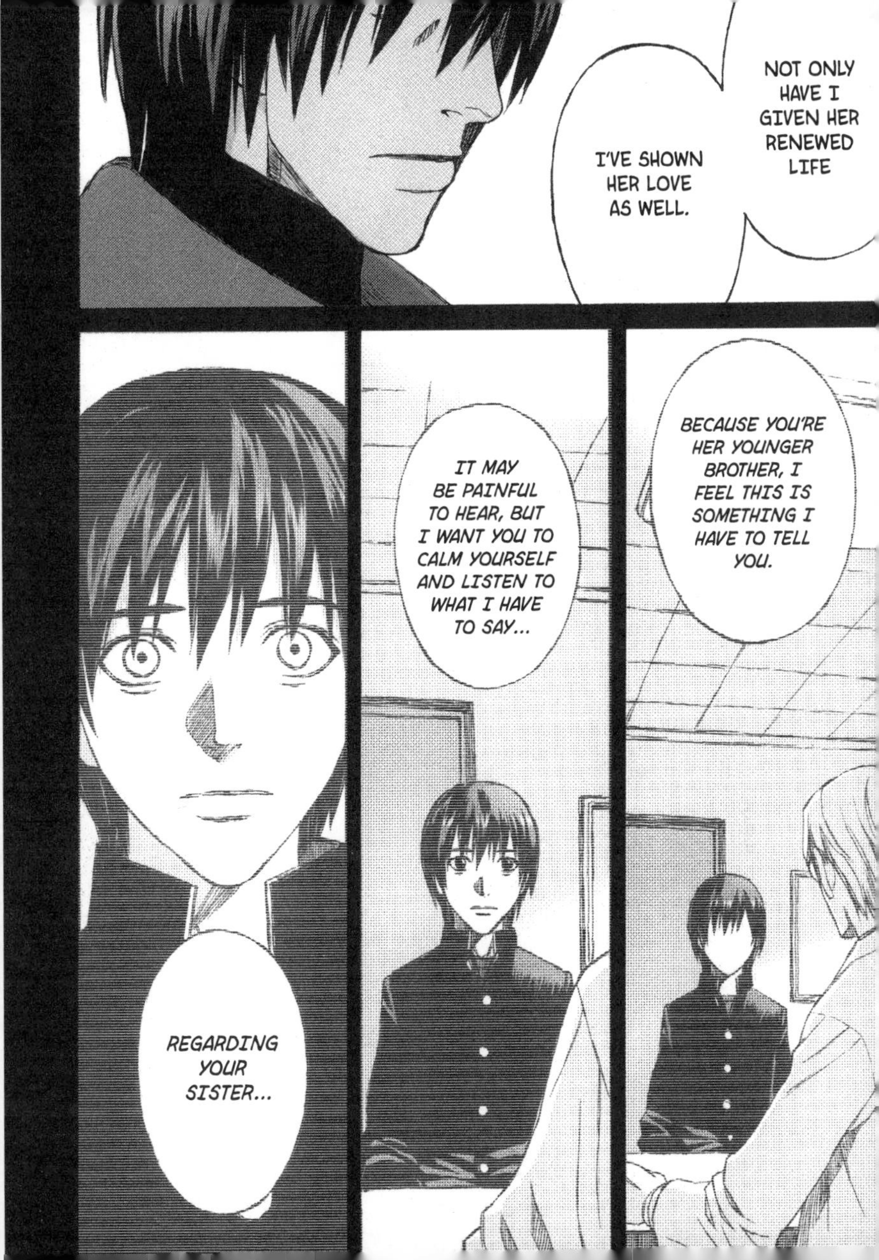

NOT ONLY HAVE I GIVEN HER RENEWED LIFE
I'VE SHOWN HER LOVE AS WELL.
BECAUSE YOU'RE HER YOUNGER BROTHER, I FEEL THIS IS SOMETHING I HAVE TO TELL YOU.
IT MAY BE PAINFUL TO HEAR, BUT I WANT YOU TO CALM YOURSELF AND LISTEN TO WHAT I HAVE TO SAY...
REGARDING YOUR SISTER...

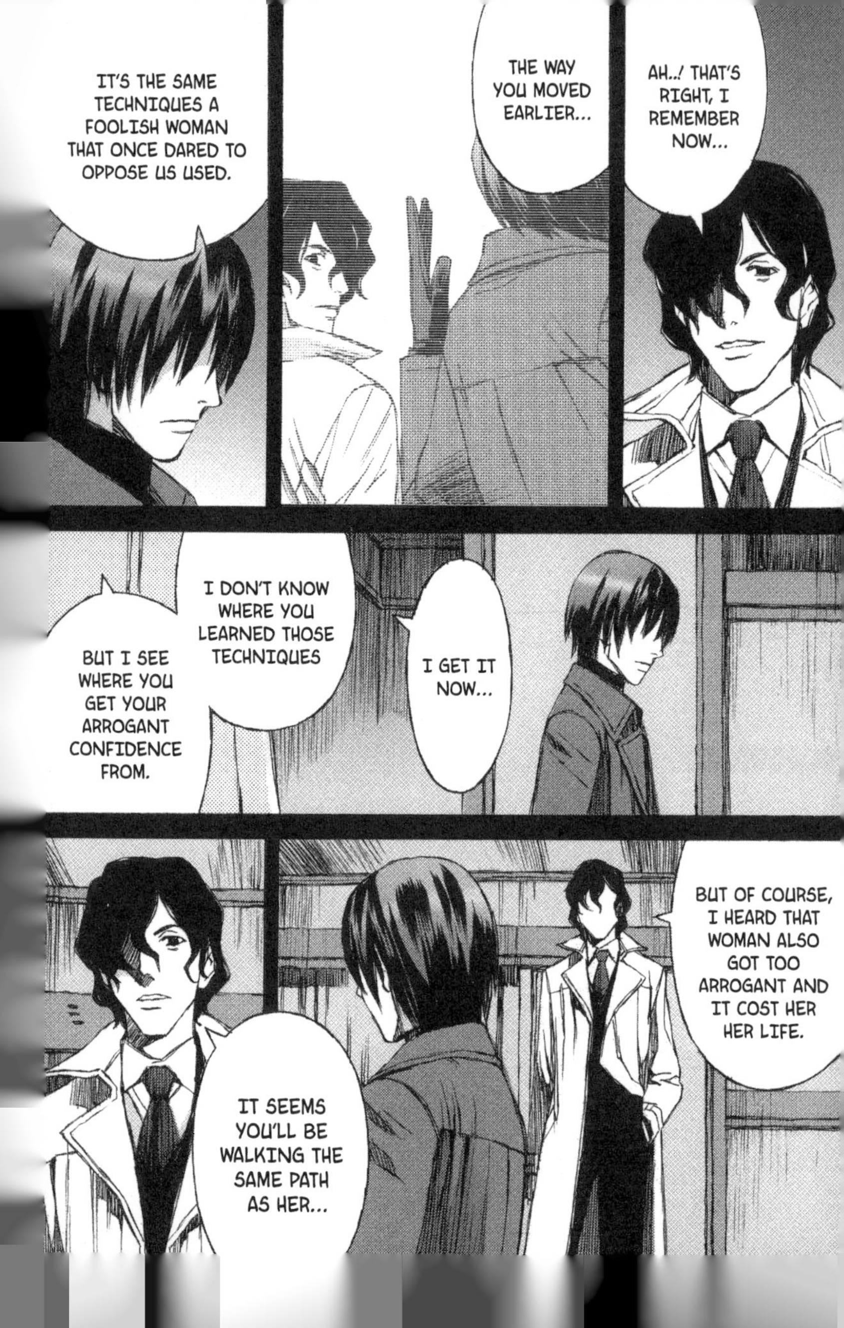
AH..! THAT'S RIGHT, I REMEMBER NOW...
THE WAY YOU MOVED EARLIER...
IT'S THE SAME TECHNIQUES A FOOLISH WOMAN THAT ONCE DARED TO OPPOSE US USED.
I GET IT NOW...
I DON'T KNOW WHERE YOU LEARNED THOSE TECHNIQUES
BUT I SEE WHERE YOU GET YOUR ARROGANT CONFIDENCE FROM.
BUT OF COURSE, I HEARD THAT WOMAN ALSO GOT TOO ARROGANT AND IT COST HER HER LIFE.
IT SEEMS YOU'LL BE WALKING THE SAME PATH AS HER...

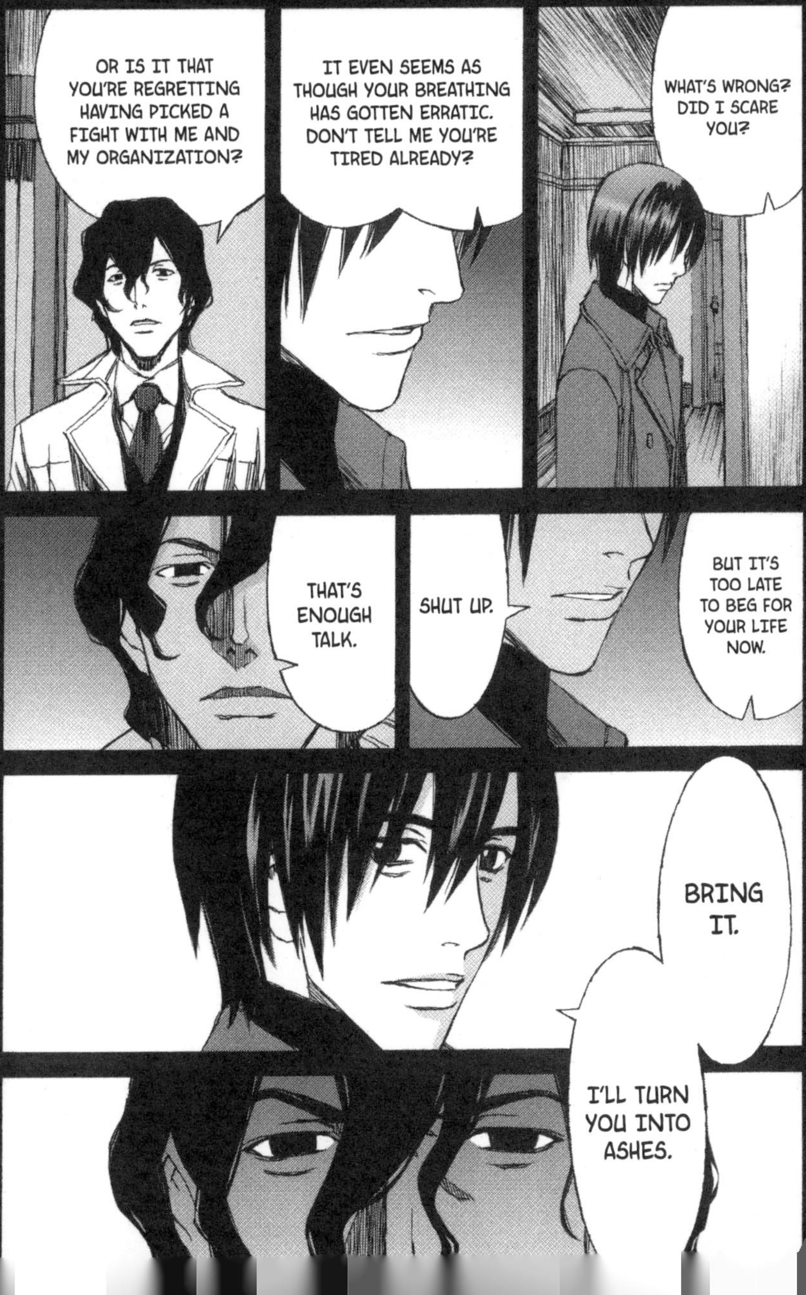
WHAT'S WRONG? DID I SCARE YOU?
IT EVEN SEEMS AS THOUGH YOUR BREATHING HAS GOTTEN ERRATIC. DON'T TELL ME YOU'RE TIRED ALREADY?
OR IS IT THAT YOU'RE REGRETTING HAVING PICKED A FIGHT WITH ME AND MY ORGANIZATION?
BUT IT'S TOO LATE TO BEG FOR YOUR LIFE NOW.
SHUT UP.
THAT'S ENOUGH TALK.
BRING IT.
I'LL TURN YOU INTO ASHES.

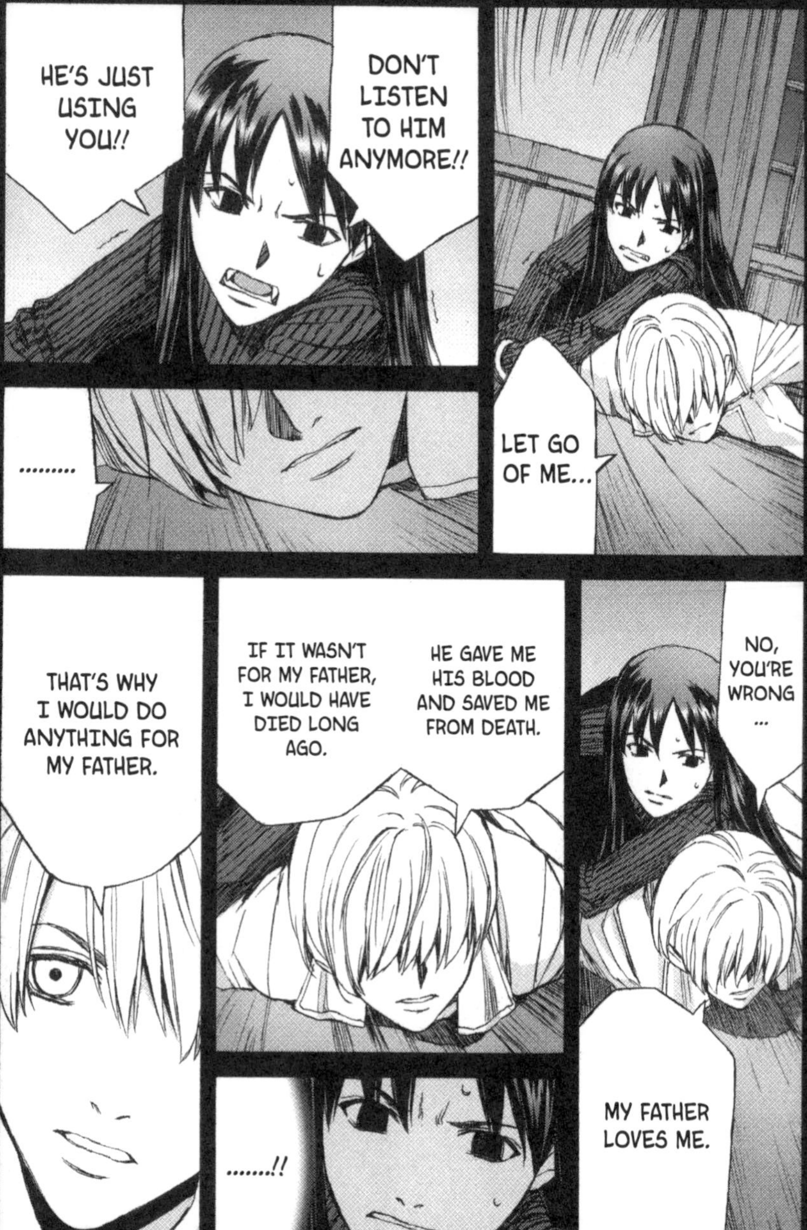
LET GO OF ME...
DON'T LISTEN TO HIM ANYMORE!!
HE'S JUST USING YOU!!
....
NO, YOU'RE WRONG ...
MY FATHER LOVES ME.
HE GAVE ME HIS BLOOD AND SAVED ME FROM DEATH.
IF IT WASN'T FOR MY FATHER, I WOULD HAVE DIED LONG AGO.
........!!
THAT'S WHY I WOULD DO ANYTHING FOR MY FATHER.

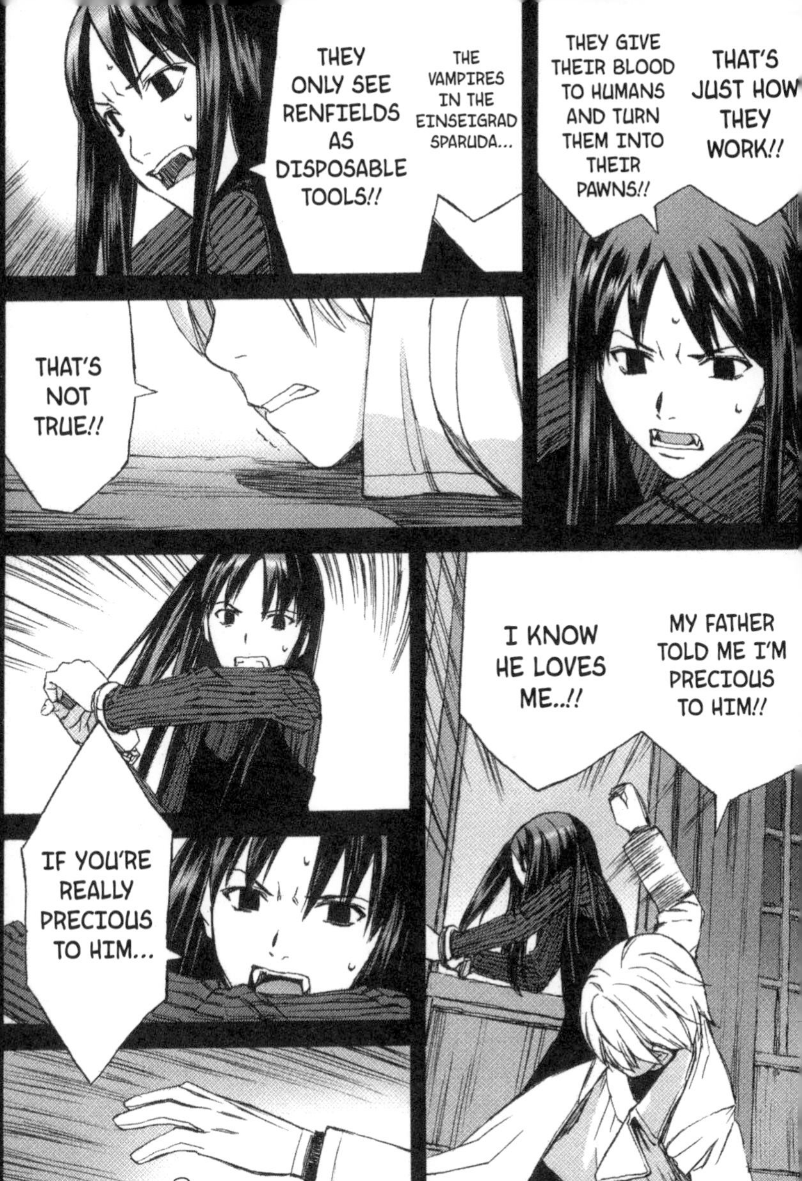
THAT'S JUST HOW THEY WORK!!
THEY GIVE THEIR BLOOD TO HUMANS AND TURN THEM INTO THEIR PAWNS!!
THE VAMPIRES IN THE EINSEIGRAD SPARUDA...
THEY ONLY SEE RENFIELDS AS DISPOSABLE TOOLS!!
THAT'S NOT TRUE!!
MY FATHER TOLD ME I'M PRECIOUS TO HIM!!
I KNOW HE LOVES ME..!!
IF YOU'RE REALLY PRECIOUS TO HIM...
REACH

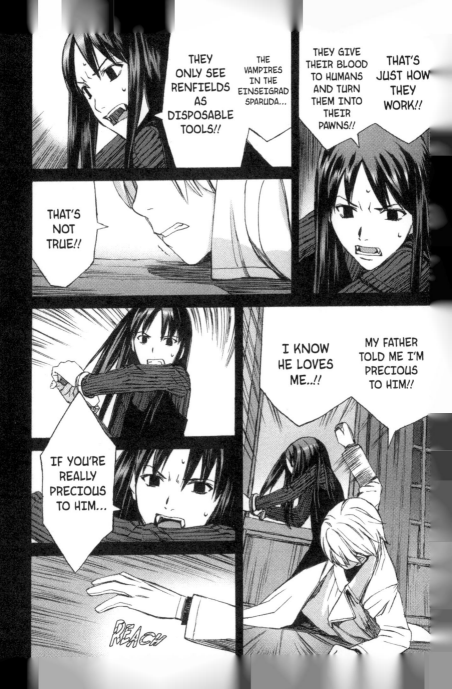

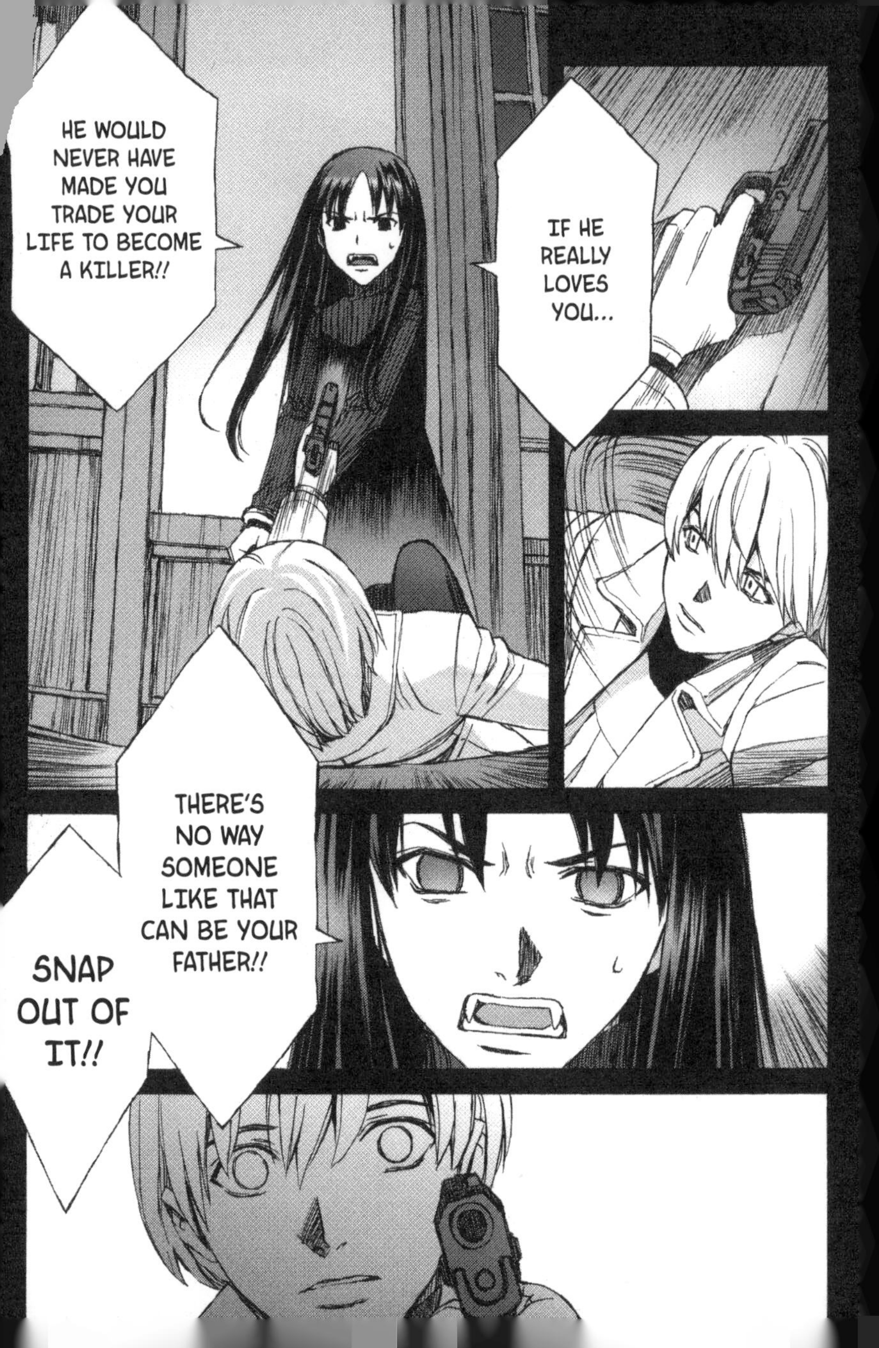
IF HE REALLY LOVES YOU...
HE WOULD NEVER HAVE MADE YOU TRADE YOUR LIFE TO BECOME A KILLER!!
THERE'S NO WAY SOMEONE LIKE THAT CAN BE YOUR FATHER!!
SNAP OUT OF IT!!

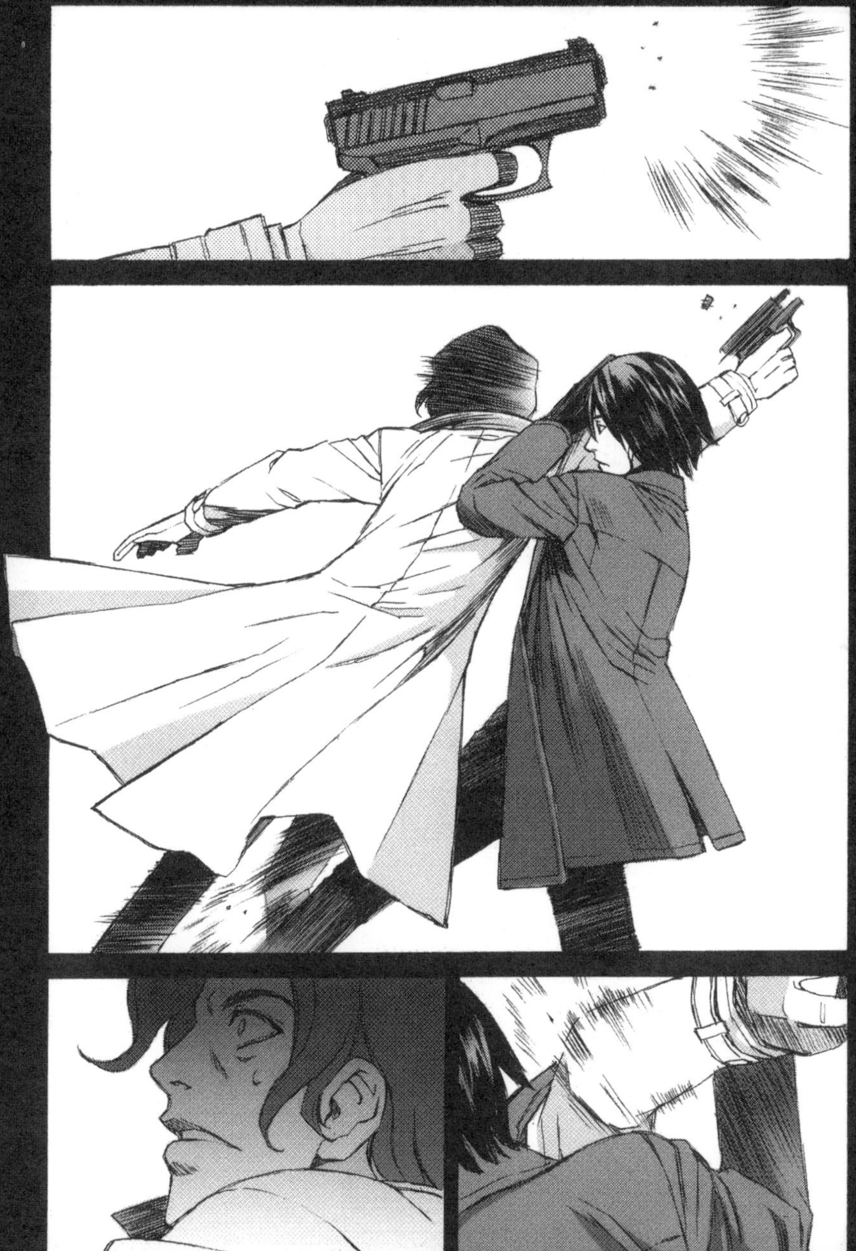

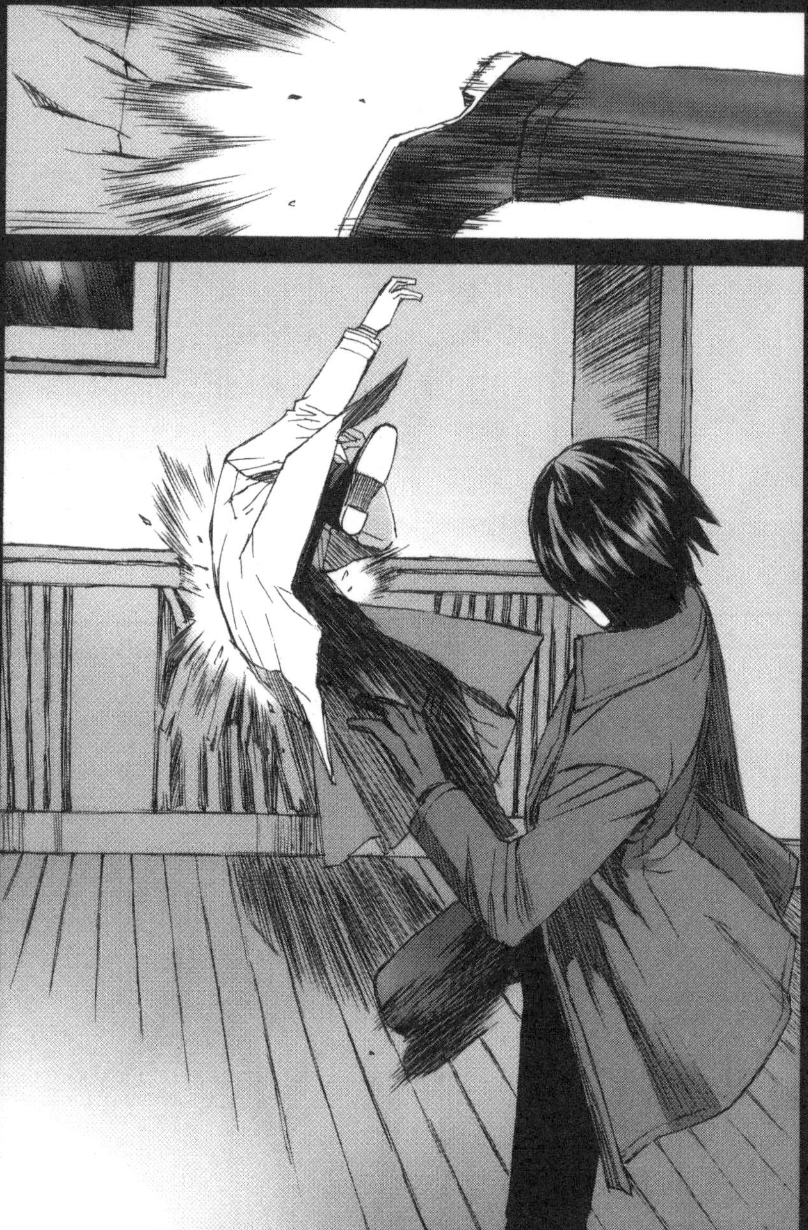

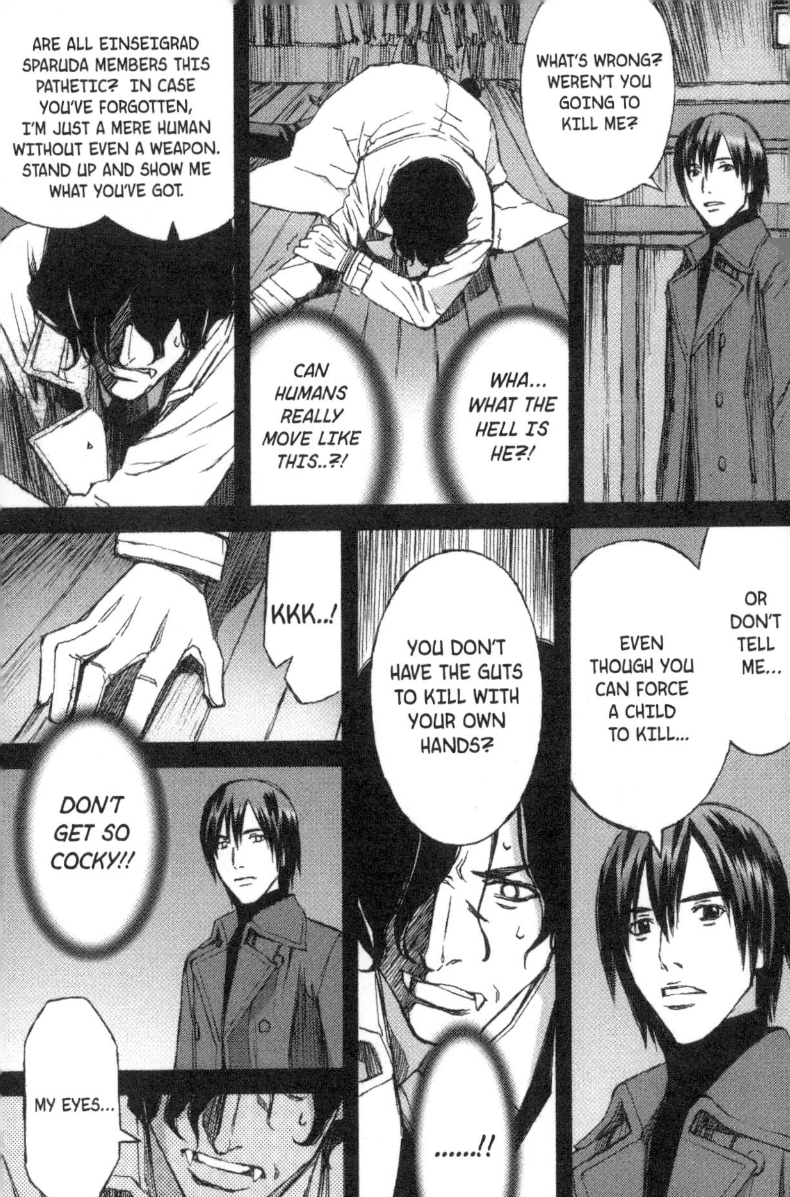
WHAT'S WRONG? WEREN'T YOU GOING TO KILL ME?
WHA... WHAT THE HELL IS HE?!
CAN HUMANS REALLY MOVE LIKE THIS..?!
ARE ALL EINSEIGRAD SPARUDA MEMBERS THIS PATHETIC? IN CASE YOU'VE FORGOTTEN, I'M JUST A MERE HUMAN WITHOUT EVEN A WEAPON. STAND UP AND SHOW ME WHAT YOU'VE GOT.
OR DON'T TELL ME...
EVEN THOUGH YOU CAN FORCE A CHILD TO KILL...
YOU DON'T HAVE THE GUTS TO KILL WITH YOUR OWN HANDS?
......!!
KKK..!
DON'T GET SO COCKY!!
MY EYES...

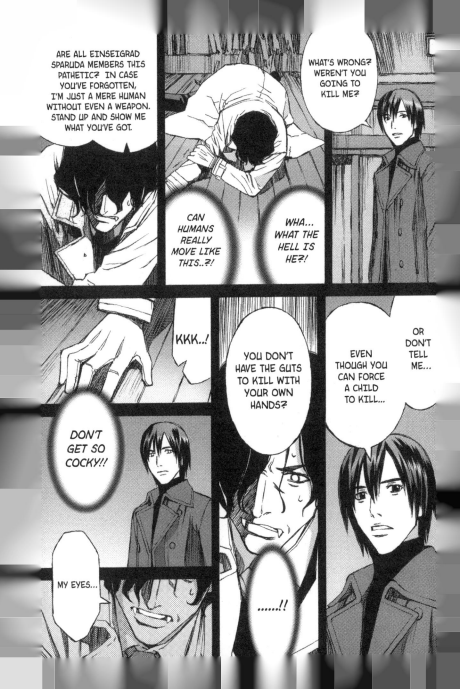

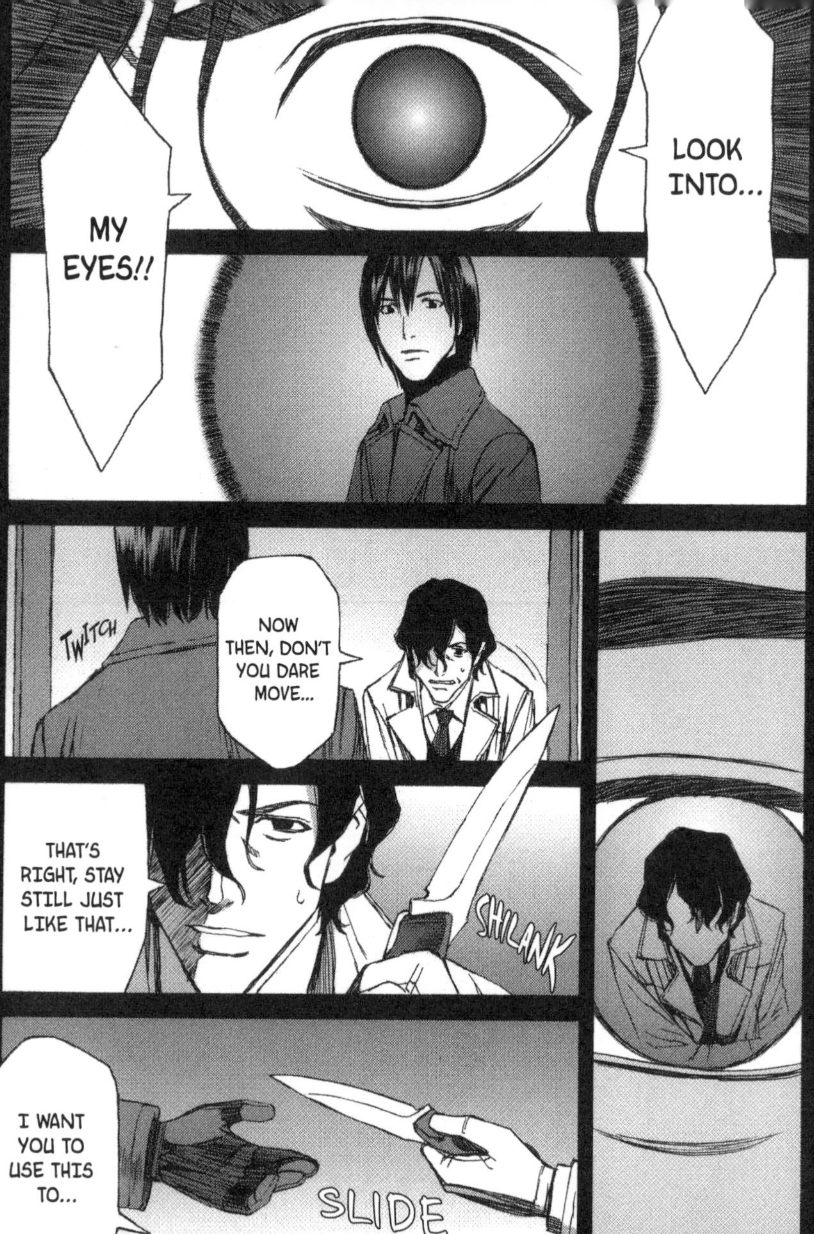
LOOK INTO...
MY EYES!!
NOW THEN, DON'T YOU DARE MOVE...
TWITCH
THAT'S RIGHT, STAY STILL JUST LIKE THAT...
SHILANK
I WANT YOU TO USE THIS TO...
SLIDE

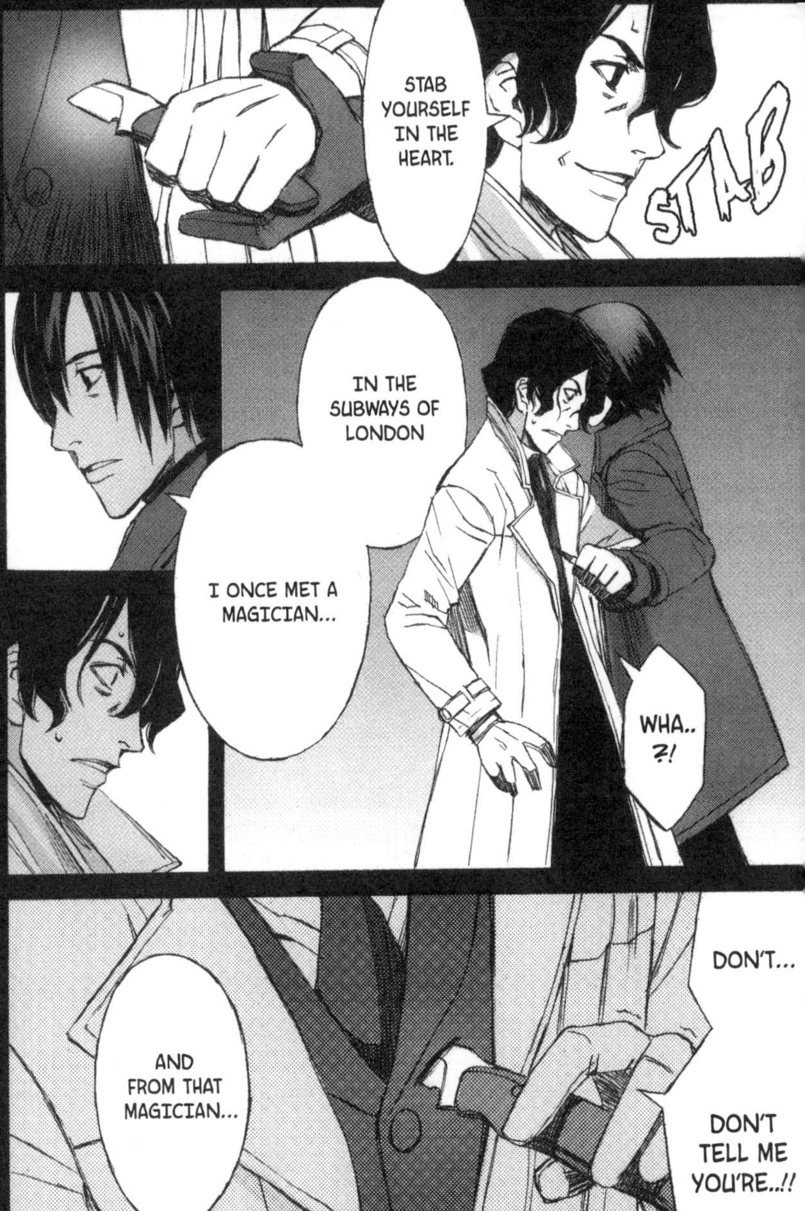
STAB YOURSELF IN THE HEART.
STAB
IN THE SUBWAYS OF LONDON
I ONCE MET A MAGICIAN...
WHA.. ?!
DON'T...
AND FROM THAT MAGICIAN...
DON'T TELL ME YOU'RE..!!

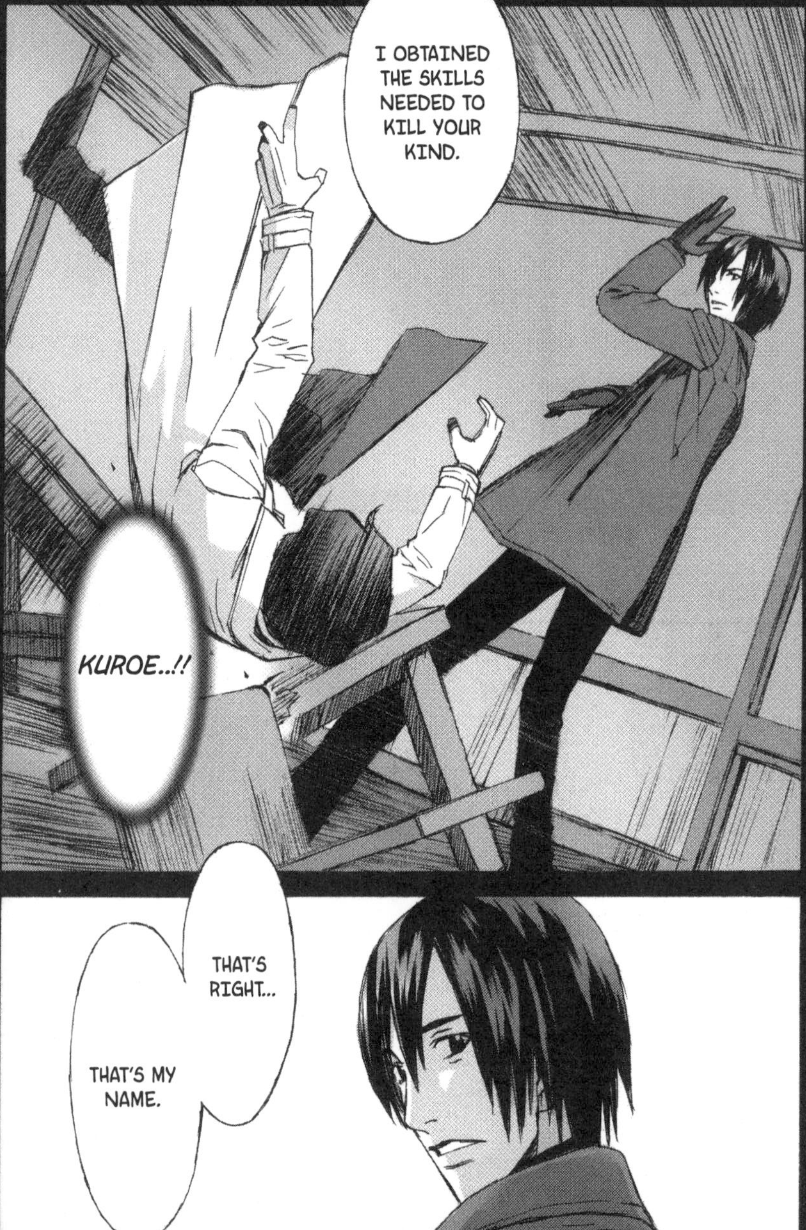
I OBTAINED THE SKILLS NEEDED TO KILL YOUR KIND.
KUROE...!!
THAT'S RIGHT...
THAT'S MY NAME.

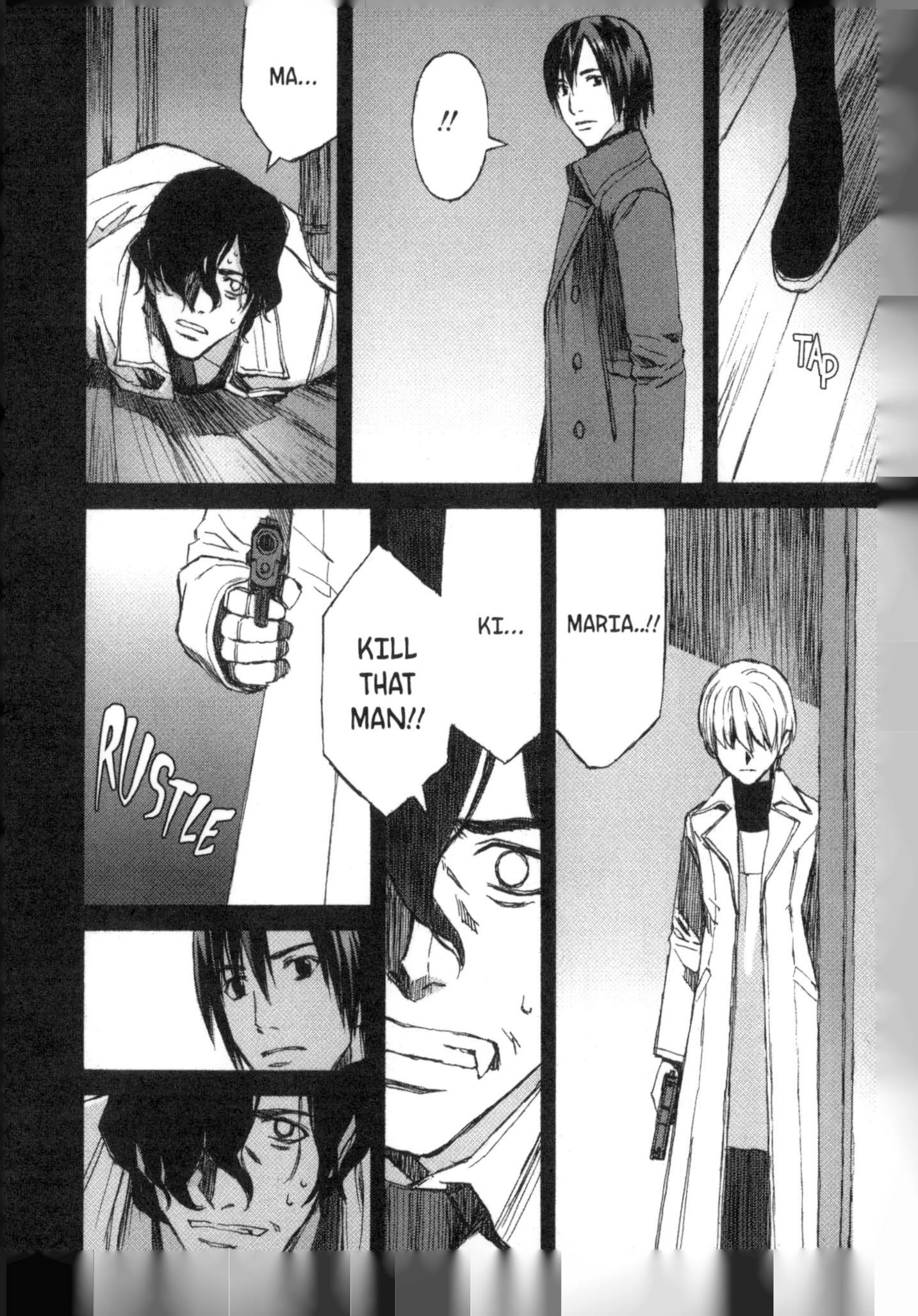
TAP
!!
MA...
MARIA..!!
KI...
KILL THAT MAN!!
RUSTLE

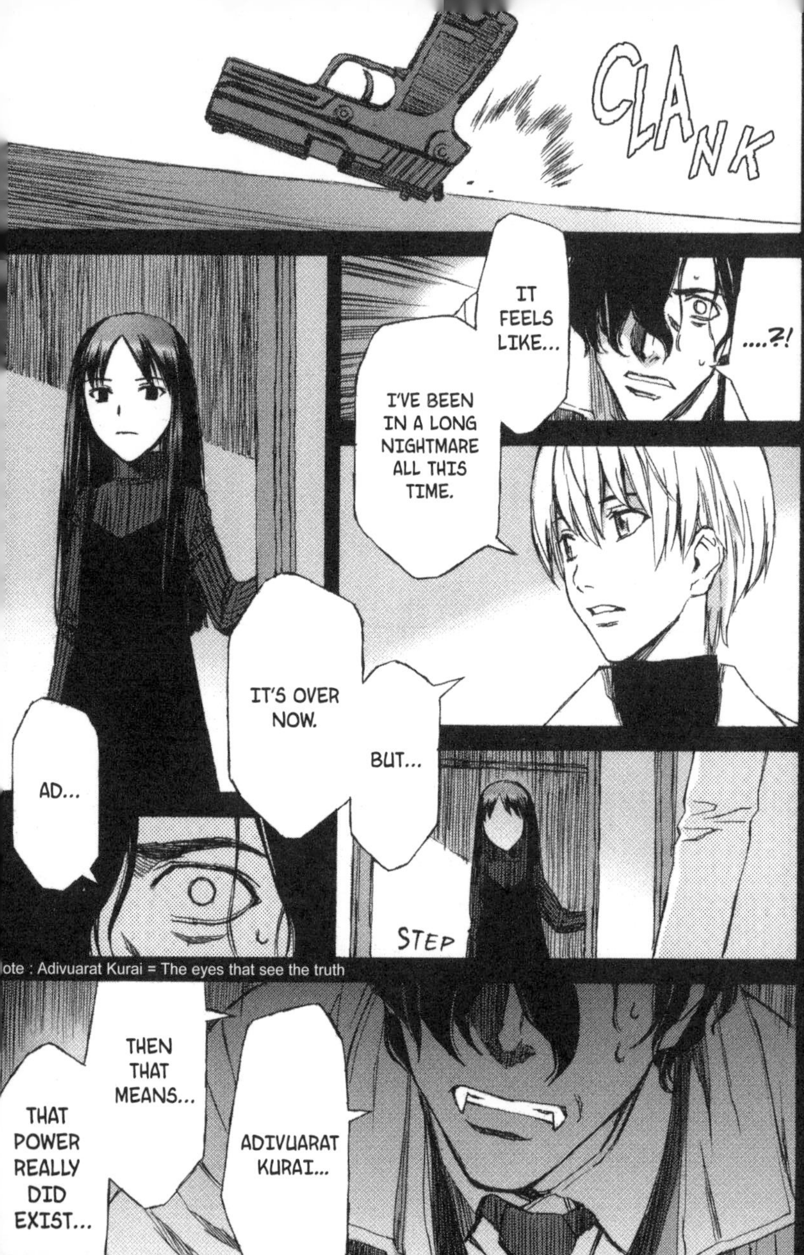
CLANK
IT FEELS LIKE...
....?!
I'VE BEEN IN A LONG NIGHTMARE ALL THIS TIME.
IT'S OVER NOW.
BUT...
STEP
AD...
ote : Adivuarat Kurai = The eyes that see the truth
ADIVUARAT KURAI...
THEN THAT MEANS...
THAT POWER REALLY DID EXIST...

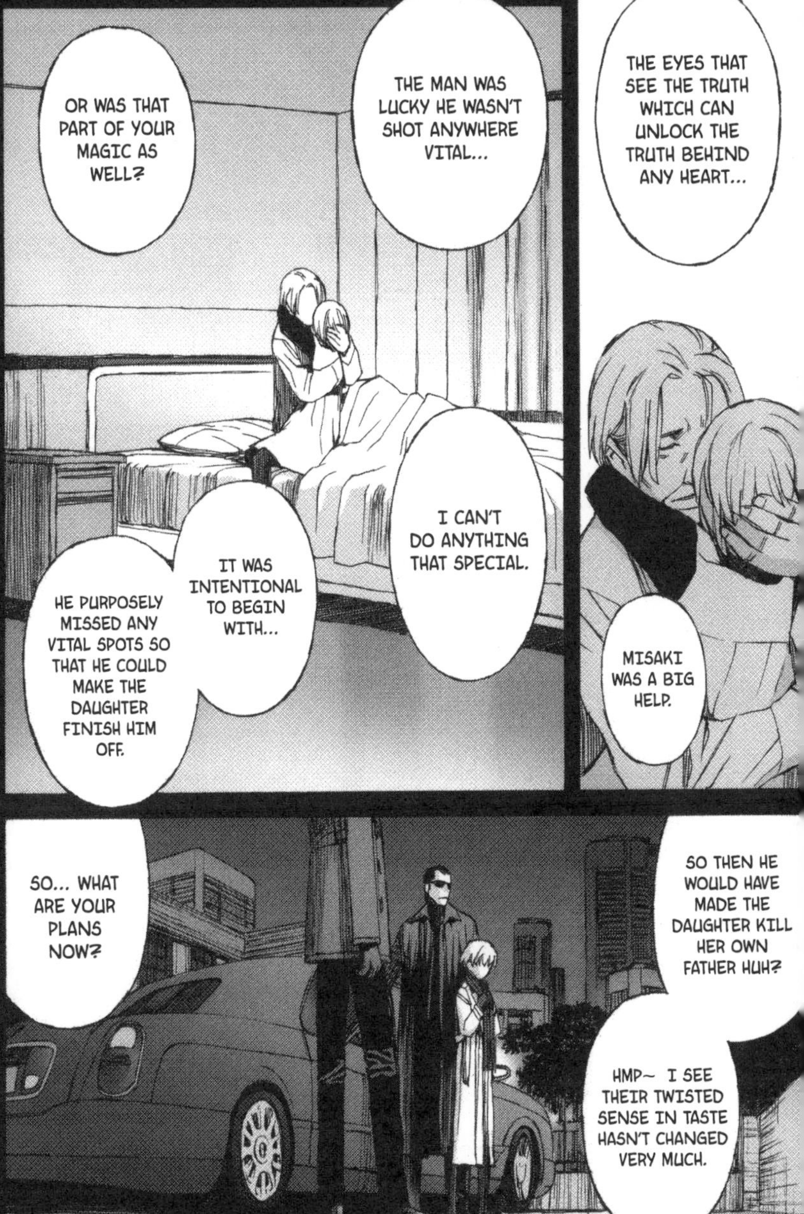
THE EYES THAT SEE THE TRUTH WHICH CAN UNLOCK THE TRUTH BEHIND ANY HEART...
MISAKI WAS A BIG HELP.
THE MAN WAS LUCKY HE WASN'T SHOT ANYWHERE VITAL...
OR WAS THAT PART OF YOUR MAGIC AS WELL?
I CAN'T DO ANYTHING THAT SPECIAL.
IT WAS INTENTIONAL TO BEGIN WITH...
HE PURPOSELY MISSED ANY VITAL SPOTS SO THAT HE COULD MAKE THE DAUGHTER FINISH HIM OFF.
SO THEN HE WOULD HAVE MADE THE DAUGHTER KILL HER OWN FATHER HUH?
HMP~ I SEE THEIR TWISTED SENSE IN TASTE HASN'T CHANGED VERY MUCH.
SO... WHAT ARE YOUR PLANS NOW?

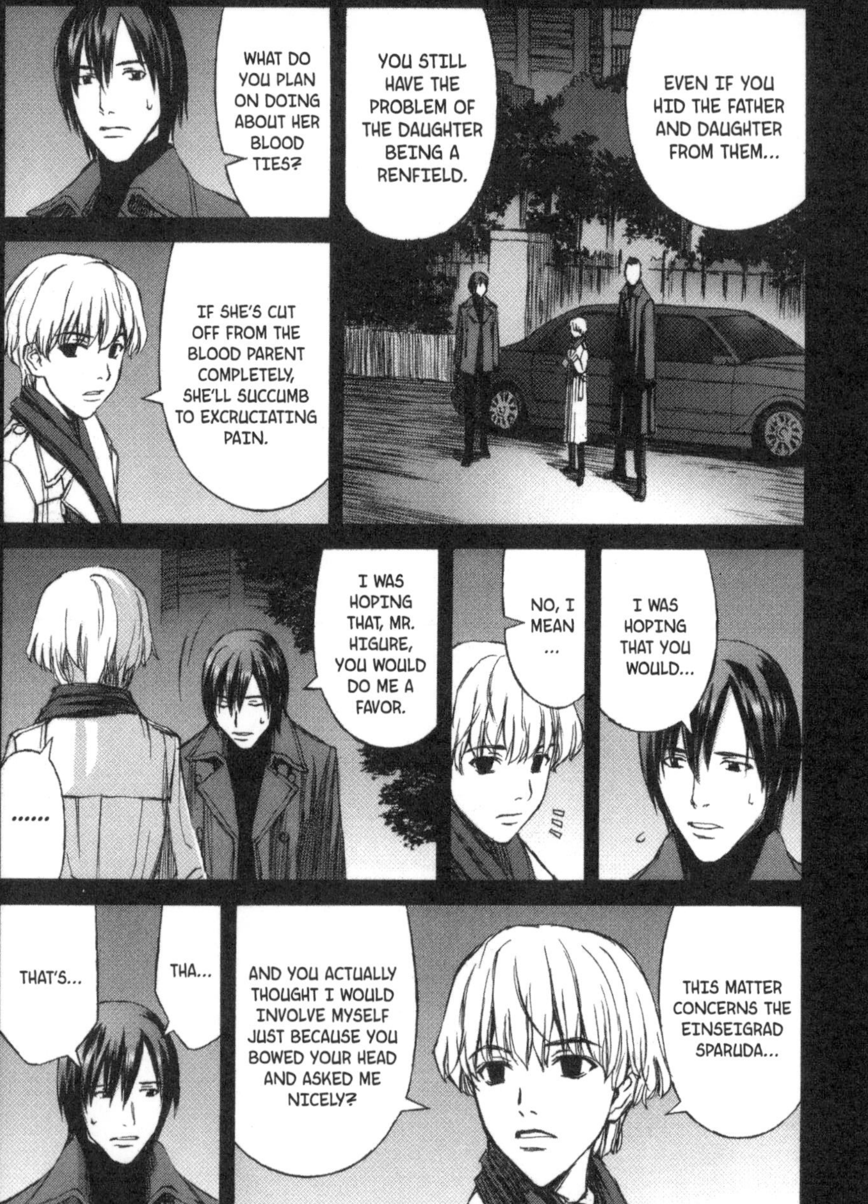
EVEN IF YOU HID THE FATHER AND DAUGHTER FROM THEM...
YOU STILL HAVE THE PROBLEM OF THE DAUGHTER BEING A RENFIELD.
WHAT DO YOU PLAN ON DOING ABOUT HER BLOOD TIES?
IF SHE'S CUT OFF FROM THE BLOOD PARENT COMPLETELY, SHE'LL SUCCUMB TO EXCRUCIATING PAIN.
I WAS HOPING THAT YOU WOULD...
NO, I MEAN ...
I WAS HOPING THAT, MR. HIGURE, YOU WOULD DO ME A FAVOR.
......
THIS MATTER CONCERNS THE EINSEIGRAD SPARUDA...
AND YOU ACTUALLY THOUGHT I WOULD INVOLVE MYSELF JUST BECAUSE YOU BOWED YOUR HEAD AND ASKED ME NICELY?
THA...
THAT'S...

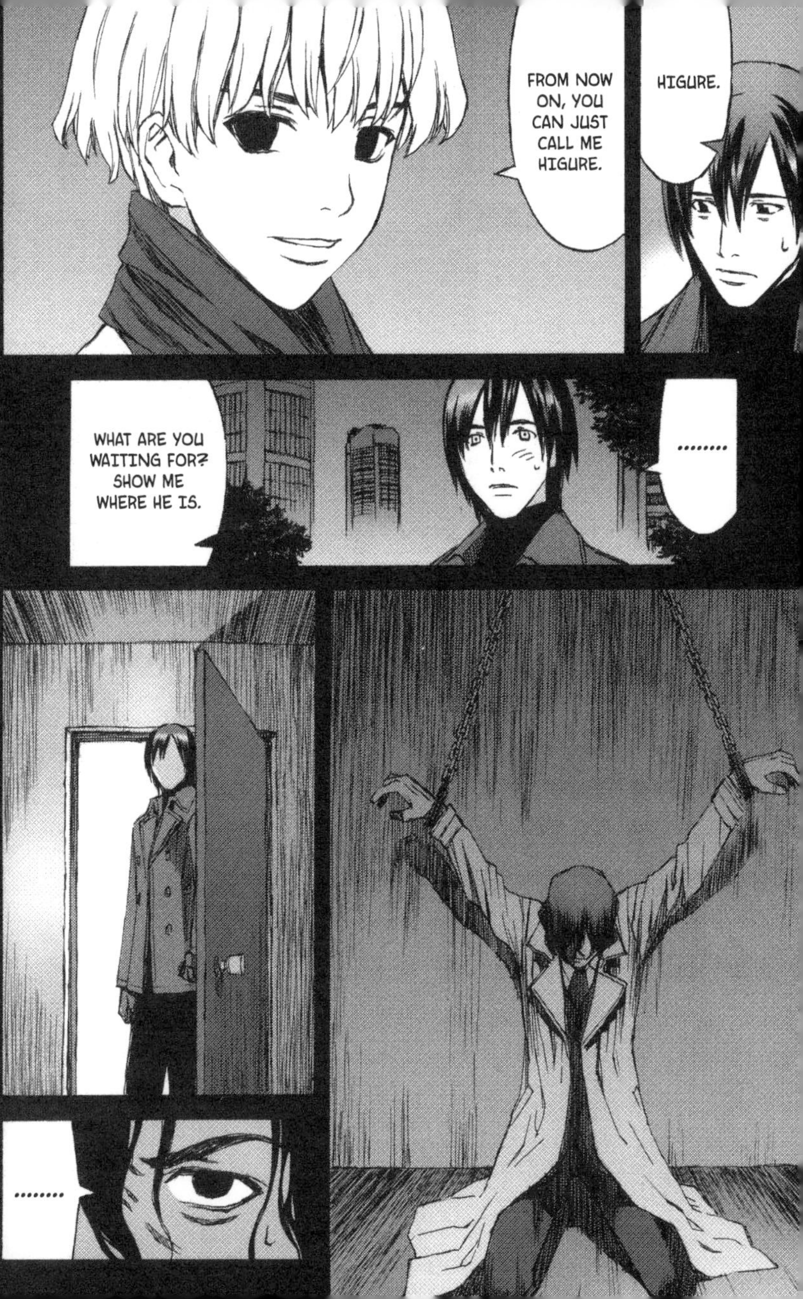
HIGURE.
FROM NOW ON, YOU CAN JUST CALL ME HIGURE.
....
WHAT ARE YOU WAITING FOR? SHOW ME WHERE HE IS.
....

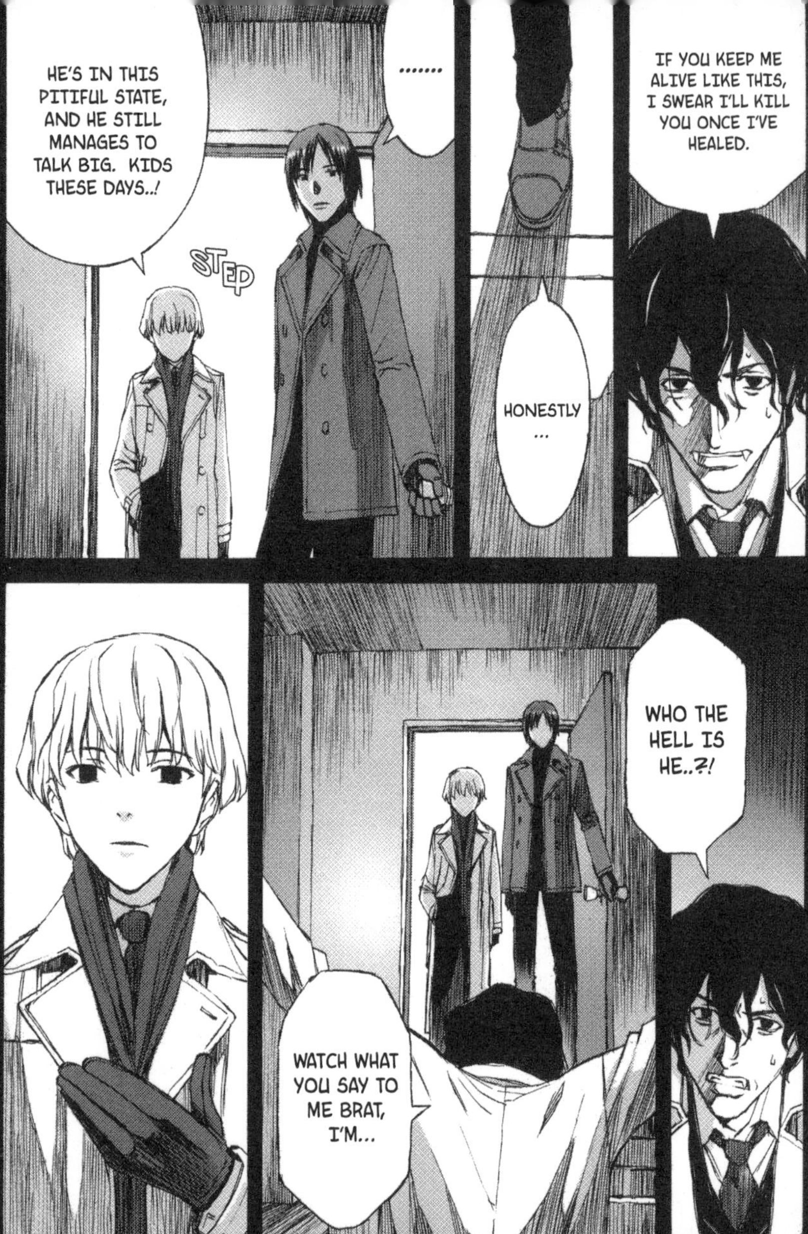
IF YOU KEEP ME ALIVE LIKE THIS, I SWEAR I'LL KILL YOU ONCE I'VE HEALED.
HONESTLY ...
....
HE'S IN THIS PITIFUL STATE, AND HE STILL MANAGES TO TALK BIG. KIDS THESE DAYS..!
STEP
WHO THE HELL IS HE..?!
WATCH WHAT YOU SAY TO ME BRAT, I'M...

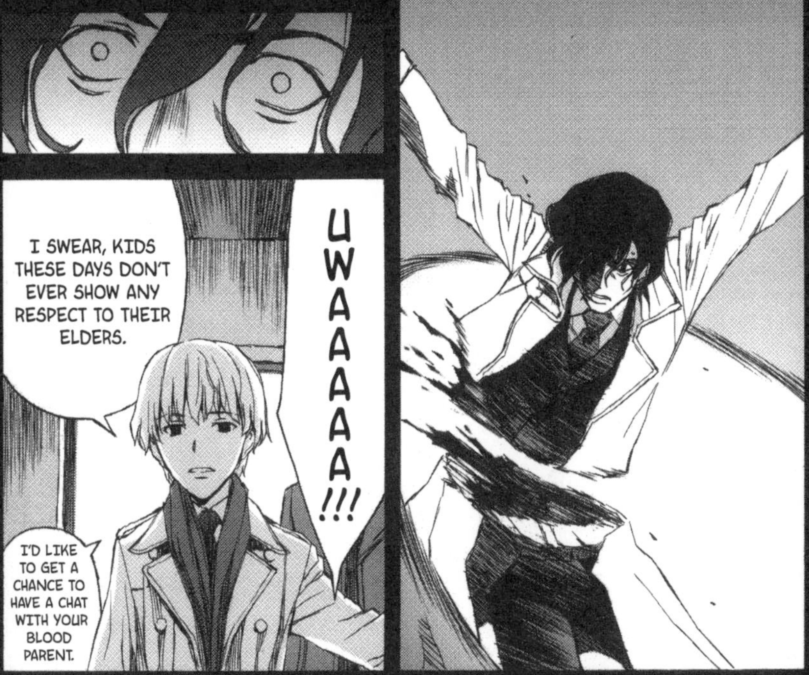
UWAAAAAA!!!
I SWEAR, KIDS THESE DAYS DON'T EVER SHOW ANY RESPECT TO THEIR ELDERS.
I'D LIKE TO GET A CHANCE TO HAVE A CHAT WITH YOUR BLOOD PARENT.

Note : Aruhiek = Elder Generation

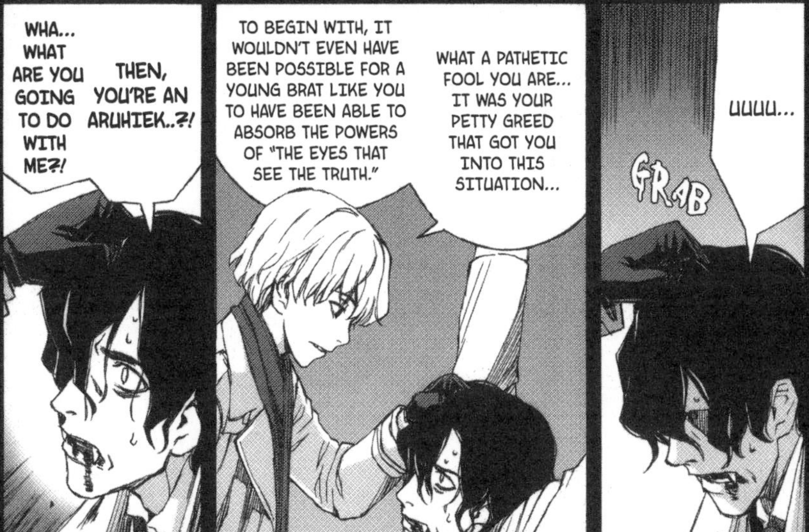
UUUU...
GRAB
WHAT A PATHETIC FOOL YOU ARE... IT WAS YOUR PETTY GREED THAT GOT YOU INTO THIS SITUATION...
TO BEGIN WITH, IT WOULDN'T EVEN HAVE BEEN POSSIBLE FOR A YOUNG BRAT LIKE YOU TO HAVE BEEN ABLE TO ABSORB THE POWERS OF "THE EYES THAT SEE THE TRUTH."
THEN, YOU'RE AN ARUHIEK..?!
WHA... WHAT ARE YOU GOING TO DO WITH ME?!

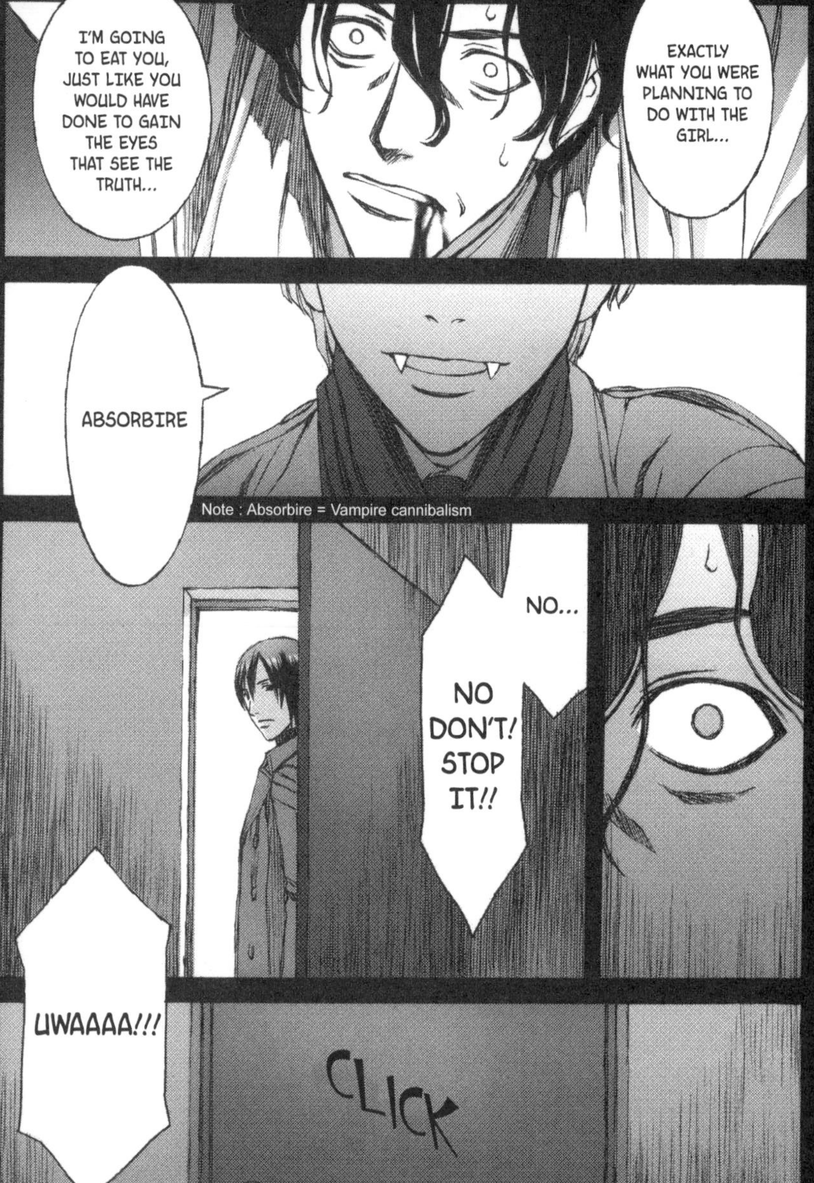
EXACTLY WHAT YOU WERE PLANNING TO DO WITH THE GIRL...
I'M GOING TO EAT YOU, JUST LIKE YOU WOULD HAVE DONE TO GAIN THE EYES THAT SEE THE TRUTH...
ABSORBIRE
Note : Absorbire = Vampire cannibalism
NO...
NO DON'T! STOP IT!!
UWAAAA!!!
CLICK

To Be Continued In Blood Alone Volume 3!!

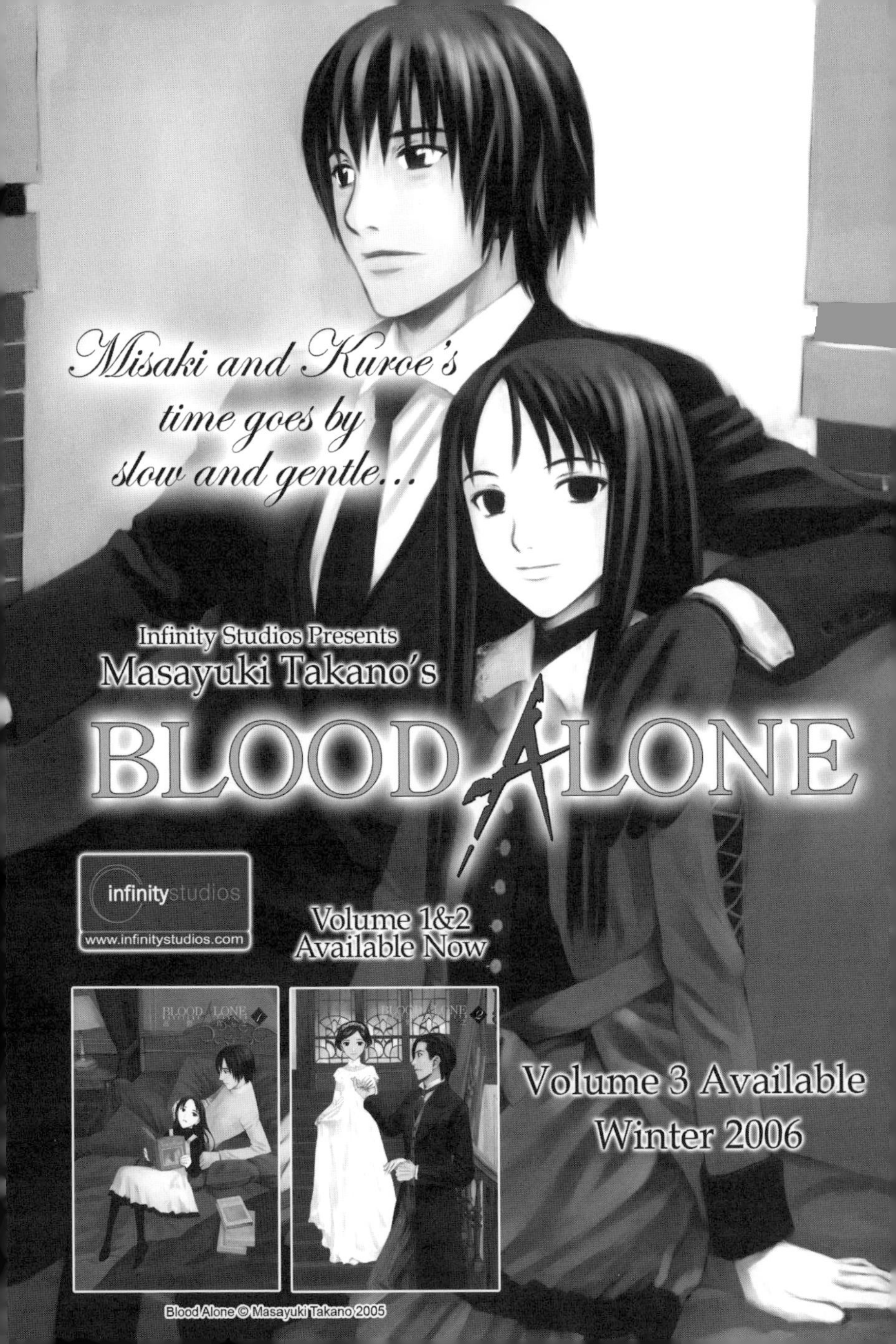

Misaki and Kuroe's
time goes by
slow and gentle...
Infinity Studios Presents
Masayuki Takano's
BLOOD ALONE
infinitystudios
www.infinitystudios.com
Volume 1&2
Available Now
Volume 3 Available
Winter 2006
Blood Alone © Masayuki Takano 2005

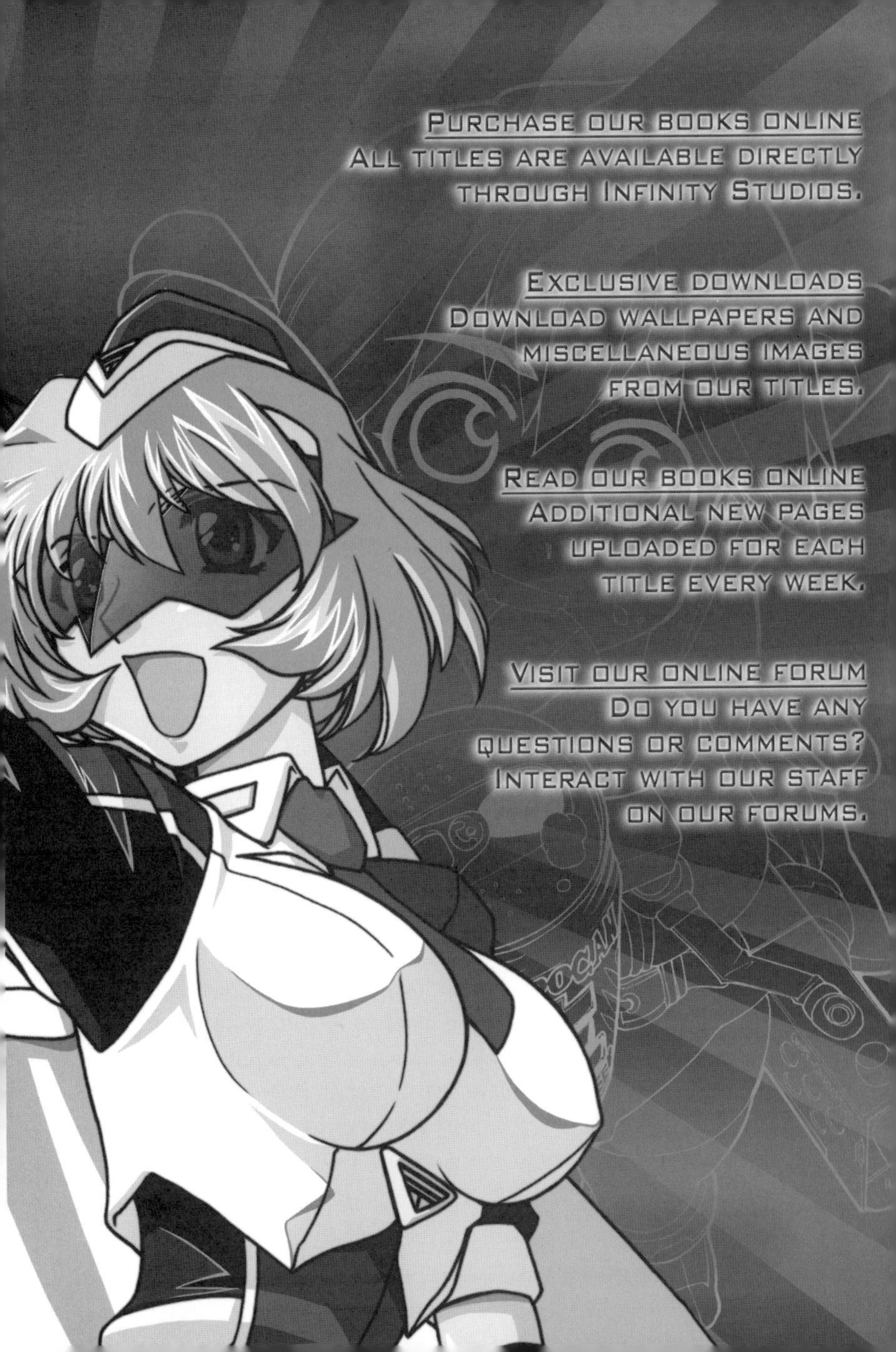
PURCHASE OUR BOOKS ONLINE
ALL TITLES ARE AVAILABLE DIRECTLY THROUGH INFINITY STUDIOS.
EXCLUSIVE DOWNLOADS
DOWNLOAD WALLPAPERS AND MISCELLANEOUS IMAGES FROM OUR TITLES.
READ OUR BOOKS ONLINE
ADDITIONAL NEW PAGES UPLOADED FOR EACH TITLE EVERY WEEK.
VISIT OUR ONLINE FORUM
DO YOU HAVE ANY QUESTIONS OR COMMENTS? INTERACT WITH OUR STAFF ON OUR FORUMS.

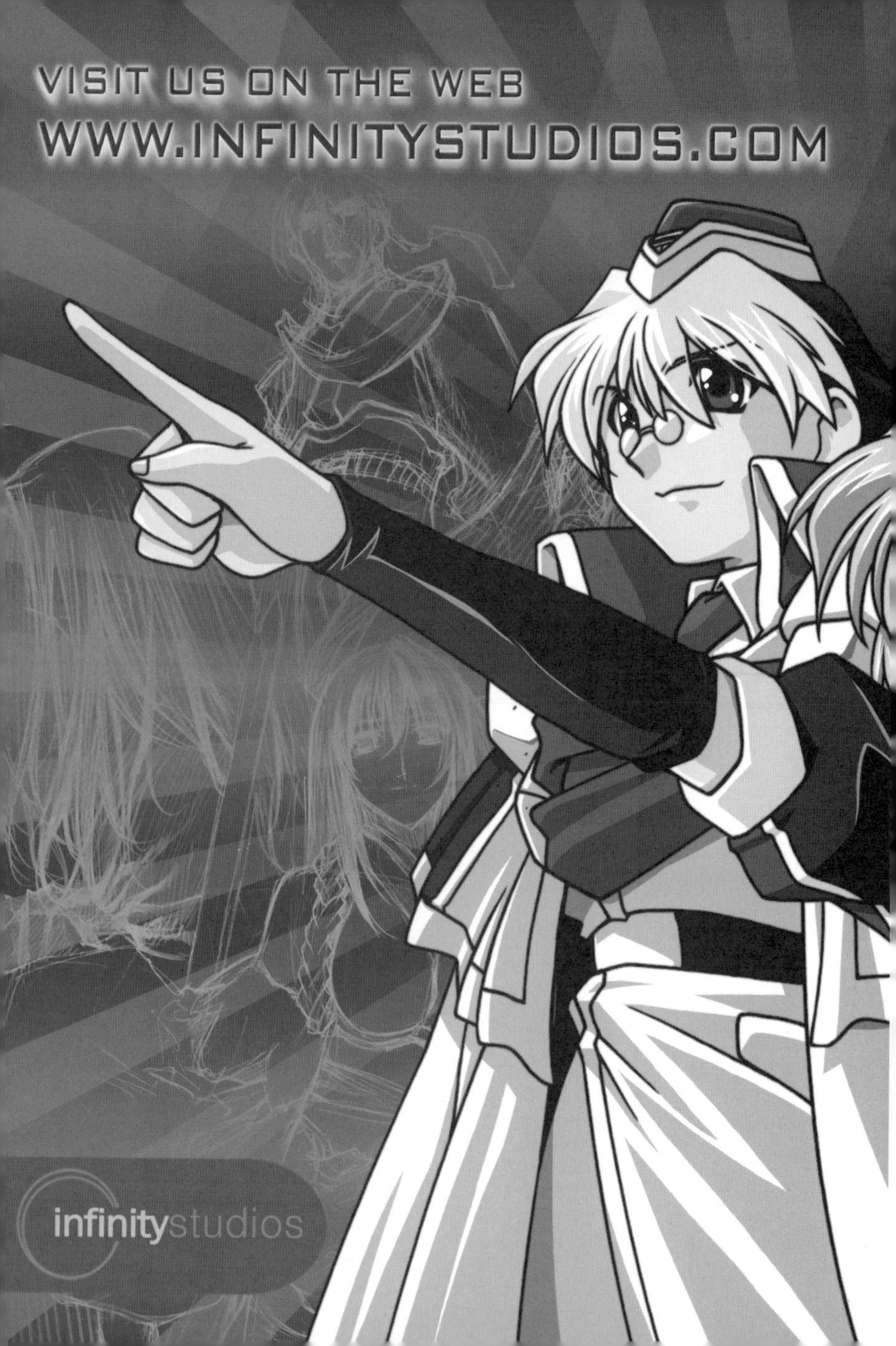
VISIT US ON THE WEB
WWW.INFINITYSTUDIOS.COM
infinitystudios

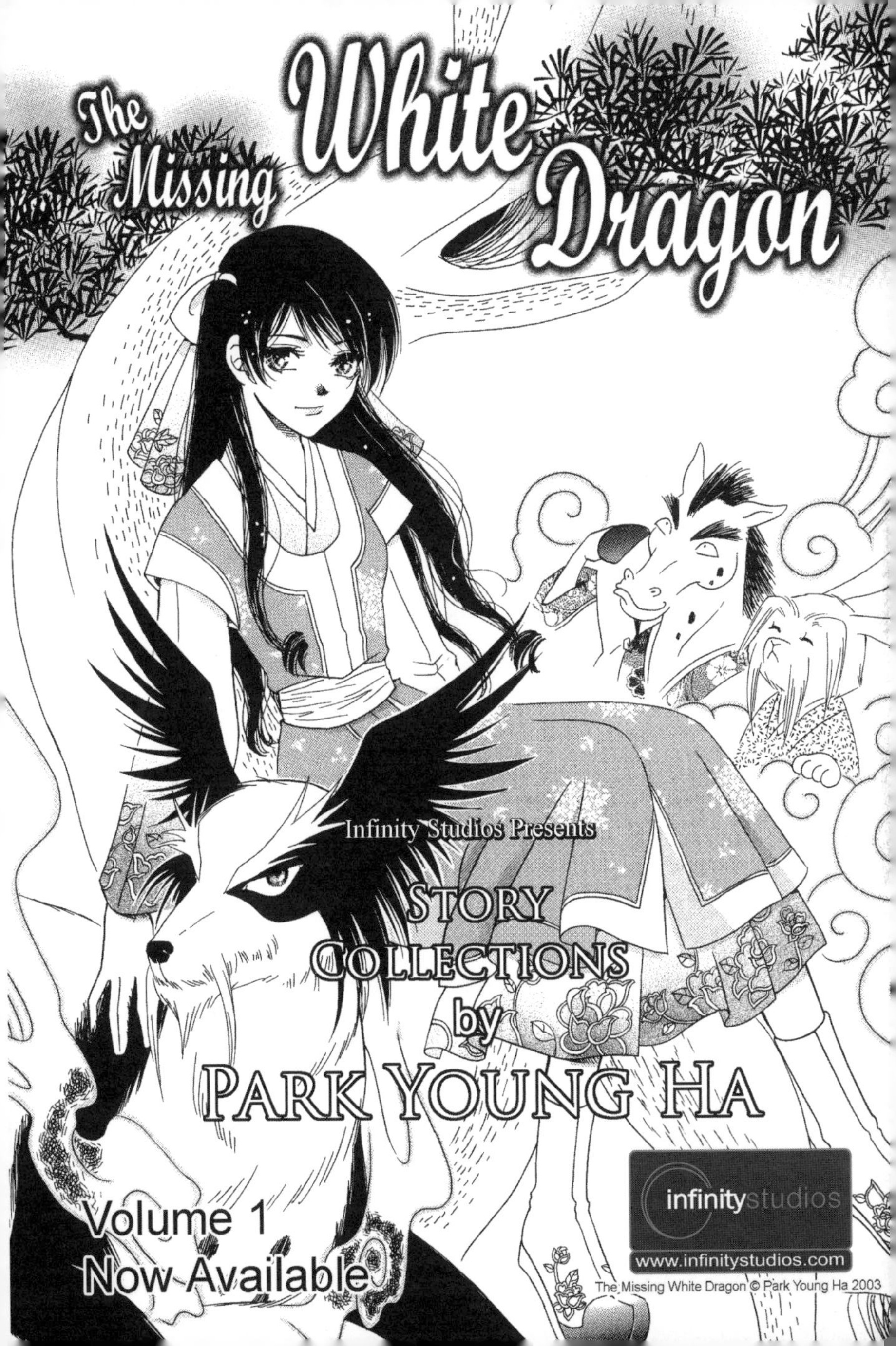
The Missing White Dragon
Infinity Studios Presents
Story Collections by
Park Young Ha
infinitystudios
www.infinitystudios.com
Volume 1
Now Available
The Missing White Dragon © Park Young Ha 2003

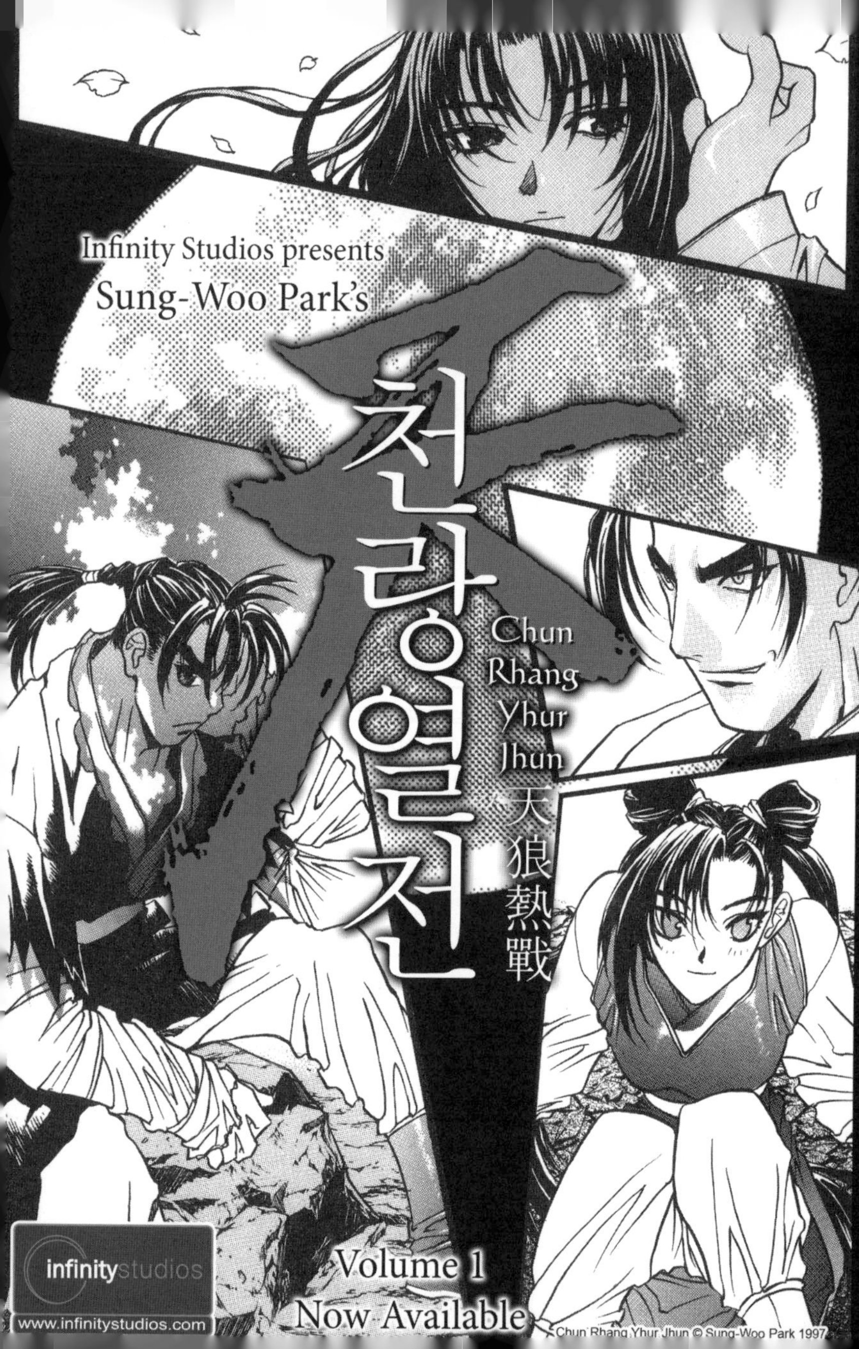
Infinity Studios presents
Sung-Woo Park's
천랑열전
Chun Rhang Yhur Jhun
天狼熱戰
infinitystudios
www.infinitystudios.com
Volume 1
Now Available
Chun Rhang Yhur Jhun © Sung-Woo Park 1997

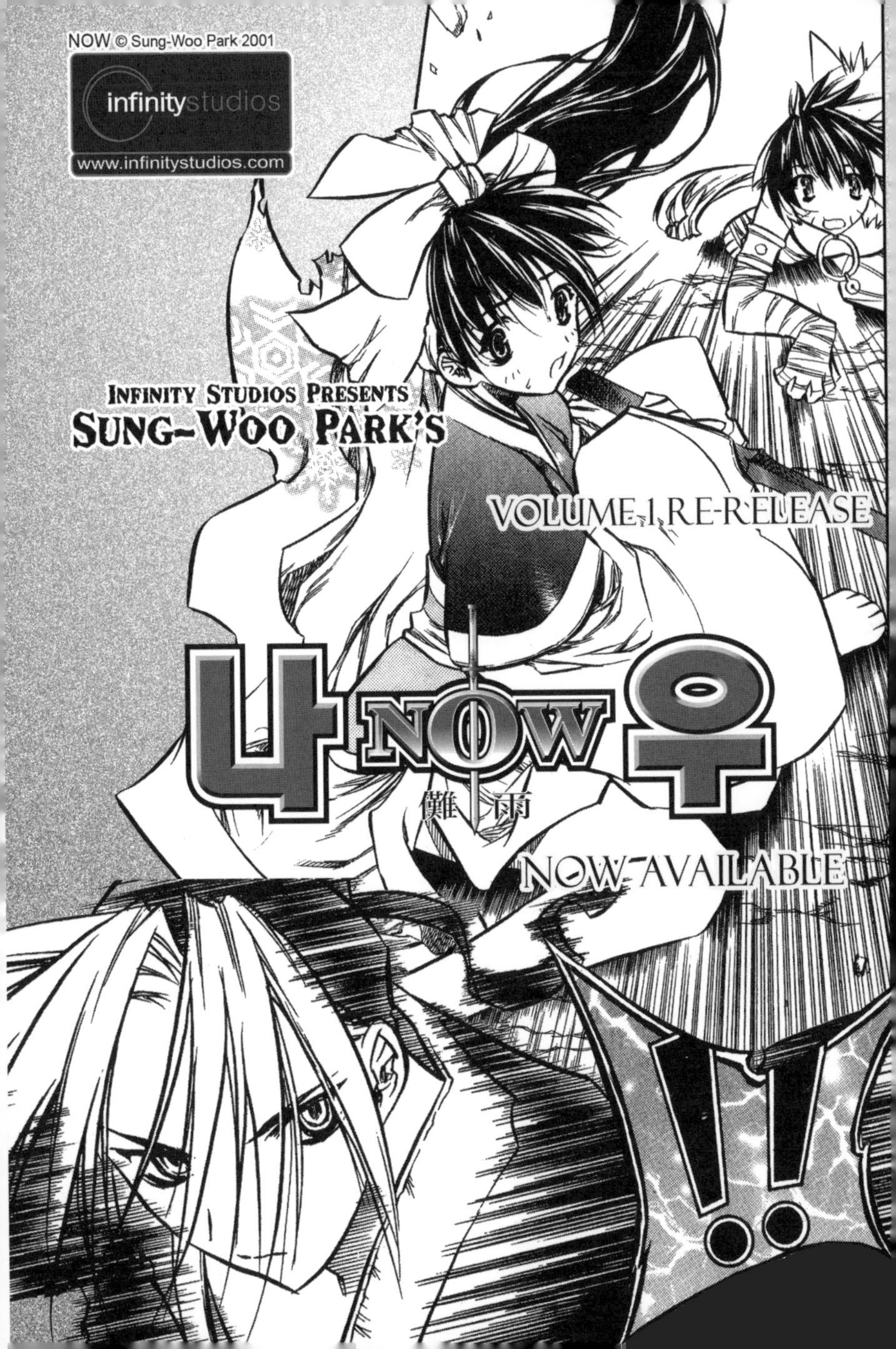
NOW © Sung-Woo Park 2001
infinitystudios
www.infinitystudios.com
INFINITY STUDIOS PRESENTS
SUNG-WOO PARK'S
VOLUME 1 RE-RELEASE
나 NOW 우
儺 雨
NOW AVAILABLE

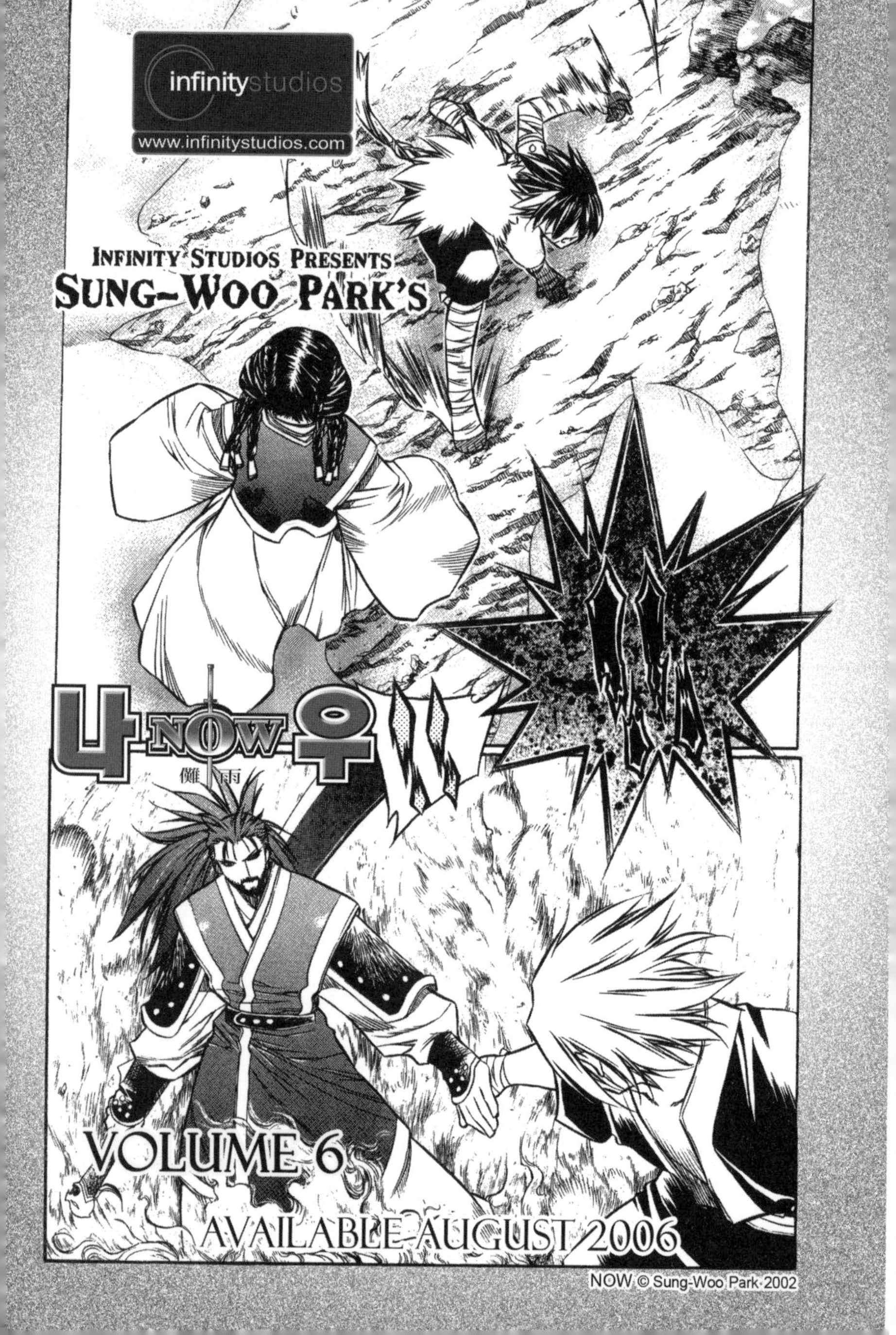
infinitystudios
www.infinitystudios.com
INFINITY STUDIOS PRESENTS
SUNG-WOO PARK'S
나 NOW 우
儺雨
VOLUME 6
AVAILABLE AUGUST 2006

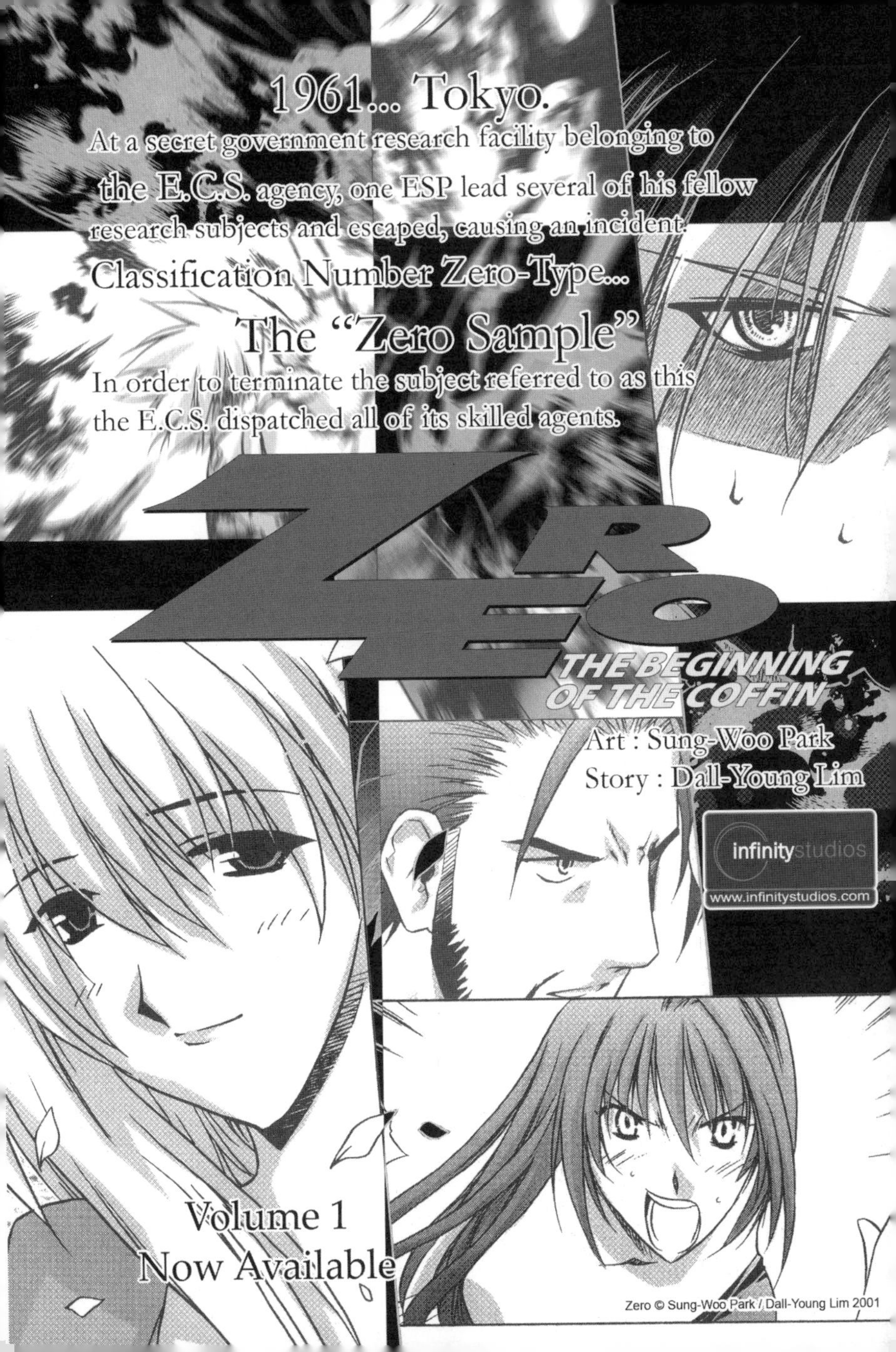
1961... Tokyo.
At a secret government research facility belonging to the E.C.S. agency, one ESP lead several of his fellow research subjects and escaped, causing an incident.
Classification Number Zero-Type...
The "Zero Sample"
In order to terminate the subject referred to as this the E.C.S. dispatched all of its skilled agents.
ZERO
THE BEGINNING OF THE COFFIN
Art : Sung-Woo Park
Story : Dall-Young Lim
infinitystudios
www.infinitystudios.com
Volume 1
Now Available
Zero © Sung-Woo Park / Dall-Young Lim 2001

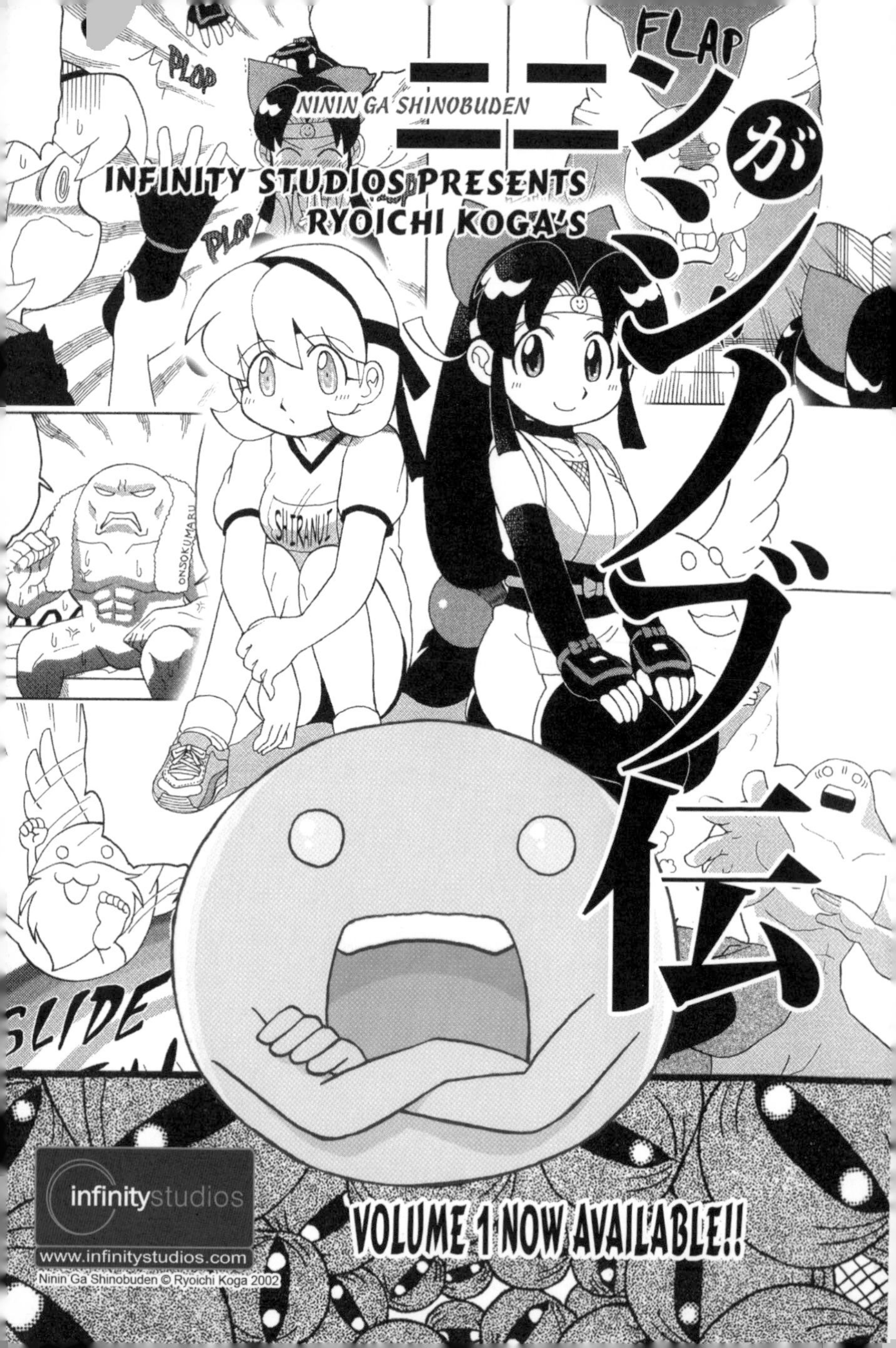
NININ GA SHINOBUDEN
INFINITY STUDIOS PRESENTS
RYOICHI KOGA'S
ニニンがシノブ伝
FLAP
PLOP
PLOP
SHIRANUI
ONSOKUMARU
SLIDE
infinitystudios
www.infinitystudios.com
Ninin Ga Shinobuden © Ryoichi Koga 2002
VOLUME 1 NOW AVAILABLE!!

스 ♥ 위 티

SWEETY

A story of a
lucky young man &
the sweetest young girl

**Volume 1
Now Available**

Sweety © Jae-Sung Park / Ju-Ri Kim 2001

Story : Jae-Sung Park
Art : Ju-Ri Kim

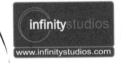

infinity studios
www.infinitystudios.com

You'd think Myung-Ho
Yoon would be happy to
get chocolates from two
cute girls on Valentine's
day, but because of them,
his high school life is
getting a little more....
complicated.